TALKING IT OUT

Stories in Negotiating Human Relations

FRANCIS M. DENG

The publisher wishes to acknowledge and thank Dr. Douglas H. Johnson for his invaluable help and support for Africa World Books and its mission of preserving and promoting African cultural and literary traditions and history. Dr. Johnson and fellow historians have been instrumental in ensuring that African people remain connected to their past and their identity. Africa World Books is proud to carry on this mission.

ISBN: 9780645759099

First published in 2006 by Kegan Paul Limited
First issued in paperback 2016

Cover design, typesetting and layout: Africa World Books
Unit 3, 57 Frobisher St, Osborne Park, WA 6017
P.O. Box 1106 Osborne Park, WA 6916

Africa
World Books
Pty Ltd

TALKING IT OUT

This innovative work by Francis Deng, the noted scholar, diplomat, legal expert and author, moves the study of negotiation out of the limited traditional context of industrial relations and resituates it in the broader arena of negotiating human relations, drawing on his childhood experiences, inter-racial and cross-cultural encounters at home and abroad, and incidents from his diplomatic career. *Talking It Out* provides an account of the author's family and background as a son of the leading Dinka Chief in a long line of leaders believed to be spiritually-endowed peace-makers, a cultural context that has helped shape his perspective on conflicts and how to manage or resolve them. His distinctive perspective became manifest in his response to the conflicts in Sudan between the Arab-Islamic North and the African-Christian South, in which he was ironically both a victim and a peacemaker. Deng's account of interpersonal relations abroad in the course of a diplomatic career that linked international civil service in the United Nations with representing his country as Ambassador to the United States, Scandinavian countries and Canada, along with serving as Minister of State for Foreign Affairs for Sudan, describes the way in which he was able to engage his domestically rooted cultural values on an international level. The volume concludes with an analytical commentary that places these experiences in a thematic framework that matches the values of his upbringing with his responses to negotiating human relations in conflict situations. Deng's unique approach to the cultural dimension of conflict management has wide relevance in today's world. This is an exceptional work by one of the outstanding cultural authorities of our time.

PREFACE

Talking It Out: Stories in Negotiating Human Relations

The stories that form the corpus of Talking It Out are elements of my lifelong experience which I have written about in other works. Indeed, the stimulus for this book was a request for editors of a cross-cultural study of negotiations for me to contribute a chapter building on my own personal experiences and observations. I contributed a chapter to their edited volume, but I also felt inspired to extend my work into producing this book.

The underlying normative cultural principle involved in the venture is that it is unhealthy to hold grievances in 'the stomach' or 'the heart,' to translate the pertinent Dinka usages. Airing differences is not only a potentially constructive way of discussing and resolving them but is also a relief to the turmoil and the unease within one's self.

Beyond the contribution to the edited volume and producing this book, I specifically presented this principle in a paper titled '*What Is Not Said Is What Divides*' that has gained considerable popularity in both Sudan and South Sudan to the point where it has become a cultural ethos in both countries. I wrote the paper in 1989 for an all-parties conference that was convened by the University of Bergen in Norway to address the North-South conflict in the Sudan. The aim of the paper was to highlight the fact that Sudanese, particularly the dominant group in the North, tried to avoid discussing issues of race, religion, and the history of slavery, which were central elements of the national identity crisis in the conflict that was tearing the country apart. My position was that unless these issues are exposed and discussed, they could not be resolved and the wars of identity that constituted obstacles to nation-building could not be ended.

It is of course equally correct and in fact more established that what is said is what divides. Words can be very hurtful and can provoke conflicts that can become violent. So, if grievances must be aired and yet speaking can provoke conflict, what is the way out of that paradox? I believe the answer lies in the manner in which grievances are aired and discussed. Both the 'what' to talk about and the 'how' to do so become equally important. If the goal is to reach an agreement that amicably resolves the conflict, then the discussion must be truthful and yet deferential. It should not be acrimonious in a way that injects a divisive wedge that deepens the wound and widens the gap to be bridged.

The stories recounted in this collection are personal and cover relations within a group, interaction with individuals outside the group, and representative discussions and negotiations between groups, organizations, and governments. It should be borne in mind that even in relations between collective entities, those directly involved in representative discussions or negotiations are individuals, with the same sensitivities and sensibilities of interpersonal interactions. It is also important to realize that although rights and wrongs in conflict situations are never fully equal, they are rarely one-sided. Each of the parties to the conflict must have a cause that subjectively justifies getting involved in the conflict.

I believe that recognizing this fact is not only essential to resolving the conflict but is also soothing to the parties insofar as it makes the conduct of the adversary more understandable, if not justifiable. Of course, airing grievances does not necessarily always succeed in resolving differences, but it at least provides the ground for potential understanding and is in any case cathartic. That is what is popularly meant by 'vomiting out' painful grievances or getting grievances out of one's chest.

For me personally, my inclination to 'talking it out' was more often successful enough to make me a strong believer in that approach as a normative principle. I also believe that it is part of my African cultural background. In the African value system, the truth in which rights and wrongs are embedded is an inherent and ordained fact that exists, if not always evident. The task of conflict resolution is to explore the truth. The word for a right in most languages also means 'truth.' And part of the wisdom of elders in the African cultural practice of mediation or conflict resolution is to look for the truth, recognize it when it comes in sight, and present it persuasively to build consensus.

It is well established that in African jurisprudence, litigation is a process of exploring the truth as a basis for finding a meeting ground on which a decision can be reached to achieve the needed consensus and effect reconciliation. It is not an adversarial process of fighting by another means. Conflicts in traditional African societies mostly concern communities. The parties were expected to return to their community or inter-communal contexts and live together in peace and harmony. Traditionally, among the Dinka, after the case was resolved, the parties were ritually sprayed with 'holy water' and blessed to go back to their community reunited to live harmoniously and cooperatively. This contrasts with the adversarial process by which the parties fight it out and end with a winner-and-loser outcome. They go their separate ways, perhaps never to meet again. In Dinka, the word for ligation or settling a dispute is *luk*, which as a verb means 'to persuade' or 'persuasion' as a noun. It is widely known to the point of being a cliché that in Africa, people gathered under a shade tree and debated issues until they arrived at a consensus.

Of course, no community is homogeneous in today's heterogeneous world and traditional African value systems are rapidly eroding and no longer secluded from external influences. But interactions between individuals and groups of varied cultures is a give-and-take process in which mutual understanding and influence are imperative and should be normative. It is therefore essential that the interactive individuals and groups know what they bring into the mix of the pluralistic context and the extent to which diversities are inherently mutually enriching. I hope *Talking It Out* can contribute further to that enrichment process.

Francis Mading Deng
Woodstock, New York
February 2023

CONTENTS

Acknowledgements   ix

Introduction   1
   An Invitation and a Comprehensive Response   1
   Negotiation in its Relational and Cultural Context 2
   Examples of Negotiation   5
   Personal Experiences as Learning Opportunities   13

Part I: Background   *15*

Chapter 1: Dinka Cultural Framework   17
   Dinka Identity   17
   The Crucial Role of Cattle   18
   Continued Identity and Influence   19
   Core Concepts of Human Relations   22
   Concepts of Dignity, Pride and Respect   25
   Reconciliatory Leaders   28
   Aggressive Youths   29
   Superior Men and Influential Women   31
   Nilotic Values and Their Implications   33
   North-South Tensions and Conflict   36

Chapter 2: Paternal Legacy   43
  The Pajok lineage of the Ngok Dinka   43
  Deng Majok   52
  Paramount Chieftainship Assumed by Deng Majok   61
  His Undaunted Innovation and Persuasive Influence   62
  His Bringing About of Justice and Peace   66
  His Unifying Role as a Respected Southerner in the North 68
  His Constructive Role when North-South Confrontation
    Took Place   79
  The Vacuum Left by his Death   90

Chapter 3: Maternal Link   95
  A Lineage Renowned for Leadership   95
  Achok Mijok as the Fourth Wife Procured by Deng Majok   97
  Maternal Relatives' Sentiments about the Marriage and
    Expectations of the Son   107
  Inherited, Nurtured, Learnt and Acquired Leadership   115
  Discussions about Responsibilities and Relationships   116
  Heritage of Maternal Ancestry   127

Part II: Internal Relations   133

Chapter 4: Tensions in the Family   135
  The Overheard Levirate Wishes   135
  The Recalcitrant Eldest Son   140
  The Transgression of Another Possible Successor   151
  Cases of Jealousy and Suspicion   152
  The Son Who Took a Stand Against Islamization   155
  The Unresolved Problem of Ongoing Marriages   157
  Retrospect   174

Chapter 5: Pieces from the Crumbling Bridge   179
  A Tragic Death and an Unsympathetic Northern Government 179
  An Accusation of Masterminding Southern Opposition
    in Europe   186

Chapter 6: Coils of the Civil War   215
  Deng Majok's Successor Installed Amid Escalating Conflict 216
  Issues with Regard to Family Unity   225
  Difficult Commanding Officers   228
  The New Chief Killed in a Massacre   233
  Increasing Disunity in the Family of the Clan   236

Chapter 7: Quest for Ngok Autonomy   247
   The Ngok Inclined, and Pressurized, to Join the South   247
   An Initiative Towards National Integration   251
   The Proposal Rejected and Chieftainship Abolished   254
   The Issues of Development and Integration Taken Up Again   256
   Family Reconciliation and Restored Chieftainship   259

Chapter 8: Arabs and Dinkas at War   267
   Suspicion, Perceptions and Antagonism   267
   Tension Increased by the Choice of a New Chief   269
   A Tragic Tribal War   271
   Talks in Various Contexts   273
   A Difficult but Successful Peace Conference   277

Chapter 9: Encroachment on National Security   285
   Deepening Hostility in a Wider Area   285
   The Call to Intervene   287
   A Presidential, but Abortive, High Level Committee   291
   Escalating Rebel Activities   296
   An Extended Mediation Process with Short-Lived Success   298

Part III: External Relations   *311*

Chapter 10: Reaching Out Abroad   313
   Establishing Communication in a Rural German Town   314
   Enduring and Confronting Biased Hatred in an American
      Residential Area   316
   A Rewarding Visit to an Antagonistic American   322
   The Effectiveness of Talking It Out in Most, But Not All, Cases   323

Chapter 11: Diplomacy of Mediation   327
   An Ambassador of a Country with a Conflatory Internal
      Agreement   328
   Influencing Sudan's Qualified Support for the Camp David
      Accords   329
   Futile Attempts to Improve Sudan's Relations with Ethiopia   337
   Talking Towards a Consensual Outcome with Regard to
      Western Sahara   347
   Reversing an OAU Chairman's Withdrawal from a Crucial
      Summit   350
   The Impromptu Establishment of Diplomatic Relations with
      South Korea   355

Part IV: Commentary   *361*

Chapter 12: Themes from the Stories   363
    Overview on the Themes   363
    Negotiating Family Conflicts   369
    Intra-State Conflicts   372
    Negotiating Personal Relations Cross-Culturally   376
    Negotiating Diplomatic Relations   381

Conclusion   391

Bibliography   395

Acknowledgements

Every book is the culmination of an incremental process that expands over a period of time and involves the contribution of people who often cannot all be identified. This is particularly true of this book whose stories of mediating human relations go back far into my youth, if not childhood, and build on values that are part of my heritage and upbringing. Of course, without the challenging request for stories from Guy Olivier Faure and the late Jeffrey Rubin, I would neither have thought of writing the book nor had the moral courage to do so. My profound gratitude goes to them. My colleague and dear friend, Professor I. William Zartman, was among the first to read the manuscript and encouraged its publication. We have indeed used the manuscript for his courses in negotiations. Another colleague, Dr. Terrence Lyons, who helped me establish the Africa branch of the Foreign Policy Studies Program at Brookings, also read the manuscript and encouraged me to have it published. I am very grateful to both of them. Professor Janie Malan of The Africa Center for the Constructive Resolution of Disputes (ACCORD) in South Africa, not only supported the publication of the book, but also did exhaustive editing, always attentive to details and making essential corrections. I am deeply indebted to him. I am also grateful to Vasu Gounden, the Executive Director of ACCORD, and Hussein Solomon, who read the manuscript and encouraged its publication. My long-time friend and colleague, Dr. Mansour Khalid, brought the manuscript to the attention of Peter Hopkins of Kegan Paul who decided to publish the book. I owe them both profound gratitude. While appreciating the role of those acknowledged here, I alone remain responsible for any defects and shortcomings in the book. Needless to say, I do not claim to reflect the African wisdom in my recollection of mediation stories from my experience, but I hope the book will at least add to the reflections of what individual experiences can contribute toward a culturally relevant African perspective on this otherwise universal challenge of negotiating human relations. Even more importantly, I hope it will stimulate others to share their own stories, experiences and reflections on that challenge.

Francis M. Deng
Woodstock, NY
September 2002

Introduction

An Invitation and a Comprehensive Response

When I began reading the letter of invitation from Guy Olivier Faure and Jeffrey Rubin asking me to contribute to a compilation of "a set of interesting and unusual negotiation stories" from which they were planning to prepare an edited volume, my interest was immediately aroused. According to Faure and Rubin (1993), "So much of what has been written about negotiation has come from a rather shallow pool of experience, based on illustrations taken from industrial societies. We wish to leave that traditional work behind and, with your help, to strike out in a more unconventional direction."

Examples of the kind of negotiation stories they were looking for were varied:

> It may be the price of a dowry as negotiated by Indian villagers, the settlement of a fishing dispute between Thais and Malaysians, trade negotiations among Central African pygmies or the Maya-quiche Indians of Central America. Or it may be a negotiation drawn from a more familiar setting. Embedded in the world of daily experience lie untold and unanalyzed accounts of ransom discussions, the exchange of baseball cards among school children, the acquisition by museums and individuals of priceless (and uncertainly valued) works of art, the

payment of bribes, the tacit exchange over the opening of a window in a waiting room, the order of procession through an unmarked traffic intersection, even the matter of finding a seat on a crowded bus.

The letter went on to say: "You have the kinds of personal experiences that are exactly what we are looking for." Even more pointedly, they wrote: "We invite *your* contributions, in particular, for two reasons: first, you have thought about conflict and negotiations over the years. Second, and more importantly, we believe your travels and other experiences have exposed you to unusual and especially interesting negotiations. It is these experiences that we want to relate."

For many years, I had considered doing exactly what was asked of me, but had always felt it both self-serving and too demanding of my scarce time. That the initiative came without my instigation made it compelling; I felt that I should respond positively and substantially. The result turned out to be an extensive selection that is almost comprehensive in scope and by far exceeds the objective of the original request. While portions will be used by Faure and Rubin for their original purpose as appropriate, I decided with their encouragement to complete this volume for separate publication.

Negotiation in its Relational and Cultural Context

The broad conceptual theme which has guided me in this framework is to see negotiation in a cultural framework of values and patterns of behavior. Having been involved in conflict resolution negotiations, both formal and informal, throughout my life, I have come to believe that negotiation is essentially management of human relations. As someone who never received formal training in diplomacy, but moved from legal studies to international civil service and on to the foreign service of my country, the Sudan, as ambassador to Canada, Scandinavia and the United States of America, and as minister of state for foreign affairs for nearly five years, I believe the same thing about diplomacy. And as I see them, these two areas are closely related. Essentially, they deal with human relations involving individuals, groups, or nations. Some people would argue that conflict is the normal state of human interaction (Zartman 1991:299; Zartman 1997). This can only be valid if it is understood to mean that grounds for conflict exist in normal human relations and that the *occurrence* of conflict is therefore normal. If it means that conflict is the normal *pattern* of life, then I would consider that position both empirically questionable and normatively ambiguous. Far from seeing conflict as the normal state of human interaction, I believe that people are more apt to cooperate and harmonize their incompatible or potentially conflictual positions, and that conflict is in fact a crisis which signifies a breakdown in the normal pattern of behavior. In this sense, conflict involves a collision of incompatible positions resulting from a failure to regulate, reconcile, or harmonize the differences. In the normal course of events, society is structured around fundamental values and norms which guide behavior and regulate relations so as to avoid a destructive collision of interests or positions. If people observe the principles of the normative code, which they generally do, the normal pattern would be one of relative cooperation and mutual accommodation, even in a competitive framework. To call that state one of conflict would be to put a negative value judgement on positive motivations and endeavors, and on a relatively high degree of success in peaceful interaction.

Perhaps an illustration with the road behavior of drivers may be instructive. There can be no doubt that drivers on the city roads and highways all compete for space in both directions and at almost the same time. And yet, the general pattern is that they all drive in relative harmony and avoid colliding with one another. The reason for this is that they generally obey the traffic laws, regulations, and road signs. Occasionally, someone inadvertently or recklessly breaks the rules and causes an accident. The word accident normally implies lack of wrongful intent, and indeed, in most cases, the worst that can be alleged is negligent or reckless behavior. Even then the crisis is often managed according to set a rules of criminal or tortuous responsibility and liability. Can one describe drivers on roads and highways as inherently in a state of conflict? It would be more accurate to take accidents as the nearest to a state of conflict, a breakdown in the normal cooperation and relative harmony expected by adherence to the traffic laws, regulations, and road signs.

Even more important than strict empirical interpretation would be the normative implications of holding conflict the normal state of existence, which would tend to foster a disposition that is fundamentally adversarial, suspicious, and conflictual. The extent to which members in a community or group reflect this disposition may depend in large measure on the culture and its normative code. Culture in this context can be defined as "a set of shared and enduring meanings, values, and beliefs that characterize national, ethnic, or other groups and orient their behavior" (Faure & Rubin 1993). As Morton Deutsch has noted: "Social interaction takes place in a social environment – in a family, a group, a community, a nation, a civilization – that has developed techniques, symbols, categories, rules and values that are relevant to human interactions. Hence, to understand the events that occur in social interactions one must comprehend the interplay of these events with the broader sociocultural context in which they occur" (Deutsch 1991:26).

Culture itself is a product of education, both formal and informal, through which the norms of behavior that a society has developed over a long period of time are inculcated from early childhood and passed on from generation to generation. The family is the institutional foundation of education, and, in particular, of the inculcation of basic cultural values. And yet, despite the pivotal role of the family and the culture in shaping values, attitudes, and operational techniques in human relations, individuals differ even within a family in their understanding, appreciation, and application of the values involved. It is this combination of the collective cultural conditioning and the individual inclination to absorb, accept and apply what is acquired that gives significance to personal experiences as particular applications of values, customs and techniques of conflict resolution and diplomacy within a specific cultural framework.

It is important to emphasize that the objective is not merely to resolve a conflict, but to resolve it in a mutually satisfactory manner. This means addressing the root causes and observing such fundamental norms as justice and human dignity. In other words, where change is urgently needed, the status quo cannot simply be supported for the sake of harmony and peaceful interaction.

Generally, as Deutsch (1991:31-32) has observed, "the characteristic processes and effects elicited by a given type of social relationship (for example, cooperative or competitive) also tend to elicit that type of social relationship." This means that "cooperation induces and is induced by a perceived similarity in beliefs and attitudes; a readiness to be helpful; openness in communication; trusting and friendly attitudes; sensitivity to common interests and de-emphasis on opposed interests; an orientation toward enhancing mutual power rather than power differences; and so on." Likewise, "competition induces and is induced by the use of tactics or coercion, threat to deception, attempts to enhance the power differences between one's self and the other; poor communication; minimalization of the awareness of similarities in values and increased sensitivity to opposed interests; suspicions and hostile attitudes; the importance, rigidity and size of the issues in conflict, and so on."

Conflict in this context can be defined as a situation of interaction involving two or more parties in which actions in pursuit of conflicting objectives or interests result in varying degrees of discord. The principal dichotomy is between normally harmonious and cooperative relations and a disruptive adversarial confrontation, culminating at its worst in high intensity violence. On the basis of this definition, conflict resolution can be defined as a normative concept aimed at reconciling, harmonizing, or managing incompatible interests by fostering a process of institutionalized peaceful interaction. Conflict resolution envisages strategies aimed at restoring or establishing the normal state of affairs and raising the level of peaceful, harmonious, cooperative, constructive, and productive interaction.

The achievement of peace and reconciliation becomes a common objective, but one that is only possible if both sides feel that the solution proposed is indeed in the mutual interest. Since both were prepared to enter into conflict in the first place, it means that each must have a subjective view of right and wrong that gives them some degree of right and places some degree of wrong on the opposing party. These subjective perspectives cannot be ignored when negotiation takes place or when proposals are made for resolving a conflict, even though they need not and should not be allowed to have too much influence on such processes. Ultimately, there is indeed a hierarchy of rights and wrongs, but the bottom line is that there is no absolute right or wrong nor is there an absolute winner or loser.

If one comes from a culture, a society, or a family in which unity, harmony, and cooperation are highly valued, then the discord of conflict becomes a disruption that is destabilizing not only to the community, but intrinsically to the individual. And if one assumes further that in any conflict there are contributing factors for which both sides share responsibility, albeit in varying degrees, then the degree of uncertainty involved must create a sense of shared responsibility for a properly tutored or nurtured member of the community. The desire to normalize the situation and restore amicable relations therefore becomes as much a societal as it is an individual objective.

Examples of Negotiation

A few examples will illustrate both the degree to which I have been involved with negotiations throughout my life, and the theme of compromise in the quest for consensus or mutual satisfaction.

5

1. The first incident goes back to my early childhood when I was still quite young and staying at the home of my maternal relatives who were very fond of me and to whom I was very much attached. My father, Deng Majok, paramount chief of the Ngok Dinka, who did not like his children to stay in their maternal homes, visited to request contribution of cattle to one of his numerous marriages. Father indicated that he wanted me to go back home with him. I am told that while he sat in a large crowd under a shaded tree discussing the purpose of his visit, I went and said to my maternal relatives with whom he was assembled that if my father was not given his request, I would have to go back home with him. The assembled crowd burst into laughter and gave me credit for the settlement of the issue. Since Father got what he wanted, he could not insist on my going home with him. As my grandparents also wanted me to stay with them, in a sense, everyone won.

2. Another incident occurred when I was in the intermediate school. My brother Bol, from a different mother, and several of his friends got into a conflict with the headmaster which almost resulted in their dismissal. The headmaster, Fahmi Suleiman, a Christian by mixed Sudanese-Egyptian parentage, was a man of great dedication and discipline. Both to encourage the students to concentrate on their studies and to protect them from the undesirable elements of urban society, free access into town on weekends was forbidden. A system of surprise roll-calls was instituted to check students' movements over the weekends.

One crucial weekend the bell rang and the roll-call showed that many students were out of the premises. Bol was among them. I had myself been out visiting some friends in the nearby Teachers Training College but had returned just before the roll-call. No one knew where the absentees were, but they were not necessarily all in town. Some, including Bol, had gone for a walk into the woods where there were all sorts of wild fruits in addition to the beauty of nature. All were to be punished by lashing. They refused to accept the punishment. Fahmi gave them a deadline within which they were to accept or be dismissed. During the crisis, the minister of education came for a visit and noticed boys in the dormitories while the school was formally assembled. When he inquired in front of the assembly, Fahmi explained, and the minister seemed to approve of Fahmi's decision. Once the specified period expired, they were declared dismissed. The matter seemed much more serious than we had thought. Something had to be done.

Bol and I were friends with Deng Mawir, a son of a leading Twich Dinka chief. Deng and I at first tried to involve the student-body into supporting the punished students. Our ground was that they had done nothing wrong by simply walking into the woods and that the rule had been unduly strict. But the rest of the students refused to be involved. We had to think of a different approach. I thought reconciliation between the headmaster and the students, if initiated by a neutral body, was the best face-saving device for both sides. There were two views to reconcile: Fahmi had declared the students dismissed and the students had refused to be lashed. It was obvious that neither of them really desired that development. Deng and I went to Fahmi's house and implored him to give the students another chance to remain in the school if they accepted their punishment.

Fahmi said that they had had their chance and that his decision had been final, but that he was impressed with our concern for the education of our fellow students and would honor it by giving them another chance. We knew that our main task would be to convince the students to accept the punishment. We also knew that many of them would be too proud to accept. All the same, we approached them and argued that accepting the punishment was nothing compared to the price of losing their education which, we said, would not only be a personal loss, but also a loss to the country; they owed it to themselves and to the country to concede and proceed with their education. The strength of our argument did not convince them to accept lashing, but it made them agree to accept a different form of punishment. As that seemed a significant concession, we rushed back to the headmaster to try to convince him to alter the form of punishment into something like cutting the grass in the school compound. He agreed after a long discussion. It was clear to us that he was not compromising from a weak position, but in appreciation of our efforts and because of his interest in their own education. Two students, a self-possessed son of a police officer, Thomas Dhol, later to join the Sudan Air Force and the Anya-Nya revolutionary army, and Ajaang Chan Nyal, a haughty son of the Awan Rek Dinka chief, refused to accept any punishment. After verbally abusing the headmaster in front of an assembled student body, they handed over their school belongings and left triumphant losers.

3. The third incident for illustration occurred when I was in the University of Khartoum. As one of the founders of a program of exchanges with German universities, which involved study visits during which we worked in factories to acquaint ourselves with working conditions in the country, I led the Sudanese team on our second trip to Germany. The group lived mostly in Berlin where the male students worked at the Siemens factory. We took our work quite seriously, observing the importance of time to the minute, respecting the hierarchy of authority in the factory, and identifying ourselves in every way with the rest of the workers. A minute's delay had to be accounted for; we stopped instantaneously when the bell rang for the coffee break; we ended work with the signal for the day's labor, when we went into our changing rooms, discarded the working uniforms, entered into our common showers, and put on our own clothes.

When the day was done, we were so exhausted that an early time to bed in anticipation of an early time from bed was the wise thing to do. As the factory was a considerable distance from our hostel, we had to rise as early as five o'clock to be at work on time. As I was the supervisor of my male colleagues, I had to work even harder to set the example.

General Ibrahim Abboud, the president of the Sudan, was on an official visit to Germany and the Siemens factory was on his schedule, perhaps in part because Sudanese students were working there. As I recall, his visit coincided with a day that would otherwise have been free. When we were informed and asked to be on the receiving line, my group members, all of them northerners, refused to meet the president, since our students union in the Sudan was militantly opposed to his dictatorial rule. Although I was the only southerner and the government was waging a ferocious war against my people in the South and pursuing a vigorous policy of forced Islamization and Arabization on southern Christians and animists, my opinion was that we should meet the president. Whatever our differences at home, he represented our country abroad and we were in Germany also as representatives of our country. It would not be appropriate to be seen in conflict abroad. We debated the matter intensely with our positions totally opposed.

Then, one of the students suggested almost jokingly that they might reconsider their position if they were given an additional day off. This was of course surprising, considering that the conflict had been over principles. But I took them up on that and negotiated with the management a deal which stipulated that if the group agreed to meet the president, they would be given a day off. As the work was hard and the Germans very strict, the idea of being offered a day off not only promised relief, but also underscored the importance our host-employers attached to our meeting the president. Even this initially met with some resistance among the students, mixed with cynicism over the compromise, but was eventually accepted.

When the president arrived, two contrasting developments took place. The minister for presidential affairs, Mohamed Hassan El Dhow, whom I had met through my father, identified me to the president. Abboud approached me very warmly to say how much he valued my father as a "dear brother" and a champion of national unity. In contrast, one of my colleagues, Tigani El Karib, a close friend, informed me later that the minister of foreign affairs, Ahmed Kheir, had asked him about me, using the name "Samuel" to connote my assumed southern Sudanese Christian identity: "Is that Samuel with you?" the minister had queried. My friend had explained to the minister that I was not only with them, but was the leader of the group. Of course, all my colleagues roared cynically with laughter, saying that I deserved what I got for pushing them to meet an unworthy delegation. I seriously considered writing to the minister to say that if *he* could speak that way, what would he expect from the street. But my colleagues persuaded me against that, arguing that he was a known eccentric and could not have meant what his words had conveyed.

Some ten years later, Ahmed Kheir would both prove them right and break the ice between him and me. I was then ambassador in the Nordic countries. While back in the Sudan on a mission, I decided to interview a number of prominent personalities for a book project on the human factor in the British administration in the Sudan (Deng & Daly 1990). Among the people I interviewed was Sarour Ramli, a tribal chief and one of the leaders of the nationalist movement who was a friend of my father. After the interview, I indicated to Chief Ramli that I wanted to interview Ahmed Kheir but had been warned that he was a difficult person to approach and quite unpredictable. Sarour Ramli informed me that they were friends and suggested that he take me to Ahmed Kheir without any need for an appointment. When we got to Ahmed Kheir, Ramli introduced me as "the son of our brother, Chief Deng Majok, who is our ambassador in Sweden." In a casual manner, Ahmed Kheir shook my hand and remarked, "You Sudanese are absolutely hopeless. Even when a man is made ambassador, he continues to butt in without an appointment the Sudanese way." The humor in his remark was obvious and all present, including myself, laughed. My interview with him was one of the best.

4. Let me move from personal situations to national issues of war and peace in which I believe the same principles apply, although the stakes are naturally much higher. Whether in discussions with northern and southern

Sudanese political leaders or with my peers on both sides, I have been involved in North-South dialogue for decades, and my personal role has been to try to explain the varying points of view in the effort to bridge the conflicting positions. In this, my task has clearly been facilitated by my familiarity with both sides, not only because of my background as a member of a southern group administered in the North, a position in which my family has historically played the leading role, but also because I had gone to schools in both the South and the North.

Through mostly personal initiatives, I was very actively involved in the long peace process that eventually culminated in the 1972 Addis Ababa Agreement. One of the most crucial phases was the preparatory meeting in London in the winter of 1972 to which Bona Malwal and I, at the request of Abel Alier, then the southern minister responsible for the talks, went from the United States and where we spent a considerable amount of time, persuading the hard-liners to moderate their demand for secession or self-determination in view of our people's suffering and Africa's commitment, supported by the world, to preserve colonial borders.

Dunstan Wai has written about Alier's efforts to involve southerners from different parts of the world and the particular role played by the London meeting:

> Alier sent four groups of emissaries to meet with Southerners in exile in an effort to avert any splits in the SSLM [Southern Sudan Liberation Movement]. These emissaries went to Ethiopia, East Africa, Zaire, and England (all of them were Southerners and they were to meet fellow Southerners who were living outside the Sudan). The group which went to London was composed of close political associates and friends of Alier and, at the time of their assignment, they were outside the Sudan. A meeting was successfully arranged with the SSLM's European representatives, Mading de Garang and Lawrence Wol Wol [with Elia Duang Arob from East Africa in attendance]. Peter Gatkwoth [Deputy Minister for Southern Affairs] was in London at the time, but kept in the background.... This London meeting between the SSLM representatives and the Alier emissaries helped both sides to iron out major disagreements on the concept of Regional Autonomy and it also enabled each side to know what the other would and would not accept. Peter

> Gatkwoth reported the outcome of the London deliberations to Alier in Khartoum; Mading de Garang flew to Uganda and thence to the Anya-Nya headquarters in South Sudan to brief the Anya-Nya high command on what transpired in London (Wai 1981:156).

At about three in the morning, everybody being tired and sleepy, I said I had a small point to make. We had to remember, I continued, that there were people who had spent many years in the jungle struggle and had adopted a form of life that gave them a dignity they had not found in the normal state of affairs in the Sudan. Some had become ministers in the rebel government, others judges, others commissioners, and many others held positions of respectability according to their forest government, which they could never have found in the normal conditions. Even the soldier for the most part enjoyed the dignity of his being a fighter for the cause. Some of these people had lived that way for as long as 17 years. Unless these individuals saw a personal gain in joining the cause of peace, they would never return. I argued that whatever system of government we adopted, we should devise a way whereby these men, whose sense of dignity was tied to fighting, could be given alternatives within peace that could substitute the sense of dignity they found in war. We had to give them a reason for wanting peace.

There was a conspicuous silence for moments that seemed incredibly long. Then, Duang, who had been lying on the couch pretending to be disinterested in the whole discussion, suddenly sat up straight and in his cryptic manner of speech, supplemented with forceful gestures of the hands, said, "That's it; that's it. Mading has just said the whole thing. That is the real point in all these discussions. I have nothing more to say." And he sunk back into bed.

Duang was followed by Lawrence Wol, who opened his comments with the remark: "Like Francis, I am going to begin by saying that I have a small comment to make and then drop a bomb." People laughed; then he continued.

By the end of that night's session, a semblance of agreement had been reached. Bona and I sat afterwards to agree on the essentials that he should write to Abel about our meeting. Central to all that was the question of absorbing the Anya-Nya forces into the various institutions of government, one of the pillars of the Addis Ababa Agreement. After he had drafted the letter, Bona read it to me and it went with Peter Gatkwoth.[1]

I had had many discussions with both Mading de Garang and Lawrence Wol on many previous occasions. Indeed, Mading de Garang was to intimate to me years later that it was I who had influenced him the most to see the point of view of the North and to make him responsive to the need for compromise. It was a very moving testimony.

5. Since leaving the government in 1983, I have continued to be involved in the search for ways and means of ending the hostilities that resumed in 1983. I have done some of this through scholarly and other intellectual endeavors in U.S. institutions, among them the Woodrow Wilson Center, the U.S. Institute of Peace, and the Brookings Institution, and some of it in collaboration with institutions and individuals concerned with the war in the Sudan, such as General Olusegun Obasanjo, former head of state of Nigeria and his African Leadership Forum, former president Jimmy Carter of the United States and his Carter Center of Emory University, and a host of other leading personalities in Africa, the United States, and Europe.[2]

In my opinion, the value of these efforts should not be assessed in terms of whether they succeeded in bringing peace to the Sudan in a tangible way or not. The process of peacemaking is incremental and each phase feeds into the next. When a breakthrough occurs, some moves may conspicuously, even ostentatiously, account for it, but many crucial steps leading to that stage may remain unrecognized and even unknown. This does not detract from their substantive and procedural contribution to peace.

The peace efforts in which I have been involved were in significant part intended to widen the circle of those concerned with the war in the Sudan, to raise the level of consciousness in pertinent policy circles worldwide, and to mobilize a variety of humanitarian and diplomatic initiatives. Judged by these objectives, I have no doubt that these efforts were not in vain. As was the case with the Addis Ababa Agreement, when peace is eventually achieved, the warring factions will be

---

1. Dunstan Wai refers to this meeting as one of the crucial phases in the negotiation process leading to the Addis Ababa Agreement.

2. For some of the initiatives in which I have been involved, see Deng & Gifford 1987, Deng 1992, Ahmed & Sorbo 1989, Deng 1993:186-215, Malwal & Kok 1992, The Carter Center 1992, United States Institute of Peace 1993.

recognized and honored for their peace achievement, even if what they do is accept principles that the advocates of peace had for long proposed and advocated. Nonetheless, that would not in any way detract from their contribution or the gratification derivable from it. Until Mading de Garang conveyed the influence our discussions over the years had had on his thinking and positions, I could not have been able to gauge the precise impact of my arguments on him, except a general sense of confidence that the exercise had been worthwhile.

Personal Experiences as Learning Opportunities

Many of the stories told in this collection, especially those pertaining to family relations, are very personal. I have told them because I believe they underscore the culture of talking it out even in matters that others might consider too private to discuss. Once the foundation of discussing such intimate matters in family circles has been established, the path is cleared for open discussions of more public matters and for welcoming third-party mediation. Naturally, some individuals are more predisposed than others to take the initiative in the process. For various reasons, I was one of those.

This book is not, however, an autobiography; I am not telling the story of my life. Nor is it my memoirs, for I am not recollecting my professional experiences in any comprehensive way. What I have tried to do is use selected evidence to substantiate how I approached negotiation, dialogue, mediation, and reconciliation as culturally oriented means of managing human relations, whether in personal relations, intergroup situations, or in diplomacy. The book, therefore, represents a policy-oriented, personalized approach to the cultural dimensions of conflict management and resolution.

Nonetheless, it is not intended to be a self-serving record of achievements or accomplishments, but a report on experiences from which I hope conclusions can be drawn and lessons learned that might shed some light on the generic challenges of negotiations as a conflict resolution technique and the role of culture and the individual in meeting that challenge. Perhaps the crucial factor in these episodes is taking personal initiatives to try to resolve conflicts. Several questions jump to mind about such initiatives: Is the "talking it out" that underlies the initiatives involved in these negotiating stories a cultural or a personal disposition? In either case, are there principles which stimulated the motivation and guided the conduct of intervention or negotiation? What about the counterparts or the actors on the other side, to what extent did they agree or differ on those principles? Was there a common framework of values relating to human relations that made communication, understanding and agreement possible? And what about the cases of failure, could they be explained in terms of differences on the framework of fundamental values, cultural or otherwise, or of personal interests or characteristics? These are only some of the questions that need to be posed and answered to help clarify the overriding issue of whether or not individual initiatives can make a difference and how individuals can be encouraged, motivated, and empowered to contribute toward the improvement of interpersonal and intergroup relations at all levels, local, national, and global.

The book is divided into four parts. In Part One, I first present elements of the Dinka cultural values that have contributed to shaping my perspectives and then proceed with an account of my family background, both paternal and maternal, that has a more immediate bearing on my experiences and responses. In Part Two, I present at some length accounts of internal conflict resolution situations from family to national, in which I have been involved. Part Three covers external relations, both personal encounters abroad in which I tried to reach out in an attempt to resolve conflicts, and situations of bilateral and multilateral diplomacy in which I tried to mediate in an effort to resolve conflicts, support conflict resolution efforts, or otherwise bridge differences. Part Four comprises an interpretive analysis of the principles that guided my mediation efforts in the negotiating stories in this collection, the extent to which my efforts succeeded or failed, and what accounted for the outcome. The conclusion is a brief summary and restatement of the main lessons of the experiences of talking it out at all levels, from local to global.

I

BACKGROUND

1

Dinka Cultural Framework

Dinka Identity

Since the stories of conflict resolution included in this collection mostly emanate from the Dinka, a Nilotic people in the Sudan, an overview of their indigenous value system may be useful in understanding their perspective on the issues involved. Among the central themes of the indigenous value system, which the people themselves highlight and which have engaged anthropological attention, are the pursuit of permanent identity and influence through procreation and ancestral continuity, communal unity and harmony as expressed in idealized concepts of human relations, and principles of individual and collective dignity and integrity. Together, these values constitute the cultural orientation that makes the Dinka, indeed the Nilotics, among the least affected by the processes of modernization or development in Africa.[3]

Although there are no reliable statistics about the ethnic populations of the Sudan, it is now widely accepted that the Dinka number several million people in a country of some twenty-three million people divided among several hundred tribes. This makes the Dinka by far the largest single ethnic group in the country. The Dinka themselves are a congeries

---

3. As Mohamed Omer Beshir observed, while some tribes accepted Islam and adopted Arab dress and a form of pigeon Arabic, "The Nilotics ... remained untouched by the influences of Islam. As long as Islam and Arabic were associated with the administration and the slave traders, they were resisted" (Beshir 1968:13).

of some twenty-four tribal groups, each one further divided into autonomous units.

The fact that the social organization of the Dinka is based on the fragmentation of the society into a large number of tribes indicates the manner in which the segmentation of the land by natural features and the economic activities dictated by the natural environment have influenced settlement patterns, economic activity, and social organizations. Some of the tribes which have now been given names that reflect a wider sense of identity were only loosely connected in cultural terms, but otherwise saw each other as different groups and even as different peoples.

The Crucial Role of Cattle

Perhaps the most striking feature about the Dinka is the extent to which cattle dominate their lives. It has been noted that "One of the determinants of the rapid or slow spread of Christianity in the South has been provided by the contrast between seminomadic cattle-breeding Nilotic tribes (Shilluk, Nuer and Dinka) and the settled agriculturalists", and that the life of the latter groups "is bound up with a cow economy, this animal being a veritable god" (Trimingham 1949b:34). Although writings on the Nilotics understate their agricultural occupation, which is a vitally important feature of their economy, they accurately underscore the crucial role of cattle, which is more than the religious or spiritual aspect implied in considering the cow a god.

The combination of cultivation and herding in the Dinka life perhaps explains the manner in which their pattern of settlements and economic activities reflect both individuality and collectivity. A family, comprising a man, his wife or wives, and dependent or unmarried children, usually lives in a settlement of several huts and a cattle-byre, with a distance of about a mile between them and the next family. A village identified by one name will usually spread over a number of miles with the same pattern repeated, either stretched out or around a wide circle of open land. Occasionally, one sees a cluster of huts and cattle-byres on one spot, indicating that it is the home of a particularly important individual, usually a Chief or a wealthy man. Sections of a tribe and sub-tribes are groups of villages spread out over a considerable distance with recognized borders.

The collective dimension comes with herding and patterns of cattle-camping, when families forming a lineage or a clan with their affiliates collect their cattle and send them with young men and women in seasonal search of good pastures and sources of water. A cattle-camp is a large temporary settlement in an area on a river or at a reliable source of water and plentiful grazing land. In cultural terms, cattle-camping for the Nilotics, even more than settlement in the villages, is the main source of pride, dignity, and the distinctive identity of what it is to be a Dinka. Since cattle are exchanged for bridewealth and bloodwealth, concepts which are considered to be interrelated, they constitute an important means of ensuring the continuation of the lineage and the race through the overriding principle of permanent identity and influence.

Continued Identity and Influence

To appreciate the fundamental values of permanent identity and influence in Dinka and indeed Nilotic society, it is important to bear in mind the close interconnection between their religious beliefs and all other aspects of life. This pervasive role of religion is almost identical to the Islamic system, the difference being that while Islam is centralized and universalized, Nilotic beliefs and practices follow a segmentary lineage system, which provides for autonomous linkages with God through the ancestral spirits, thereby allowing for a measure of religious pluralism and freedom. The flexibility inherent in these values permitted the Nilotics in the past to selectively adopt aspects of foreign religions and cultures, and more recently to accept the Christian mission as an inherent aspect of education or development, with which they complemented their indigenous spiritual, moral and cultural values. Change for them was thus a process of adoption and adaptation of desired elements and not a wholesale radical transformation of society. What is generalized as resistance to change is therefore a selective process involving continuity with change and resisting a radicalism that would undermine the system.

This continuity is seen in terms of intergenerational succession with deep emotional ties to the legacy of the ancestors but with the dynamics of adjustment to changing conditions of the present and the future. Chief Arol Kacwol of the Gok Dinka, then in his late seventies, articulated these values when he said: "It is God who changes the world by giving successive generations their turns. Our forefathers, who have now disappeared ... managed the affairs of their world. Then God changed things ... until they reached us; and they will continue to change. When God comes to change your world, it will be through you and your wife. You will sleep together and bear a child. When that happens, you should

19

know that God has passed on to your children, borne by your wife, the things with which you lived your life" (Deng 1978:50; Deng 1980:51-52). Writing on the Mandari, Jean Buxton quoted similes and parables to make the same point: "People are like fields. They are the grain of the Creator. They are born, grow up, and die .... When grain is ripe and ready it is cut by man and finished. The field is left and then re-sown with new seeds. So it is with man" (Buxton 1973:29). A Dinka chief, Thon Wai, spoke in almost identical words when he said, "Man is like a tree, the tree that grows in the forest; and man is like grass, the grass that grows from the earth. One group goes and another group grows .... Generations die and other generations grow. People never finish" (Deng 1980:172).

Godfrey Lienhardt (1961:26) highlighted the Nilotic value of permanent identity and influence embodied in what the Dinka term *koc-e-nhom*, standing the head upright, when he wrote: "Dinka fear to die without male issue, in whom the survival of their names – the only kind of immortality they know – will be assured."[4] A man who dies without issue to carry on his name is said to perish, *riar*, and become truly mortal. Even then, members of his family are under a moral obligation to marry a woman for him, to live with a relative and beget children to his name, according to what anthropologists call "ghost marriage". Equally, a man who dies leaving behind a widow of childbearing age devolves a moral obligation on his kinsmen to have one of them cohabit with her to continue bearing children to his name in accordance with the custom of "levirate". The amount of cattle paid as compensation for homicide is approximately equivalent to the average amount of bride price paid in marriage and is in fact used to procure a wife to beget children to the name of the dead man. Sharon Hutchinson observed of the Nuer that "The social identity of every woman is fundamentally rooted in her procreative powers and the children they create" (Hutchinson 1980:375).[5]

---

4. A common way to express willingness to die is to say that one has had children to continue the name. Chief Ayeny Aleu, determined to speak his mind, whatever the risks, said, "Let us die as long as we leave our children behind to continue our names" (Deng 1978:47). And in the same vein, Chief Stephan Thongkol remarked, "I am a man who does not fear death. If I die, then I have children" (Deng 1978:47).

5. Immortality through procreation is a widely shared value not only in African traditional society, but also in Islamic culture. Radcliffe Brown (1960:13) observed: "An African marries because he wants children .... The most important part of the 'value' of a woman is her child bearing capacity."

To emphasize the continuance of one's identity and influence in this world even after one's death is not to be understood as implying that the Nilotics do not believe in any form of existence in the unknown world of the dead. Admittedly, their belief on this matter is complex and unclear. They categorically discard the Muslim and Christian concepts of life hereafter as introduced to their converts and insist that once a person is dead he cannot live again and be judged in a second life. On the other hand, apart from calling upon the dead in prayers, which implies a recognition of some form of existence, they sometimes speak of joining their dead and of reporting to them matters of interest or significance among their still living relatives.

The existence in the next world and the continued participation of the dead with the living are not in conflict, but interdependent. People die and disappear, but the reality of their one-time existence remains. They become part of the unknown which largely depends on genealogy, memory, and belief. Continued participation is therefore a physically, socially, and culturally explainable phenomenon.

By emphasizing the survival of every individual through a lineage, the Nilotic concept of continued identity, participation, and influence gives importance to both the individual and the group. This is significantly illustrated by the system of naming in which no one family name is applied to successive generations, but instead, each person bears his or her own name, which is equivalent to the first or Christian name in the western system, and the first name of the father, the grandfather or other ascendant is then added for relational identification. This addition of the personal names of ascendants continues according to the requirements of the particular circumstances. While a father's own name is frequently used to identify the family link, there is no one family name used by the extended family or generations within a family as is the case in the West. This way, the line becomes a chronicle of individual names linked by their relationship in the lineage. The western system also combines the individual with the group identity, but it leaps from the individual's Christian name to that of the original ancestor from whom the family name is derived, leaving out the Christian or first names of the intervening ancestors. Among the Nilotes, even a married woman retains identification with her father and the family line in her genealogical name.

Every child is taught from a very early age to recite and be proud of the father's genealogy to the most distant ancestor remembered. Each ancestor's biography is related to the present status of his lineage. The identity of the lineage and its influence are thus explained in terms of the achievements of its founder and individual descendants and successors.

The communal aspect of the concept is also evident in the fact that continuity creates a chain of ancestors and their descendants, seen as clans or lineages. In the system of naming, people trace their genealogy through individuals; but the clan, the lineage, or the family, as the case may be, is collectively called by the name of its founding father in a manner comparable to that of Arab genealogies or tribes. Alternatively an explicit identification of the descent group as that of so-and-so is made. This segmental significance of permanent identity and influence elucidates the nature of the common, the competitive, and even the conflicting interests of individuals and groups at the various levels of society. There is however no question that the societal ideal is unity and harmony and in many ways this is also considered to a degree, to be the norm.

Core Concepts of Human Relations

Dinka notions of unity and harmony are expressed in a concept called *cieng*, which, as a verb, means "to live together", "to look after", "to order or put in order", "to inhabit", and "to treat [a person]". As a noun, it means "morals", "behavior", "habit", "conduct", "nature of", "custom", "rule", "law", "way of life", or "culture". And these last ten are in addition to the noun forms of the verbs above. As these words indicate, *cieng* may be used in purely descriptive terms, but more often its usage is normative and implies a judgment of values. To emphasize such judgment, the Dinka add appropriate adjectives and adverbs: "bad *cieng*", "good *cieng*", "to *cieng* well", or "to *cieng* badly". To say that "this is *cieng*" or "that a person knows *cieng*" is to evaluate positively; to say that "it is not *cieng*" or that a person "does not know *cieng*" is a negative judgment.

Although some of these meanings may not show it clearly, *cieng* is a concept of human relations. It puts "human" values like dignity and integrity, honor and respect, loyalty and piety, and the power of persuasiveness at its core. Material values are dependent on human values and can therefore be used to express moral sentiments. Thus, traditional education, rather than emphasizing knowledge for its own sake, aims at promoting that which makes for good human relations. In Dinka economy, *cieng* lays stress on sharing produce and providing for the needy rather than on increasing production beyond subsistence. Cooperation in production is important, but the objective is more human than economic. When a man holds a feast and invites his age-mates, friends, and neighbors to work in his field, their aim is to help him produce his normal yield, not to increase production for its own sake.

Cieng does not merely advocate unity and harmony through attuning individual interests to the interests of others; it requires assisting one's fellowmen. Despite the violent nature of Dinka society, good *cieng* is opposed to coercion and violence: for solidarity, harmony, and mutual cooperation are more fittingly achieved voluntarily and by persuasion.

Cieng has the sanctity of a moral order not only inherited from the ancestors who had in turn received it from God, but also fortified and policed by the ancestors. Failure to adhere to its principles is not only disapproved of as an antisocial act warranting temporal punishment, but also, more importantly, as a violation of the moral order which may invite a spiritual curse – illness or death according to the gravity of the violation. Conversely, a distinguished adherence to the ideals of *cieng* receives temporal and spiritual rewards.

Whether it is a way of life or a set of standards, *cieng* begins at home with the family and follows the fiction of the tribe as a family. In fact, *cieng* implies "people" living together in the family, home, village, tribe, or country. The focus of all its various meanings is their way of "living together". This implies both individual and collective identities. The Dinkas believe that in the interest of unity and harmony, differences must be openly voiced, discussed and resolved. To hold grievances "inside" is believed to cause stomach disorders and is therefore unhealthy. Children are encouraged from a very young age to voice their grievances against their elders, politely but assertively.

In line with the inclusive and exclusive character of the lineage system, the society is decentralized and functions through a complex process of the well-documented "segmentary lineage system."[6] Unity in disunity is thus the outcome of the individualized yet collective quest for permanent identity and influence. The concept is essentially individualistic in that it is generated by the individual-oriented importance of enhancing and immortalizing the self. While the self extends into communal identities, the sentiment and united action involved are

---

6. For the system among the Nuer, see Evans-Pritchard 1940, and among the Dinka, see Godfrey Lienhardt 1958. As a result of historical influences from the Arab North, combined with their anomalous position under the Condominium rule, the position of leadership among the Ngok Dinka of Kordofan as will be seen later, is more centralized than among other Dinka tribes.

concentrated in the immediate circles. Since anyone not a member of this immediate group is an outsider, inclusive identifications are increasingly reduced by the multiplicity of intermediate identities.

This system of segmentation applies to and reinforces the whole social organization laying stress on the autonomy of the segments within the segmented unity. As Godfrey Lienhardt (1958:117-118) explained of the Dinka:

> [They] positively value the unity of their tribes, and of their descent groups, while also valuing that autonomy of their component segments which can lead to fragmentations. The basis of this occasional contradiction of values lies in each Dinka ambition .... A man ... wishes to belong to a large descent group, because the greater the numbers of his agnatic kin who have still not formally segmented with separate agnatic groups, the wider the range of people from whom he can hope for help ... in quarrels either within the tribe or outside it. On the other hand, each man wants to found his own descent group, a formal segment of the sub-clan which will for long be remembered by his name, and wants to withdraw from his more distant agnatic kin in order not to be required to help .... These values of personal autonomy and of cooperation, of the inclusiveness and unity of any wider political or genealogical segments and the exclusiveness and autonomy of its several subsegments are from time to time in conflict.

Evans-Pritchard (1940:148-149), describing the system among the Nuer, who are considered perhaps the best example of the acephalous societies with the segmentary lineage system, where social order is maintained through balanced opposition, wrote:

> Any segment sees itself as an independent unit in relation to another segment of the same section, but sees both segments as a unity in relation to another section; and a section which from the point of view of its members comprises opposed segments is seen by members of other sections as an unsegmented unit. Thus there is ... always contradiction in the definition of a political group, for it is a group only in relation to other segments of the same kind and they jointly form a tribe only in relation to other

> Nuer tribes and adjacent foreign tribes which form part of the same political system, and without these relations very little meaning can be attached to the concepts of tribal segment and tribe… Political values are relative and … the political system is an equilibrium between opposed tendencies towards fission and fusion, between the tendency of all groups to segment, and the tendency of all groups to combine with segments of the same order … Hence fission and fusion in political groups are two aspects of the same segmentary principle, and the Nuer tribe and its divisions are to be understood as an equilibrium between these two contradictory, yet complementary, tendencies.

Permanent identity and influence and the implicit values of the segmentary lineage system also account for the Nilotic personal and collective sense of dignity. To be remembered and honored, one must be respected as an individual, honored as an ascendant and eventually revered as an ancestor. This in turn fosters personal pride and dignity in the individual, a phenomenon which accounts for the degree of deference or respect accorded every person in dispute settlement.

Concepts of Dignity, Pride and Respect

Dinka notions of dignity are subsumed in the concept of *dheeng*, the adjective of which is *adheng*. An initiated man who comes of age, legally and socially, meriting the respect due to the status of adulthood is referred to as *adheng*, a word which can only be translated in English as "gentleman." But *dheeng* like *cieng* is a word of multiple meanings – all positive. As a noun, it means nobility, beauty, handsomeness, elegance, charm, grace, gentleness, hospitality, generosity, good manners, discretion, and kindness. The adjective form of all these is *adheng*. Except in prayer or on certain religious occasions, singing and dancing are *dheeng*. Personal decoration, initiation ceremonies, celebration of marriages, the display of "personality-oxen", indeed, any demonstrations of an aesthetic value, are considered *dheeng*. The social background of a man, his physical appearance, the way he walks, talks, eats, or dresses, and the way he behaves towards his fellowmen are all factors in determining his *dheeng*.

Although *dheeng* relates to social relations, it should not be confused with *cieng*: *Cieng* provides standards for evaluating conduct, *dheeng* classifies people according to conduct; *cieng* requires that one should behave in a certain way, *dheeng* labels one virtuous for behaving in that way; *cieng* is a normative concept – a means – *dheeng* is a concept of status – an end.

A remarkable feature of Dinka culture is that it gives everybody some avenue to dignity, honor, and pride. The degree varies, the means are diverse – there are the sensuous means concerned mostly with appearance, bearing, and sex appeal; there are the qualities of virtue in one's relations to others; and there are the ascribed or achieved values, material or spiritual, which help determine one's social standing. Some people distinguish themselves by their sensuous gifts; most people try to win recognition by adherence to the norms of *cieng*. Yet others depend to some extent on the social class into which they are born or which they achieve. These ways are interrelated and cannot really be separated, but only by seeing them as alternatives and by realizing that all ways lead to the same ends can we understand why every Dinka has some share in the values of self-respect, inner pride, and human dignity.

In order to appreciate the dignifying value of *dheeng* to all Dinka it is perhaps useful to have a closer view of who follows which avenue from what status to achieve what alternative status. As material and inherited means to *dheeng* are mostly controlled by the male elders of the lineage, young men and women preoccupy themselves with such values as singing and dancing which, though engaged in by youth in any society, are given a special function by the Dinka as substitute values. This way, the desires of the have-nots are satisfied and their latent hostility pacified.

Although *dheeng* is opposed to obstreperousness and aggressiveness, these are attributes, which Dinka childhood stresses as components of courage and the development of physical strength. At the threshold of adulthood they must be controlled and usefully channeled. Young men are encouraged to engage in activities which require courage, adventure, and endurance without causing destruction or unreasonable risks. They travel far to fell trees for drums; they herd in far-off camps for better grass; they hunt wild animals dangerous to livestock and men; they compete in gymnastics and sports; they punish age-mates who disgrace them with moral wrongs; and, of course, they defend the land and the herds from aggression or otherwise sublimate their aggressiveness with war-songs and dances.

The sublimation of aggressive dispositions in youth is remarkably evident in the significance young men and women give to cattle, in particular bulls and oxen. They sharpen their horns and encourage them to fight. Castrated bulls (that is, oxen) symbolize the qualities of gentleness and submissiveness on the one hand and of aggressiveness and physical courage on the other. In their ox songs, young men and women praise their oxen or the oxen of their husbands or boyfriends for their aggressiveness and valor even as they criticize them for the same. To a young man or woman an ox symbolizes wealth. The pride in one's family's wealth is usually expressed in ox songs and in relation to one's ox. Thus, by owning an ox or a few oxen, a young man, his wife, or girlfriend feels as rich as his/her father who controls the herd. The fact that oxen, though castrated and subdued, are pivotal in the esthetics of cattle is symbolic of the fact that young men and women, though subordinated to elders, occupy a high position in the esthetics of Dinka society.

The central value behind *dheeng* as a concept of pride and dignity is respect, known as *atheek*, a notion of obsessive preoccupation for the Dinka. Respect carries with it several connotations and is manifested in various ways. Ideally, it implies recognition of the attributes considered exemplary for the status of the individual involved, whether as a gentleman, a father, an elder, or a leader. But it also means recognition of an attribute that invokes awe or fear. Similarly, respect may be manifested in a close interaction or by maintaining a distance through avoidance. One respects one's elders with whom one maintains close family relationships.

In the relations with in-laws, especially between the sexes, respect requires that a person be self-composed and behave with great care and constraint in the presence of his/her in-laws, especially of the opposite sex. One does not speak face to face with a senior relative-in-law of the opposite sex. It is common to see a man on one side of a tree and a woman on the other side, or one inside a hut while the other remains outside, the two solemnly discussing an issue which may not be all that serious. When a man meets a woman on the road, he snaps his fingers loudly saying, "May we meet?" "May I come?" or "May I pass?" to which she replies, "Yes, with virtue." When a Dinka woman approaches her sitting males-in-law or any men who might fall into that category, she kneels quite a distance away, announces her appearance, and approaches on her knees, stopping several yards away to talk. From a western-oriented liberal perspective, these practices may reflect gender disparities, but to the Dinka, they signify respect. It is also the respect of avoidance which prevents the mother of a married son or daughter from sitting on their marriage bed.

Another form of respect is to avoid encounter with sources of danger, whether "relatives" or adversaries. For instance, respect for deadly creatures like snakes and wild animals, which are ritually adopted as clan deities and therefore relatives, requires meeting such obligations as making offerings to them, but otherwise keeping a safe distance. In their war songs, tribes brag about being avoided in respect by their adversaries. In that sense, respect means fear. It is indeed the quest for this kind of respect or, to put it in reverse, the desire to dispel disrespect that encourages violence among young warriors.

Evans-Pritchard (1940:181-182) captured this aspect of Nilotic culture with reference to the Nuer who represent perhaps an extreme example of what are otherwise common characteristics: "That every Nuer considers himself as good as his neighbor is evident in their every movement. They strut about like lords of the earth, which, indeed, they consider themselves to be. There is no master and no servant in their society, but only equals who regard themselves as God's noblest creation ... In his daily relations with his fellows a man shows respect to his elders, to his 'fathers,' and to certain persons of ritual status, within the circuit of its reference, so long as they do not infringe on his independence."

Reconciliatory Leaders

Despite Nilotic egalitarianism and individual sense of pride and independence, leadership is of critical importance to their value-system. Traditionally, a chief is not a ruler in the western sense but a spiritual leader whose power rests on divine enlightenment and wisdom.[7] In order to reconcile his people, the chief should be a model of virtue, righteousness, and, in Dinka terms, "a man with a cool heart," who must depend on persuasion and consensus building rather than on coercion and dictation. Godfrey Lienhardt (1963:828) wrote:

> I suppose anyone would agree that one of the most
> decisive marks of a society we should call in a spiritual
> sense "civilized" is a highly developed sense and practice
> of justice, and here, the Nilotics, with their intense respect

---

7. Cole and Huntington (1985: 7) have noted: "At the center of Dinka religion are The Masters of the Spear, among the Ngok it is the great chief, *bany dit*, who is holder of the Sacred Spears."

for the personal independence and dignity of themselves and of others, may be superior to societies more civilized in the material sense... The Dinka and Nuer are a warlike people, and have never been slow to assert their rights as they see them by physical force. Yet, if one sees Dinka trying to resolve a dispute, according to their own customary law, there is often a reasonableness and a gentleness in their demeanor, a courtesy and a quietness in the speech of those elder men superior in status and wisdom, an attempt to get at the whole truth of the situation before them.[8]

Evans-Pritchard (1940:164) himself observed of the Nuer settlement of disputes: "The five important elements in a settlement of this kind by direct negotiation through a chief seem to be (1) the desire of the disputants to settle their dispute, (2) the sanctity of the chief's person and his traditional role of mediator, (3) full and free discussion leading to a high measure of agreement between all present, (4) the feeling that a man can give way to the chief and elders without loss of dignity where he would not have given way to his opponent, and (5) recognition by the losing party of the justice of the other side's case."

The chief's mediation between individuals and groups, using largely persuasive strategies, was a feature of this all-embracing responsibility toward the dual worlds of man and spirits, but in terms of political and governmental power, not less significant. As Chief Yusuf Deng points out, to the Dinka the power of persuasion is more durable than the power of the arm. "The Dinka used to say that a man defeated by strength of power comes back ... But a man who is defeated with words does not return" (Deng 1980:195).

Aggressive Youths

Despite the emphasis the chiefs and the elders place on persuasion, Nilotic society was very violent not only in its confrontation with outside aggressors, but also within itself. It can indeed be argued that the emphasis placed on the ideals of peace, unity, mediation and persuasion emanates from the pervasiveness of violence. Internal violence can in turn be attributed to generational distribution of roles and functions and the

---

8. See also Lienhardt 1961:248

sense of dignity young members of the warrior age-sets acquire from their identity and status as warriors, defenders of the society from aggression.[9] Young men are organized into age-sets in their mid-teens when they undergo an initiation involving a physical ordeal from which they graduate as "gentlemen" with gifts of spears and bulls, "personality oxen", as symbols of their identity as warriors and herders. Boys start to train for the warring and herding roles from an early age through a wide variety of games and sports. In this, they are supported and encouraged by corresponding women's age-sets, which correlate to men's and by the society as a whole, including the elders, who view them with great favor and admiration.

In fulfillment of their esteemed role, young warriors exaggerate aggressiveness and disposition to warfare so much so that the slightest provocation, whether through the violation of territorial integrity of grazing lands or sources of water, or something as trivial as a slanderous song by an adversary, would provoke hostilities. Once a tribal war has broken out, all generations of men fit to fight and women following them to render support, will join in. Those who are old enough to be experienced with warfare and to have procreated, yet young enough to be fit to fight are the ideal soldiers, although often times, it is the newly initiated who have not yet married, or are newly married, who are eager to demonstrate their manhood. As Jean Buxton (1963:124) observed of the Mandari, "The still active older men fought on the outside ... while the young inexperienced, and unmarried with no sons to bear their name, were placed on the inside." Although the chiefs themselves are peacemakers and not warriors, the "generals" who plan and direct the fight among the older, more responsible managers of warfare are members of chiefly clans with the divine authority to "bless" in addition to transmitting their war skills. It will not be until a later stage that the role

---

9. Evans-Pritchard argues that the age-sets among the Nuer "have no definite military functions" even though "youth who have recently been initiated are anxious for their first raid, and consider that they ought to earn for their set a reputation for valor, and it is likely that raids were generally conducted in the main by men of the most junior set." Evans-Pritchard (1940:253) however sees the role of age-sets as a cross-cutting one that both supplements and modifies the kinship system. P.P. Howell (1951:258) has noted that "the age-set system ... appears to have a greater functional meaning among the Ngork [sic] than any other Nilotics, Dinka, Nuer or Shilluk of whom I have had first hand experience." For a detailed discussion of the age-set system among Nilotic societies with special reference to the Atuot, see Burton 1980:146-160.

of chiefs and elders as peacemakers is then invoked to negotiate or mediate reconciliation.

The delicate balance between the violence of youth and the peacemaking role of leaders was articulated by Chief Arol Kacwol, reacting to the anthropological assertion that the Dinka are among the chiefless peoples where force was the deterrent behind the social order: "It is true, there was force. People killed one another and those who could defeat people in battle were avoided in respect. But people lived by the way God had given them. There were the Chiefs of the Spear. If anything went wrong, they would come to stop the people from fighting. Each side would tell the chief its cause and he would go to each side and settle the matter without blood. Men [chiefs] of the [sacred] spear were against bloodshed. That was the way God wanted it from the ancient past when he created people" (Deng 1980:58-59).

And in the words of Chief Giir Thiik, "There was the power of words. It was a way of life with its great leaders. If anything went wrong, people would get up and travel to [the] Chief. He would be called upon to say his word. He would say, 'do it this way.' It was not a way of life of the power of the arm" (Deng 1980:42). It is clearly paradoxical but perhaps logical that a society in which violence was so pervasive would be almost equally preoccupied with persuasive strategies and peacemaking.

Superior Men and Influential Women

Another paradox of Nilotic society relates to the status of women. The male-oriented lineage system implies that men are superior to women in much the same way that elders are considered superior to youth. Since children in perpetuation of the male-oriented ancestral line were the main objectives of marriage and the family, men could marry as many women as they could afford, while a woman could marry only one man and had to respect the fidelity of the one-sided exclusiveness of marriage. This had the effect of generating in the women an endemic tendency toward jealousy and divisiveness. Lack of a clear voice in decision making also fostered in them a tendency toward manipulative techniques for influencing their husbands and sons, which were suspect as inherently divisive to the male members of the family, the lineage, and the clan.

And yet as women are indispensable to the attainment of those societal goals, they are at the center of the value system and can be said to provide the motivation for virtually everything men do. Even the young

31

warriors' propensity toward violence is aimed at impressing women. Not only are they wives and mothers, active or potential, but in that capacity they are vital to shaping the child's character and agnatic loyalties. Maternal kin are in many respects, especially in terms of the spiritual powers to bless and curse, considered more important than the paternal kin. Through the system of bridewealth, women are also the medium for wealth exchange and distribution. They also play a supportive role in cattle husbandry and even in warfare, for as Jean Buxton said of the Mandari, "If the fighting was near home the women and boys followed to pick up spears and arrows and assist the wounded" (Buxton 1963:124).

The Nilotic attitude of domination with respect toward women has sometimes led to extreme views about their place in society with some alleging a form of enslavement while others maintain that "The position held by the woman is a high one, and she is considered man's equal" (Titherington 1927:153, 159). Writing on the Nuer, Sharon Hutchinson (1980:371) explains the degree to which men and women are interdependent in a manner that approximates equality despite appearances to the contrary: "[T]he dependence of men upon the reproductive and nurturing powers of women assures the latter an important source of control: mutual dependence implies a mutual independence. Women have an exclusive realm of activity and hence an exclusive domain of control and influence. Moreover, they can subvert political alliances and aggravate divisions within the male hierarchy through the manipulation of their children's loyalties ... These bonds of mutual dependence uniting men and women ... outline some of the sources, characteristics and limitations of male domination and authority."

Jean Buxton (1973:209-210), after explaining the ideological foundations of women's position in Mandari society, seeing it largely in the context of their superior creative reproductive capacity, observed that "there is ... a direct connection between the high status of women and the explicit ideology", but that "the ideal of female value is often contradicted in daily life by the ambivalence inherent in actual male/female relationships. Further, Mandari women, though displaying dignity of person, independent-mindedness, and influence, are, from the point of view of property-ownership and the exercise of political power, much less advantageously placed than men. Greater creative importance is balanced by subordination in executive affairs and femininity involves paradoxes alien to the simpler maleness."

The bottom-line, however, is that there were significant inequalities in the value-institutional structures and processes of traditional Nilotic society. As society was stratified along the lines of descent, age and gender, distributional patterns were structured along those lines. Leaders descended from predetermined lineages, elders predominated over youth, and men over women. Positive and negative traits were attributed to the structural position of the individual or the group in the hierarchy, with the privileged reflecting a higher degree of conformity to the ideals and the disadvantaged popularly perceived as depicting negative traits. As representatives of the ancestors and the deities, the chiefs symbolized the ideals of the social order; elders stood in close association with the spiritual leaders in upholding the ideals; youth displayed the aggressiveness from which they derived their dignity; and women were revered as "mothers" who nurtured life, particularly in the womb and in infancy, and were valued as sources of wealth distribution through "bride price" in marriage, but were ambivalently criticized for alleged propensity toward jealousy and divisiveness which threaten the unity of the larger family and the clan.

Nilotic Values and Their Implications

It is important to remember these values and practices as the cornerstones of Nilotic identity, cohesiveness, and cultural continuity. As alternatives were limited, conformity was the general pattern. Nevertheless, in extreme instances, individuals and groups might disaffiliate themselves and move to settle elsewhere. In fact, the segmentary lineage system so characteristic of Nilotic society is attributed by anthropologists to this process of disaffiliation and segmentation. Even then, the ancestral values of the clan system are preserved, affiliation into the clan is maintained, although new sub-divisions might emerge, and the rules of exogamy which prohibit marriage among members of the clan, however distant the relationship, are observed.

A number of implications emerge from the foregoing Nilotic value system. Perhaps the most important and pervasive is that it gives the age-long issues of religion – origin and the destiny of life – a worldly orientation that makes the people intensely religious, ethical and moral, constantly preoccupied with the word of God, fearful of committing wrong, by commission or omission, or through inadvertence. According to the Seligmans, "The Dinka, and their kindred the Nuer, are by far the most religious peoples in the Sudan" (Seligman 1932). Writing on the Nuer, Evans-Pritchard (1971:17) observed, "[I]f a man keeps in the right – does not break divinely sanctioned interdictions, does not wrong others, and fulfills his obligations to spiritual beings and the ghosts and to his kith and kin – he will avoid, not all misfortunes, for some misfortunes come to one and all alike, but those extra and special misfortunes which come from *dueri* faults." As Lienhardt (1961:46-47) has observed: "God is held ultimately to reveal the truth and falsehood, and in doing so provide a sanction for justice between men. Cruelty, lying, cheating, and all other forms of injustice are hated by God, and the Dinka suppose that, in some way, if concealed by men, they will be revealed by him." Chief Thon Wai reflected the Dinka view when he said: "Even if a right is hidden, God will always uncover the right of a person … It may be covered for ten years, and God will uncover it for ten years, until it reappears … God never loses sight of the right" (Deng 1978:66).[10]

Another implication which is correlative to the almost religiously ordained Nilotic view of themselves and their heritage, is a deep sense of pride in their race and culture which approximates ethnocentrism and fosters in them a conservative approach to change. It is a subjective sense of self-esteem that does not impose racism on others, nor does it want to be imposed upon.

A third and equally important implication of the segmentary lineage system is a deep sense of autonomy not only for the groups at various levels of the social structure, but also down to the individual. In particular, the Nilotics are uncompromisingly resentful of coercive authority and any interference with their independence and freedom. This has been a major problem in the democratic process since every Nilote sees himself entitled to leadership and subordinate to none.

A fourth implication which may sound contradictory to the Nilotics' spirit of egalitarianism, but is not really, is the importance they attach to a notion of leadership. Their respect for a worthy leader quickly approximates spiritual veneration, linked with ancestral legacy, real or assumed. In the traditional order of things, there was no room whatsoever for an authoritarian leader, except through the awe of spiritual power that could only be effective if morally justified.

A fifth implication, a corollary of the Nilotic sense of uniqueness, is their aversion to assimilation by others even though they are more amenable to assimilating. This does not mean that individuals in a foreign context are not adaptable. Quite the contrary, a deep sense of dignity and pride could propel a person to adapt and integrate in order to win

---

10. Cf Deng 1980:154-55.

acceptance and respect by the standards of the new context, while the society as a whole remains prone to the preservation of its ethnic and cultural identity. Although the Nilotics practice exogamy, prohibiting marriages among relatives by blood and affinity, resistance to assimilation implies opposition to tribally, and certainly racially, mixed marriages. Their attitude in this respect does not differ much from that of the Muslim North, but since their prejudice against mixed marriage is regarded as mere convention or tradition, it is not given the degree of recognition or significance accorded to the religiously ordained prejudice of the Muslim communities. Furthermore, despite the prejudice against marriage outside the group, once marriage has taken place, it is expected that the outsider be fully accepted as a member of the family without any discrimination attaching to the parent or the offspring.

These Nilotic values have been consistently highlighted and sometimes exaggerated by observers. One observer, for instance, wrote that "the Nilotics have 'no respect whatsoever for the wisdom of strangers, all of whom they despise as beggarly, cattleless wretches, inferior in every way to Nilotic gentlemen who were Lords of the Earth'" (Khalid 1989:47). In an almost identical language, another observer wrote: "They consider their country the best in the world and everyone inferior to themselves. For this reason they ... scorn European and Arab culture ... Their attitude toward any authority that would coerce them is one of touchiness, pride, and reckless hatred of submission ... They are self-reliant, brave fighters, turbulent and aggressive, and are extremely conservative in their aversion from innovation and interference" (Butt 1952:116).

Nilotic comparative perspectives on themselves and others have, however, been described in more tempered language. Trimingham (1949a:34), explaining the need to understand the Nilotics' value system in order to design an appropriately sensitive approach to the Christian mission among them, wrote that they "are intensely conservative and very proud of their civilization," and went on to observe: "They have acted as a bastion against the penetration of Islam by having proved impervious to its seductions. Christian work amongst them demanded from the first a distinctive treatment and they have only just begun to respond in some degree to the treasures of the Christian Gospel. Consequently, it is very important now – the barriers are beginning to be broken down – to the penetration of new ideas and ways of life, that the missionary effort should be intensified among them, so that with the Christianizing of their civilization their unique ethnic qualities may still be preserved and they may find a true sphere within the structure of the wider Sudan."

North-South Tensions and Conflict

Pride in race and culture are, needless to say, shared even to a greater degree by the Arabs. It is no exaggeration to say that the incompatibility may not be so much due to the differences as to similarities of otherwise parallel systems of values and institutions. One major difference worth emphasis is that the Nilotics, unlike the Arabs, do not wish to impose their mold on others. The ethnocentrism of Nilotic self-image is based on feelings of distinctiveness as a people rather than on assumptions of domination and superiority over others, except insofar as they take themselves as the standard of what is normal in God's creation of humankind and its dignity. Having been dominated and ruled by others and having seen the technological superiority of others over them, their sentiments of human worth are more in the realm of moral and spiritual rather than material values.

Pertinent in this context is the modern, pluralistic framework of the nation-state, with its conflictual North-South dichotomy. Most of the experiences of negotiation within the domestic context in this volume relate in one way or another to the North-South conflict that has raged intermittently in the Sudan for nearly four decades. It is ironic that the civil war in Sudan should be the result of the country's greatest promise as a microcosm of Africa and a bridge or crossroads between the continent and the Middle East. The racial, ethnic, cultural, and religious diversities in Sudan's composition are most often described as falling into North and South. The North, two-thirds of the country in land and population, is inhabited by indigenous tribal groups, the dominant among whom intermarried with incoming Arab traders and over centuries, dating back to time immemorial but heightened by the advent of Islam in the seventh century, produced a genetically mixed African-Arab racial and cultural "hybrid." The resulting racial characteristics look very similar to those of the African groups in the continent below the Sahara: Ethiopia, Eritrea, Djibouti, and Somalia in the East, Chad and Niger and Mali in the center, and Senegal to the West. Indeed, the Arabic phrase, *Bilad El Sudan*, from which the Sudan derives its name, means "Land of the Blacks" and refers to all these sub-Saharan territories.

Unlike the situation in these countries where people identify themselves as Africans, the northern Sudanese see themselves as Arabs and deny the strongly African element in their skin color and physical features. They associate these features with the Negroid race which they see as the mother-race of slaves, inferior, and demeaned. Having been permitted by Islam and the assimilationist Arab culture to pass into the supposedly superior Arab-Islamic identity, northern Sudanese "Arabs" vehemently resist any attempt by the non-Arab population to identify the country with Black Africa.

There are also non-Arab communities in the North which, though large in numbers proportional to the Arabized tribes, have been partially assimilated by their conversion to Islam and adoption of Arabic as the language of communication with the other tribes. Since Islam, Arabic, and the racial and ethnic concept of Arabism are viewed in the Sudan as closely intertwined, these groups have been virtually adopted by the dominant Arab groups as "orphans" of Arabism, redeemed from the degraded status of their slave origin as Blacks. While the North was undergoing Arabization and Islamization, mostly through the Egyptian connection, the South remained isolated, protected by natural barriers and the resistance of the Nilotic warrior tribes, primarily Dinka, Nuer, and Shilluk. This isolation was punctuated, however, with the violent incursions by waves of adventurous invaders from the North in search of slaves, ivory, and gold. The Nile was their link with their victims and their eventual redeemers.

Aggression from the North peaked during the mid-19th century when a semblance of administrative control by the Turko-Egyptian rule of 1821-1885 enabled slave hunters and traders to recruit and deploy local armies for the purpose. The Turko-Egyptian administration's attempts at stopping the slave trade only made it more organized and adventurous. It also won Mohamed Ahmed, the self-declared Mahdi, the support of the slave traders for his revolution that ousted the Turko-Egyptian rule in 1885.

The British, who jointly with the Egyptians reconquered the Sudan in 1898, administered the two parts of the country as separate and unequal entities. The North received more economic, social, and cultural development along Arab-Islamic lines and was the first to become politically conscious and to spearhead the nationalist movement in collaboration with Egypt. In the name of protection from the North, the South was "closed" to outside influences and was preserved in its natural milieu, modified only by the activities of the Christian missionaries, whose task it was to introduce Christianity and the rudiments of Western civilization, reflected in basic education and medical services. Whether the country eventually would be united or partitioned, with the South becoming a part of Uganda or Kenya or an independent state, was left unresolved until the dawn of independence.

In 1947, only 9 years before independence, the British, under pressure from the North and Egypt, decided abruptly to reverse their separatist policy and to evolve the country toward independence as a unitary state. From that time on, relations between the North and the South were set on a turbulent course. The fears of the South increasingly intensified. In August 1955, only 4 months before independence, violence erupted and rapidly spread as a result of widely shared fear that independence was going to mean a change of masters – from the British to the Arabs – and could entail the return of the slave trade. The mutineers eventually were persuaded to lay down their arms by the outgoing British Governor-General, who promised justice. When the northern parties also pledged to give serious consideration to the southern call for a federal system of government, the country united behind the declaration of independence of January 1, 1956.

It soon became evident, however, that the North was not intent on honoring the pledge for a federal constitution but, quite to the contrary, sought to impose Arabization and Islamization on the South in an attempt at achieving national unity through uniformity. There was even a serious call for the adoption of an Islamic constitution. In response, hostilities were reactivated under the leadership of the Southern Sudan Liberation Movement (SSLM), better known as Anya-Nya, the name of its military wing, whose objective was the secession of the South and the establishment of an independent state. In 1972, however, the movement agreed with the military government of Jaafar Mohamed Nimeiri on a compromise solution, the highly acclaimed Addis Ababa Agreement, which granted the South regional autonomy.

Nimeiri's unilateral abrogation of the Addis Ababa Agreement – by dividing the South into three regions with reduced constitutional powers and then, in alliance with the Muslim Brotherhood, imposing the so-called September (Islamic) Laws – led to the resumption of hostilities in 1983 by the Sudan People's Liberation Movement (SPLM) and its military wing, the Sudan People's Liberation Army (SPLA). Initially, the declared objective of the SPLM/SPLA was not the secession or the autonomy of the South, but rather the creation of a new Sudan, united and free of racial, religious, cultural, or gender discrimination. Developments have since moved the SPLM/SPLA toward the demand for self-determination for the South and other marginalized areas.

In 1985, two years after hostilities resumed, Nimeiri was overthrown by a popular uprising. A transitional government coaxed the country back to parliamentary democracy within a year, but military rule returned on June 30, 1989, in a coup led by previously unknown middle-ranking officers proclaiming a "Revolution of National Salvation", which became even more rigorous in imposing Shari'a and the Islamic agenda. This development was pivotal in generating internal differences within the South on the objectives of the movement, with the breakaway faction demanding independence. The call for self-determination for the South and other marginalized areas represents a compromise around which the South is forging a unity of purpose.

Much of my adult life has gone into efforts to address the North-South problem and other conflicts related to it. The mere fact of the conflict, however, does not explain each individual's involvement or the particular approach he or she brings to the process of negotiation or peacemaking. For this reason, the contextual background of the negotiating individual, including culture, family, personality, education, and outlook are all significant factors to understanding a particular approach. It is certainly relevant to understanding my negotiating perspective that my country is not only divided by race, culture, and religion, into North and South, but that I come from the Ngok Dinka, on a border area between North and South where hostile Nilotic and Arab tribes meet, interact, conflict, cooperate, or coexist.

A pertinent aspect of the conflicting value systems in North-South relations is the way negotiation is measured by the yardstick of moral and spiritual values in the role of leadership. If negotiation is perceived as a game of wits in which the outcome depends on cleverness, rather than on the discovery of the truth and a fair allocation of rights based on that truth, it is hard to conceive of it in the context of the Nilotic scheme of values. Indeed there is no equivalent concept in the Dinka language.

Of course, life itself is a process of daily negotiations in many small, different ways, but in a situation of open or pronounced conflict, the Nilotic mode of resolution implies a third party mediation. But mediation is more than a neutral search for the truth, however conceived, for the mediator cannot be successful unless he or she can persuade the parties to see and accept the truth. Indeed the Dinka word for mediation is *luk*, which means "persuasion".

It is in this area of the moral and spiritual values that the Nilotics are particularly condescending to the northern Sudanese. The history of animosity between the two parts of the country and the series of promises made and broken or never intended to be met in the first place have left the South with a deep sense of mistrust of northerners as morally corrupt, and they see this corruption as racially and culturally inherent.

The history of North-South relations has indeed been one of promises made and dishonored. The low and high points in the relationship can be correlated directly to agreements and their breach. There are times when agreements promised in a mutually acceptable framework are accepted, and times when the agreements are dishonored: the North attempts to impose its Islamic Arab vision on the whole country, and the South falls back on its violent resistance.

As a result of this historical evidence, even after the highly acclaimed Addis Ababa Agreement of 1972, southerners in general and the more experienced tribal chiefs in particular remained skeptical of the long-term prospects of the Addis Ababa accord because of their mistrust of the northerners.

Chief Makuei Bilkuei advised the southerners to take the Addis Ababa accord with cautious reservations: "The Arab said, 'You South, let us unite.' Is that not what the Arab said? If you accept, you open one eye and close the other eye ... Let one eye speak with the Arab and let the other eye remain closed" (Deng 1980:79).

Chief Stephan Thongkol was even more emphatic that the Addis Ababa accord was merely a pragmatic, self-interested concession from the North that did not resolve the real issues dividing the two sets of people. In other words, it was a superficial, clever ploy not based on acceptance of the deeper truths. To him, the conflict continued:

> When they found that the thing was ... difficult ... and that it was also killing some of them, they introduced other policies. But the war is going on. We cannot say we are relatives. The war is still on. There is no relationship .... Respect towards people is missing. Our chiefs don't have a salary that is respectable. We are still being insulted. Some people still call us slaves. Some of us are still actually slaves .... We cannot marry among them. They take our girls and turn them into prostitutes, and when they have made them prostitutes, they send them back. They are still controlling our economy: they are the people who own the shops; and all the money is still in their hands (Deng 1980:130).

If, as experience seems to show, negotiation for the South is identifying the truth with the help of mediators, agreeing on the basis of that truth, and holding to it, but for the North it is a game of wits in which one aims at carrying the day in a tactical maneuver that alters with the changing climate, then there is no common moral ground from which to talk. This indeed is the crisis of North-South relations.

In their moral conviction that in every conflict there is a truth embodying the relative rights and wrongs involved in the situation and that what is needed is to explore that truth, the Nilotics encourage voicing grievances and a candid discussion of the differences. I should hasten to add that the existence of an objective truth in the belief of the people does not invalidate the normative value of apportioning rights and wrongs to cater for the interest of both sides and promote a consensus. That the truth largely favors one party does not absolve that party from the moral obligation of responding to the perceived rights of the other, if only to save face or compensate for a loss. Toward that end, dialogue and mediation are encouraged. "Talking it out" is therefore a Nilotic trait, very much in keeping with the fundamental values of the social order. This does not necessarily mean that the specific manner in which I responded to the conflict situations involved in my negotiating stories included in this volume claim to represent the way all or even most Nilotics would respond. The extent to which individuals observe the normative code of their society differs considerably.

2
Paternal Legacy

The Pajok Lineage of the Ngok Dinka

If the argument that perspectives on negotiations in terms of both disposition and techniques are at least partly influenced by cultural and social conditions and that these in turn are products of education in the broad sense in which the family figures prominently, then it goes without saying that an individual's family background is crucial to appreciate his or her perception of the issues involved. The degree to which culture and personality is the determining factor becomes a matter of detail that can be debated.

Without prejudging the question of whether my negotiating disposition and techniques are culturally based or individually geared, a word about the family background may be instructive. I come from a family, the Pajok lineage or clan, which for many generations has provided leadership for the Ngok Dinka on the volatile borders between the Arab Muslim North and the African South of the Sudan, an area in which the pastoral warrior Arab and Nilotic tribes interact and often clash over pastures and sources of water. Even prior to the colonial intervention, these leaders entered into diplomatic relations with their Arab counterparts and negotiated pacts which provided their people with significant protection against slave raiders and fostered cordial ties that transcended racial and religious differences between their respective peoples. This history is frequently recalled both to explain the deterioration that has taken place in recent years and to uphold standards that are not only desirable but also achievable, and indeed were once achieved.

Despite centuries of contact with Arab tribes and the adoption, adaptation, and assimilation of certain northern cultural traits, the Ngok have remained distinctly Dinka and in some respects more so than their compatriots further south. It is easy to theorize that, placed at the point of contact with the outside world and confronting a forceful, assimilationist civilization that claimed universality, their instinct for cultural self-preservation has been commensurate with the threats of inequitable integration. Paul Howell, a British anthropologist-administrator who served in the area, in a work published in 1951, noted, "To the casual observer ... the Ngork [sic] Dinka may appear deeply affected by Arab influences. Closer observations show that the so-called process of 'Arabization' is only skin deep ... 99 per cent of the Ngork, despite generations of contact with the Arab, are quite unaffected by any form of Islamic traits and are as completely Dinka as their Dinka neighbours to the South" (Howell 1951:248).

With the advent of colonial rule, Ngok leaders sought protection for their people from the central government to the North by affiliating themselves into Kordofan, one of the northern provinces. By virtue of their early contact and agreement with the colonial rule, Ngok leadership was viewed by the southern Dinka as providing a protective shield in their adversarial relations with the Arabs, mostly through diplomatic representation and management or resolution of conflicts on those highly sensitive borders.

Oral history, which embodies mythology, is generally associated with the legends of leadership. Being a people at the frontiers of contacts with the hostile world to the North, the Ngok Dinka have been particularly dependent on the role of their divine leadership which they trace back for over ten generations and which links up with more mythical prototypes of original leadership, allegedly from the Byre of Creation.

Ngok Dinka society, like other Nilotic societies, is organized on the basis of territory, clan or lineage, and functional age-setting. There are nine sub-tribal groups in Ngok society, now known as *wot* (singular *wut*), literally cattle-camps, or by the Arabic word *omudiya*, each of which is headed by a sub-tribal chief, *beny*, known as *omda* in Arabic. Since some of the names of these territorial entities and their chiefs will keep recurring in this book, introducing them at this stage may be useful. Listed alphabetically, they include Abyor, sub-tribe of the paramount chief, Achak, Achweng, Alei, Anyiel, Bongo, Diil, Mareng, and

Mannyuar, the sub-tribe of the second leading lineage in the tribe. Each sub-tribe is further divided into two or three sections, each headed by a chief known by the Arabic word *sheikh*, perverted by the Dinka into *macheik*. As individuals move and settle wherever they choose, over time, clans or lineages cut across these territorial entities. But within the section, the lineage is recognized as a political entity headed by a *nomgol*, "clan head". Age-sets are organized on sub-tribal bases as warrior regiments. It is between sub-tribes that tribal wars were fought, using spears. Within sections, fights were considered internal and only clubs were permitted as weapons of war. In the major wars, the various sub-tribes would align themselves into two main alliances headed by Abyor and Mannyuar.

Ngok leadership is associated with two clans or lineages, Dhiendior and Pajok, which are found in most of the sub-tribes, but associated principally with Abyor and Mannyuar, and both trace their direct lines over ten generations. Although these two clans have intermarried at almost all genealogical levels to foster cooperation, they remain intensely competitive. It is generally believed among Dinka tribes that the Dhiendior are the most spiritually powerful, being the descendants of the legendary Longar, the spiritual hero of the Dinka. Jok, the founder of Pajok, whom methodology relates to the original Dhiendior lineage, is said to have branched out and founded his own line that became the principal competitors of the original line. Among the Ngok Dinka, the descendants of Jok progressively assumed the leading role until colonial intervention confirmed them as the predominant government rulers in the area. As a consequence, the myths of original leadership have tended to be reinterpreted to justify and reinforce the contemporary preeminence of Pajok. But, although the role of the Dhiendior has largely been relegated to that of an opposition group, the competition remains intense.

According to the now dominant myths of the Pajok lineage, Jok is believed to have emerged from the Byre of Creation with the two Sacred Spears that have been passed down from generation to generation as symbolic sources of spiritual powers. It is conceded even by Pajok that Longar of Dhiendior, presented as an older brother of Jok, was initially in the lead, but proved ineffective, when Jok then assumed the supreme leadership. It is said that they came to a river which they could not cross because of powers in the river which were killing the people as they tried to cross. These powers are sometimes described as spirits and sometimes as "White." Jok eventually gave them his daughter, Achai, which made the powers withdraw and the waters parted, allowing the people to cross on dry land. Jok is said to have also won other spiritual contests with Longar, leaving him the unchallenged leader of his people, even though the claim of Longar's descendants to leadership has persisted.

Jok's descendants have retained leadership through the observance of primogeniture, by which the most senior son of the most senior wife succeeds, even though circumstances may be complicated enough to permit a latitude of choice among the sons of the chief. In their descending order, the lineage includes: Bulabek, Dongbek, Kwoldit, Monydhang, Allor, Biong, Arob, Kwol, Deng Majok and, in rapid succession, his sons Monyyak (Abdalla), Kwol (Adam) and Kwol (Adol).[11] Ngok history is largely traced through these leaders. The competing genealogy of Dhiendior comprises Longar, the founder, Jiel, Juic, Akonon, Bagat, Mithiang, Ajuong, Ajing, Allor, Jipur, Chol, and several more from collateral branches changing leadership positions through internal rivalry.

While much of the history and political dynamics among the Ngok tend to focus on Pajok as the principal leaders and players, behind virtually every counteraction against them, there is nearly always some significant elements of Dhiendior involved. Much of the disunity among the Ngok, which has often played into their relations with the Arabs, relates directly to the rivalry between these two factions, with lesser groups aligning themselves behind them. It is a structural, functional dichotomy that represents the summit of the balanced opposition of the segmentary lineage system elaborately expounded in anthropological literature. The picture is not, however, one of consistent opposition, for, to offer the tribe effective leadership, these two lineages must also cooperate, an objective often fostered through intermarriage between the corresponding sections at every genealogical level. The reality, then, is a more complex picture reflecting both rivalry and cooperation between

---

11. After tracing the history of the Ngok from Jok, Paul Howell (1951:264) observes, "The position has been held in this line ever since and according to strict primogeniture, the office descending to the eldest son of the oldest wife in each case." Howell (1951:264) goes on to say, "Such political power as is backed by the Government in the present system of administration was naturally accorded to the Chief of the spear by the Ngork [sic] themselves, and not only to the principal Pajok family, but also to the minor leaders who are all Chiefs of the Spear, either of the Pajok clan or the Dhiandiar [sic]." Howell (1951:242) also reports that "Jok ... had four sons and a daughter: Aiwel, Bulabek, Dhion, Biar, and ... Achai ... Biar became leader of Twij [sic], Dhion of the Rek, Aiwel and Bulabek, of the Ngork." This would justify the Ngok claim for Pajok as the original leader of all the Dinka.

elements on both sides. David Cole and Richard Huntington of the Harvard Institute for International Development (HIID), who were involved in a project of integrated rural development in the area in the 1970s, commented on the degree to which internal rivalries and intrigues, which they attributed to the segmentary lineage system, were ultimately harmful to the collective good of the people.

> A segmentary social structure facilitates an ever narrower and shorter-term perception of self-interest allowing an adversary to pursue a policy of divide and rule. The Ngok know painfully that it is the very essence of their society that provides for such extremes of unity and division. In their experience, the negative divisive element appears to predominate. This divisiveness depresses them in the face of their ideological awareness of their potential familial unity. Often during these difficult times, Dinka lament, "We are a terrible people; we bring destruction upon ourselves through constant disunity and betrayal." ... The divisiveness of recent years making Ngok society vulnerable to external advances is directly attributable to the jealousies among the members of the chiefly lineages. Furthermore, among those with chiefly credentials, there is a further hierarchy at the apex of which stand the direct descendants of the recent paramount chiefs. Always there are chiefs who stand to gain by the diminution of the status of those closer to the center than they .... As the Ngok polity has become increasingly stratified, the negative and divisive aspect of the segmentary social structure has come to predominate (Cole & Huntington 1985:36-37).[12]

It is important to bear this in mind as a factor behind the process by which internal settlement or reconciliation is undermined by the intrigues of disenchanted individuals resorting to external sources of support for personal benefit against the collective interests of the community.

The first of Jok's descendants to establish and sustain cordial relations with the Arabs is said to be Arob Biong, our great-grandfather. Arob even fused blood with his Arab counterpart to create a blood bond

---

12. See also Deng 1986:263.

that would pacify their people from enemies to relatives.[13] And during the Mahdist revolution, Arob, escorted by his Arab "relatives" and accompanied by Allor Ajing from the Dhiendior clan, paid a visit to the Mahdi to seek protection for their people. Dinka oral history presents them as having gone to *Jenna*, the Muslim paradise, but does not support the Arab contention that they converted to Islam. They are, however, reported to have prayed with the Mahdi. Dinka accounts have it that as they were praying, their heads bent down, Allor Ajing asked, "Arob, do you see God?" Arob replied, "Allor, I do not see God, but let's leave it at that." Their attitude toward the Mahdi was simply the traditional Dinka reverence for men of God, whatever their clan spirits or religious affiliation.

Arob's son, Kwol, consolidated the cordial ties between the tribes which his father had established. The British placed Chief Kwol Arob in charge of all the neighboring Dinka tribes to the south, including the Twich and the Ruweng, from whom he collected taxes and heard appeals. This remained the case for a good part of the Condominium rule. Ngok leaders for the British were therefore not only instrumental to law and order within their own jurisdiction, but were also a vital point of entry and penetration into Dinka society, extending further south.

The role Ngok leaders have played in promoting peace at the North-South borders through their connections with Arab tribes and successive administrations in the North is widely acknowledged among the Dinka, both in Ngokland and in the South. "It is only the family of Biong [Arob's father] who, when disaster occurs as it has now occurred [in the Arab-Dinka hostilities of 1977], sacrifice their own lives", said Chol Piok. "And even when they suffer a major destruction, they will still remain patient and work for the good of the tribe. A Chief does not hold his country through the force of arms; he holds the country with his tongue.

---

13. Unlike most Dinka groups who had revolted against the Turks only to face the Mahdists, there was hardly any Turko-Egyptian presence in Ngok area. Although the Mahdiya period was one of the most violent chapters in southern history, it was a relatively peaceful time for the Ngok. When the non-Mahdist Homr, led by Hamadan Abu Ein, were thrown out of Dar Messirya, the Ngok accommodated them in the swamps of Baralil and continued to give them protection until the Condominium. See Henderson 1939:69.

Even when the people of the tribe have died and died and died, it will be for him to hold the land eventually."[14]

Atem Muoter of the Twich Dinka was even more exalting: "Our land is tied to Arob Biong and it was Arob Biong who used to rescue our people and return them from slavery ... Rian [the Chief of the Twich] ... encountered the Government in the home of ... Kwol Arob. Then they found Boldit [Chief of another Twich tribe] as a religious leader and gave him power to be a government Chief as well ... Arobdit was the Chief of all these areas. And when Arob's son, Kwol, came, the country continued to prosper under his leadership." In the words of Chief Makuei Bilkuei of the Paan-Aruw Dinka, "It was [the family of Arob Biong] that saved us with the tongue of [their] forefathers" (Deng 1980:84). "Most Dinkas didn't know what was going on," said Chief Giirdit of the Rek Dinka. "We didn't know anything. Only the Ngok knew the Arabs .... And even the fact that there are Dinkas today – people are here because of [Arob]. It was [Arobdit] and [his son Kwol] who saved the people" (Deng 1980:42, quoted in Deng 1986:47).

Beginning with the Mahdiya, Chief Giirdit elaborated on the history of Arob's role in North-South relations, depicting the confederate nature of relations among Dinka leaders that is never reflected in the literature: "Word came that the Mahdi was liberating the people. So, contributions of remaining cattle and sheep and goats would be made and sent to the Mahdi through [Arobdit]. Then [Arobdit] would pass them on. It would be my father [Thiik] here gathering things from his tribe, sending them to [Arobdit]. Yor Mayar on his side, Agwok, would bring his contributions to [Arobdit]. Mawien Ariik would come from the side of the Luach. And ... Akol Arob would come from the Kongoor side. All those Chiefs would gather and meet with [Chief Arob]" (Deng 1980:43; 1986:47). In another context, Giirdit enumerated more chiefs from other Dinka areas and added: "It is the big things of the country and how they would run their country that they would meet and talk about. Such things as how people should relate to each other on the borders. Those were the ways of those big leaders of the past" (Deng 1980:43; 1986:47). Chief Makuei Bilkuei added more leaders to the list: "There was a man called Biem and my father Bilkuei, and a man called Koc, and the man called Kwol Arob. Those were the ancient leaders who confronted disaster" (Deng 1980:84).

---

14. From unpublished portions of an interview for the biography, *The Man Called Deng Majok* (Deng 1986). Unless included in the book and indicated accordingly, undocumented quotations are from the unpublished portions of the interviews on Deng Majok.

Later, part of the Twich broke off to join the South under the leadership of Rian, who had been Arob's protégé. The partition was sanctioned, if not initiated, by the British on the grounds that the area was too large for the administration of one chief. The Ruweng were subsequently severed from the jurisdiction of Ngok leadership on the same basis.

The administrative status of the Ngok in Kordofan remained an anomaly with which the British were not entirely comfortable. Paul Howell (1951:240) wrote: "[T]he Ngork Dinka of Western Kordofan are something of a problem. Situated as they are between the Baggara Arabs of the North and the main body of the Nilotic peoples in the South, they are in a peculiar position and the problem is whether they should be included in a Rural District Council in which Arabs must always predominate or whether they should be joined to kindred tribes further South. Should tribal and racial boundaries remain intact or should territorial associations be created in which tribe or race is of no consequence? There are purely practical arguments in favour of both such lines of political development."

K.D.D. Henderson, another British administrator who had served in the area, also commented on the anomaly of the Ngok situation on the North-South border:

> Tidy-minded persons – British and Sudanese alike – were always suggesting that the Ngok be transferred to Southern administration. I resisted this partly because it would have been impossible to draw a fair boundary between them and the Homr, but chiefly because their presence in Kordofan provided an invaluable buffer-state and meeting ground and gave the Northern administration knowledge of and sympathy with the Nilotics. Further West, the Malwal and the Rezeigat were perfectly at loggerheads. To the East, the transfer of the Rueng to the Upper Nile Province had given rise to endless friction. But the relationship of the Ngok was excellent with the Homr on one side and the Twij [sic] on the other. Arabs with a grievance against the Twij or the Hijeir [Rek], and vice versa, always approached Kwal in the first instance to act as an intermediary.[15]

---

15. In a written response to the questionnaire for Deng 1986.

Later it appears that the administration had changed its position and decided in favor of the Ngok joining the South. The government encouraged, indeed instigated, the southern chiefs to persuade Chief Kwol Arob to join them. Chief Giirdit later recalled the discussion between them and Chief Kwol: "We talked – [Kwol] was brought by the Government – the Great Kwol, son of Arob; and [the Government] said, 'You, Kwol, you are among the Arabs, but you are a Dinka. I would like you to unite with the other Dinka and become the District of Gogrial'" (Deng 1980:39; 1986:49). Chief Makuei Bilkuei also recalled: "I talked to Kwol and said, 'These people will disgrace us later on. So why are you after [them]?' ... This is the word I said to Kwol, a word that was to come true" (Deng 1980:74-75). By that Makuei was alluding to the internecine conflicts that would erupt between the Arabs and the Dinka in a northern context which favored the Arabs against the Dinka.

Kwol Arob chose to remain in the North for strategic reasons. After a public announcement of his refusal to join the South, he pulled Giirdit aside and spoke to him: "Son of my father, what you tell me it is not that I do not know it. The Arab is a thief. Even though I am with him, I know he is a thief. If I were to pull away from him, he would destroy my things ... Even this land which is mine, he might say, 'It is my land'" (Deng 1980:39-40; 1986:50). Kwol Arob's words were prophetic, for that was precisely what happened later when the Dinka sought to reverse that historic decision which he had meant as a protective strategy.

Thus, while recognizing the unity of the Dinka, Kwol argued that his presence in Kordofan was in the strategic interest of the South in general and the Dinka in particular. He maintained that position, balancing between North and South until the end of his days. His image remains towering in the memory of his people and the neighboring leaders to the North and the South, all of whom acknowledge that he was a Chief of great virtues and charisma. Nevertheless, Kwol Arob's era marked the end of the cohesiveness of the tribal system, built upon deference for the spiritual authority of the leader and the tribal consensus on the values and the institutional structures of traditional society. Under the leadership of his son, Deng Majok, external involvement, whether by the neighboring Arabs or by the central government reinforced rather than supplanted traditional norms and structures, thereby rendering the authority of the chief more effective. The negative side of that effectiveness, however, has been the gradual but irreversible erosion of the traditional system of authority and control, leading to the eventual collapse of the autonomy of Dinka society.

Despite the important historic role played by successive Ngok leaders on the South-North borders and especially by Arob Biong and his son, Kwol Arob, there is a general consensus that Deng Majok was the most pivotal in consolidating the authority of the Ngok chief and the position of Abyei area in Kordofan as a symbol of national unity. This was in part due to his personal ambitions and need for allies in the North and in part a continuation of the family legacy of leadership at the crossroads. With a more developed view of national unity than his forebears, Deng Majok metaphorically considered himself the needle and the thread that mended the two parts of the Sudan into one whole. Ngok area became a national crossroads and a microcosm of the Sudan, in much the same way that the Sudan is a microcosm of Africa.[16]

Deng Majok

Because of his pivotal influence not only on his people, but also on the Dinka-Arab situation as a whole, Deng Majok's reign calls for a closer look treatment. His rule was indeed paradoxical in that it mobilized and utilized the external forces of the Arabs and the central government to consolidate effective power within the tribe, while at the same time ensuring a jealous protection of the autonomy of the tribe and his own power. And yet, while that succeeded for the most part during his period, it certainly opened doors which many would use later in a fragmented attempt to promote individual interests through external connections. Deng Majok's main avenue to power and success in imposing an unchallenged "sovereignty" over his tribal territory would eventually become tantamount to opening the pandora's box. Reaching out to more powerful foreign allies became not only legitimate but indeed popular and open to any opportunist with some prospects for advancing the cause of the foreign players in the region. This inexorably undermined the system and led to its virtual collapse, the stage the Dinka are in at present.

The process which has led to this tragic end is inherent in the manner by which Deng Majok achieved the leadership of the tribe. Indeed, the

---

16. K. D. D. Henderson (1965:164n), after explaining that "if the South, while remaining essentially Southern, could yet become an integral part of an independent Sudan it could help to bridge the inevitable gulf between Muslim and non-Muslim, Asian and African, white or brown and black, in the African future", goes on to say, "The Ngok Dinka, on the Bahr el Arab, had joined Kordofan Province at the reoccupation and had played precisely such a role as intermediaries between the Homr Baggara and the Dinka of the Bahr al Ghazal."

story is a drama of personal ambitions transcending traditional boundaries and the role of outsiders in influencing internal decisions. Chief Kwol Arob engaged Nyanaghar, Deng Majok's mother-to-be, and paid part of the bridewealth. She rejected him, however, in favor of another man with whom she even chose to elope. Kwol withdrew his cattle, leaving one cow-calf as a token of his ancestral claim on her. Meanwhile, he married another girl, Abiong, and brought her home. Shortly afterwards, Nyanaghar became seized with a disease that was diagnosed to be the curse of her having rejected the chief. The family persuaded her to change her mind and she eventually consented. They apologized to the chief and begged him to accept her. He did. The marriage was rapidly concluded and Nyanaghar joined Abiong as Kwol's first two wives.

Elders of Anyiel sub-tribe, which traditionally played a leading role in the rituals of installing the paramount chief of the tribe, were then called upon to bless the brides and pray for their procreational success. The elders sacrificed animals to the ancestors over the brides and prayed for their productivity. To Kwol's surprise, they invoked the spirits to let Nyanaghar beget a son to be the heir to the leadership, while they prayed for Abiong to beget a daughter as her firstborn to be then followed by a son. Kwol protested, insisting that Abiong, the first to accept him, be considered his first wife and the one to beget the heir. The elders argued that Nyanaghar was not only the first to be chosen, but was the one the ancestors had pursued by inflicting on her the disease that forced her to accept the marriage. The fact that one cow was left in the marriage, despite her rejection, was a symbol of the bond which continued to bind her to the family in marriage.

The will of the elders came to pass; Nyanaghar begot Deng Majok and Abiong begot Agorot, followed by Deng Makuei (also known as Deng Abot). Kwol still maintained that Abiong was his first wife. She was given the cattle dedicated to the senior clan spirits and Kwol himself acquired the name of Wun-Agorot, Agorot's Father, according to the tradition of designating a man by the name of the firstborn of his first wife, whatever the gender. Deng Makuei also received the color patterns associated with the senior son, of which Mijak, called Majok in Rek and Twich Dinka dialect, a pied black and white pattern, is the most important. The other Deng was given the second-class patterns, of which Marial, a different version of black and white formation, and Miyom, brown with a white spot on the head, are the best known. That is why among the Ngok Deng Majok was known by the praise-name of Deng

Arialbek, the Red-bill Stork; Deng Awet, the Crested Crane; and Athok-Yom, the White-Spotted Brown.

What became his official praise name, Majok, which acquired the image of the most senior color pattern, was in fact a clever twist of the nickname, Majoh, "the doggish", which he acquired from his love of a dog with whom he shared milk and food. The southern Dinka, Twich, Rek, and Malwal, not realizing the origin of the name, thought it was the Ngok dialect for the color pattern Majok and changed it accordingly. The ambitious Deng, preferring the southern version to the Ngok Dinka nickname, adopted Deng Majok as his official name, giving him the appearance of being the senior son of his father, which he was indeed biologically, but not in terms of leadership seniority.

Deng Majok's mother died early, leaving six children, three sons – Deng Majok, Biong Mading, and Arob – and three daughters – Ayan, Awor, and Abul. Although their step-mother, Abiong, treated Nyanaghar's children well, the fact that they had no mother left them at a disadvantage. The two sons, being close to each other in age, were raised almost as equals and when they became of age, were both appointed by their father as his deputies, but Chief Kwol still made it clear that Deng Makuei would be his successor. Deng Majok resented this and endeavored to excel over his half-brother to prove that he was the one best qualified for the top leadership. The tribe itself looked upon him as more able than his half-brother, but Kwol remained adamant on Deng Makuei and for the most part the tribe conformed to his will.

Despite the antagonism between them, it is said that Deng Majok was keen to appease his father and was in the habit of initiating reconciliation whenever they quarrelled. His maternal relatives, who were wealthy and very supportive, willingly gave him cattle to propitiate his father in the customary practice by which material gifts, especially of cattle, are made as a token of apology and appeasement. According to Chol Piok, a sectional chief (*sheikh*) from Anyiel sub-tribe, and a relative who observed the situation closely:

> He would quarrel with his father to the point where
> everyone would know that they had quarreled and that
> Kwol was angry with his son. Then, at night, he would
> come with a cow and say, "Father, I appease you with this
> cow." His maternal relatives were a family of great
> wealth. Whenever he wanted anything from them, it was
> given to him the same day. So he would appease his
> father and their quarrel would end. That is the way they

lived and lived. And he would quarrel with his father because his father had a tendency to suppress the rights of his mother's side of the family. That is what he would not accept (Deng 1986:63).

Deng's attitude toward his father was part of a more general pattern, for he is said to have combined physical courage and tough-mindedness with an ability to reason and a disposition toward conflict resolution and reconciliation. "When he was still a child, [he] was very hot-tempered," began Pagwot Deng, Omda of the Bongo sub-tribes.

He was very easily provoked. But he was a man who reasoned well with words. His was the hot temper of a man who could also speak well! He would not overlook anything that touched him. He would pursue the matter to the end. And yet he was for good relations. Among his companions, even if he fought with another child, he would insist that they sit and eat together. He did not believe in nursing grievances into a continuing bitterness. He believed that people should fight but then sit and eat together, leaving aside the conflict. That was the way he behaved (Deng 1986:63).[17]

A theme that emerges in the complex relationship between Kwol Arob and Deng Majok at this stage is that Kwol recognized Deng's qualities, especially in the modern administrative context, but still felt that Deng Abot was the senior son for leadership in accordance with Dinka tradition, for he never wavered on the status of Abiong as his first wife and therefore the mother of the heir to the throne. Indeed, the more Deng Majok distinguished himself in modern terms, the more Kwol Arob saw him as a threat to Deng Makuei. "Why Kwol was rather negative about Deng Majok was because he thought that Deng Majok would overwhelm Deng Makuei and deprive him of his rights. He realized that Deng Makuei's heart was not the same as that of Deng Majok. Deng Makuei would despair angrily. But Deng Majok would never despair. Those were the things Kwol used to say" (Deng 1986:67).

---

17. Eating together is a gesture of reconciliation in much the same way as abstaining from sharing food is a gesture or symbol of conflict or serious disagreement.

Achwil Bulabek, the Omda of Abyor, the sub-tribe of the leading family, agreed:

> What his father feared was that Deng Majok would capture the chieftainship. That was why he tried to trim him down. Abiong was, of course, the surviving wife. It was she who had a wife-husband relationship with Kwol. Those were the small issues that caused problems between them. Whenever Deng noticed mistreatment by his father or his father violated any right that was his, he would not overlook it; he would quarrel with him and people would then say, "Deng and his father had a quarrel." But Deng never committed a wrong against his father. It was only that he insisted on representing the position of his dead mother .... Kwol feared that Deng was going to capture the chieftainship (Deng 1986:67-68).

The paradoxes of the transition the Dinka were in became clear. To Kwol Arob, there were certain societal norms to be observed and honored. Deng Majok was not the heir to the leadership, however competent in modern administration or even in traditional terms he might be. In the cohesive system of the past, matters would have ended there. Deng Majok might not even have allowed his aspirations to grow beyond that point. But the situation was in flux and Deng Majok knew it. That combined with a genuine sense of injustice by his father made him look elsewhere for a remedy. It did not matter much to him that in doing so he would be upsetting tradition, even though he sought to interpret tradition or the facts of the situation in order to ensure a degree of legitimacy.

It was the quest for traditional legitimacy that made Deng Majok seek the authoritative opinion of his great uncle, Bulabek Biong, father of Achwil Bulabek, the chief of Abyor, who would become his right hand man and principal ally in the bid for chieftainship. Achwil, who was present at Deng Majok's meeting with his father, gave this account of the conversation:

> Deng Majok came to my father and said: "Grandfather [Great Uncle] I have come because I have heard that you are dying. Our people have their own traditions. It is said that the people of our clan do not contest for chieftainship; that if chieftainship is contested, it will cause death. That is why I came to ask you. Here we are

both under our father. Our father is of course still strong. The spirit of death does not distinguish between children and elders. If it chooses to kill a child, that child will die. If it chooses to kill one's father and the father dies, then a son is expected to step into the position of his father. What I want is the truth. What should I do if the question of succession arises in the future?"

My father then said, "You, Deng, I am going to tell you the truth. I am not going to live any longer. And I am not going to leave you with a word that might lead you to the curse of death. I have nothing more to gain from trying to win your friendship. You will no longer buy me any clothing so that people can say Bulabek has become a friend of Deng. Let me tell you that it was to the wedding of your mother, Nyanaghar, that we, the sons of Biong, all went; we did not go to Kwol's second marriage, the wedding of Abiong, the mother of Deng Abot. That was performed by your grandfather, Arob, alone. But all the four of us (half-brothers of Arob) went to your mother's wedding. When our marriage to your mother was rejected, our ancestral spirits followed her until she was brought back to us. That was something the sons of one man did together. So, with respect to chieftainship, if the people of the tribe should oppose your becoming chief, leave it; do not push for it. But if the tribe should want you to be chief, then accept it willingly. You will not be accursed with even a headache if seniority is the qualification. Your mother is the senior wife. So, no illness will befall you on account of seniority. And now, give me your hand." Deng extended his right hand. My father held it. Then he raised it up: he raised it up three times. Bol, the son of my mother was there; and Miyan, the son of my father was there. They were witnesses. Deng cried. He cried over his dying Uncle (Deng 1986:53-54).

That opinion would become the legitimizing point in Deng Majok's struggle for power.

Deng Majok focused his efforts on winning the support of the Ngok public, the neighboring Arab and Dinka tribes, and the British administrators. Combining his deferential attitude toward people, verbal skills, well-known generosity, administrative competence, and drive toward ending tribal wars, Deng Majok increased his popularity within and beyond the Ngok tribe. "Whenever tribes came into conflict in the grazing area of the *toc* [dry season wetlands]," observed Matet Ayom, one of Deng Majok's closest associates, "it would be Deng Majok who would initiate moves for peace. He would approach the Twich and he would approach the Rek, and he would make peace between them. If there were a conflict between Bongo and Abyor, he would rise and make peace between them. If Anyiel and Bongo were in conflict, indeed, if any tribal groups were in conflict, he would rise, call for peace, and hold meetings. He did all this before he was the chief. His were only the words of a son of the chief" (Deng 1986:70).

Matet goes on to give an account of an incident in which Deng Majok distinguished himself as a peacemaker:

> One time, the Abyor section went to raid the Twich for cattle. That was when the Twich first recognized Deng Majok as the future chief. Deng got up and went to the camp of the Twich. There he found an elder by the name of Rian Gorkwei, the chief of the Twich. Deng went with some people on horseback. The horses entered the cattle-camp in a display of riding skills. That was the traditional Arab way of honoring their hosts and announcing their arrival. Our people adopted it from the Arabs. The best riders raced their horses to the home of the hosts, who would then get up to hold and unsaddle the horses. On this particular occasion, Bol Bulabek, one of the companions, raced his horse into the herd, knocking down cattle as he went.
>
> The elder called Rian Gorkwei got up and said, "O people of Arob Biong, is this an intimidation or a raid?" Deng Majok responded: "Uncle, it is only that the horse got out of control; no offense was intended. It is neither raid nor intimidation. Please cool down and welcome us as visitors. I have come accompanied by these people to see you. I shall tell you what I have come for when we are seated."
>
> Rian Gorkwei turned to his people, who had grabbed their spears and were about to fight. He said: "O Twich, stop! The wrong is shifting to your side. Deng Majok has

reversed the situation. He has passed the responsibility to you. Should you harm anyone after this, the wrong will be on your side."

The spears were then laid down and the visitors were led into the camp. The horses were unsaddled. After they were seated, Deng Majok said: "The reason I came was to tell you to graze without fear of any attack by our people. The Abyor tribe will move this way. And here you are camping in this area. We should graze our cattle in peace. Even if the cattle should mix while grazing in the daytime and a man from Abyor offends a man from Twich, I would like you, Uncle Rian, to call me and we shall settle the matter together. I myself will come in front of you because you are my elder. We shall discuss the matter and make peace for our people to graze together in peace."

Rian Gorkwei said, "My son, they say you are Deng, the son of the second wife of Kwol, but that you were the first to be born. Whatever people may say about the seniority of mothers, you will be a leader of men in accordance with the words you have just spoken." Rian said these words as an agreement of peace was concluded between them. Then Deng left. His father, Kwol, was informed, "Deng Majok has made peace between the Ngok and the Twich, so the two tribes are now grazing amicably together."

Kwol's only comment was, "I see" (Deng 1986:70-71).[18]

---

18. The British had not yet fully succeeded in establishing law and order on the South-North border. After describing Baggara Arab raids under Ali El Gulla of the Missiriya, Henderson (1939:71) observes: "The Dinkas were their own worst enemies, for the Twij and Malwal resistance to the Government, which lasted into the nineteen twenties, cut them off from any chance of redress. A particularly flagrant raid in 1915 was heavily punished, however, and the reoccupation of Darfur curtailed the area of irrepressibility." This uncertain state of affairs underscored the role of the chief as a peacemaker, and Kwol Arob had established in his area a more advanced state of civic order. See Henderson 1939:71.

Achwil Bulabek tells of another occasion involving another tribe, the Rek, in which Deng Majok adopted a different strategy for peace, also before he had become chief:

> We had captured the herds of the Rek. The Rek rose up in arms to attack us. Kwol Arob and the government came to prevent the fight. They went and spent the night near our cattle-camp. Kwol gathered the cattle and returned them to the Rek. We then proceeded to the *Toc*. The Rek went and grouped their camps together to prepare for an attack. Deng Majok and Deng Makuei had their horses saddled and went to the Rek, accompanied by the government police led by an Arab sergeant-major called Mekki. The Rek were under the leadership of Lual, the brother of Chief Yor Maker. Deng spoke to the son of Lual, also called Deng, and said, "Deng, son of Lual, here you have come with your tribe, Ajuong. You are now camping at Baarngop and we at Nyiel. We have now settled that matter. If I should hear of any provocation from your side, then your head and mine will remain here in the *Toc*. I will not do anything to offend you, but should you think to yourselves, 'The Ngok once raided our cattle so we, Ajuong, should avenge,' then know that you and I will face one another in single combat while Ajuong and Abyor face each other in battle" (Deng 1986:72).

Apparently, that threat was effective in ensuring peace between Ngok and the Rek in the grazing lands of the *Toc*.

Babo Nimir, the paramount chief of the neighboring Missiriya Arabs to the north, reports an incident involving the Dinka and the Arabs in which Deng Majok intervened for the cause of peace while Kwol Arob was still the chief.

> I remember when his father was still chief, some people among the Abyor and the Kalamna Arabs fought toward the area of Fadhalla. I was not there. Deng came to the scene. When he came, he said, "You, Kalamna, here you are holding the leadership, and you also want to show your manhood by fighting. Do you want to keep them both, leadership and manhood? No! Either you hold onto your manhood and surrender your leadership, or you keep

your leadership and surrender your manhood." They were pleased by his words. They said, "It will be according to your words. We shall abandon manhood; leadership is enough for us" (Deng 1986:72).[19]

Paramount Chieftainship Assumed by Deng Majok

As a result of internal wars between the warring alliances initiated by Abyor Bongo, in which he proved to be administratively more competent than his father and half-brother, the colonial administration urged Kwol to retire into a position of honorary leadership, while one of his sons assumed administrative responsibilities. The British also contrived a situation in which Deng Majok, supported by his young uncle, Achwil Bulabek, the chief of their sub-tribe, Abyor, was chosen to take over his father's responsibilities. Chief Kwol Arob was left with the Sacred Spears to symbolize his on-going spiritual leadership of the clan, on the understanding that they would pass on to Deng Majok after his death.

Kwol died two years later, and contrary to the earlier understanding with the British authorities, bequeathed the spears and the spiritual leadership they symbolized to Deng Makuei, which would divest Deng Majok of much of the traditional authority behind his leadership. In a move unprecedented in Dinka experiences, Deng Majok, now supported by the Ngok, with the exception of Abyor, contested the will, triggering a confrontation that almost provoked a civil war in the tribe. The British administration intervened and after a public debate in which the government's preference for Deng Majok coincided with that of the Ngok majority, he was "elected" the paramount chief. The Sacred Spears were forcefully seized by the state and handed over to him. The government also banished Deng Makuei to the North, where he remained under preventive detention. Deng Majok thus combined the spiritual authority of the spears and the secular power of the government behind him. The legal fiction was that because his mother had been the first to be betrothed to Chief Kwol Arob and one cow-calf left in her bridewealth even after her rejection, she was indeed the first wife, the one accepted by the ancestral spirits to be the mother of the heir to the throne.

As for Deng Makuei, after a period of banishment and detention, Deng Majok persuaded the government to return him to the tribe and

---

19. The idea here is that leaders are peacemakers and not warriors, while the warriors tend to show off their masculinity through aggressiveness and valor in warfare.

install him as his deputy in order to neutralize the opposition within the family and the tribe. Even as he had shattered the principle of unity and harmony, he now endeavored to reverse the negative image and turn himself into a champion of the ideals of Dinka society. But in this, Deng Majok continued to be an embodiment of intrinsic contradiction, torn as he was between respecting the traditions of his society and at the same time undermining them in a fundamental way. This contradiction represented the crisis of a people who, while proud of their identity and its heritage, were being incorporated into the wider political arena of the state, dominated by alien races and cultures whose interests were different.

His Undaunted Innovation and Persuasive Influence

Throughout his reign as chief, Deng Majok continued to strive to prove to both his people and the government, and, tragically to his dead father, that he was indeed the right person for the leadership of the tribe. But he also realized that his conflict with tradition, which his father represented, was unresolvable. Indeed, in sharp contrast to the Dinka tradition in which the forebears are always exalted over their descendants, Deng Majok never shied away from projecting himself as having performed better than his father. The conflict of tradition and modernity, of father and son, would continue to drive his passions and actions for all of his life. In essence, this is what made his life both one of outstanding accomplishment and a tragedy, for both himself and his people in the long-run.

Within his tribe, and in close cooperation with the colonial authorities, almost as though he were following the logic that had brought him into power, Deng Majok took a firm stand against tribal wars through both peacemaking measures and severe punishment of those responsible. As a result, he ended warfare in his own tribe, turning it into an island of peace in an area where tribal wars occurred with intractable frequency among both the Arabs to the North and the Dinka to the South. He strengthened the administration of justice and the rule of law in the traditional order and the modern framework of the state. Through the policy of indirect rule, he was the administrator and the judge, the supreme ruler whose judgments were hardly ever contradicted by the national authorities. He introduced education, modern medicine, veterinary services, market economy, and the police as a security force. All in all, Deng Majok was an embodiment of both tradition and innovation, an individual whose authority and influence went far beyond his own tribe and became a symbol of national unity. But much of this was very personalized, for he was an individual out of step with the mainstream of the society he led.

Among the personal attributes for which Deng Majok was known as a person and a leader, several stand out: his ability with words and an immense power of persuasion; a striking capacity to reconcile and unite people by reaching out to the person or the group farthest removed from him, sometimes at the expense of those closest to him; an almost compulsive generosity which made his home an open house for food and accommodation and his wealth a source of welfare to the needy, whoever and from wherever they might be; and an ironic display of moral and physical courage which had given him an early fame as a young warrior, before he was pacified by his appointment as deputy to his father.

Some of his attributes endeared him particularly to the Arabs because they were in conformity with Islamic values and very striking in a person who did not profess Islam. In traditional Dinka society, almost everyone, including children, drank the local beer, which was low in alcoholic content and was made available only on special, festive or seasonal occasions: solicitation of collective labor on farms, marriages, entertainment of special guests, or offerings made to God and ancestral spirits. Deng Majok never drank; he argued that it compromised one's dignity and sense of judgment. Nearly every adult Dinka, man and woman, also smoked a pipe or chewed tobacco, but not Deng Majok; his reason was that craving sometimes forced smokers to beg for tobacco, thereby also compromising their dignity and integrity. Deng Majok would not eat the meat of any animal not slaughtered according to Muslim requirements, and he always kept a Muslim, usually an Arab, in his house to slaughter according to the Islamic rites; his argument was that he did not want his guests to have any doubts about the food they were served in his home. But Deng Majok went even further than that: he always had religious men, both Arab and Dinka, around to offer spiritual protection, and would even drink the water used to wash off Koranic verses written on a plate as a blessing. Furthermore, though performing Dinka rituals and observing the requirements of traditional religion, he also celebrated Islamic occasions, especially from the perspective of social festivity.

These attributes were of course noticed and appreciated by the Arabs. Ibrahim el Hussein made this observation: "Deng had a secret quality. He practiced what the Arabs do, sought the spiritual protection offered by Muslim Holy men. He made use of them. He had a large number of Koranic verses wrapped up. I once saw him give five cows to a Muslim

Holy man to perform protective rituals. I saw him with my own eyes" (Deng 1986:121).

"Deng Majok did not eat bad things," said another Arab, Abdalla Hamadein. "He never smoked. He never drank alcohol of any kind. And he never told a lie" (Deng 1986:121).

Notwithstanding his embodiment of all these attributes, which were the ideals postulated for leadership, Deng Majok was not so much obeyed out of the deference and reverence which the Dinka accorded their divine rulers or leaders, as out of fear for the government power behind him. This accentuated his temper and propensity for combat through the law. He was no longer using the threat of personal violence against his adversaries, but he still projected a verbal assault against wrongdoers which made the threat of official action real and awesome. Deng Majok was again an embodiment of a contradiction between the ideals of Dinka spiritual leadership and the counter-ideals of a warrior now armed with the weapons of state power represented by the modern court, police, and prisons. While persuasion had been the key to the effectiveness of traditional leadership, it was for Deng Majok an added value, an icing that mitigated the violence of state power and paradoxically enhanced his image as a peacemaker and a man endowed with exceptional persuasive powers.

But there was more to Deng Majok's effectiveness than the power of the government or his verbal skills. As part of his strategy for unifying the tribe and broadening his circles of influence and loyalty, Deng Majok went far beyond any precedent in Dinka history by marrying over two hundred wives and maintaining a close-knit polygynous family that was most striking in the degree to which unity and solidarity were upheld and internal rivalries and jealousies, though acknowledged as inevitable in such a setting, were ruthlessly suppressed and repressed. Even at the average of three children to a wife, that gave him several hundred sons and daughters, all of whom were raised within a framework of rigid discipline and normative order.

Even this aspect of Deng Majok's life is closely associated with his quest for power and the contest of wills with his father. It is said that he was cursed to love by a maternal uncle whose daughter he had seduced and impregnated in contravention not only of the moral code but also of the rules of exogamy. His uncle willed that women would be his disease. Deng Majok did not believe in the curse or did not mind it; he resisted attempts to make him repent and pay his uncle or his heirs the customary appeasement for atonement. Far from it, most of his marriages represented an assertion of his will against his father, pursuing women who had already been betrothed to other men or whom his father otherwise disapproved of for a variety of reasons, and in the process, outpacing by far his half-brother who was by tradition senior to him and had priority over him even in matters of marriage.

Deng's family was spread over several villages in different areas of the tribe, but he maintained three areas as his regular homes: his original village at Noong where the eldest wives remained, assisted by a few younger wives, his administrative center in Abyei, where he regularly resided, and a resort village at Nainai, the home of his ally, Achwil Bulabek, where he occasionally went for a change of venue and pace.

The family was administratively divided into three "doorways" or "houses", under the leadership of the top three wives, Nyanbol Arob, otherwise known as Nyanboldit, the first wife (*dit* signifying seniority), Nyanbol Amor, and Kwei. These wives had their homes at Noong, his original village. In each of the other villages, they were represented by the most senior wives from their groups in that area. At Abyei, his administrative center, they were represented consecutively by Amel, Nyanawai, and Amou. In every village, all the wives were administratively classified into these three groupings and the order of seniority was strictly observed with respect to authority.

Wherever Deng Majok was, his home was constantly crowded with family members, tribal elders, and the many people who came to plead their cases in his court, which was almost permanently in session, informally at home and formally under a large shaded court tree. From 6:30 in the morning, when he would come to his public sitting room for tea, the crowds would begin to gather and some cases might even be heard that early. By the time he rose to go to the court tree, he would be followed by scores of people who would have been waiting outside the sitting room, many of whom would struggle to have his ear for a word. The court tree would soon be filled with elders, litigants, and spectators. Hearings would last all day, sometimes non-stop to the late afternoon, when the crowd would move back home for a collective meal, with food flowing from the three sections of the family and from individual wives. He would then have a siesta and reemerge in the early evening for a resumption of litigation or discussion of public affairs. The day would end with the evening meal, again shared by a crowd, some of whom were strangers in the area and needed accommodation for the night.

As might be expected, Deng Majok had enemies, some of them bitter ones. They included educated liberals who saw him as a dictator, young men whose girlfriends ended up as his wives, and opposition leaders who saw in his marriages and the size of his family a ground for corruption. Cases were raised against him by daring individuals, all of whom failed and ended up in prison, guilty of false accusations and political agitation. Indeed, he narrowly survived an assassination attempt by an aggrieved young man, Kwol Chol, against whom he had passed a judgment that deprived him of a woman with whom he had eloped and had a child. It was alleged that her family intended to give her in marriage to the chief. The man, said to have been mentally unbalanced, served a prison term, and was later released to return a lunatic for the rest of his life. But although Deng Majok's leadership was controversial on internal matters, the Ngok Dinka and indeed the Dinka tribes to the South saw in him paradoxically a dependable protector against his own allies, the Arabs and the government, both provincial and central. All things considered, Deng Majok was a chief of unprecedented power and authority, reinforced by both tradition and modernity, and fortified by the strength of his own personality and ingenuity.

His Bringing About of Justice and Peace

Of his many accomplishments, his role as a peacemaker and a champion of law and order with justice stood out most conspicuously. As Patal Biliu, a Ngok elder, explained: "Deng began to bring those who had been against him close to him and turned them into his people (supporters). Most of the people who were court-members under him were people who had rejected him. The people whom he saw to be opposed to him were the people he brought into his inner circle" (Deng 1986:116).

Matet Ayom, a close associate with whom he later developed an ambivalent relationship, also stressed Deng Majok's lack of grudge against those who had stood against him in the dispute over succession: "Deng Majok did not turn against those who had opposed him. Anyone with a cause Deng would give his rights without prejudice. And even with those who had supported him, if one had no cause, Deng would say, 'Let go of this, it is not yours'" (Deng 1986:116).

Elaborating, Matet went on to say: "It was Deng Majok who brought peace and unity to the people so that they stopped tribal wars and laid down their spears and their shields. He would call a nobleman from one tribe and call another nobleman from another tribe and call yet another nobleman from a third tribe and gather them together near him to become his companions. It is because of Deng that our people have now mixed and united to become one people (Deng 1986:118).

Achwil Bulabek confirmed Deng Majok's broad-based selection of his court members and his impartial justice even against his own clan and went on to say: "Let me tell you that where Deng Majok far excelled Kwol Arob is in the fact that none of our people died anymore on the tip of the spears of war. Our wars ended with the war of Nainai between us – Abyor – and Bongo. When Deng imposed severe punishment on those responsible, people were deterred and stopped provoking wars. Where Deng Majok excelled your grandfather is on the issue of the sons of Adam living without fearing death from war!" (Deng 1986:118).

But Deng Majok's decisions were not just backed by coercion; tact, diplomacy, and the art of persuasion were also among his main tools. As one of his wives put it: "There was no power greater than the power of his tongue. It was with his tongue that he managed this tribe. The power of his tongue has never been seen and will probably never be seen again" (Deng 1986:135).

"When a case was too formidable for Deng Majok," remarked Matet Ayom, "he would use diplomacy and the art of persuasion, patiently explaining the roots of the problem and avoiding premature expressions of opinion until he got fully to the roots of the issue. Then he would make his statement" (Deng 1986:135). But, according to another Ngok elder, Mithiang Aguek, one of the reflective victims of Deng Majok's justice, "Whenever Deng said a word, he never changed it!" (Deng 1986:135). On the other hand, he would not leave the victims of his judgments without convincing them of his reasons. In the words of Achai-Jur, one of the senior daughters of Deng Majok, "[W]henever he ruled against a person and that person felt disfavored by him, he would send for him some time later and would talk to him at length to explain why he had decided against him and advise him about how people should relate to one another. He would talk to the person that way until the person fully appreciated his position." The strategy applied not only to those against whom he had passed judgment but also to his political adversaries: "Even if a person turned against him and gossiped to the public, Father would remain calm and work to win him over. Eventually, that same person would turn to Father and become the one to speak to the public in his favor" (Deng 1986:135-136).

That, indeed, was often the case in his ambivalent relations with Matet Ayom, who was imprisoned and sent to the district headquarters in Fulah because his brother had eloped with Kwol Arob's daughter and he,

Matet, opposed his brother's marriage to the girl. "When he came to Fulah and we were reconciled, Abiem Bagat said to him, 'Deng Majok, now that you are again bringing Matet close to you, you will quarrel again. When you do, know that we are not going to involve ourselves again.' Then he said, 'Abiem, my plan is not to push Matet away from me. I keep him close to me because he will one day be of great service to me. And what I am now claiming from him is not the same as what he will one day do for me'" (Deng 1986:136).

His Unifying Role as a Respected Southerner in the North

Apart from maintaining law and order within the tribe, an area in which Deng Majok's leadership was most pronounced was his bridging the North and the South in the border area under his control. In 1951, the British again gave the Ngok the option of joining Bahr el Ghazal or Upper Nile in anticipation of Sudan's independence. Their argument was that the Ngok were racially and culturally different from the bulk of the people with whom they shared the district and the province. It was therefore expedient for them to join their kindred groups in the South.

The Governor of Bahr el Ghazal, Richard Owen, who had been District Commissioner of western Kordofan, influenced the Dinka chiefs of Bahr el Ghazal to persuade Deng Majok to join the South. Again in the words of Giirdit:

> More recently ... we spoke with Deng Majok. We went and talked to him ... The British told him, "You are wanted by your people of the South." We were all gathered: Ajuong (Yor Maker), Boldit, the family of Rian, and others. We talked a great deal. I said ... "You, Deng Majok, ... we discussed the matter with your father a long time ago. And your father told me the truth. But what my uncle told me no longer holds. We must now leave it and unite with you ... We will make you our shield. And you cannot take our shield and turn it to the Arabs."... We discussed the matter a great deal ... Then we left the matter, hoping we would meet again to discuss further (Deng 1986:223-224).

The Arab elder, Ibrahim el Hussein, a descendant of the Arab leader, Azoza, with whom Deng Majok's grandfather, Arob Biong, had entered into a pact of friendship, gave this account of the consultations that ensued on the issue:

> Deng consulted with us. He got on his horse. And with him were all the omdas and a number of sheikhs ... We were on the farm in the area called Ajbar. The crops were ripening. We poured in from the villages on the surrounding highlands ... We found them settled on the farm. I brought a bull with me, a fat young bull. I told the young men to slaughter it. It was slaughtered. The chiefs were seated. We went and brought grain from the farm for their horses. As we left them to rest, Deng said to us, "I would like you all to come back this evening. I would like to talk to you." The Arabs left and then returned in the evening as Deng Majok had requested. This time they came with their elders. He said to us, "I went to see the governor, the Englishman. And he said to me, 'The English are about to leave. Their period of rule in the Sudan is coming to an end.' And he said to me, 'Join the south.' I said to him, 'Why should I join the South?' And he said, 'Listen to my advice; join the South.' And he said to me, 'You see, you have a brother on the White Nile; he is going to be a member of the Senate.' I told him I was going to consult with my people. So I have come to seek your views. What is your opinion?" (Deng 1986:224).

The Arabs were apparently stunned by what Deng Majok had told them according to El Hussein's recollection: "Our fathers, who were elderly people, did not even understand what he was saying. 'Son Deng,' they said, 'what sort of a thing are you saying?' I said, 'Listen Deng, go and tell that Englishman who asked you to join the South that he found you a northerner. The English found us as brothers from a long way back. We were brothers when the Turkish government came. The Mahdiya also found us brothers. And when the English came, they found us sitting together on one rug. The South is not for you; it is not for you.' We said a great deal to him" (Deng 1986:224-225).

Deng Majok then revealed to them his own intentions, which were in full accord with their position: "In front of all the people assembled he said, 'Very well! That was what I wanted. We are not going to the South. That is my opinion'" (Deng 1986:225).

Deng Majok was asked by the British to visit the South before finally making up his mind on the issue. He went on a tour of Bahr el Ghazal Province accompanied by chiefs and elders. They went to Aweil, Wau, and Tonj and then returned for final consultations with the people. But he was already predisposed to remain in the North and nothing he saw in the South persuaded him to change his mind.

In the opinion of the Dinka, Deng's decision to remain in the North was not a rejection of the South but indeed a means of ensuring the protection of his people, including the southern tribes, against their Arab neighbors. According to Matet Ayom, he argued: "Should we join the South now, the black people will be harassed and reduced to a small entity. It is our path which stretches the height of the black people. And it is our path which guides the black people. And one day, should tragedy befall this country, the survival of the black people will start here at Abyei … Should we abandon this land with all its blessings, our descendants will one day blame us" (Deng 1986:226-227).

This argument implies that at least to some Ngok Dinka joining the South was misconceived as entailing a physical move from the area rather than a mere change of administrative affiliation and borders on the map. But the main point in the argument of Deng Majok was that the Ngok Dinka, in particular the leadership, should continue to play a bridging role on the North-South borders. To some people, by choosing to play that role Deng Majok was simply continuing the tradition of his forefathers. His grandfather Arob had established the link; his father, Kwol, had taken a determining position; and, as the Ngok elder, Chol Piok, put it, "Deng Majok decided to follow the word of his father" (Deng 1986:227).

Nazir [Chief] Babo Nimir defended the unity of the Missiriya Arabs and the Ngok Dinka on the historical grounds alluded to earlier by Ibrahim el Hussein. "The relationship between the Ngok Dinka and the Missiriya, in particular the Homr, is one that predates me and Deng. It predates even our fathers and our grandfathers. It is a relationship that goes back a long way. Our fathers came and found this relationship prevailing. And we came and found the relationship prevailing" (Deng 1982:59). On the other hand, Babo concedes that "The strong cordial ties which prevailed between the Arabs and the Dinka Ngok during the last phase were very much due to the brotherhood between me and Deng Majok" (Deng 1982:61).

Ibrahim Mohamed Zein recalled an incident during Deng Majok's visit to the Arab town of Muglad in 1952 or 1953; while in Muglad, Deng Majok called on the school and made generous gifts to the students and the faculty. "We, the teachers, met and decided to pay a courtesy call to the chief in his house to thank him for what he had done. So, I went to him accompanied by a number of teachers ... Three bulls had been slaughtered for the public ... A public dance was in progress. He received and greeted us very warmly. And we thanked him for his generosity to the school. I recall his precise words to us: 'The English have tied my neck with a turban and they are pulling me chanting, "South," "South;" and I am also pulling myself the opposite direction chanting, "North, North."' He said, 'I am doing all that in order to find people like you and schools like yours for our children; so that they can learn'" (Deng 1986:228).

Ibrahim el Hussein believes that Deng Majok chose to remain in the North because of the recognition and respect he enjoyed from both the Government and the Arabs: "Here in the North, Deng was highly respected by the government of the English and ... by the Arabs as a leader ... When an Arab woman saw him pass by, she would take pleasure in greeting him, 'Nazir Deng, peace be upon you.' [A]ll the Arabs, the Ajaiyra and the Felaita ... regarded him highly" (Deng 1986:228). This again highlights the degree to which Arab acceptance of Deng Majok was largely personal, almost as though he were a unique Dinka. The cordiality of relations between the Ngok and the Homr was thus perceived as inherited from the ancestors, but mostly consolidated and ensured through the Arab bond with Deng Majok personally.

With his identity recognized and respected beyond the dividing line, Deng Majok could then afford to be assertive in his demands on the Arabs and the government without endangering his leadership. That way he was able to acquire material benefits for his people through his northern connections. Monyluak Rou, a Ngok elder, stressed the practical considerations behind Deng Majok's decision. "Deng Majok used to say that he could not join the South because the standard of living of the people of the South was not as good as that of the people of the North. The reason why [he] liked the people of the North was because of the things we wear, these clothes. There was nothing else. Where people told us to go had little to offer" (Deng 1986:229).

Nyanjur, one of the middle daughters of Deng Majok, elaborated on the attraction of the North for her father in this way: "It was Father's own efforts that made Abyei what it is today as a town. And how did he do that? It was not because of his relations with the South; it was because of his relations with the North. That was how Abyei came to build shops, a dispensary, schools, and other services. Father left Abyei in a 'Thank

God!' situation. All that was the result of his relationship with the Arabs"
(Deng 1986:229).

But according to Nyanbol Amor, Deng Majok's second wife, his
preference for the North over the South was only a matter of degree, for
he felt a sense of belonging to both: "He was able to combine ... the
South and the North, though the North was a little more favored by him.
Most of his activities outside his tribe were toward the North, but he also
maintained friendship with southern chiefs, with whom he met
periodically. And those among the southerners who knew him well were
not disturbed by his close relations with the Arabs because they realized
that he benefitted the Dinka through those relations" (Deng 1986:229).

"Deng Kwol was like a guard at a gate between the Arabs and the
Dinka," said Chief Chier Rian of the Twich Dinka. "He was the Dinka
voice among the Arabs. He felt that if he moved from the Arabs, the
Dinka would have nobody looking out for them among the Arabs. That is
why Deng Kwol remained in the North" (Deng 1986:230).

Malith Mawlen, also from the Twich Dinka, shares the view that
Deng Majok's refusal to join the South was a ploy in favor of the South.
"Deng Majok said that if he came to the South, the Arabs would be
frightened by our unity and would treat us as strangers. If anything that
belonged to us were plundered, nobody could reclaim it. The Arabs would
say that we are aliens. But now that I am on the border, they fear me. If I
went to reclaim something that belonged to the Twich, the Nuer, or the
Malual, they would say that Deng was the person responsible on the
border" (Deng 1986:230). Malith Mawien concluded: "At this point I
cannot comment on whether the Ngok should come here to the South or
not. What I can say is that the descendants of Arob Biong are well known
as the people who guarded our borders with the Arabs" (Deng 1986:230).

Although the decision to remain in the North initially strengthened
relations between Dinka and the Arabs, the inclusion of the Ngok in the
newly formed Missiriya District and Rural Council, in which they
comprised only ten percent of the membership, was a development which
threatened Ngok autonomy and eventually aroused tensions between them
and the Homr. Confrontation first came when Babo Nimir was selected as
Paramount Chief to be the administrative and judicial head of all the tribal
chiefs in the district, a move which Deng Majok opposed on the grounds
that despite his being in the North, his tribe was ethnically and culturally
'southern,' and therefore had to be governed by Dinka law and custom,
akin to that which prevailed in the South. The British agreed with him and
the Ngok remained autonomous in their unity with the Homr.

A foundation for this special status had already been laid, for, in accordance with a special order by the Governor-General, Ngok courts were governed by the Chiefs' Courts Ordinance, 1931, which applied to the southern Provinces, and not by the Native Courts Ordinance, 1932, which applied to the North. But whereas in the South appeals from Chiefs were heard by their own peers through an elaborate inter-tribal court system, the Ngok Paramount Chief was virtually the final authority in matters of customary law and a very powerful ruler, whose decisions were rarely challenged. Because the Ngok Chiefs had such a grip on the situation, law and order, and therefore peace and security, became more effectively entrenched there than anywhere else in the Dinka world. Internal warfare totally ceased, and despite occasional attempts, inter-tribal wars involving the Ngok also virtually disappeared. The Ngok area became a harmonious point of contact, a secure bridge, and a free market between the North and the South.

It is important to emphasize that their moral and spiritual values, their deference to their divine leaders, and the impact of governmental power all combined to make the Ngok Dinka remarkably responsive to law and order, especially in comparison to the Missiriya who are notoriously militant and unruly. Under Deng Majok, the Ngok became particularly responsive to law and order. Sir Gawain Bell, who served in the area as District Commissioner from 1947 to the end of 1949 shortly after Deng Majok had assumed full leadership, had this to say about him and his people: "I can't remember that we ever had any serious crime in that part of the District. Among the Baggara of Missiriya, there were frequent tribal quarrels and fights and disturbances. There was a good deal of serious crime: murders and so forth; and the same applies to the Hamar in the North ... [T]he Ngok Dinka were a particularly law-abiding people. Deng Majok kept his people happy and content, looked after their affairs, saw that justice was administered, and I cannot recollect that either within the tribe or as between the tribe and the Baggara, they ever had any serious trouble when I was down there" (Deng 1986:137-138).

Deng Majok, unlike the Arab chiefs, followed gun control laws to the letter, ruling out any illegal possession of arms in his area, while the Arabs accumulated weapons illegally in large numbers. As one Ngok elder explained: "The Arabs started their illegal acquisition of guns while Deng Majok was still alive ... Chief Deng Majok would never tolerate anybody doing anything against the law even if it were done very discreetly ... He did not behave the same way Arab chiefs like Babo did. Had he permitted the Dinka, he would have died leaving his people armed with guns ... But ... Deng Majok believed that all his people should follow a straight and clear path."[20]

Although fear of government reprisal was a factor in this approach, the Ngok Dinka believe that Deng Majok's rigid conformity to the law was largely the result of his commitment to what is inherently right and to the avoidance of wrong. His effectiveness in securing the obedience of his people to his legal and moral code is in turn attributed to his combined secular power of government and spiritual authority of divine leadership. Babo Nimir is said to have recognized that dimension of Dinka leadership and used it to explain Deng Majok's superior performance in commanding the obedience of the Dinka:

> When the Government asked Babo during the last destruction (1965), saying "When Deng Majok says his word, that ends any problem; all his people listen to what he says. Nothing else goes wrong among his people. But your people continue to go and destroy [other] people. Does this come from you or do your people think of it by themselves?"
>
> Babo said, "But I am not like Deng ... Deng has two authorities; he has the Government power to arrest a person. He also has something else. When people contravene his words, he has Big [Sacred] Spears. If he says to a person, 'So and so, is it you who does this and that to my people? The spear of my Father will kill you,' that person will die. That is why the Ngok fear him. It is not that he has frightened the people himself; it is the Spears. He has two authorities, the chieftainship with which he kills people and the government power with which he arrests people (Deng 1980:331).

Ironically, the authority and influence of the Ngok Chief is attributed not only to divine leadership, complemented by government power, but also to Arab cultural influence. As David Cole and Richard Huntington (1985:37) observed, "The Ngok Dinka are the most hierarchical of all Nilotic peoples, a situation that seems rooted in Ngok traditions, deepened through Arab contacts and exacerbated by the colonial state." At the same

---

20. Chief Pagwot Deng, unpublished portion of an interview for Deng 1986, Kadugli, September, 1977.

time, the relative isolation of the Ngok from both Arab hegemony and government domination is said to have enabled them to develop a cohesive system that effectively amalgamated their own traditions with external influences. Paul Howell (1951:263-264) has observed:

> The Ngork [sic] have not been subjected to an intensive system of administration. Their country is practically inaccessible during the rains from May to November, the nearest point which can be reached by car during that period being Muglad, 130 miles away ... Administration consisted mainly of occasional visits by the District Commissioner rarely totaling more than a few weeks in the year. For this reason, and because of their remoteness from any of the main lines of communication, the lack of a permanently navigable river and the absence of commercial enterprise by merchants from the South, the Ngork have been subjected to less external influences than most Nilotic tribes today. Moreover, administration ... has for the most part been conducted by men who had relatively little experience of Nilotic peoples and did not speak their languages. This has had a definite result in the political organization of the tribe.

According to Howell (1951:263-264), the remoteness of the Ngok and the administration's need for local representation combined to reinforce Ngok leadership along the lines of Arab centralization of authority.

> There was therefore an attempt to find some institution equivalent to the Baggara "Nazirates" or the "Sultans" or "Meks" of Nuba and Dagu of the District. One reads early reports which describe the most important *Bany de Ring* as "Nazir," "Sultan" or even "Mek" (king) of the Ngork ...
>
> [A] Chief with considerable autocratic powers has been in the process of evolution over a number of years and if Kwol Arob was not a Nazir to begin with, he soon became the Dinka equivalent. His son, Deng Majok, has carried the evolution a stage further and has a burning ambition to pattern himself on the Ali Gulla "Nazirate" of the Homr (Baggara) with all the pomp of state visits to Khartoum, tribal gatherings, and in addition the Dinka

ideal of wealth, a company of wives. There is no serious danger in this except that former administrative policy has tended to build up an effective autocracy in an essentially democratic society; a system which might prove a stumbling block to the introduction of a democratic system of local administration.

Howell's message both in substance and in tone should be seen in the light of his experiences among the other Nilotics, particularly the Nuer in whose area he served and on whom he wrote his doctoral thesis.[21] Nuer society, described by Professor Evans-Pritchard (1940:296) as "ordered anarchy," has been perceived by anthropologists as typical of the "acephalous" societies with a segmentary lineage system described by Middleton and Tait (1959) as "Tribes Without Rulers." Since Evans-Pritchard and Howell admired the Nilotic democratic spirit, the authoritarian system of the Ngok leadership must have been an undesirable anomaly. Be that as it may, the centralization of autocratic authority was not only the outcome of the three sources of influence described above; it was, at least under Chief Deng Majok, consciously fostered and consolidated by the Ngok leadership's jealous protection of its autonomy.

It is in this regard that Deng Majok was most successful in harmonizing the contradictions of his personal power position. He had generated change through the involvement of outside forces, the Arabs and the central government, but he saw to it that their accessibility was limited to him as their sole representative in the area. That way the temptation to resort to foreign allies or outside sources of justice would be effectively curtailed. According to one elder:

> Deng Majok, talking to the Government representatives about what he deemed to be the best way of ruling his area said, "In my area, people used to fight to the death in the past, particularly the tribes of Abyor and Mannyuar; but my main concern now is to see to it that no further fights take place, and should this be realized, there will prevail a better atmosphere for security, education, and progress. And to achieve this, the official contact or communication between the authorities and the people

---

21. See Howell 1954.

should be solely through me; I should be the only link between the government and my people. If there is a direct communication with individuals, anarchists will take advantage of that and the whole area will be in chaos. Whatever message the Government wants to convey to the public should first come to me and I will transmit it to the people through the Omdas, sheikhs, and the clan heads, until it reaches the individual. I can assure you that this system will work the best." Deng Majok, through this policy, managed to be the only person in the entire area to whom the authorities talked and listened. And when the government representatives left the area after their short visits, he would for his part summon his chiefs to pass on whatever he deemed fit to communicate to them.[22]

Apparently, government's policy of indirect rule and the remoteness of the Dinka made Deng Majok's shrewd policy of restricted contact and communication between the officials and the people quite appealing. Deng Majok became virtually the ultimate authority over his people. As one elder put it: "Deng Majok was the governor. And he was the judge. And he was the chief. All three were his responsibilities in his own tribe. If a major problem should come to his tribe, the government would only come to assist him in assessing the punishment in the case of a major offense ... If it were compensation for homicide, he would settle that. If it were an imposition of fines, he would also do that. And his decisions would be backed up wherever the matter might go."[23]

Ngok autonomy was possible not only because of the diplomatic successes of their leaders on a very sensitive racial, tribal, and religious cross-roads, but primarily because the central government under the British provided protection from their neighbors. Independence considerably diminished this third party protection, as the central government was occupied by people identified as Arabs and therefore with one of the parties. Deng Majok tried to counter this imbalance by reaping the fruits of his earlier investment in identifying himself with the North. The value of unity with the North which he had defended against

---

22. Mithiang Aguek, quoted in Deng 1986:137.

23. Chol Piok, quoted in Deng 1986:140.

the British now came in handy in his relations with the new rulers in the Arab North.

Deng Majok indeed ensured the government's relative neutrality through his unwavering commitment to unity manifested in his staunch stand in favor of remaining in the North. As Ibrahim Mohamed Zein recalled, he distinguished himself in the Missiriya Rural Council through his unity line: "I used to hear a great deal about his personality, and among ... the things that were said to have been said by Deng Majok ... was: 'I consider my being in Abyei for the Sudan as a whole to be like a needle and a thread which binds the two parts of the *toub* [a sari-like dress] into one piece.' Those words ... made people look to Chief Deng Majok as a great leader and thinker" (Deng 1986:230-231).

Not only did Deng Majok object to Dinka appeals being heard by Babo Nimir, but in the words of Ali, one of his senior sons, he "would never accept being placed in a subordinate status" (Deng 1986:231). In the view of some people, Deng Majok much preferred remaining in the North because being a Dinka chief among Arabs would give him a unique status that was superior to being classified as either a northerner or a southerner. Hassan Biong Deng elaborated on his father's sense of pride as a Dinka in the northern context:

> He was always stressing, in every move he made, that he had a special status ... Every single time he found difficulty breaking through, he would draw the attention of the authorities to the fact that he was not racially or culturally part of Kordofan's administration. This was especially the case whenever there was an issue which required the approval of the majority in the district. If he felt that something would prejudice Dinka interests ... he would always draw the attention of the administration to the fact, arguing that he should not be regarded as a member of the same cultural group as the other tribes or be required to adhere to the cultural ways of the other members of the district. But he would never lag behind in matters that required the full representation of his tribe as a separate entity ... He never gave up the fundamental cultural identity and values of the Dinka (Deng 1986:230-231).

And yet, according to Biong, Deng Majok was fully integrated into the Arab context: "To confirm that he was fully accepted into the northern community or the district, he was elected president of the Council by the Arabs in the district" (Deng 1986:230-231).

That incident, in which the Arab chiefs rebelled against their paramount chief by supporting, indeed engineering, Deng Majok's election as president, was the climax in the political rivalry between Babo Nimir and Deng Majok. Although dictated largely by the internal differences among the Arab chiefs, his election by the Arab majority was, and has remained, a symbol of Deng Majok's stature as a hero of national unity between the South and the North.

Once he had secured their trust, Deng Majok could afford to pursue his rights as a Dinka leader in a predominantly Arab Muslim context. Through his unflinching defense of his people, his self-assertiveness as a Dinka among Arabs, and his acceptance by the Arabs not only as an equal but even as a leader of their combined Dinka-Arab council, Deng Majok gave the Ngok much to be proud of, even though they were a minority in the northern Arab context. It is in this area that the Ngok Dinka most appreciated his leadership. In the words of the Arab elder Ibrahim el Hussein: "Deng kept the Arabs in one hand and the Dinka in the other hand. He protected the Dinka and he protected the Arabs. He guided the Arabs with words of wisdom as he guided the Dinka. And the Arabs fully accepted his word. The Arabs looked to Babo's chieftainship only when they were back in Arabland. But when they were in Dinkaland, their chief was Deng Majok" (Deng 1986:232-233).

Even though he and Deng Majok became rivals, Babo Nimir himself confirmed Deng's popularity among the Arabs: "By God, we in our area had not the slightest doubt that no man who went before Deng Majok would ever leave feeling that he had been treated unjustly ... With Deng Majok, we felt assured of the protection our people would get whenever they went there ... Whenever there were problems among my own Arab tribes, I would send for him and he and I would get together to solve the problems. And the Arabs would accept his word. He was very highly respected by the Arabs" (Deng 1982:59).

His Constructive Role when North-South Confrontation Took Place

Just as the friendship between Babo Nimir and Deng Majok fostered cordial relations between the Arabs and the Dinka, their inherently conflictual political rivalry symbolized and contributed to the deterioration of Arab-Dinka relations. This was compounded by Babo's link to the inner circles of the sectarian power structures at the center. A leader of a people who had been among the staunch supporters of the Mahdiya, Babo cemented his relationship with the Mahdi family by marrying the daughter of Sayed al-Fadhil al-Mahdi, the niece of Sayed Abdel Rahman al-Mahdi.[24] During the 1954 elections for the Constituent Assembly, Babo invited his father-in-law from Omdurman to stand for the Umma Party in the combined Dinka-Homr constituency. Sayed Abdullahi el-Fadhil had never been to that part of the country before, and the arrangement offended the Ngok, who interpreted it to be giving away their country as a bride-price, but of course, he won the elections.

Ngok sub-tribal leaders, certainly not without Deng Majok's discreetly concealed knowledge, acquiescence, and perhaps instigation, raised a criminal case of electoral corruption against Sayed Abdullahi el-Fadhil, the first such charge to be brought against a prominent member of the Mahdi family. Mohamed Ahmed Mahjoub, a well-known lawyer who was to successively hold the positions of Foreign Minister and Prime Minister, defended the accused. Not surprisingly, Sayed el-Fadhil was acquitted and Deng Majok succeeded relatively well in distancing himself from the case, even though Babo and his associates were sure that he had been involved.

From the point of view of the Ngok, the merger with the Homr in one constituency, the invitation of Sayed el-Fadhil, and his election to the parliament were all indicative of the change of policies in favor of the Homr. But it did not end at that. In the Council, things generally went the northern way. The language of the proceedings was Arabic, which many of the Dinka delegates could not understand fully, and usually only Deng Majok spoke. Other matters, relating to the distribution of government cars, the council officials and the like, convinced the Ngok of subjection.[25]

It was perhaps during the South-North civil war of 1955-72 that Deng Majok's identity as a southerner and the ambivalence of being a Dinka among Arab tribes became most pronounced. For a considerable part of the war, Ngok area remained sheltered from its effects, and to a

---

24. Babo Nimir divorced all his wives to marry her, but after producing several sons, well-raised and educated in close association with both families, the marriage was dissolved, according to Babo's account to this author, because she was condescending and could not adapt herself to the conditions of his tribal context.

25. Arob Kwol, the youngest brother of Deng Majok, lamented the change in a song that recalled the glory of the Pajok leadership in the history of Arab-Dinka relations and the indignity that had befallen Ngokland. See Deng 1973:180-181.

large extent was the only secure area in the southern cultural-ethnic-geographic complex. However, as the war continued to intensify, the Ngok began to sympathize and identify more and more with the South, and some of their young men began to join the military wing of the southern movement – the Anya-Nya – and even assumed leading positions in the struggle.

One of the local rebel leaders was Ahmed (Arob), the eldest son of Deng Majok. After his secondary education at Hantoub in the North, one of the leading secondary schools in the country, Ahmed was appointed by the British as a local government officer and on the request of his father, was posted to Abyei. A power struggle with his father and the Arab resentment against his position led to his premature downfall and eventual rebellion, despite the fact that he was a Muslim, culturally Arabized, and at Hantoub had been a Muslim Brother.

During the mid-sixties, rumors began to reach Abyei that the local Anya-Nya might attack under the command of Ahmed Deng. This naturally heightened the anxiety of the Arabs. One incident after another fueled the fire that ignited the 1965 Ngok-Homr hostilities in which several hundred people, and many estimate a lot more, lost their lives. As it was during the dry season, when the Arabs were on their seasonal migration southward, the war was fought on Ngok soil and the Arabs initially suffered defeat. But, with superior arms, they retaliated later with a vengeance that devastated the Dinka.

Abdelbasit Saeed, from the Missiriya, a university lecturer who later became Under-Secretary in the Ministry for Peace in the post-Nimeiri government of Sadiq al-Mahdi, has given a detailed account of the developments in Ngok-Homr relations and their linkage to the North-South confrontation with commendable objectivity. He attributes the 1954 hostilities between the Ngok and the Missiriya to an attack in September by the Anya-Nya rebels in the southern town of Gogrial, in Bahr el Ghazal province, where some Missiriya had settled as merchants, and the events of December 6, 1964, in which northerners and southerners clashed in Khartoum, as a result of rumors surrounding the delay of the southern Minister of the Interior, Clement Mboro, from his fact-finding and goodwill visit to the South. "Subsequent to this incident, scores of southerners fled Khartoum to the southern Region carrying with them the frustrating stories of the Sunday genocide of Southerners in Khartoum" (Saeed 1982:215-216).

Although news of the Gogrial raid had spread in Missiriya territory, the Arabs could not revenge because it was during the rainy season and they were still far north in their permanent residences. Their outrage was manifest as soon as they got to the river in their seasonal migration southward. As far as they were concerned, the conflict was with the ethnic southerners, the Ngok included. By the same token, the news coming to Ngokland about the Khartoum "genocide" provided the Dinka with a cause for outrage. "This chain of national and local struggles in 1964 served to create a bench-mark in tribal relations in Abyei District subsequently" (Saeed 1982:216).

> The Missiriya believed that any Nilote was a party to the conflict and a potential object of revenge. The conception of tribal identification and association did not serve the Missiriya to objectively distinguish between friend and foe among those groups they encountered; for the Missiriya, the Nuer and Shilluk were also Dinka. The ... Nilotes ... also took every Arab whether Ajairya, Falaita or a merchant from farther Northern Sudan, for a potential enemy, and objective of skepticism, mistrust and possibly revenge.
>
> Knowing that one of the sons of Deng Majok [Ahmed Deng] ... was one of the leaders of the Anya-Nya forces, the Missiriya could not believe that the Ngok were not party to or involved in the raid onto their brethren in Gogrial (Saeed 1982:218).

Thus, "the ground was set for violent confrontation, the primary causes for which were anchored in the national struggle between North and South. But it was relegated by provincial authorities to 'tribal' conflict" (Saeed 1982:219).

A series of gruesome incidents of violence took place. In one, "The Kelabna Arabs fired at Higair [Rek] Dinka, killing two and the others fled. Police investigations later found that the arms of the dead had been amputated, and the corpses mutilated. The Dinka claimed that the Arabs amputated the arms and used them for beating the Missiriya ceremonial drums (nuggara)" (Saeed 1982:219). Furthermore, the Arabs resorted to setting fires on Ngok villages, looting and killing at random.

Deng Majok and his Arab counterparts, Babo and Ali Nimir, were then at El Obeid, the provincial capital, to receive the Queen of England, who was paying an official visit to the country. But an accusing finger is pointed at another member of the leading Arab family: Police records say that the President of the local Court at Al Muglad was the suspect; and that ... he had been seen burning deserted Dinka huts ... [H]is presence in Abyei during the crisis was confirmation of his involvement. The suspect was immediately suspended ... and ... the District Commissioner ... demanded that charges be pressed against him and that he should be put to trial" (Saeed 1982:221).

Abdelbasit Saeed, citing police reports, went on to explain that the Arabs used to transport fighting squads from Muglad, neighboring villages and camps of the nomads to battle fronts southward employing commercial lorries belonging to the local merchants, and that the Arabs used firearms, "to the detriment of the Dinka who were using locally made spears" (Saeed 1982:221-222). And yet, with surprising lack of scruples, the Arabs "sent delegations to the central government demanding that the Missiriya should be armed so that they may be able to fight back the insurgent Southern outlaws" (Saeed 1982:222). According to the police reports, "In fact, this claim is unfounded and baseless, because there is no evidence of a single case of death among the Missiriya during the fighting in which a victim was killed by a firearm. On the contrary, it has been proven in many incidents that it was the Missiriya who were using firearms" (Saeed 1982:222).[26]

Perhaps the most devastating events occurred farther north in the Missiriya towns where southerners became victims of inhumane brutalities. In the atmosphere of tension and violence that prevailed southward, "people from the South in these Northern towns became open targets for assault, looting, murder, and at least intimidation by the resident northern majority" (Saeed 1982:224).

Although southerners sought protection from the authorities or asked to be transported back home, "subsequent events showed that they received no protection even when in the custody of police" (Saeed 1982:224). Eventually, people were transported to Abyei from El Fulah, Al Muglad, and Babanusa, but some of those in Babanusa met with the worst massacre in the conflict. According to a police report which Abdelbasit Saeed describes as "extremely self-incriminating," police protection at Babanusa, if it existed at all, was the worst:

> Humr [sic] masses of women and children invaded the police station where Southerners had gathered seeking government protection, and had been accorded such status by sheltering them in available rooms inside the police

---

26. File No. M.R.Sh. 66-D-1, Al Fula, 1979, quoted by Abdelbasit Saeed.

station. [Arab] women and children were armed with kerosene onto the defenseless Southerners and set fire to them. When the local government district Commissioner arrived ... in the afternoon, everything had gone. Fire was still burning on the dead corpses inside the rooms. He found the master-sergeant policeman who was in command of the police station and the *Nazir* of the Missiriya sitting under a tree in front of the police station ... All the inhabitants of Babanusa refused to assist in putting out the fire ... There was no way out except to let the fire complete its mission. Seventy-two Southerners were burnt to death ...

The police station was equipped with seventeen trained men who were armed with rifles, and had four tear gas bombs at their disposal. The fact that they did not apply the tear gas facility against the attackers raises many questions (Saeed 1982:225).

The long legacy of relatively cordial relations between the Homr and the Ngok was thus immersed in the North-South conflict which went far beyond right and wrong.

Not only did an armed police unit give *de facto* approval for a group of "women and children" to burn to death a group of defenseless southerners; but also the entire town of Babanusa apparently engineered a conspiracy of incredible magnitude; leaving the genocide to the so-called "women and children." This crime clearly testified that in that particular situation, it mattered not whether any particular victim was from Ngok or any other Nilotic group. The fact of being a southerner, who happened to be among that group, was sufficient cause for him/her to be burnt to death. It was even more saddening that the whole town refused to help in digging the graves for the dead ... Since the "Dinka-on-fire were southerners, who could have otherwise been fighting on the sides of the Anya-Nya forces, let them meet their fate" (Saeed 1982:226).

Although demonstratively outraged, Deng Majok, now back in his area and, as expected, loyal to law and order, cooperated with the authorities to restore peace. Ibrahim Mohamed Zein recalled the predicament which then confronted Deng Majok, torn between loyalty to his people and a sense of duty toward promoting law and order in cooperation with the Government: "Despite his clear stand with us [the North] ... things deteriorated ... between the Dinka and the Arabs ... [H]e worked very hard to restore law and order. A delegation went from here (Khartoum) comprising Rasheed El Tahir [Minister of Justice] and Ahmed Jubara El Awad [of the Interior]. They went and held a very large meeting between the tribal leaders in order to reach a peace settlement. There was of course bitterness in the speeches, but the end-result was commitment to the unity of the country and a reaffirmation of his leaning towards the North. His attitude had a considerable effect on the restoration of peace and stability. The result was a recognition of strong bonds between the Dinka and the Arabs" (Deng 1986:239).

The peace conference that would affirmatively reconcile the two parties was convened later. Pending the conference, Tigani Mohamed Zein witnessed the depressed mood Deng Majok was in then:

The deterioration was immense. Muhktar El Tayeb [the District Commissioner] happened to be on a trip to see the elections there. So, we joined him. Then we left on our way back. I believe the time was about 5:30 in the morning. Muhktar El Tayeb said, "Let us pass by Deng Majok's house! Let us see whether he is up or not." We went and found him awake and sitting in his court house ... with ... tribal elders and ... Abdullahi Dugul from the Arabs. Mubhtar El Tayeb greeted him and said, "Nazir Deng, I am now leaving. I came to see the situation and must now go to report to the Governor. I thought I would stop to bid you farewell."

He said, "I would like you to take a message to the Governor. Please tell him that I say, 'Here we are afflicted with a problem that has burned down a large number of villages. Many people have left for the Northern towns. There is no grain and there are no homes to live in. We want him to let us know whether we should build on our old spots or in new areas. And tell him that whether we build our homes to the South or the North of the River Kir, we will still remain in Kordofan; whatever the amount of death or the burning of villages, we are in

Kordofan and nobody is going to force us out of Kordofan.' Just tell the Governor that" (Deng 1986:239).

At the peace conference held at Abyei in early March, 1965, Deng Majok maintained his firm identification with Kordofan and therefore the North rather than with the South. According to the District reports: "[He] reiterated his Northernliness and his Kurdufan [sic] identity. He ... denied any association with the insurgency in the South. He reaffirmed his cleanliness of heart toward the Missiriya. He mentioned that he was absent at the outbreak of hostilities; that the Dinka ceased fighting after his arrival and the arrival of army troops, whereas the Missiriya continued the killing and the burning and destruction of property. He also referred to the massacres at Babanusa, and the embarrassing situation he had been put in, in front of his following" (Saeed 1982:228).[27]

By then, Deng Majok's sympathy for the rebel movement and the southern cause in general was relatively established and known. His unequivocal claim to be a northerner must therefore be understood as a shrewd political tactic which Babo sought to expose at the conference by placing the responsibility on the Ngok and specifically on Deng Majok because of the attacks on the Missiriya in Ngokland, the failure to expel southern tribes from the area, and the involvement of Deng Majok's son in the southern insurgency.

After long deliberations, a peace agreement was eventually concluded with the help of prominent tribal leaders as *ajaweed*, mediators. The agreement stipulated the termination of acts of violence, restriction on display of arms, guarantee of the safety of members of each group in the territory of the other, return of all property captured during fighting, preparation of an inventory of persons and property lost during the hostilities, the administration of oath-taking by each group according to its beliefs, the Muslims on the Koran and Dinka on the sacred spears, and cooperation with the local authorities in the maintenance of peace and security (Saeed 1982:229-230). Apparently it was agreed that no *dia*, the customary bloodwealth of cattle, would be paid for those who had been killed on both sides. All that was forgiven as part of the peace and reconciliation agreement, a unique arrangement in the history of tribal warfare and peace agreement that would later haunt Ngok-Homr relations.

---

27. Report of the Commissioner of Police-South Kordofan on Tribal Conflicts, quoted by Abdelbasit Saeed.

Generally, the Ngok remember the Arab mediators as having been fair and just. As preeminent leaders of tribes, they had their own "indigenous" standards for judging, which seemed to stand apart from the moral vacuum of North-South dichotomy. For those leaders, the fact that Deng Majok, a Dinka, identified himself with the North, filled that moral vacuum. In any case, some of those leaders saw the aggressive profile of the Missiriya in a broader framework of inter-tribal conflicts in the region as a whole. According to Ngok sources, the Chairman of the mediation conference, Moneim Mansour of the Hamar Arabs of Nahud District in Western Kordofan, said to Babo, "Babo, how can you alone dispute the land with the Rezeigat [in Darfur] and with the Hamar [in Western Kordofan] and with the Nuba [in southern Kordofan] and go to that ... distant land of Deng [Majok] and even as far as Paan- Aruw? What kind of behavior is that?"[28]

As indicated above, Deng Majok's absolute consistency and therefore credibility on the issue of his loyalty to northern identity in the North-South cleavage, while winning the Arabs, was a more complex strategy than they realized. Deng Majok fully identified with the southern cause, but chose to play his role in the most constructive way he knew and was within his control. He wanted to avoid identifying the central government with the Homr Arabs. He felt that it was essential to the Dinka cause to force the central government into the moral position of a third party, judge or mediator, even though in fact he realized that the shared Arab identity of the Homr and the central government favored the Arabs. It was a case of upholding virtue to moderate evil; to foster objective judgement that could only work in favor of the Dinka. There is every reason therefore to believe that Deng Majok emphasized his identification with the North as a means of winning some favor from the central government and therefore ensuring a degree of justice against the Homr, but it was obvious to him in any case that the Government would not have allowed his joining the South. Nor was there much to look to in the South under the devastation of the civil war conditions.[29]

At the peace conference, the Arabs claimed that the fertile North-East area of Ngokland known as Ngol was theirs. In the words of Abdelbasit

---

28. Chol Adija, in the interview for Deng 1986.

29. According to Chief Pagwot Deng, "When this problem first occurred, if we were in the South, there would be no single Ngok alive today. The Arabs would have destroyed us totally" (Deng 1980:275).

Saeed, "Nazir Babo Nimir ... claimed that it was his father, Nazir Nimir Ali al Gulla who ... permitted the Ngok in 1939 to move further North into a place known as Ragaba Zarga [The Black River Neck]" (Saeed 1982:164). To the Dinka, that he could fabricate such a claim was the epitome of Arab unscrupulousness and lack of moral standards in their relations with the Dinka. In a way, it ironically proved the point Chief Kwol Arob had emphasized in his arguments for remaining in the North, that if he identified with the South, the Arabs, instead of appreciating his generosity by allowing them to graze and water their cattle in Ngokland, could claim the land to be theirs. With the North-South hostilities reflected in Ngok-Homr relations, the calculated ambitions of the Arabs over Ngok territory were already manifesting themselves. But as Chol Adija recollected, Babo was criticized by the conference. Among the things Moneim Mansour, the Chairman of the conference, is remembered to have said to Babo was, "Why are you after a soil as dark as the Dinka? What do you want from the dark soil of the Dinka? ... You are a people who simply go after grazing areas in the three months of the dry season. How can a person of three months' residence dispute the land with the settlers of all seasons? Babo was found to be in the wrong."[30]

Matet Ayom, who was also at the conference, recaptured the mood of the tense discussions that ensued and the competing claims to the land articulated in genealogical terms: "Deng said, 'You Babo, this land is not yours. Your ancestors do not reach ten, while my ancestors go at least that far. Which of us therefore found the other on this land?'... Ngol became established as ours. But Deng's contention was that he should swear with Babo over Denga (Muglad) itself ... He argued that Muglad itself was our area" (Deng 1986:240).[31]

Despite Deng Majok's fierce defense of his people and their land, the Arabs realized that only he among the Dinka could represent the interests of both sides, especially during such times of racial animosity. Ibrahim Mohamed Zein reports more evidence from his conversation with the district commissioner, Mukhtar El Tayeb, as they left Abyei early in the morning during the heat of the conflict: "We met Arabs on the way.

---

30. Chol Adija, in the interview for Deng 1986.

31. Muglad (or Denga), the Homr Arab town and headquarters, was settled by the Alei sub-tribe of the Dinka before they moved further South to their present territory. Indeed, its name is believed to be derived from an Alei chief by the name Deng, whose home was in that area.

Muhktar El Tayeb ... said to them, 'Here I am leaving, what I want to tell you and ask you to tell every Arab who might not understand the situation well, is that Deng Majok is the only person who binds the South and the North together. If we lose Deng Majok, it means that we will have lost this vital link and things will happen that only God knows'" (Deng 1986:240).

Only days after the conclusion of the peace conference, the Ngok Dinka filed a complaint alleging Arab violation of the terms of the agreement. The Dinka retaliated and a series of incidents ensued. According to one incident, a group of Dinka going to report to the police station was attacked by a group of Arabs. "The Dinka took refuge at a nearby army truck. They handed over their spears to the soldiers, in compliance with the latter's order, and demanded protection from their approaching assailants. The presence of the armed soldiers, who were also northerners, did not deter the Missiriya. A situation similar to the cold-blooded murder of unarmed Dinka at Babanusa took place. The Missiriya attacked the unarmed Dinka and murdered them, whether outside or inside the army truck. They also fired and punctured the tires of the truck. The soldiers did not fire at the invading Missiriya claiming that the master sergeant in command did not give such orders" (Saeed 1982:231-232).[32]

As Abdelbasit Saeed observed, "The circumstances of this incident of genocide confirmed to the Dinka any doubts they might have had about the neutral stance of government troops. It provided the Dinka with sufficient reason to believe that the position that had been taken by the police during the Babanusa genocide was supportive of the Missiriya Arabs against them ... nor were soldiers on the scene charged with complicity" (Saeed 1982:231-232).

The Ngok, having now lost faith in the prospects for peaceful coexistence with the Missiriya and in the justice of the District's administration "demanded that a separate rural council seated at Abyei should be established for them, or that they may be annexed to the southern Nuba Mountains Rural Council seated at Kadugli. The Ngok argued that they could no longer remain with the Missiriya as subjects of the same administrative unit, since they could no longer reconcile their deep-seated differences. They demanded that all Missiriya policemen

---

32. Reports of the Commissioner of Police-South Kordofan, presented to the Kadugli Conference on Missiriya-Ngok Conflict.

stationed at Abyei be transferred immediately" (Saeed 1982:230).[33] Abdelbasit Saeed pertinently observed that "the Ngok did not demand disassociation from Kordofan Province as a whole", a position which he regarded as "consistent with Nazir Deng Majok's argument by deposition of all allegiance to northern Sudan, and with disassociating himself from any affiliation with the revolution in the South" (Saeed 1982:230). He went on to acknowledge that "after the resolution of the civil war in 1972, and subsequent to [Deng] Majok's death, the tendency towards accession to the Southern Region gained ground and became the center of differences among the Ngok themselves at the local level, and between Ngok and provincial administration" (Saeed 1982:230).

Ironically, because Deng Majok continued to identify himself with the North for calculated strategic reasons despite his bitterness against the Arabs, Ibrahim Mohamed Zein contends that this itself was evidence of his love for the North and dedication to national unity: "I can truly testify to the fact that Deng Majok was a man whose sense of national unity and love for the North remained strong even in the most critical moments of relations between the Dinka and the Arabs" (Saeed 1982:240-241).

The Vacuum Left by his Death

As the South-North war intensified and extended into his area, Deng Majok became increasingly vexed about the fate of his border area and according to the evidence of many, there is reason to believe that his vexation contributed to his ill health and eventual death in August 1969, an unparalleled calamity for the Ngok and other Dinkas further South and indeed for the Arabs of southern Kordofan too.

When the news of Deng Majok's death reached Twichland, according to the Twich Dinka elder, Atem Muoter: "One felt that the world was destroyed. And that is what it is: the world is not only spoiled; it will continue to be spoiled. Nobody seems to be able to bring it back under control. If Deng Kwol were alive, he would have checked the Baggara Arabs ... Deng would tear the Arabs apart with his teeth. And indeed, we and the Arabs have always been cannibalistic with one another. People run away from a person when he is brave and strong or when he has some supernatural powers. The power of Deng Kwol was unique" (Deng 1986:269).

---

33. District reports, File No. MRDM-66-3-A. Tribal Conflicts-General, Al Fula, 1966.

Babo, a man who had turned from being a very close friend into a political adversary, also saw disaster in the death of Deng Majok: "'O God!' we thought. 'What a loss!' It was as though the link binding the Missiriya and the Dinka had been broken. Once Deng was dead, the door was open to the young men who had gone and studied in missionary schools in the South, men who did not have the spirit of Deng Majok. We thought, 'Now that Deng is dead, these men will find the freedom to unleash their aspirations. The area will certainly be in trouble'" Deng 1982:61.

And, "Truly, after the death of Deng Majok," commented Tigani Mohamed Zein:

> many problems occurred which people believe are due to his death. The present generation is different from the older generation. Today leaders, whether they are sons of Deng Majok or others, are educated and their view of things is different from that of their older generation. This is also true of the North. Of course, the traditional society in both the North and the South has remained the same because education has not affected the predominant position of the population. But there was special wisdom in the manner with which Deng Majok was managing the affairs of the area. The tribe has not found anyone who can fill the position of Deng Majok. So Deng Majok has left a vacuum; his death has created a big gap. This is my opinion (Deng 1986:270).

"Of course, God always gives a leader something special and unique to him," observed Ibrahim Mohamed Zein.

> For instance, the Prophet Mohamed, who was very dear to God Almighty, was from Ghoreish Tribe, and during the days of ignorance, all the Arabs, with the exception of Ghoreish Tribe, used to go naked. The Ghoreish were dressed and their women used to be veiled. This was a special blessing from God to the Ghoreish because it was from them that He would select his Prophet.
>
> And so it was with Deng Majok, God gave him special qualities so that he could fill his unique position. Among his greatest assets for leadership was that he was a man of unusual intellect and wide comprehension of issues. In politics, for instance, one felt that he always achieved

whatever objective he had set for himself. No situation ever confronted him that he was not in full command of. His broad outlook and unique capability placed him in a natural leadership position. He was always able to make delicate and precise calculations in any decision-making situation in time of peace or of war. He always gave great attention to showing hospitality to visitors; gifts must go to visiting dignitaries. These are qualities which are not possessed by everyone; they are the qualities of leadership. He treated problems with wisdom, with full understanding, and he went after whatever he wanted to achieve, clarifying his objective quite clearly and pursuing it with diligence. These are rare leadership qualities (Deng 1986:270).

"Deng had the qualities of a true leader," said Babo Nimir. "He was just, generous, and hospitable. He never feared the truth. If one was bad, he would tell him so" (Deng 1986:270).

A former governor of Kordofan Province, Mohamed Abbas, a northern Sudanese, concluded about Deng Majok:

I knew many of the tribal chiefs of the South. With some exceptions, they tended to be instrumental, waiting to carry out instructions, rather than being suggestive. Deng Majok was a man of ideas. He was so paramount that you could hardly apply to him the North-South distinction of measurement.

Chief Deng Majok could compete favorably, both in performance as a chief and in strength of character and dignity with the best chief in Kordofan or elsewhere in the Sudan. In his clean white Jibba and turban, he looked like a pyramid (Deng 1986:270-271).

Ibrahim Mohamed Zein, an educator from Khartoum, summed up widely shared sentiments when he said, "Deng Majok is a loss to the family, he is a loss to the area of Abyei, he is a loss to the whole area of Dar Missiriya, he is a loss to Kordofan Province, and he is a loss to the Sudan. He was the guarantor of stability in the area; he was the hope for a stabilizing leadership. Once he was gone, the situation began to shake and shake until it fell apart" (Deng 1986:7).

As the problems in Abyei became progressively worse and assumed national dimensions, that sentiment was to be echoed over and over again, not only at all levels within the Sudan, but also abroad in the interested circles of the Middle East.[34]

Many of the negotiating stories in this volume, whether within the family or at higher levels of the social and political structure, touch on the relations between the Dinka and the Arabs. And although their relations have evolved over the centuries, Deng Majok has been a pivotal character in the recent developments, which is why his name figures prominently in any negotiations. As the unchallenged authority, Deng Majok exercised a remarkable control over his tribe and relations with the Arabs. But that control was precarious at best and artificial at worst. It represented an outstanding accomplishment of an individual who felt unjustly treated by tradition and sought to liberate not only himself, but his community from the weight of traditional values, structures, and attitudes, even as he sought legitimacy from them. It was an awesome task that became a passionate preoccupation for him.

Deng Majok's success depended on alliance with the more privileged Arab neighbors and the superior powers of the central authorities. He saw to it that the door he was opening to those outside forces did not open too widely to encourage others in his tribe to seek the same opportunities for external alliances, which he feared might lead to anarchy. Given the potential for conflict in the highly individualistic, yet communalistic system of the Dinka, Deng Majok ensured that external linkages and the flow of information were strictly controlled. He became the only legitimate channel of communication with the higher authorities. All those who tried to circumvent or side-step his authority did so at their own peril and always ended up the victims of law and order.

---

34. This was particularly the case around January and February, 1983, when many among the Ngok elite, including leading sons of Deng Majok, were arrested, accused of instigating and masterminding the renewal of rebellion in the Ngok area and in the region of Northern Bahr el Ghazal. The chief of National Security, who was also vice-president of the Republic, threatened to charge them with treasonable offenses. The contrast between Deng Majok's commitment to unity and the position of his sons was highlighted in the press. On the other hand, when after several months of mediation, reconciliation was effected between the Ngok leaders and the authorities of Kordofan with the sympathetic involvement of the National Security Chief and the President, the occasion was celebrated in the media as if it were a second Addis Ababa Agreement. This in itself represented the importance of the area as a link and a potential source of conflict between the North and the South.

With his death, the tenuous connection through one individual was broken, the door to the outside circles was left wide open without a guard, and the stampede by those who saw themselves disadvantaged by the Deng Majok order, including previously loyal, but repressed political allies, would result in a catastrophic chaos for the tribe as a whole. The man who had initially posed a challenge to the traditional order, became the sole protector of his people and when he died, the Dinka became orphans – to use a popular metaphor.

That was the man we as his children observed as we grew up and whose ways we watched closely, sometimes emulated, at times disapproved of, and in some instances wanted to correct in our own lives. It would, therefore, be too simple to conclude that the values or attributes associated with Deng Majok are reflected in his children. Not only would some attributes be accepted and others rejected, but the result of the selective process would also vary with the individual for reasons that may have to do with each personality and the possible influence of the mother and her side of the extended kinship circle.

More than most of my brothers, at least of my generation, I was particularly close to my maternal relatives. Their keen interest in me and my future in the Deng Majok family and indeed in the tribe must have played a considerable role in shaping my aspirations and performance in public life. Indeed, on several occasions, elders have drawn to my attention the extent to which my attitude on public issues and my manner of speaking are the products of my dual heritage from both the paternal and the maternal lines. A word about my maternal background is therefore in place.

3
Maternal Link

A Lineage Renowned for Leadership

The Dinka bias in favor of the paternal line implies that the mother's genealogy is generally far less traceable than the father's line. But just as the child is emotionally closer to the mother, though rationally more identified with the father, so is the special bond that ties a person to his maternal kin. Their affection, support, and reinforcement are recognized as unfailing and could be pivotal in shaping the character and destiny of a person.

What is striking about the influence of my maternal link on me is that it both reinforced a strong sense of identification with my father and provided me with an alternative yardstick for the traditional Dinka ideals of leadership in the combined political and spiritual sense. This is particularly so since my maternal relatives were themselves descendants of a lineage that was renowned for leadership, which in the modern context they no longer had, except in the spiritual sense. They clearly had aspirations for power through their daughter's marriage to the chief, but they also realized that as a relatively junior wife, her progeny would be disadvantaged. This combination, the ambition for leadership and the disadvantages of tradition, combined to present me with a challenge that was somewhat reminiscent in kind, though not in degree, of Father's experience.

Like Father, I strove hard to meet the qualifications for leadership, but realized my disqualification by the traditional rules of succession, and while Father eventually sought the intervention of outside forces on his behalf, I saw the prospects for my future in education and job opportunities in the modern sector, more specifically in the government. This eventually qualified me for a leadership role in the interlocking circles of power that affected my people in one way or another, from local to global. The negotiating stories in this volume, particularly the initiatives I took on behalf of the area, reflect this dynamic.

The dependency on external forces which the family had historically used for the benefit of the tribe and which Father had consolidated to reinforce his control, however, proved to be a double-edged sword. At times, it was a non-partisan source of justice, which the Dinka desperately needed, but at times, it was a source of interference in their internal affairs and a gross violation of their dignity and integrity. This, more than anything else, created the swinging of the pendulum between success and failure in the negotiating processes at various levels. Whatever was achieved at one level was soon undermined by subversive elements seeking advantage in the diversity of interests and the proliferation of centers of power.

The main question, however, is why I felt motivated or propelled to initiate the peace processes in which I was involved and what accounted for the techniques I applied, including the orientation toward achieving a consensus. The answer, I believe, has much to do with a sense of obligation or responsibility which was nurtured in me from my childhood years. If it is at all possible to make any causal connection, I believe that was an underlying motivation in my education, and has been a driving force in much of what I have done. Once that premise is established, the principles and techniques which guided me can be interpreted with an eclectic reference to both indigenous Dinka values and the enrichment of cross-cultural perspectives. The explanation for such an eclectic process rests as much with the model my father offered, as with the motivation, the coaching, and the support I received from my maternal relatives. I must emphasize, however, that their values were not to govern in the governmental sense, but to offer a leadership that would conform to the ideals of the moral and spiritual values of traditional Dinka society. This is perhaps why my writings on my father have been credited with a delicate balance between filial admiration and scholarly objectivity. My father offered me an inspiring model, but a close scrutiny of his leadership revealed a mixed bag of great accomplishments and tragic consequences, whether they were the results or the implications of what he did.

This chapter on the maternal link will help explain, I hope, how the son of a fourth wife could dare to aspire not only to a status of equality, but assume that it was his call of ancestral duty to be part of the leadership of the family, indeed the tribe, and eventually achieve and sustain a linkage of varied levels of responsibility, from local, through national, to global.

Achok Mijok as the Fourth Wife Procured by Deng Majok

Most of the account in this volume will center on my generation of brothers and sisters from the first four or five wives of my father. My mother, Achok Mijok, followed three senior wives: Nyanbol Arob (Nyanboldit), Nyanbol Amor, and Kwei Deng, all of whom he married in close succession. Of all three, only the marriage of Nyanboldit was uncomplicated by rivalry with other men. In what appeared like a repeat of Nyanaghar's story, Nyanbol Amor was in love with another man and had indeed eloped with him before she was returned and given to Deng Majok. But unlike Nyanaghar, Nyanbol claimed that she was resisting being a second wife, an argument which seemed to have won Deng Majok's sympathy. Although she became a second wife, she competed favorably for a special treatment so much so that it was popularly known that she enjoyed a unique place in Deng Majok's consideration. Although Nyanboldit still occupied the respected status of the first wife, this favoritism created considerable tensions between the two women and their respective groups. Deng Majok and Kwei were dance partners and although she became betrothed to another man, a romance developed between them which resulted in her pregnancy. The clan insisted that she be married because of the child.

After marrying Kwei, Deng became engaged to Aker Tiel from a leading family in Twichland. But before completing Aker's marriage, he married my mother, Achok Mijok, and brought her home. For that reason, there was always a degree of ambiguity about the seniority issue between Aker and Achok. One was betrothed first while the other came first, the very dilemma that had afflicted grandfather's first two wives. It seemed, however, generally agreed that my mother was fourth.

Deng Majok's marriage to Achok was complicated by the relationship between Chief Kwol Arob and Achok's father, Mijok Duor. Achok's lineage, Dhienagou, had been the divine chiefs of the Biar section of Bongo tribe. As a result of a blood feud, Mijok's grandfather, Maluk, had migrated from Bongo to Abyor, at the time of Kwol's father,

Chief Arob Biong. Maluk's father, Dau, and Arob's father, Biong, had maintained cordial ties as leaders of preeminent lineages. Maluk had therefore been well received and honored by Arob Biong and the whole of Abyor. He and his descendants had quickly established themselves as exceedingly talented with words, renowned for wisdom, and as divine leaders, endowed with curative powers. From that time on, they had been close associates and advisors to the line of paramount chiefs. Achok's father, Mijok, who was a member of Kwol Arob's age-set, Koryom, was the latest in the line.

"Your mother's father, Mijok Duor, was not originally from Abyor tribe, "said Monyluak Rou, an elder from the Bongo tribe.

> He was from our tribe, the Bongo. Even your grandmother, the mother of your mother called Ayak Deng Ngor, was a girl of our tribe. Our home was Ngol, the land we now dispute with the Arabs. Our section was called the Biar. Your maternal kin were the central members of Biar section. And Biar is the largest section of the entire Bongo.
>
> Your maternal relatives were our Divine Chiefs. They were the Dhienagou clan. Any illness or disaster that befell the tribe was cured by them. Today, nobody has remained who can claim the leadership of the Biar other than your maternal relatives. Had the descendants of Maluk returned to Bongo and claimed the Chieftainship, people would have stepped aside and said to them, "Yes, this is your position. Take it."
>
> Your maternal kin have always been known for wisdom and verbal skill. For instance, with your grandfather, Mijok Duor, if he were absent from his age-set, Koryom [The Locusts], people would wait for him before talking. If it were a subject which required the gathering of the age-set for consultations, they would say, "We must wait for Mijok before we open the subject for discussion."
>
> When your grandfather begot children, the first set of children came as girls. And Ngor was born last. Ngor is a member of Chuor [The Hawks] age-set. And when the Chuor used to meet and discuss as an age-set, Ngor used to be waited for if he were away. He is a man who weighs

words this way and that way. The whole Abyor would recognize him immediately as Mijok Duor, his father.[35]

Pagwot Deng, the Chief of Bongo, also said of Achok's kin: "The section called Biar was theirs. They were the leaders of Biar. In those days, there was no Government, but Chieftainship was determined by divine authority. So, they were the divine Chiefs of Biar" (Deng 1986:154).

"Your maternal kin were the center of the very ancient Bongo," said Achwil Bulabek, Chief of Abyor.

> Maluk Atokbek, son of Dau, was the man who immigrated into Abyor tribe. That is why you hear of the war song of Abyor: "Milk the Cow, Ayan, of Maluk, the son of Dau; Milk Ayan of Maluk, the Buffalo."
>
> When Arob was the Chief, he called your grandfather and said, "Mijok, here is my son (Kwol); take good care of him." Mijok and Kwol were of the same age, Koryom. They were also very close friends (Deng 1986:154).

"Your grandfather, the elder called Mijok Duor, was a man of exceeding wisdom and verbal skill," commented Matet Ayom. "He was a man who spoke extremely well and spoke great words. He was also a great friend of Kwol Arob."[36]

The story of Achok's marriage as told by her brother, Ngor, and her daughter, Ayan, provides insights into Dinka attitudes toward marriage as a business transaction and an affiliation of families with a mutual interest in promoting a genetic synthesis in procreation, the fundamental objective of marriage in Dinka society.

According to Ngor, after two of Mijok's daughters allegedly committed suicide (supposedly by infringing on a dietary taboo against drinking the milk of sacred cows during menstrual period) in opposition to their proposed marriages, he declared to his ancestral spirits and God that he had abandoned cattle, normally acquired through marriage. He therefore gave his subsequent daughters away in marriage for virtually nothing. Then, he changed his mind when his daughter, Achok, came about. He slaughtered a bull to propitiate God and his ancestral spirits and

---

35. From an unpublished account for the project of the biography, *The Man Called Deng Majok* (Deng 1986).

36. From an unpublished account for the project of *The Man Called Deng Majok*.

performed other rituals to signify his change of mind. Ngor's account continues:

> Mading, it was then that a man called Kweng came and said, "I want the daughter of Mijok Duor." Kweng spoke to his mother, Achai, from your clan Pajok [the daughter of Arob Biong]. Achai came to see the girl. She saw Achok and approved.
>
> When the people came back to negotiate the marriage, father said, "Achok is the daughter with whom I intend to raise my children. If a man wants to marry her, he must make a betrothal payment of twenty cows. As she has not yet reached puberty, this payment will only be for betrothal. When she reaches puberty, so that the man is more assured of her becoming his wife, I will then say my word."
>
> The people went and returned with twenty cows and two excellent bulls: a huge tawny bull and a dark bull with a white stripe across the shoulders (Mabil). They were brought. I was now old enough to be aware.
> The following year as the rains began to fall, Achok went to a dance. Deng Majok and Deng Makuei were at the dance.

After the dance, Deng Majok approached Achok to make her acquaintance.[37] The conversation between them as recounted by Ngor, represented the typical way of inquiring into the girl's parentage and ancestral background which indicates the importance the Dinka attach to kinship and heredity as factors that must be weighed in choosing a marriage partner. Shortly afterwards, according to Ngor, Deng Majok went and told his father, "I want to marry the daughter of Mijok Duor."

> Chief Kwol said, "She is already engaged to Kweng, the son of Achai."
> Deng said, "No, I will not accept that."
> Kwol said, "Deng, you will not marry from the family of Mijok Duor. You will bring conflict into my relationship with Mijok. This Chieftainship of mine is protected by the

---

37. Approaching girls to establish acquaintance that might lead to courtship especially after a dance was a perfectly accepted practice which did not imply any impropriety of conduct beyond conversation.

family of Maluk. Abyor has prospered because of the family of Maluk. You will not marry Mijok's daughter. You will only drag our relationship into problems. If you were not already married, I would have encouraged you to take your wealth to marry the daughter of Mijok as your first wife. But you have married several wives. Your wealth has already been too depleted for you to afford the daughter of Mijok. And as you know, Mijok has lost his senior daughters. It is from the marriage of this girl that he hopes to acquire sufficient wealth to maintain his children."

Deng said to his father, "I will not accept your word."

Kwol then said, "In that case, consider me out of this matter."

They discussed the matter a great deal, but could not agree. Kwol remained opposed while Deng persisted.

Deng went to Kweng and said, "Leave the girl and take back your cows."

Kweng said, "How can I take back my cows from a girl I have married?"

Deng said, "Take them back!"

Kweng said, "I will not, son of my maternal uncle; I will not."

Then Deng said, "In that case, we may have to kill one another."

Kweng said, "That would be better; I cannot withdraw my cattle from a girl I want to marry."

Ngor then proceeded to give an account of a violent confrontation which I have not heard corroborated by any other source and may well be an over-dramatization of the competition for his sister:

Later, at a public dance, Deng Majok just attacked Kweng and started to dart him with spears. He darted and darted him, barely missing him, until Kweng ran and jumped into the river. Deng went after him and continued to spear him in the river.

It was then that a man called Biong Ngar-Chol stepped in to defend Kweng. Deng and Biong began to throw spears at one another until they were eventually restrained and separated.

People said, "Deng, why did you try to kill the son of your paternal aunt?"

He said, "If anyone wants this conflict to end, then let him fetch Kweng's cattle from the marriage."

Achai, the mother of Kweng, Deng's paternal aunt, then approached him and said, "Deng, this is a child whom I raised and weaned among you, the sons of Kwol. His father died and left him with me. And this is not a girl that you yourself had courted before my son saw her. She is still a small girl. And I have chosen to marry her because I want someone who will raise the name of my son. If you are determined to have her as your wife, and you succeed in doing so, I will not part with her; you will have her together with me; you will have us both. But I will go all the way to get her for my son. Even if you should offer a hundred cows, I will fight for her."

Deng said to her, "Aunt, even if your eyes should shed tears that have never been seen before, she will never be your son's wife."

Achai said, "In that case, I shall move to the home of Mijok Duor. Achok's feet and mine will move together."

And indeed, Achai moved to our home.

My father decided to stop his daughter from attending dances. The situation was most bewildering. People did not know what should be done. Kweng himself no longer went to the cattle-camp. And he could no longer attend the dances.

The age-set, Koryom, which was the age-set of both your grandfather, Kwol Arob, and my father, came to our home at Nok-Jur. They came on horses. They all gathered there and tethered their horses. Father slaughtered in their honor and after entertaining them he said, "Gentlemen, my dear age-mates, what brings you? Is anything the matter?"

They said, "We have something to tell you."

He said, "Very well! What is it?"

They said, "You have lost two of your daughters. This issue of Deng Majok is going to associate your daughter with blood. No one will be able to face the feud of Deng Majok. Please, give up the cattle of Achai. Your daughters are still small. They should not be confronted with this. We say, leave the girl for Deng."

Mijok said, "Gentlemen, is that why you came?"

They said, "Yes!"

He said, "Is the man for whom you are speaking without a father's voice behind him?"

They said, "There is no one to speak for him with the tongue. He himself has spoken with the spear. And he stands alone."

"But where is the voice of Kwol?" he asked.

"Kwol has excused himself to us," they said. "He said, 'Gentlemen, my age-mates, I am out of this. Deng is putting Mijok Duor and me in conflict. Should Mijok accept, Deng will not be able to meet his aspirations. So, I better keep out of it.'"

Again, the importance the Dinka attach to the consent of the father makes Ngor rationalize the position of Kwol as ambivalent and even contradictory:

Kwol Arob would talk to Deng Majok privately and say, "Go ahead my son. Take the girl. No one should surrender marrying into this kind of breed. Work hard to win her. But let me keep out of it."

A man called Matiok Malek overheard Kwol's conversation with his son, Deng Majok. He came to my father and said, "Mijok, what you are really struggling with is Kwol Arob behind the scene. He has been instructing his son not to give in."

Mijok said, "I know that."

The issue was most bewildering. People could not find a way of resolving it.

My father then summoned his clan, the entire clan, and said to them, "Sons of Maluk, I have surrendered. And let me tell you what Deng Majok once did to me when he was only a small child. Our age-set, Koryom, had laid down their spears in the home of his father, Kwol Arob. So many were the spears that they covered the tree on which they rested. Deng Majok came and examined all the spears. When he came to my spear, he placed it in his lap. And when the people came to leave, his father said to him, 'Son, give the spear to your uncle. 'Deng refused. And when people tried to take it away from him, he threatened to pierce the spear into his stomach. So, I told them to leave the spear with him. That is one thing Deng once did to me.

So, if his father has unleashed him against me when I am only beginning to reacquaint myself to cattle, to raise my children, then I have surrendered to their will."

Some people said, "And why are you imposing on yourself all this trouble?"

He said, "I do not want blood to be associated with the name of my daughter. And I have even smaller children to protect. As for the mind that went after my spear when he was still a small child and is now following me openly in the tribe, I ask you to leave that challenge to me."

That way, he persuaded our family to give in.

After he had persuaded them, he turned to Achai and said, "Achai, I am going to release your cattle. You have been defeated."

He took the cow Dan-Akol, sun-spotted-brown, with wide-spread horns, which was his personal milch cow, and gave it to her, saying, "This cow is to appease you because your cows have been milked here and because you will be eyeing my daughter away from you. Go and quarrel with the members of your own clan. If you should cry, and thereby threaten a curse, I will find myself forced to resort to what I have as the son of Duor Maluk."[38]

Achai's cattle had multiplied so much within only one year that calves were running and kicking all over the plains.

Mading, all those cattle were sent back.

People then stayed. Achok reached puberty. Father then approached Deng Majok and said, "I will give you your wife. All I want from you are the cattle of the clan spirits.

---

38. He was implicitly threatening to use the awesome spiritual powers of his own clan to curse.

You have paid eight cows; give me four cow-calves to dedicate to the spirits."

He went and brought a brown cow and a cow-calf of brown and white colors. Then he spoke of the cattle he intended to pay. My father went ahead and gave him the girl.

My father then called Dau Maluk and said, "I have given the girl away. Give me the bull, Mading, to be sacrificed for the spirit *agorot* [which, according to custom, must be done when a girl is betrothed before puberty. Unless done, it is believed that she may not be able to have children]. Give me Mading with horns yet untampered with [according to the traditional way of training horns to grow into desired shapes]; that is what I want. That is the bull we should sacrifice for Achok's *agorot*."[39]

Dau Maluk went and released Mading.

My father called the members of his clan and said, "Let us take this Mading to be sacrificed [in Deng Majok's home]. Let us go and invoke Mading; let us go and pray to God."

He left with a number of people. Among them was a man called Chol Minyuon, an elder. And with them was Miyar Kac, an elder. And among them was Deng Michar, an elder. He called a number of elders. And they went. They stood their sacred spears in the ground and prayed. My father said, "God, what I have to say is not much. We ask you to give Achok a son whom we shall name Mading after the bull we are about to sacrifice. That is all we ask of you."

My father and the elders with him prayed over the bull, Mading. They prayed and prayed and then sacrificed him. Then they left. They said, "It is now up to God to decide whether to accept our prayers or to reject our word."

---

39. The symbolism of horns untampered with, means that Mijok wanted a raw material which would be shaped and guided by the vision and the spiritual powers of his divination for the offspring of his daughter, to be born after the sacrifice of *agorot*.

Needless to say, the event sounds like a replay of the prayers over the mothers of Deng Majok and Deng Makuei. And like those prayers, my maternal relatives' prayers for a son were answered.

> After you were born, my father convened the elders of his clan and said, "Chol Minyuon, do you not see anything pleasing to your heart? You will die. And I will die. And all of us assembled here will die. I have only one word to tell you. Is there any other name besides that Mading?"
>
> They said, "No, there is only that Mading."
>
> He said, "Then I am giving you a lamb with which to wash your hearts and pray to God and say, 'God, our hearts are now pleased; we no longer have anything bad in our hearts, now that we have our Mading. He will one day hear all these words.'"

Apparently, my paternal relatives gave me the name, Arob, after Father's grandfather, in disregard of my grandfather's expressed wish to have me named after the bull he and his family elders had sacrificed in prayer for a son. On hearing that I had been given another name, grandfather Mijok was infuriated. He went to Noong very early in the morning and met with Deng Majok and Deng Makuei together. According to Ngor, he said to them: "All I wanted from the marriage was that head which drove the cattle away from my daughter's engagement and imposed his will on me. And I appealed to God for divine justice. If God has responded by giving me my Mading, how could you think of naming him Arob Biong? This Mading of mine, never ever call him by any other name."

And he threatened to take his daughter and baby with him. He was eventually prevailed upon to leave her to follow later. Deng Majok then followed him with a number of elders to apologize and returned to tell his family, again quoting Uncle Ngor, "I do not want to hear this child called Arob any more. He will be Mading."

> Later on, my father sent for the elders of his clan and said to them, "I do not know the day my end will come. I want to leave you my word today. If any one of you should ever think of raising a claim against Deng Majok on account of Achok, that person would have invited a deadly curse, a curse that will destroy that person. Anyone who would raise a case of cattle against Deng

Majok, know that he is cursed to destruction. Leave that whole matter as it is; it will remain my own affair."

Maternal Relatives' Sentiments about the Marriage and Expectations of the Son

I was weaned among my maternal relatives, which meant that I left home around the age of two or three and lived with them until about age four or five. This is considered to be particularly important for a firstborn who is an important link between the two lineages. Ngor's account reveals a most moving incident of which I was not aware at the time:

Then you became ill when you were still an infant. You were beginning to walk. My father was extremely fond of you. He would watch you keenly as you played around. And very often, he would want you to sit on his lap or hold you and bounce you about as he chanted words of praise for you.

One night, while you were severely ill, he did something. It was raining very heavily, with frightening thunder and lightning. He decided to take you out in the rain that night. My mother objected; but he insisted. She cried as she tried to restrain him from going outside with you. At one point, he said to her, "Ayak, did I not fetch you with my sacred cows?"

"Yes," she said.

"And how could you question my ancestral duty? Open the door and let me go out."

She opened the door and he went outside with you in his arms. Then he prayed, "God, why are you thundering this loudly, is it in your heart to take him away from me? If you are thundering because you want to take him, then I pray that you take me instead and leave him for me. Take me this very moment as you are angry, raining and thundering. And if you should decide not to take me tonight, then let me return into the hut and let your water, which has fallen on him, be a blessing so that he can sleep well and wake up tomorrow morning to smile and play for me to see."

You were crying as he held you and prayed that way. The next morning, you woke up miraculously well. He held you in his hands and seated you in his lap. And he smiled into your face as he saw you well and smiling.

Then the following night, he woke up my mother and said, "Ayak, are you awake?"

My mother said, "Yes."

Then he turned to me and said, "Son."

I said, "Yes, father!"

He said, "Get up and sit here. Listen to my words very carefully. Did you not witness what happened last night?"

I said, "Yes, I did."

He said, "Well, I surrendered myself to redeem Mading. I will die. And after I am dead, what you hear happening in Abyor about the Chieftainship will come true. Don't you hear that Deng Majok will take over the Chieftainship from his father, Kwol Arob?"

I said, "Yes!"

He said, "The Head that imposed its will on me will make that happen. And should it happen that way, this Mading of mine will one day force his way and find a position there. When you grow up, never complain to your brother-in-law, Deng Majok, that he has not paid your sister's bridewealth. Never tell him.

"And you, Ayak, when you used to say that we should give our daughter to Kweng, I am going to die and you too will die. You and I might have found in Kweng's wealth a great deal for our life-time consumption, but what about something to be found by our children in the future?! We do not know which of us two will die first. But even when we are both gone, Mading will not miss inheriting from the Head of Deng Majok; and he will not miss inheriting from my own Head, I, Mijok Duor. From these two Heads, something will emerge in him. Should he inherit from the Head of his father, Deng Majok, that too will have become mine. And should he inherit from my own Head, that too would have become mine. That was all I wanted, my dear wife, Ayak, daughter of Deng Ngor. With my Mading, I have compensated for the loss of cows."

At the age of about five, Father sent me to school with three other brothers of my generation. It was the first school to be opened in our area and it was located in the tribal headquarters at Abyei where Father had just established a second home. It was in the early days of my first year that the tragic news of my grandfather's death reached me one evening. I felt as though my world was totally shattered. As a child, I did not even cry out loud, although tears quietly streamed from my eyes. I was later to learn from Ngor what had transpired:

> When he ... got seriously ill ... people said to him, "Mijok, shall we send for Mading to come?"
>
> He said, "No!"
>
> They said, "Why not?"
>
> He said, "I do not want him to be involved in this. I have already given him my blessing."

Ayan's account of her mother's marriage is far more positive and conciliatory than her uncle's:

> Our mother, Achok, was one of the youngest of the daughters. Achok was then betrothed by a man from the Abyor tribe. She was still a small child. She had not yet even reached puberty. Achok rejected the man to whom she had been betrothed. She rejected him with great determination. Her father also joined her in rejecting the man. But their entire clan was in favor of the man, saying, "This man has offered too large a bridewealth to be rejected. We cannot leave him." The man was from the marital family of our father's aunt, Achaidit.
>
> Our father then said, "I cannot miss from the daughters of Mijok Duor, the Great Strong man who leads Abyor in both courage and wisdom; I cannot accept not marrying into his family." Our paternal grandfather, Kwol Arob, then said, "But, my son, I am rather embarrassed that it is the son of my sister who has engaged the girl."
>
> Father said, "I will not accept."
>
> He debated the issue with our grandfather for a long time.
>
> Uncle Biong Mading then said, "This thing will never be! Deng, son of my mother, if we leave this girl, where shall we find a similar crop to marry in this land of the Ngok? What our father wants is a disfavor for us the children of Nyanaghar. This is the old story that he did

not love you but Deng Abot. This is why he says you
should not marry this girl. He does not want your name
to rise ahead."

Father then said, "That, I will never accept. So, Biong
Mading, let us release our own cattle for the marriage."

Father and Biong Mading then went ahead and collected
the bridewealth by themselves. But our grandfather,
Mijok, rejected the cattle and said, "Why should I receive
bridewealth from children? I must hear from your father."

So they returned and spoke again to their father, Kwol
Arob. Kwol then said, "My sons, there was nothing I
disliked about marrying into Mijok's family. Mijok Duor
is my partner in the leadership of this tribe. If you want
to persuade your aunt's son to leave the girl for you, and
you want to appease him with cattle, then I have no
objection."

That is when our grandfather, Kwol Arob, sent his word
to Mijok Duor. Mijok Duor then said, "Kwol Arob, I do
not want cattle from you. I am not in need. I will give
Deng Majok my daughter with only a few cows as a
token of bridewealth so that you know that it is not the
need for wealth that has induced me to give her to your
son."

Matet Ayom gave a version that was also conciliatory about the manner in
which Deng pursued Achok and Kwol's reaction to the proposed
marriage.

Mijok Duor had reacted rather negatively, saying, "Deng
Majok, if yours is a marriage of a son without the
involvement of his father, then I shall not accept. Kwol is
my age-mate and my associate. If he has not shown
interest in the marriage of my daughter to his son and it is
only the desire of the son, I cannot accept."

When Kwol heard this, he sent a message to Mijok Duor
saying, "Please tell Mijok Duor that he is not a man I can
reject. It is just that my respect for him inhibits me. I have
already married for Deng Majok with a lot of cows. I am
afraid of his getting involved with Mijok's daughter at a
time when he does not have the same number of cows at
his disposal as he had for his first wives. I fear that Deng

may not afford a bridewealth appropriate for the status of
Mijok Duor, a great man in whom I find support, for it is
with the words of Mijok Duor that I am running this
tribe."

Kwol had attended the marriage of Aker Tiel, who had
been married in Twichland and had not yet come home
when Deng Majok wanted to marry Mijok's daughter.

The marriage of Biong Mading, your father's brother,
came immediately after that. The cattle he had were not
sufficient. He would take some cows and send them to
Biong's marriage. And then Arob, his younger brother,
made a girl pregnant. So his own marriage was also added
to these other marriages. All four marriages were
performed by your father at about the same time.

But your maternal grandfather was a cool-hearted man.
He said, "Tell Deng Majok, if his father says that it will
be for his son to perform his marriage with me, then let
him not concern himself with paying me the bridewealth.
Let him occupy himself with other urgent matters. I have
cattle for my food; I am not in need. I shall also not reject
his marriage on account of cattle. Let him perform the
marriages of his younger brothers."

That attitude from your grandfather was very pleasing to
your father (Deng 1986:155).

Deng Abot gave the friendship between his father and Mijok Duor as the
reason for Kwol Arob's opposition to the proposed marriage:
Mijok was a very dear person to my father, a friend with
whom he shared one bed ... When your father wanted
your mother, my father said, "Mijok, Deng is going to
create problems between you and me. He and Deng
Makuei are now independent. Each one must now pay
for his own marriages. I fear that Deng Majok will not be
able to afford a good bridewealth for your daughter. It is
better to let him find a wife wherever else he can and you
and I remain in the close relationship our families have
enjoyed for long. You and I have been very close; your
father and my father were also very close; your
grandfather Maluk was also very close to my grandfather;
and your great-grandfather Dau was also close to my

great-grandfather. Let us not allow this proposed marriage
to generate conflicts between you and my children."

That was how my father refused. He was concerned
about a close relationship that might be affected by the
marriage. Both families had important roles to play for
the welfare of the tribe. Your maternal relatives were
also people of divine authority. If disease appeared in the
tribe, my father would call upon Mijok to perform
curative rituals (Deng 1986:155-156).

Chol Piok, a close relative, saw a different motive for Kwol Arob's
opposition to Deng Majok's proposed marriage to Achok: "Why your
grandfather Kwol Arob refused at first was the fact that Deng Majok was
already marrying more than Deng Makuei. That he did not like. That
disturbed him deep inside. He did not want Deng Majok to be an equal of
Deng Makuei. You see, that grandfather of yours, if Deng Majok had not
stood firm, he would have been left far on the periphery of things" (Deng
1986:156).

Ngor concluded his own account of my mother's marriage and my
grandfather's aspirations and expectations for me with these words: "So,
you, Mading, you are a child of destiny. I pray to God and to my father to
keep this destiny. All I want is the path my father had set forth. My
father said that he was not after winning men of influence; nor was he
after the power of magical charms; nor was he ambitious for any
particular leadership position. As he was dying, he said to us, 'What I
wanted in my heart, I have told you. If you should have any grievances
aching your hearts, tell me about them.'"

And of course in Dinka faith, the dead father continues to watch over
his family and provide counsel and protection as needed.

Although I grew up aware of the sentiments of my maternal relatives
and their expectations of me, my own situation in the family as the son of
the fourth wife was less secure, precarious, but challenging. I was my
mother's only son among four daughters, the second son having died in
infancy. My immediate companions were Bol, who later adopted the
Christian name of Zachariah, second son of the first wife, Nyanboldit, and
Kwol, who first converted to Christianity as Adrian and then to Islam as
Adam, first son of the second wife, Nyanbol Amor.

Bol's eldest sibling was a sister, Adau, from whom Father derived his
"procreational" name as Wun-Adau according to the custom by which a
man is deferentially called with reference to his firstborn from the first

wife, son or daughter. Next to Adau was Chan, Christianized under the name Lino, who, from childhood, was afflicted with the disease of epilepsy that threw him into fire and left him disabled. Next to Bol was Monyyak, who later converted to Islam as Abdalla.

Kwol's older siblings were sisters, Abul, who gave their mother her procreational name, Man-Abul, and Achai, who was known as Achai-Jur, "Achai the Arab," because she was unusually light for a Dinka. Kwol's younger brothers were Monylam, who became Ali, and Mijak, who converted to Islam under the name Osman.

The firstborn of Kwei, the third wife, was Arob, making her Man-Arob. He became Ahmed as a Muslim. Partly because of his mother's pregnancy before marriage and the death of the firstborns of the first two wives, Arob was the oldest in the family.

Next to him was Achai-Monyjang, "Achai the Dinka," because of her exceedingly black skin color and to distinguish her from Achai-Jur. Kwei's remaining children were daughters, Ayan and Nyannyob. It was popularly known that Kwei's childbirth was terminated prematurely because of a conflict with Father, attributed to her insubordination and insult. The resulting feud between husband and wife would later extend to the father-son relationship. Being the oldest, Arob was the first to go to school in the North, and after completing his secondary education, was recruited into the local government by the departing British administrators and posted into the Dinka area on Father's request. Soon, memories of the conflict between Father and Mother, which were rumored to have been fanned by the maternal kin, contributed to the power struggle that triggered Arob's downfall and eventual doom.

The generation of Monyyak and Monylam included Aker Tiel's firstborn, Bulabek, who converted to Islam under the name Abujabar, and Miyar, whose Muslim name was Mekki, the firstborn of the sixth wife, Nyanbol Deng. Bulabek had several sisters and Miyar had one sister.

Chan's misfortune and Arob's disastrous adventures left our generation of Bol, Kwol, and me in the senior position. The three of us grew up together as close companions. We were virtually the same age, although Kwol was a little younger than Bol and me. We were also later somewhat separated from Adam as we proceeded with higher school education, while he dropped out at the elementary level.

After finishing elementary school, the British director of education in the South persuaded our father that it would be in his political interest to have some of his children educated in the South. That way, he would have his feet in both the North and the South. In line with that policy Bol and I (initially with Chan who was later withdrawn because of his illness) proceeded to schools in the South with two cousins, Lino Ayong, whose mother was adopted by our grandfather from a slave background (a sensitive issue in the family), and Justin Deng Aguer, the firstborn of Father's sister, Awor. While Lino and Justin went to missionary schools, we went to Tonj Primary school which the British had established for sons of chiefs and government officials. After Tonj we went to Rumbek Junior Secondary which was later transferred to Tonj as an intermediate school. Father, who had always preferred the northern system, then insisted on our transfer to Khor Taqqat Secondary school, one of the top three in the country. After Khor Taqqat, we were both admitted to the University of Khartoum, I in the Faculty of Law, my first choice, and Bol to the Faculty of Arts and Economics, which was not his first choice, being an ardent scientist, whose ambition was to study medicine. Consequently, he sought and obtained a scholarship in East Germany and later transferred to Italy. Joining the University of Khartoum with us was Uncle Bonaventura (Bona) Bulabek, a junior son of grandfather Kwol Arob, whose destiny would later pose a crisis in the North-South context. A recognized genius, Bona was always top of his class and even jumped several grades. Although behind us, he caught up with us and even went a grade ahead. Conditions of the civil war in the South set him back by one year so that we sat for the high school certificate examination together where he came top in the country. He was admitted to the medical school but chose to give his position to a southern colleague who had been admitted to the faculty of law instead of his first choice, which was medicine. Uncle Bona, who had already been granted a scholarship to study in the United States, took his colleague's position in the faculty of law, pending his departure to the States. For some reason, his trip was postponed by immigration formalities which would have meant losing a year. Rather than wait, Bulabek accepted an alternative scholarship to study medicine in Padova, Italy, with his colleague and friend, Justo Muludiang, where Bol eventually joined them.

Even for the brief period which he spent in the faculty of law pending his departure to Italy, Bona already distinguished himself as an excellent law student. His genius was a quality that applied to any subject he studied. The story in the tribe was that when grandfather Chief Kwol Arob was dying, he asked for his baby-son, Bulabek, to be brought to him. Placing a pencil in his right hand, he said, "This is what I bequeath to you." From that time on, that prophecy was reinforced and from the time

Bulabek entered school, he reflected an excellence and a lead on which he never faltered.

As for Kwol, who never took his studies seriously, after Abyei elementary school, which was modelled after the southern system, he went to the North and started all over with elementary schooling in the Arabic system and although he flirted with Comboni Intermediate School in El Obeid for a year or so, never went beyond that level.

Inherited, Nurtured, Learnt and Acquired Leadership

During our vacations at home, however, the three of us always resumed our circle as the closest companions. In that circle, I occupied an ambivalent position. On the one hand, I felt equal to Bol and Kwol and indeed often found myself as their spokesman, especially in formal discussions, including those with Father. I once asked Bol how I happened to be the one who spoke for us, at the risk of always being assumed to be responsible for the positions we took, some of which were not at all pleasing to Father. With the characteristic humor that always accompanied our reminiscences, Bol replied that it was because I had a "clever mouth," was "well-spoken," and "diplomatic." And indeed, both among my maternal relatives and in my father's family, I knew that I had that reputation from early childhood. My performance in my father's court, where I was very popular with the elders, even became a matter of concern for my mother, who worried that I might attract the evil-eye and be bewitched.

Some of that must have been innate and spontaneous, but some of it was nurtured, both by the environment and by my own aspirations or ambitions. I was highly motivated to observe and emulate Father as a model of what I should be. Oftentimes, I would close my eyes and daydream, fantasizing myself in his role as the chief, with all the social standing, his numerous wives, and the responsibilities his position entailed. How I assumed that role, whether I replaced, succeeded, or merely assisted my father, I do not clearly recall. But an element of succession after death must have been involved because I fantasized having inherited some of his favorite wives. According to the levirate system widows of childbearing age are inherited by relatives, including senior husbands, to continue to bear children in the name of the dead husband. Reality had it that as a son of a fourth wife in a highly structured society in which the rules of primogeniture determined leadership, I barely figured in the traditional order of succession. On the other hand, I felt not only equal to my brothers, but indeed justified in my aspirations for leadership in the family and the tribe.

Father must have observed that with some scrutiny. This was one day indicated to me by a small incident. Chan had insisted on going fishing. Cousin Justin Deng Aguer and I joined him to watch over him in case he got a convulsion. That was precisely what happened. When Father heard of that, it was reported to me by Mekki as Father having remarked: "Why does Mading's name have to be in everything that happens?" Obviously, I was hurt by the report as I had only volunteered to be of help. Whenever we confronted Father and I spoke on behalf of the brothers, he would always turn to Bol and Kwol to say, "I have heard Mading, let me hear what you have to say," as though he questioned the degree to which I represented a collective point of view, or thought I had instigated the brothers and was therefore their ring leader.

Much of my leadership profile certainly had to do with the subtle, but effective influence my maternal relatives exerted on me. And indeed my mother's family, particularly my grandfather, invested a great deal in me during my most formative years. It was from my maternal grandfather and those around him that I first learned to value listening to elders and learning from their wisdom. I recall sitting with him in the evening as he chanted hymns or responded with prayers to the voices of animals who symbolized clan spirits. I also remember him anointing the deadly snake, the puff-adder and placing melted butter in front of it to lick, as he sang hymns or prayed to it as a symbol of a clan deity. Much of my research and writing would depend on elders as my principal source of information, and I believe my early experiences with my maternal grandfather had a great deal to do with that.

Discussions about Responsibilities and Relationships

Among the stories I would hear being attributed to me by my maternal relatives was that someone questioned me on how I expected to be a chief when my mother was the fourth in seniority, considering especially the traditional rule of primogeniture in succession. I am reported as having replied that in the world of the future, it would not be one's mother's order of seniority but one's competence and abilities that would determine one's qualification for leadership. There is little doubt that Father's case must have played a role in the thinking which was attributed to me.

But, although I felt that I met the standards required of my position as Deng Majok's son, spoke well, was polite and responsive to my duties, running errands for Father and other elders, interpreting in his court, even though he had an official interpreter, drafting his most important letters, even though he had a secretary, advising him on public issues at his request, and representing him where necessary, I still felt a gap of paternal love and affection which I translated as dissatisfaction. And whenever he was explicit about his approval, it was a source of great joy to me. Once I wrote a letter to a Nuer chief which was carried by a Ngok Dinka who had a claim against a Nuer. The man came back later and told Father that the clerk of the Nuer chief, having had difficulty in reading the letter, had said to the bearer that Chief Deng Majok should get himself a clerk who could write. Father laughed and remarked: "Anyone who finds something wrong with the writing of my Mading must have something wrong with his reading." On another occasion after I had drafted a sensitive letter to a chief of another tribe about a proposed marriage to a girl in his tribe and read it back to Father, he remarked with satisfaction, "You can always count on my Mading's ability."

When we were in our final year of secondary school at the time Father was quarrelling with Ahmed, he tried to persuade me to consider running for the forthcoming national Parliamentary elections. He asked me which of us, Bol or me, was older. I said he should be the one to tell us and not me to inform him. He then said he thought I was older than Bol and that he wanted me to run for Parliament. I was then still in high school and certainly not of age to run. I told him so, but he said the age issue could be arranged, for as I had no birth certificate, I could be assessed to be older. For me, of course, this was another indication of my father's faith in my qualification for leadership, one which played an important role in balancing the insufficiency of paternal love and affection that I continued to feel from him.

These incidents were most elating to me. And yet doubts lingered on. And the more I felt or suspected his dissatisfaction, the more I strove to improve my performance to win his approval. And yet, I nursed a certain degree of bitterness or anger toward my father.

When I was in the University of Khartoum and Bol was studying in Europe, I once returned home on leave and decided to have a man-to-man talk with my father about our relationship. He had come as close as Sennar, but had returned without proceeding to Khartoum. And he did not write to me. Even the things he wanted to be done for him, such as guns to be repaired, were brought to my attention by the people he had sent and not with a message from him directly.

Shortly after I got home, I requested a meeting with him. He asked his retainers to place two chairs some distance away from the crowd and to see to it that we were left alone. I said,

Father, as I grew up, I saw small things which have disturbed my heart considerably. But I have not let them come out in the open.

We have heard you say quite often how your father had treated you and how you yourself have corrected your father's attitude in your treatment of us, your children.

But when I see the way you treat us I feel that there is a small but significant shortcoming which I have not understood. How could you come as close as Sennar and not send me a letter or even a word of mouth? Even your things that had to be done in Khartoum were brought to my attention by your messengers on their own initiative. I have been wondering what it is that has generated this attitude from you. What have I done to my father?

You see, a son does not feel that his father loves him simply because he has sent him to school and pays for his education. Nor is love expressed merely by providing maintenance. There is something which makes a child feel that his father loves him beyond these material considerations. It is not even a question of calculation that this son will one day do this or that for me. It is merely a feeling of love between a child and his father.

So, what have I done to deserve this small but important shortcoming of love I feel from you? Is there anything you see in me which has disappointed you and which deserves this attitude from you?

I had no way of predicting Father's response. It was quite likely that he would rebuke me for my silly talk and dismiss me without any substantive response. But he did not. Instead, he spoke very movingly. He retold the story of his relations with his father and his own relations with us, his children.

He went on to say that according to Dinka practice, a man's view of his child is influenced by his view of the child's mother. Then he went on to praise my mother:

I see your mother Achok as the wife who even if I am away, I trust that I have someone responsible at home. I do not see Achok as junior to my senior wives. I see Achok as though she were a first wife, as senior as Nyanboldit.

So, there is nothing I can hold against you on account of your mother. And as for yourself, it is you and Bol I look to for the future of my family and the tribe. From the time you were still small, the British administrators and later the Sudanese officials kept telling me that you would be the children who would in the end prove to be my strength.

Two more incidents occurred which prompted me to have another talk with Father. He had allotted Bol and me an allowance from his salary, to receive in Khartoum on a monthly basis. Then Bol left Khartoum University, where he was studying economics, to study medicine abroad. Later on, when Bol returned on vacation and went home while I was in Khartoum, Father asked him whether I had sent him money. Bol acknowledged that I had been sending him the money. Father then remarked: "Then Mading has truly proved himself a man." Bol later reported that to me.

On another occasion, as I was at home on vacation, and about to go back to the university, Father called Kwol [Adam] and asked him: "How much money do you think Mading needs for pocket money?" As Kwol and I had been walking together when Father called him, I asked him what it was about. Kwol told me what father had asked him. When Father later came on a visit to Khartoum, while I was in my last year at the university, I approached him on these issues. I told him: "Father, I understand that you said I have proved myself to be truly an honest man by having sent the money to Bol. Did you believe that I would be dishonest and not send Bol what you had allotted to him? Did you realize for the first time what I was because of having sent the money to Bol? Another issue arose as I was leaving home. You called Kwol and asked him how much money I needed to go to school. Does Kwol know where I live to be in a position to tell what I need?"

His uncle, friend, and ally, Achwil Bulabek, chief of Abyor sub-tribe, was with him. This time Father reacted with apparent anger. First he said he did not remember what he was alleged to have said. But assuming that he had said them, what was wrong with asking my brother how much he thought I needed or praising me for having delivered my brother's money which I might have used instead? When I continued to complain, he became enraged. Turning to Achwil, he said: "Why don't you advise the child!?" Achwil intervened to moderate between us. Then we stopped and I left. When I did not return to see him the next day, word reached me that Father was asking about me. Eventually, he sent someone to fetch me. I was afraid that Father may misread my attitude as a rebellion by a son who was about to graduate with a law degree, establish his independence, and turn against his father. I saw his disappointment with Arob coming back to his mind. So I went back and we resumed our normal relationship. I then accompanied him to his official meetings with ministers and senior government officials and organized a large tea party to which I invited Deng Teeng, a Dinka cabinet minister, some diplomats, the principal of Comboni College (the chaplain of our university Saint Augustine's Society of which I was the secretary-general), and my Sudanese and German student friends.

As I reflected on the story of Father's life and in particular his relationship with his father, I felt that my relationship with my father was almost a replay of that drama, albeit at a lower level of intensity and magnitude. In this respect, Father's own perspective on his relationship with his father and its relevance to us was reassuring to me in an ironic way. He used to say to us that a child loved by God was better off than a child loved by his father. He is reported to have gone beyond that to say that the son of God is not equal to the son of man. And there was no doubt what he considered himself to be in the equation.

Uncle Ngor was later to tell me of a conversation he had with one of Father's relatives and closest associates, Deng Korow, which reflects my relative position in the family, Father's expectations of me, and what I felt about both:

> There was a year that you and Bol were on leave. As you came to go back to school, you sold a number of cows for your school fees and pocket money. I believe each one of you sold about four cows. I spoke to Deng Korow and said, "What is all this wealth of cattle being spent for?"
>
> He said, "Ngor, there is something important in this. And that son of your sister has caught the attention of his father. Deng Majok has begun to focus on him. He even says in a low voice: "That child you see will one day be my Head. Now I realize that what my father was saying has come true. When I was about to give up on Achok, he said to me, 'Son do not surrender, even though I will not join in myself. As long as she is the daughter of Mijok

Duor, then go after that Head.' That Head which my
father was talking about is apparent in my son, Mading.
He will one day be my Head."

"So you see, Deng Majok gossips in admiration of your
sister's son."

I said, "But why is it that when the children come
running, Kwol jumps onto his lap while he praises
Mading with a certain distance. Why does he do that?"

He said, "What you see..." and I must stress that Deng
Korow did indeed say this, "What you see, when they
grow up and reach the age of maturity, you will see that
child cared for by others. The close tie you see now will
pull them apart and you will see that child cared for by
others ... You will see that with your own eyes. As for the
son of your sister, he now turns to look around. He
notices that there is a small something [negative] in his
father's attitude. He may brush it all aside, but he notices
all the same."

Applying the logic of Father's argument in his relations with his
father, a child who is shown much love merely for his being without
regard to the qualities of his mind or behavior may become too spoiled
and unmotivated to improve himself. Sadly, that would be the case with
both Kwol (Adam) and his brother Mijak (Osman), both of whom had
enjoyed the greatest favor from Father. By an extraordinary coincidence,
Bol and I once came across a note which must have been from a diary
Kwol kept. It was a lamentation for not having taken his studies seriously;
if only he had done so, he wrote, he would not have been left behind from
his brothers. Osman, whose irresponsibility I heard Father criticize during
his terminal illness by saying to him, "Should I die you will turn into a
dog", was later to make this moving response to the questionnaire on
Father's biography:

By God, Mading, the implications of my father's death
for me, I believe I am the most affected. I have lamented
his death beyond description. Why? As you know, I never
completed my education. I always leaned on my father
and was totally dependent on him. It never crossed my
mind that my father would die. I could not imagine it. I
was so comfortable with him that I was incapable of
conceiving of his death. But nothing can be done about it.

121

> One only nurses the pain in one's heart and otherwise remains silent. Father cannot return. If only one could live twice, die and return to life! But one does not! Father is forever gone (Deng 1986:254).

As I look back on the family, those who accomplished the most are those who either through their position as individuals or through their mothers felt some need to prove themselves, primarily to Father, but also to society.

One of the people who was very close to Father and who always gave me a positive reinforcement was Matet Ayom, whose relations with our family would deteriorate from ambivalent to hostile. Matet, then an outstanding personality in the positive sense, used to call me Ba'ashoum, "the Arabic Fox", which I always understood as praise, implying intelligence or cleverness. But when my lingering curiosity led me to ask him in the course of an interview on the story of my father what he had meant by calling me "the Fox", Matet gave a cryptic explanation that still leaves me wondering whether it was praise for cleverness or a subtle condemnation of Father and me along with him for self-indulgence:

> Why I used to call you the Fox was because of an incident that took place at Noong. We were visiting Noong. And then your father asked that corn be roasted on cobs for us. It was at the beginning of the harvest. And you were a very small boy. And when the corn on cobs were brought, your father said, "Mading, take the corn and offer it to the people." The corn was in a tray. You then took the corn and brought it to us. As you were reaching us, you picked the largest corn and placed it down and then you picked up the tray with the rest of the corn and offered it to the people.
>
> People burst into laughter. You were then asked, "Mading, whose corn is the one you have left behind on the ground?"
>
> You said, "I shall come back to it after I have offered the guests these ones."
>
> After offering, you then returned to that corn and took it for yourself. I then said to your father. "Deng Majok, this son of yours is a Fox. You see the size of the corn he reserved for himself? That is what you do when you distribute cattle. You pick up the best for yourself and distribute the rest, the less attractive cows, to others."

122

That became a permanent nickname by which I called you "The Fox". You were a very clever boy. Whenever you were sent on errands, you would do the errand correctly. Whenever you were asked any questions, you always gave an intelligent answer. So, I said to your father, "This foxy son of yours will be like you one day."

According to Matet, he and Father had a conversation about me during my last visit to the area after my graduation and before proceeding to the United Kingdom for graduate studies. I had been top of my class in the first year and had won an attractive prize for the rest of my years in Khartoum. After our final examinations three of us had been appointed members of the teaching staff and offered scholarships to pursue our graduate studies in London, after which we were to return to teach at the Faculty of Law. According to Matet: "Your father spoke to me and said, 'Matet, this son of mine whom you used to call 'The Fox', your words have come true. The cleverness of my son Mading, which made him put aside the biggest corn and offer the rest to the others has now materialized. He has succeeded very well in his education." Matet concluded his account with the following words: "Mading, I started praising you very early in your growth. Although you have not done me any personal favour, I have always praised you as the true image of your father. Even Deng Majok before he died, I used to tell him, 'Deng Majok, this Chieftainship of yours, no son of yours will be able to shoulder it. The only one who can is Mading, but if we bring Mading into your position, it will not suit him; it will be too small for him. Mading's position is truly big.'"

In that respect, Matet was treading a treacherous course, for it was not only what I saw as Father's preferential treatment that made his story relevant to my situation. Another respect in which his relations with his father seemed applicable to me was that I felt sure Father saw in me qualities that he admired and thought might benefit him, the family, and the tribe in the future, but for precisely the same reasons, was ambivalently afraid that what had happened between him and his father could happen again. He was afraid that one might aspire to his chieftainship and possibly out-wit him the way he had out-witted his father. Considering the educational gap between us, the danger seemed larger than the one that had prevailed between him and his father. And indeed, his earlier experience with Arob had not been reassuring.

Accounts of elders reflect in Father an ambivalent appreciation of his sons as having fulfilled his expectations and fear of sharing power with them. According to Ajuong Deng Tiel, a close cousin and chief of Anyiel, "Deng Majok found what he was looking for in his children."

> He had children about whom he made some confidential remarks to people like myself whom he liked as his special relatives from the maternal line. When he was alone with such people, he would say, "Don't you see? What I used to say has come true! Don't you see that son of mine is already showing a great deal of usefulness." He began to speak of how right he had been about the question of children when he was still going strong. He would say, "There is always that one child who will promote the name of his father. There is always that one woman who will bear the child that will reflect the good name of his father. Now I have already seen the children who will bring value to my people." And the people have come to recognize what he was talking about. They came to accept his words (Deng 1986:258).

"He knew you, his sons, well," commented Achwil Bulabek. "After you were grown up, he knew where you were heading. For instance, he knew that you had become too well educated to remain in the tribe and that your education would take you farther away into the national government. And that is what happened today" (Deng 1986:258). As for sharing power, Ajuong explains,

> He knew that youth have their own way of behaving ... Your father felt that if he were to share power with a young man, a young man who might jump here and jump there and jump here, such a young man might introduce his own view of things into the leadership. He might come with his own words and change things. Or he might do things that might undermine his father ...
>
> That was why your father was reluctant to appoint one of his sons as his deputy. Your father's heart was afraid. You see, your father handled his leadership with great care (Deng 1986:259-260).

Connected with this issue of a deputy was the issue of eventual succession and there too Father remained ambivalent, as Achwil explains:

He had his two sons Abdalla and Kwol under him to assist him. But according to the word of his own heart, which I knew, he wanted Kwol to be the chief. Then we would ask, "Why?" The matter dragged until Abdalla committed adultery with his father's wives. He went with two wives. That was Deng's main grievance against Abdalla. He then argued that Kwol should inherit his leadership. He said, "The household of Nyanbol Amor has not impurified my bed!" That was an issue which he and I used to debate. I would say, "This is wrong! Abdalla will be the chief!" And Abdalla became the chief. But your father was against that. He even wrote a letter on the matter. This was not an issue he simply talked about; he had it written down on paper. He said, "I will place Abdalla in El Obeid, the Province Headquarters, to be my representative there and Adam will be the chief at home." That was what he used to say.

As for you and Bol he left you up there! You had distinguished yourselves in education and your names had become associated with success in education very early. That was your father's word; he wanted chieftainship to go to Kwol (Deng 1986:259-60).

Ajuong believes Deng Majok later changed his mind about Kwol:

At first, he said, "Kwol is the person to assume chieftainship." Why? When we looked into the matter, we found that it was what his heart had considered, but in his explanation to the people, he would put it discreetly by saying: Kwol was born first; Kwol also learned the law from his services in the police. So that is why I say that Kwol is the one who should be chief."

But later he began to reconsider the situation. Kwol had started to drink heavily while Deng was still alive. Deng would be pleased with Kwol when he saw his appearance walking, but when he heard him speak, in situations involving Kwol and his brothers or strangers, he would look at Kwol's behavior with disfavor. That is how he began to withdraw from his earlier position about Kwol (Deng 1986:259).

Although Father took Bol and me as having transcended tribal ambitions, it seems that he had lingering concerns about the implications of my legal studies. After my first year in law school, I went home to conduct research into customary laws. Word began to go around: "Mading is being prepared to be appointed as the man in charge of all the appeals from Dinka courts." Matet Ayom even congratulated me for the expected appointment. Uncle Deng Makuei said to me when I went to investigate into Dinka law in his court: "I saw it in your eyes from the time you were a baby." He went on to express appreciation for my collecting information from his court: "When I heard you were studying Dinka law in your father's court, I was afraid that you might collect your father's lies and call them Dinka law," he remarked, still reflecting their on-going rivalry for leadership.

When I saw the rumors so rampant, I told my father: "I will no longer sit in court to listen to cases; there are rumors which I hear going around and which disturb me; I will only investigate with elders and chiefs at home and avoid sitting in court." Father heard me and laughed in the manner of a person who knew exactly what I had in mind and liked my reaction.

During my third year, I returned home with an English lecturer in law and a finalist student to continue investigation into Dinka law. Father asked me, "Mading, this recording of customary law, is it being conducted throughout the Sudan or is it only in the Ngok area that it is being done?"

When I graduated and accepted the academic appointment to be lecturer in the Law Faculty instead of becoming a judge as had been expected, many relatives and tribal elders expressed surprise. Being a judge for them was a position of power, status, and public service. When Uncle Ngor asked me for an explanation and I said that being a lecturer was a recognition for my academic performance and therefore an honor and that it was in any case better paid than being a judge, he was outraged. "Leadership requires a priceless service to your people," he argued. "How can you, son of the lineage that has provided leadership since creation, choose money over service to your people?"

My father's reaction was more measured. He was clearly not overjoyed by my choice, but he did not oppose it either. Instead, he chose to explain it to his people, "Mading will be a teacher of judges!"

In a way Ngor's perspective reflected the unequivocal ambition his father and maternal relatives in general had for me while my father's reaction betrayed the ambivalence he felt about a successful son who vied for a position of power with the potential for competition and conflict with him on that ground. It was a conflict inherent in the contradictory logic of permanent identity and influence – continuity and change. It was a conflict not shared by the mother and her side of the family since it posed no threat of stepping into their shoes.

Heritage of Maternal Ancestry

Ironically, while the Dinka are preoccupied with the principle of permanent identity and influence as a perpetuation of the male line, accounts of my role in the family always project my maternal kin alongside my father's and the continuation of the paternal line. Matet Ayom is one of those who highlighted the maternal heritage in my attributes:

> You are a product of two persons. The man who begot your mother was a man of great wisdom. He helped keep this tribe in order with the power of his great words. And so was your own father. So, both the bull and the cow who begot you are people of equal stature. If anyone should associate you with your mother, he will not have associated you with a bad side. And if anyone associates you with your father, he will not have associated you with a bad side either. The person who says that you resemble Mijok Duor, your mother's father, and the person who says that you resemble Deng Majok, none of them has associated you with a bad side. Both were great men who maintained this country with the power of wisdom and the truth. So, we shall now end our words, but I again urge you to think of your people and what you should do for them.

Some years ago, I made a public speech to the Ngok Dinka in Abyei on the theme of our role on the South-North borders, upholding and reinforcing our ancestral heritage of being bridge-builders or the link between the Africans of the South and the Arabs of the North, thereby assuming the important symbol of national unity and integration. It was an attempt to turn the negatives of a disputed area into positives that could give the area a national significance and promise considerable advantages to the people. As I left the meeting, paving my way amidst the security forces and the crowd, Patal Biliu, one of the leading personalities in the tribe, managed to draw my attention and say, "Mading, just remember that the words with which you speak so well are not merely those of your father, Deng Majok, or even of your grandfather, Kwol Arob; they are also the words of your maternal grandfather, Mijok Duor, and your line of maternal ancestors. Just remember that."

And needless to say, Uncle Ngor has continued to believe that his father's vision and expectations about me have largely been fulfilled. Ngor sees a comparative advantage for my maternal side, arguing that instead of preoccupying themselves with short-term gains of power, they look into the future to serve the long-term interests of the society.

> Mading, I want to tell you my word, a word to leave with you even after I join our ancestors. Our kind has always been known for predicting the future. Our kind can tell what will come in the very distant future. Mading, our kind are rich in heart and mind. Even if a person may be lacking in material wealth, the words they say are never poor in substance. And our type never look at other people's things; there is no envy in our type. But our kind excels over all others with the wisdom of their words. Our type can tell what will lead to disaster in the future and they can tell what will lead to the good of the land. I tell the members of our clan: "Mading is a crop of our breed. He is the crop of our breed because he is Mading, son of Achok, daughter of Mijok Duor." You see, Mading, man dies and passes on, but he leaves behind a progeny to continue the name. The word of the son of man, the way I am now talking, will be recognized. It will go on and on, never letting the name disappear: and if some good should come out of the earth, people will look around for the available names.

Nor did Ngor limit his vision of procreation and the values of permanent identity and influence to my immediate role in Dinka society or even in the Sudan. Quite the contrary, he saw my role abroad and even my foreign marriage as aspects of widening the circles of kinship, participation, and continuation. Ngor reports having said to his kin-group after my return to the Sudan:

> When [Mading] was in America in a secure environment, my heart was at peace. I was happy because I knew he was well and names also benefit from the extension of circles. He was extending our ancestor's circle to those

distant lands ... What is needed is a crop for the future. And when people speak of a crop, it is not anyone who is valued as a crop; it is the crop of a person of prudent heart and mind who, if he is hidden in safety somewhere, even if the land should be destroyed, it will one day return to peace and order. When it does, that crop will return and will enquire in the air about the whereabouts of his people. He will be told, "So and so is there and so and so is there." He will go after them and collect them to become a group again.

Ngor concluded his impassioned account with words that combined his flexible global view with unwavering commitment to Dinka identity and influence in the wider framework of interracial and cross-cultural family ties: "So, Mading, those are my words. Take care of your children and they will continue the name. People now say, 'What does Mading say about this or that. It is Mading to whom we look for protection.' Mading, the land is the land of your forefathers. But these children are now in your hands alone. If you are with them to pass your heritage on to them, then they will be Dinkas. That is why I pray to God and to my father that you live to raise them and pass your heritage on to them the way you and I have now talked." Ngor even predicted that in accordance with the will of his father, "that is the way it will be."

The balance I now feel towards the heritage of my paternal and maternal lines is of course a late realization. But I have no doubt in my mind that in all kinds of subtle ways, the message about the heritage of my maternal ancestry has always been there, discreetly but effectively filtering through the depths of my consciousness.

Several factors combine to distinguish my position in the family from that of my peers. One is that I was the first born of my mother and they were not. My mother is known as Man-Mading, a promotion my peers did not receive from their mothers' procreational names, since they were junior to their sisters. For the same reason, my maternal relatives placed their aspirations and expectations in me and my future in my father's family; to the best of my knowledge, that was not true of them. While our father's marriage had much to do with procreation, it was a collective aspiration that did not focus attention on individuals. Father was indeed reported to have said that the reason for wanting many children was that they would, combined together, contribute various qualities and complement each other to produce the ideal that would immortalize his name. In response to a critic, Deng Majok is supposed to have explained:

> There is a snake called the python; it is said that this snake begets all the different kinds of snakes. It begets the brown snake called *biar*, and it begets the snake called *akelek*, and it begets the black snake called *pien*, and it begets the snake called *kuryath* (the puff-adder), and it begets the snake called *gor*, and it begets the snake called *bok*. It begets snakes that can inflict instant death and it begets benign snakes that will not harm.
>
> So what I am doing is not because of the beauty of sleeping with women; it is the desire to beget children. In the future, there will be a child among these children who will live up to my character and there will be a child who will deviate from my image. It is like the case of the snake; there is a snake which kills instantly and there is a snake which does no harm and both are from the same parent-snake called the python (Deng 1986:208).

According to another source, Deng Majok wanted a large number of children that could one day become a clan and perhaps a tribal section. In a way, it was as though he intended to take over the Abyor through the power of sheer numbers in order to conquer their opposition to his leadership. "Deng Majok used to say," according to Malith Mawien, "that he wanted to have a whole tribal section known by his name. He said that through his marriages, he would increase the size of Abyor tribe: he might have four children with one wife, five with another, three with another, and four with yet another" (Deng 1986:206).

And in the report of yet another source, Deng Majok explained, "If a woman bears three or four or five children, among these women will be a woman who might bear girls, another woman who might bear a useless child, yet another woman who might bear a child to compensate for all you put into her marriage. And with respect to the children of a chief, if they are few, there is always the chance that they might all turn out to be useless. But if they are many, then the chances of their all not turning out to be useless are much better" (Deng 1986:206).

Although we grew up being told by Father and others what was hoped or expected from us in the future of perpetuating the name or the image of our father, none was spotlighted as the chosen one by our paternal kin. In sharp contrast, my maternal kin impressed upon me from an early age what was expected of me personally in projecting a role that would meet their aspirations in the context of my paternal leadership. In this connection, while our father projected an innovative profile, my maternal relatives appeared to be proponents of what they regarded as the ideals of Dinka tradition. It is therefore no surprise that I grew up keenly interested in Dinka traditions and would be the only member of my family thus far who has been committed to documenting, promoting, upholding, and applying their cultural norms and practices to the modern context.

I should, however, emphasize that neither my concerns nor the initiatives I have taken in trying to address the problems in the family and the tribe make me unique among my brothers and sisters. The differences I have mentioned are by and large matters of degree, not of essence. As David Cole and Richard Huntington (1985:18) have observed of the sons of Deng Majok, "all of them, for whatever comfort and prestige their education has granted, remain passionately committed to the welfare of the Ngok people although they often disagree fundamentally among themselves about the best political course for the tribe. Additionally, they are competitive among themselves since there are always more qualified sons of Deng Majok than there are opportunities for scholarships, offices, or notoriety."

I have given my family background in some detail for two main reasons. One is that my responses to the situations with which I was confronted may have much to do not only with the cultural context of the society from which I come, but also with the family in which I was raised, both paternal and maternal, and the values which were inculcated in me by the legacy of the two strands in the family. The other, perhaps even more obvious, reason is that many of the negotiation situations in which I was involved concern relations between the Arabs and the Dinka at the North-South border that have been a preoccupation of my family for centuries, a responsibility which largely fell on me by virtue of my position in the family and in the country and my disposition to perpetuate the bridging legacy of the family. Let me now describe the conflict situations in which I have been involved and the principles which I tried to follow in those experiences, beginning with domestic relations by which I mean those internal to the country, from the family to the national levels.

II

INTERNAL RELATIONS

4

Tensions in the Family

Since I have emphasized that negotiation and conflict management or resolution are aspects of everyday life and since life begins in the family, and disputes of varying degrees of magnitude and intensity are frequently encountered at that level, it is appropriate that this collection of negotiation stories begins with family episodes. Although unity, harmony, and solidarity were emphasized in our family, the very nature and complexity of the family meant that serious tensions and even conflicts were inevitable. The key issue in the relationships within our family was polygyny and the tensions built into such a large "clan." While jealousies were the result of rivalries in a wide variety of situations, the central issue was competition for father's love and affection. Father himself maintained a jealous guard over his wives and even his sons were not above suspicion, especially as some of his wives were the same age and even younger than his sons. As his sons, we too kept a discreet distance from his junior wives, attracted to them as we inevitably were at times. But grounds for suspicion were abundant.

The Overheard Levirate Wishes

The year when things first began to go wrong was the year we were spending our vacation at Noong, visiting Abyei only occasionally to obtain such supplies as tea, sugar, and other town commodities. At Noong, we slept in my mother's hut, and while she took care of our special provisions like tea, there were a number of young wives who attended to our comforts in other respects, cleaning our hut, making our beds, serving our meals, and sometimes keeping us company in a purely conversational sense. My mother's hut was conveniently located apart from the other huts and close to the road so that we were the first to be encountered by a visitor. In the evenings, we sat around a fire some distance from the hut and rather central to the whole compound. There, women came to join our conversation and withdrew according to the circumstances of the particular situation.

During one of the occasions when we sought reinforcements from Abyei, this time asking for a milch-cow, in addition to our usual needs, we noticed that our father was unusually reserved. But we still thought that it might be his not so unusual way of appearing to ignore people when he felt overwhelmed by the pressures on him. Several times, we tried to draw his attention and voice our needs, emphasizing that we had to return that day and that it was getting late. Then at one point, he got up and walked towards the market. Thinking that this was an opportunity to secure some of the commodities we wanted, we went after him. When we reached the shop of the leading trader, Ali Beshir, he went into the veranda, where he was received and seated. As Ali ordered coffee for him, Father told his accompanying policeman or security officer that he did not want anybody to disturb us, and asked us, Bol and me, to sit. It sounded quite serious, especially as he dismissed Osman, his favorite boy, on whom there were hardly any limits.

It was impossible to conceive what was in his mind. Then he began to speak, giving us the history of his relations with his father and his stepmothers. He told of how he knew no inside of the huts of any of his father's wives, except that of Abiong, the mother of Deng Makuei, who was the oldest and his closest stepmother. He recalled the words of a great uncle who had said to him while he was still a child, "Son, we have a curse in this clan against anyone who goes with another man's wife. Do not even smile with the wife of another man!" He said he had followed that advice and had hardly ever smiled, even with his father's wives.

It was obvious that we were in trouble. I could not think of anything, but something had certainly gone wrong. He then proceeded to tell us how much he thought of the two of us, how many administrators, British and Sudanese alike, had told him of the pride he should feel about us as the future promise of his family, and how he looked to us not only for the leadership of the family but the tribe. I was beginning to feel more relaxed. Suddenly, he said he had received information about some of his junior wives at Noong which he thought he should share with us! According to the information, some women had been heard voicing wishes for the sons to inherit them after his death.[40] One was reported to have said, "If only I could be inherited by Mading!" When I heard my name, I felt my inner self-collapsing, my mind and senses seemed to stop suddenly. This was more serious than anything I had expected. But the next thing he said was ironically more consoling, for Bol and I were placed in the same boat and I knew that the chances of our being believed as innocent were better if we were accused together. According to Father, another wife had said in response to the wishes of the first wife, "And if only Bol could inherit me!" I felt relieved because from the way Father told Bol's side of the story, I thought he felt we were both innocent. He said that he had told us the story because of his confidence in us and because he wanted to clear the issue.

Then followed a moment of silence. I felt one of us had to talk, and since I had become used to my brothers expecting me to speak for them, I took onto myself the burden of first response. I told Father that it was difficult to speak under those circumstances, but that it was necessary to do so. I said the whole matter was not only shocking to us but totally inconceivable. I only hoped he really meant what he said about his faith in us and that he did not think we were in any way associated with whatever wishes anyone might have expressed. All the same, if it had occurred, it was deeply saddening to us. Bol spoke in the same vein, dramatizing in a way how surprised and really shocked we were that this could have happened.

Father showed a degree of restlessness as we threw the suspicions away, perhaps out of embarrassment that he credited the rumors enough to confront us with them. He virtually interrupted us, once more stressing his confidence, but adding that he planned to convene a family council of all the wives and children, and once it was established that these women had said what they were reported to have said, he would expect us to punish them by beating them ourselves. Anyone who would be reluctant to punish the woman who had desired him would be giving evidence of his own interest in her. And that would be the determining factor in Father's attitude towards us. He went on to say that the matter was of utmost

---

40. According to the levirate custom whereby a widow continues to bear children with a relative, including a senior son, to the name of the dead husband.

confidentiality and that it should be confined to him and us, and should under no circumstances go beyond.

Then, almost as though he had overstated his case and needed to compensate us for doing so, he granted all our wishes, most generous with all our requests. We left for Noong that evening, not sharing our secret with anyone, not even with Kwol, who for some reason had not come to Abyei; he was at Noong when we got there.

About two days later, as we sat around our evening fireplace chit-chatting among ourselves, I felt that the conversation the women were having some fifty yards from us had something rather important to do with us. This was simply a feeling perhaps based on over-hearing something I could not substantiate. So, I kept it to myself until Kwol's mother, Nyanbol Amor, came and informed us of the latest news from Abyei. The whole story, as our father had told it to us, was brought by the latest arrivals – none other than one of the accused wives, the one alleged to have wished for me. I should say that the two wives were from our respective sides of the family.

According to the story, more fully developed by the account, there was a third woman within hearing distance outside the hut while the two wives allegedly made their wishes. The third woman, Awut Kiir, an attractive woman whom our father had met and married in a town, was from the Rek Dinka, without a clearly established family affiliation.

Kwol, to whom all this was news as he had not gone to Abyei with us, reacted spontaneously and distinguished himself with the pertinence of his observations. He wondered how we could possibly have heard our father's report without insisting on knowing his source of information and why that source had not first informed us. According to him, our first quarrel should be with the woman who had bypassed us and gone straight to our father, implying that we were involved in the plot of wishes. She should be the first for us to punish before we punished those who had supposedly made the wishes. Kwol said he had no doubt in his mind that if he were us and he knew the woman who had reported to our father, he would beat her first and then turn to the wish-makers. But since there was no way of knowing who had really talked to our father, except through Father himself, he would insist on urging him to expose his source before we could take any steps against the accused wives. Kwol seemed so right in what he said that our submissive reaction to our father seemed embarrassing.

What was even more perplexing was Father telling us to keep the matter a secret and then proceeding to reveal the affair. According to the account the woman brought which was surprising in its details and candor, she went to ask her husband for some jewelry. After ignoring her for some time, he asked sarcastically, "Do you want the jewelry to attract your step-son!" The woman responded with, "What do you mean, Chief?" Father then rebuked her, "Get out of my sight, I do not want to see you. The sight of you nauseates my heart."

More than that, Father had already talked to two of his senior wives in Abyei, Amel and Amou, who were respectively in charge of Nyanboldit's and Kwei's sections. When the wife left his room, she heard the story circulating around. We felt persuaded by the logic of Kwol's argument and betrayed by Father's violation of the secrecy he himself had imposed. Kwol instigated us into leaving the next morning to confront our father.

We quickly secured an appointment with him, protected from the on-looking crowds by the police. We did not consider it prudent to blame him for exposing the secret, but we impressed upon him our indignation for being kept in the dark by his source and demanded that he reveal the source. As was typical of Father, he turned the tables around, displaying a restlessness about our indignation, and reasserting that he was waiting for the district commissioner to leave after which he would convene the family, reveal the whole story, and ask us to punish the women. If we did not, then he would suspect us of involvement with them. He went further to say that he might draw the conclusion from our impatience that there was a degree of discomfort on account of some guilt. Father was always good at making the innocent feel guilty, so that he himself would feel innocent. We went back to Noong with no new dimensions to the episode.

At Noong, the woman who was accused of wanting me and the one my father had talked to, sent me a relative with a message. According to the message, she regretted what had happened and expressed the hope that I did not hold it against her. The message did not clarify whether she had or had not said what she was alleged to have said, and yet she wanted to secure my sympathy. I decided to play her game back by saying that I had no position since I did not know whether she had indeed said what she was supposed to have said or had been wrongly accused. The messenger tried to be solicitous by urging me to say simply that I was not angry with her. That would have implied that whether or not she had done what she was said to have done, I held no grudge against her. I certainly did not want to risk any further complications. So, I simply told the messenger to deliver my message as I had articulated it, nothing less and nothing more. I never heard from her on the subject again.

The whole affair seemed to disappear quietly. We never heard of the matter from Father again for, as was typical of him, when he was convinced by an argument, he would not expressly concede but would eventually act or not act in accordance with the opinion. He must have concluded that convening a family council and forcing us to punish the women would probably not be the best thing to do. So he quietly dropped the whole affair.

The woman who had reported the matter soon became known and as was to be expected, there was a widespread animosity towards her behavior. When she was later afflicted with a prolonged illness that eventually killed her, it was widely believed that it was a spiritual punishment for her evil deed in provoking a family feud unjustifiably. As for the women, I later learned that they were among those who dropped out, leaving no children, no traces, and probably not even a scandal beyond that episode.

The Recalcitrant Eldest Son

Although our group of brothers, Bol, Kwol and I, stayed among Father's wives without scandals, there were to be scandals in our family, not only involving wives, but also sons. Perhaps the first and the most dramatic involved Ahmed [Arob]. But Ahmed's case was primarily a power struggle and sexual conquest was only an aspect of that struggle, in turn a reflection of the dynamics in the relations between the parents.

As noted earlier, while Ahmed's mother, Kwei, was the third wife of our father, he was Father's eldest child. Even allowing for the deaths of the first and second borns of the first and second wives, Ahmed's seniority in age could only be accounted for by the fact that he was conceived and born before his mother's marriage to Father. After her marriage, she soon demonstrated a tough-mindedness that brought her into sharp conflict with her even more tough-minded husband. The conflict focused on smoking. Although smoking the pipe and chewing tobacco were common among the Dinka of both sexes, Father, who never smoked, forbade his wives from smoking, but Kwei was either addicted to tobacco or too independent-minded to observe the prohibition. She not only smoked but also chewed tobacco. A series of confrontations and conflicts culminated in Father abstaining from Kwei's food and bed, which led to Kwei's having only four children, all fortunately surviving.

Apparently, Ahmed grew up not only with the complex of having been born out of wedlock, but also, at least in the view of his maternal relatives, of his father's mistreatment of his mother. Arob was the first member of the Deng family to go to school and acquire higher education. With the special concern the British had about the post-colonial position of the Dinka in the context of Arab dominion, they quickly groomed him and promoted him from a clerk in the district headquarters, to local government executive officer, which was then a position of considerable power, in some respects superior to the chief's authority.

Ahmed came in very high-handedly. He was extremely severe on those who defaulted or delayed in tax-payment. He was known for tours of terror across Dinkaland, collecting taxes in money or cattle, arresting those who failed to pay, turning them into carriers, and "hanging" the insubordinates among them by tying their hands to high branches of trees and having them whipped. In one case, Ahmed was said to have ordered his local retainers, tribal police, to run after an escaped tax evader and to bring him back "alive or dead", implicitly ordering them to shoot, if the escaping prisoners did not heed the stop order. The retainer was reported to have returned, breathing heavily to report to Ahmed, "Sir, I did as you ordered." Ahmed, back to his senses, suddenly realized the gravity of what might have happened and the seriousness of the orders he had lightheartedly given. "What did you do!?" he asked.

"I shot him," the retainer answered, "but I am sorry I missed him, Sir."

"Thank God," Ahmed thought to himself, but the reputation had already gone. Not only did he "hang" his own people, he even ordered their execution for reasons of tax evasion.

As though his unpopularity with the public was not enough, Ahmed ironically seemed to disapprove of his father's autocratic rule and went out of his way, perhaps unwittingly, to give the impression that he was the redeemer from his father's power. He became popularly misperceived as having a combined judicial and administrative authority to check and balance his father's alleged abuse of judicial and administrative powers. In the eyes of the dissident groups, this made him an appellate authority with the power to oversee his father's decisions and, if necessary, reverse them. The Dinka were quick to pull on that string and many among them took their grievances to Ahmed, even when they did not necessarily present formal appeals. With the competitiveness of Dinka politics, word went to and fro between Ahmed and his father as to who was doing what against whom, and political tensions rocketed high. In the face of the seeming superiority of the central authority invested in Ahmed, he was more on the aggressive side while Father seemed to retreat and shrink in the confrontation, a most uncharacteristic response from him.

Ahmed was socially as ostentatious as he was politically ambitious. His huts were among the best built in Abyei, with attachments that added to traditional architecture, and well furnished with whatever modern-type furniture was locally available. What was more, he divorced his Ngok Dinka wife and married a Catholic teacher, the daughter of a Dinka chief from the Twich tribe further South, a marriage which had been opposed by Christian missionaries and had been concluded only with the intervention of state courts. Although in a Dinka-Muslim surrounding, where the place of the woman was inside the home, Ahmed introduced a modern approach to husband-wife companionship. They sat together, ate together, walked together, and generally appeared together in a manner that was totally unknown to the Abyei community and was reminiscent of the days of the visiting British district commissioners.

Within a short time, Ahmed had established his image as a force to be reckoned with in political power, social prestige, and even charisma. His rising position was primarily seen as a limitation on his father's, and to make things worse, they were neighbors so that they held their respective home courts in close proximity, but separately, a fact which accentuated the tension and competitiveness of the atmosphere.

It was rumored that Ahmed's attitude of confrontation with his father was the result of pressures from his mother and maternal relatives who reminded him of the past in the relations between his father and mother and disposed him towards using his position to avenge the indignity his mother had suffered in the hands of his father, especially her untimely termination of procreation. Ahmed did not seem to realize fully that Father was an old hand in power politics and that just as he had successfully coached the promotion of his son among both the British and the Sudanese, especially as his appointment to that senior executive position was unpopular among the Arabs, he was capable of arousing sentiments against his son. It was during this period that Arab administrators intensified their efforts at convincing our father that Ahmed was not in his long-term interest and that the promise for the future lay more in Bol and me.

One day, having come from Noong where we were spending our leave, we got so delayed that we decided to spend the night in Abyei. We planned to sleep in the structure where our father held his home-meetings, but while it sheltered from the sun, it did not provide adequate protection against rain. So, when it suddenly began to rain at night, the obvious alternative seemed to be the attachment in front of Ahmed's guest-house, then occupied by Dominic Wol, a one-time class-mate of ours who had left school at the intermediate level to marry and was then employed as an agricultural expert. Ahmed refused us permission to use that room on the grounds that it was too close to the room which his guest occupied with his wife. This was despite the fact that a closeable door separated the two rooms, and in any case, the situation was one of emergency which was understandable, even if it imposed any inconvenience on the visitor. Infuriated by Ahmed's attitude, we sent word to our father, who had to be awakened, to find an alternative among his wives' huts. Father got out of his hut in great sympathy and directed that a hut be evacuated for us. While angered at Ahmed's behavior, he seemed ironically pleased to see us become alienated from him, for, as he said, "Now that he has done it to you, his brothers, you will understand better what I am facing with Ahmed." Father went as far as telling us that the British had wanted Ahmed to join the Army and that it was he who had rejected that suggestion, preferring Ahmed to be in administration to assist him, a decision he now seemed to regret.

Arob's eventual demise was paradoxically to come from a politically motivated case against our father in which he was initially an accomplice but increasingly assumed the responsibility of the principal culprit. While we were back in our final year in school, word reached us that Chol Jipur, one of Father's two deputy paramount chiefs and the leading personality from the Dhiendior lineage, had raised a case of corruption and misappropriation of public funds against our father and Ahmed. Ironically, Chol Jipur was made by Father, for he had been installed deputy paramount chief in succession to his father, Jipur Allor, of the main branch of the Dhiendior clan, against the wishes of the majority of his tribesmen who wanted Deng Akonon, the son of the daughter of our grandfather, Arob Biong. Deng Akonon claimed that his father had been the one rightfully entitled to succession and that Jipur Allor had succeeded simply because Deng's father, Akonon, had been under age. He therefore felt qualified to claim his father's succession. My father thought that since Jipur Allor had assumed leadership and had died while he was deputy paramount chief and in the good books of the government, his heirs should not be deprived of succession, and among his competing sons my father preferred Chol Jipur, who had now turned against him.

Chol seemed to carry such an air of revolutionary power against the supposed tyranny, autocracy, and corruption of our father's power that he seemed to represent a formidable force for radical change, especially as he was instigated or at least supported by Babo Nimir, Father's friend, turned enemy. Having been told by central authorities that the matter would be investigated, Chol returned home with the euphoria of a hero while our father and Arob were still in the North attending council meetings. Rumors had it that the end was about to come for Father.

Corruption and misuse or misappropriation of public funds were popular grounds, because they seemed to make an easy case in view of Father's extensive marriages and the unprecedented size of his family. But while this particular case was receiving greater attention and interest than all that had preceded it, we also knew that such attempts had previously ended in disgraceful failures on the part of the opposition members, who almost invariably ended in prison. Indeed, it wasn't long since Matet Ayom, the very articulate sectional chief of Alei, one time close friend turned enemy, tried to tarnish Father's image and power with the central government and eventually lost, served a prison term, and returned to recultivate old ties. Another sectional chief, Ajang Deng Kwei of Bongo, had also tried with similar consequences. He was later to tell Bol and me, "Your father is like the huge tebeldi tree. It would be foolish for anyone to think that he can fell it alone. With many people working together, it is possible that a tebeldi tree can be cut down. So, quite honestly, if I found many people united to pull down your father, I will not lie to you and say that I would not join them. But alone, I will never think of rising against your father again." So, while we always worried that something unexpected might happen as a result of these accusations, we did not really believe that anything could happen to our father.

When the confrontation eventually materialized and the central government authorities came to investigate the case, Chol Jipur, like those before him, failed dreadfully and was arrested and deported for falsely accusing his superior. The atmosphere of jubilation among the opposition suddenly turned into panic as Father came back fully in control and his opponents were frightened of his retaliation. He did not retaliate other than by replacing the deposed Chol Jipur with the man the tribe had wanted in the first place, the then aging Deng Akonon, that time through fresh and free elections with which Father ostensibly chose not to interfere.

But the opposition did not fail altogether, for while Father was fully exonerated, the prima facie case against Ahmed was established, pending further enquiry and eventual trial. I think it would be fair to say that those who held the case against Ahmed to be at least worth further investigation also realized that he was no longer in his father's good graces and that Father would at least be ambivalent about his son's fate.

Things were to get worse for Ahmed. While he was awaiting further investigation and trial, two of our father's wives confessed that he had committed adultery with them and had made them pregnant. According to the news reaching us in school, the effect of these events was dreadful and understandably so, considering the degree of Father's jealousy over his wives. Ahmed's fortunes were suddenly on a downhill slide. Now in extreme conflict with his father, having committed an offence the Dinka consider not only morally depraved but spiritually contaminating, accused of a crime and threatened with imprisonment, dismissal, and disgrace, Ahmed soon became a haunted man, a social reject, a rebel without a cause, and a deteriorating loner. He withdrew some seven miles away from Abyei to Akechnhial on the River Kiir (Bahr el Arab) where he built himself a hut and a *rakuba* on a beautiful spot. For the most part, his companions were a few subordinates with lingering loyalties and some traditional members of his age-set, Chuor, who would never have been anywhere near his social circle during his hey-days.

In sharp contrast to his earlier culturally alienated attitude towards tradition, Ahmed suddenly developed a keen interest in the Dinka ways; song, dance, cattle-complex, and institutionalized courtship. He composed politically motivated ox songs in which he explained his reasons for leaving Abyei, which he blamed on his political opponents and his hate for the Arabs, whom he called butchers whose only interest in cattle was meat. He dared his opponents to take away the spiritual powers of his clan or the power of his pen – his education – both of which he placed above the power of the government that he had abandoned. He implored his father not to permit their mutual enemies to pull them asunder, but, instead, to reconsider his heart and maintain the bonds of father-son relationship. Otherwise, he sang in praise of his bulls, about distant camp grazings to which he said he could not go but nevertheless felt close to, and of course, he flattered the people, and especially the girls of Akech-nhial, his new home whose name means "Standing High," a concept with which he elevated himself as closer to the spirit of the legendary Achai, who was sacrificed to the river spirits by Jok, the founding father of the leading Pajok clan, so that the waters would part and permit his people to cross.

Although we had heard in school about the gravity of the conflict between Father and Ahmed, and could imagine our father's reaction, it was not until we returned home and witnessed the situation ourselves that we fully realized the impact of the developments on our father.

Shortly after our return home on leave, there arrived a delegation of medical students from Khartoum University, accompanied by their Scottish professor on an academic tour. Together with our father we took the delegation to the river at Akechnhial, quite close to Ahmed's spot, and since a number of the students had been Ahmed's colleagues, indeed friends, from his days at Hantoub Secondary School, they requested to see him. Ahmed was duly informed. When the group arrived at Akechnhial, he came to meet them. Ahmed greeted the guests but did not approach our father for greeting. In sharp contrast, since we were meeting him for the first time since our return from school, we greeted him with an embrace. Father was watching, outraged, but composed.

That same afternoon, he called a meeting of all his sons. Present also was his sister, Awor. Father spoke about the moral principles that had been handed down by our ancestors on the question of social, let alone sexual, relations with married women and in particular, stepmothers. He repeated what he had told us about his own attitude as a young man growing up among his father's wives, and the extent to which he had avoided even their huts. Turning to what Ahmed had done, he said it had first crossed his mind to shoot him, forget the chieftainship, and face trial for murder. He had decided against that. However, the least he could do was to sever Ahmed from his family and never again to be regarded as his son. He said he had been shocked to see us greet Ahmed with such enthusiasm. We had to make a choice between Ahmed and himself. Those who chose to be with Ahmed had to leave the family and join him. Those who were on their father's side were not to have anything to do with Ahmed and were to immediately sever all ties with him. He said he was planning to convene a general assembly of the family at Noong and carry out the rituals of Ahmed's severance from the family.

Father spoke in such a bitter and categorical tone that it was unthinkable for anyone to contradict him. It was even difficult to find adequate words of support for him. So, I spoke, supported by the brothers, simply to reassure him of our agreement with the moral values he had expounded, to express our indignation at what Ahmed had done, and our sympathy for his feelings on the matter. We said nothing directly connected with the issue of the ritual severance of Ahmed, but by omission, we seemed to acquiesce to his decision.

Aunt Awor was obviously not in favor of our passive stance on the issue of severance of blood ties. She went to her brothers, Biong Mading and Arob, and received unequivocal support against the idea. They in turn chose to talk to us instead of to our father directly. In a serious business-like meeting, they told us that sons were the most appropriate persons to confront their father on such a matter as what was at issue between Ahmed and our father; that there was no way Ahmed could be disaffiliated, for, however much he was denied by the family, he would remain the blood and social member of the family and his image anywhere would remain part of the family. They said it was our responsibility to check our father in his design to sever him from the family. They expressed disapproval at our implied support for our father's position and urged us to undo it by initiating a talk with him immediately. They were obviously persuasive in their argument.

Before we could approach our father, a letter came from Ahmed addressed to Father but sent to me to read to him. I knew this was bound to be an unpleasant assignment, but one I had to perform. After going through the letter, I waited for Father and approached him as he emerged from his bedroom and was going to his morning tea-time assembly in his home courtroom. As I intended to read the letter in privacy, I said I had a letter for him from Ahmed, hoping he would listen to the whole letter before going into his public assembly. Very impatiently, he asked what the letter was about. I told him it was about the quarrel between him and Ahmed. He said, "And what is he saying about it?" I tried to summarize the letter, but there was no way of softening Ahmed's substance and tone which essentially was a reaction to what Father had said in his meeting with his sons. How Ahmed knew, I do not know. Essentially, he said he had heard of Father's intentions to sever him from the family. Ahmed wrote of how saddened he was that his father had not only disaffiliated his son from him, but would go to the extent of severing him from his brothers and the family. He wrote, and I reported faithfully to Father, that God would be his judge. To that, Father's patience was taxed beyond limits; he said, "So be it, may God be the judge between us," and he would permit no more translation of the letter, which anyway had nothing more of substance to add.

Having decided to talk to our father on the issue of Ahmed, we sought an appointment as we had always done on such important occasions. He granted the audience. As always, the brothers designated me to be the spokesman on their behalf. I spoke reaffirming our stand behind the values he had espoused in the earlier meeting and our sympathy with the motivation behind his decision to sever Ahmed from the family. Reiterating the argument of Aunt Awor and Uncles Biong and

Arob, I told Father that there was no way he could strip Ahmed of his family label and that wherever he went, he would still be Deng Majok's son. What was more, I said, Ahmed had been his father's top partner in tribal power in which there had been and still were many critics and enemies. If Ahmed were to be totally disaffiliated and be forced to take the side of the enemies and reveal the secrets of father-son association, might it not be damaging to Father? People might then feel that by virtue of his position of confidence, Ahmed certainly knew the facts and however ill-motivated and false what he said was, there would be a tendency to believe him as someone who ought to know the facts. Such embarrassment, we thought, should be avoided in order not to give our enemies a chance.

The strength of the argument seemed to antagonize Father even more. After hearing his other sons speak, all in support of our agreed line of argument, Father said angrily that he had never realized he had a bunch of cowards for sons and that if we had all become intimidated by Ahmed, then he would stand on his own and proceed with his plans for disaffiliating him from the family, even without our support. "Let him do what he wants to do, I do not care or fear!" was his concluding remark. Of course, we argued beyond our normal limits of courage, but he was clearly not to be persuaded otherwise. Our meeting ended with no positions changed, but certainly with a full exchange of views. On our part, I felt satisfied that we had adequately performed our duty as senior sons.

No family council was ever held as planned by Father, and, knowing that he was never the one to admit being in the wrong or that he had been persuaded otherwise, we watched with interest the passage of time without action on his part and convinced ourselves that our message had registered and that Ahmed would not be disaffiliated from the family after all.

In fact, Father's attitude improved considerably with time and although he never forgave Ahmed publicly, he never did anything to disavow him publicly either. When Ahmed's trial eventually came, he did not do much to defend or protect him, but he was less than openly negative towards him. Yet, everyone knew that Ahmed did not have his father's affection, let alone political backing and protection. Ahmed faced the case as a loner and in the realistic world of law and politics, there can be no way of divorcing the finding of guilt from his deprivation of his father's sympathy and protection. This was particularly apparent when he was sentenced to a prison term that could have been replaced by pecuniary payment, which Father could have done, had he chosen to do so.

Many years later, Ibrahim Mohamed Zein, then the headmaster of Abyei School, was to recall a conversation he had with Father at the crucial time of Ahmed's arrest:

> I recall one incident. His son Ahmed was then the executive officer of the Council. Some problem occurred between Ahmed and Mukhtar El Tayeb, who is now a Commissioner of a province and was then the District Commissioner. Mukhtar El Tayeb gave instructions to the police to have Ahmed arrested. Ahmed was not only an executive officer, he was also the son of the chief. On his way back from court, Deng Majok passed by my house and told me all that had happened with Mukhtar El Tayeb, adding, "I left because I could not tolerate watching what was happening and I was afraid also that any one of the Dinka might be provoked into committing an offense, seeing my son who is also their officer treated that way. It would be difficult to tolerate."
>
> Then he proceeded to tell me, "But to tell you the truth, there is something deep inside me between me and my son. First of all, I educated him until he completed his schooling. I then said to the authorities that I was the man controlling this very difficult area between the North and the South: Here was my son educated, knowing both English and Arabic, knowledgeable in every aspect of modern government, 'I would like you to help me by appointing my son an executive officer and bringing him here to be with me.' Thanks to them, they appointed him executive officer and brought him here. I said to him that he should not view himself as simply an executive officer, but also as the chief of the tribe and my righthand man. I gave him my full authority and responsibility.
>
> "I am a man of many responsibilities, both public and family, and I have many children in various schools. Ever since Ahmed became an officer, he has never given me a helping hand with the education of any of his brothers. Second, he left our girls here and went to the South to marry a girl who cost me considerable wealth. I

paid all that, brought the girl, built her a home close to me, and made her settle as a member of my family.

"I began to see one of my most beautiful wives whom I loved dearly go frequently to my son's house. I called the woman and told her to stop going there because that was the house of my son's wife who was an outsider, and in any case that I did not want people to get the impression that my wife might be interested in the things available in my son's house, which might be better because he was educated and an officer. I asked her to stay at home and be content with my own way of life. Yet I noticed that she continued to go to him. I had a feeling that the situation was not normal.

"One day, I sat the woman down and questioned her very closely. Then I found out that Ahmed had been sleeping with her. I became extremely angry. I called his maternal uncles and explained to them what the son of their sister had done. His mother, I said, was one of the most senior wives. 'But from today,' I said to them, 'her position is relinquished; she no longer occupies that status and I bear no further responsibility for her.' That conduct from my son affected me very deeply. But God Almighty has acted on my behalf. I am his father and a father is the second God to a person. He has offended God and God has punished him for raising his head above me and against me. But, despite all that, he is my son and I cannot feel good to see him treated that way in front of me" (Deng 1986:216).

As it was, Ahmed went to jail in far-off Nahud, suffered a greater emotional ordeal on account of his father's disregard for his fate, lost a dedicated wife who died while in Nahud, trying to provide him with some care and consolation (an occasion for which I wrote and sent him a poem), and ultimately served his full term and survived to the extent he did only because of his resilience and strength of character. Moving from job to job, humiliated and disparaged, increasingly dependent on alcohol, Arob suicidally drove himself into an early death. All that was widely believed to be, at least in part, due to his having lost his father's favor and perhaps drawn down a curse. According to Ali: "In a way, it is very much in line with what the Dinka say that if a father is unhappy with his son, he can inflict great harm on him through the will of God. Even though it is fashionable these days to say that this is a Dinka superstition, one feels that if your father's heart is offended with you, God can inflict harm on you. Arob's end came from the time he committed adultery with Father's wives. Since then and until his recent death, we never saw anything good on the part of Arob" (Deng 1986:215).

The Transgression of Another Possible Successor

Ahmed's case was apparently far more significant than anyone seemed to realize at the time. It was the tip of the iceberg, and other scandals soon followed in rapid succession, involving relatives both within and beyond the immediate family. Although loyalty and faithfulness remained the norm, and violation of them a most resented exception, the unfaithful were not without sympathy in the family. Monyyak (Abdalla) and, ironically, the wife concerned in the second case of adultery with a son, both confided their secret to a younger brother, Charles Biong – and won his sympathy:

> Monyyak discussed the situation with me even before he committed adultery with Father's wife. At first, he started by posing the general question of what would be the position of a son if he did such a thing. I told him that no one among us could possibly think of doing such a thing. Then he presented an argument assuming that the deed was done not on the initiative of the son but the woman. We discussed the issue along these general lines and agreed that the son should resist such a temptation. And then, later on, he told me that there were women after him ... I still encouraged him to resist.
>
> But then he began to come to me and say that he could not resist any longer because the woman was so persistent. Later on, I was forced to talk to the woman. At first she did not want to talk to me. But I talked to her very frankly, trying to warn her and to discourage her from doing any such thing. That was when she came to explain to me her point of view. She confronted me with a situation about which I could not blame her or Monyyak. She told me that she thought it would be wiser to go with the son of Deng Majok and have a child within the family. "But if you people say that you cannot do that, if

you reject me, I will be forced to go and pick any man regardless of who or where he is. The child I would beget would also be called the son of Deng Majok. I am ready to take anything. The child will carry your name anyway. Whether your father accepts it or not, he or she would be my child. It is because I respect your family that I want a child by Deng's son" (Deng 1986:217).

Biong's account of the case goes on to show how, as expected, Father reacted to the affair: "For a period of at least two months, he did not talk to Monyyak. Then he called Monyyak's mother [Nyanboldit] – I recall – and rebuked her. The only person who tried to help the situation was Uncle Biong Mading. In the end, he managed to reconcile Father and Monyyak. Father had taken an oath not to regard Monyyak as his son anymore, something similar to what he had done with the late Ahmed, Arob Deng. But even after they were reconciled, his opinion about Monyyak was never what it had been before the incident" (Deng 1986:217).

All this, of course, goes to explain the dilemma Father was to have about his successor: Bol and I had drifted away from the tribal context and were no longer relevant to the issue of succession; Adam, whom he had always favored for succession, had adopted the habit of drinking which Father deplored; and Abdalla, who would have stood a good chance on account of his traditional position as son of the first wife, had committed a mortal sin by committing adultery with his father's wife.

Cases of Jealousy and Suspicion

The year Ahmed committed adultery with Father's wives, we were to encounter a different case of tension in the family. We were then graduating from our third year at Khor Taqqat and due to join our final year. As the third year exams had been interrupted by a strike, we were expected to sit for the exams on return and were therefore supposed to study during our vacation. This necessitated finding an alternative to the normal living conditions of our family, which were utterly prohibitive to any studies. We succeeded in taking over an abandoned old brick wall and corrugated iron-roof house of the medical assistant which had two rooms. So, for the first time in our life, Bol and I lived in a house with two separate rooms, each one of us occupying his own room with a door between us. This was perfect, except that it made possible an unfortunate incident that revealed the ugly side of jealousy in a polygynous family.

It is of course no secret that there is a great deal of jealousy in a polygynous Dinka family, but we also took pride in the fact that such jealousies were severely repressed in our family and that the sons, especially our age-mates, were above them. Bol and I felt even more above them than might be the case with most members of the family. This was demonstrated one day when Aker Tiel, my mother's competitor in the seniority order and the second in Bol's section of the family, came to see Bol. As the door between our two rooms was closed, she thought I was nowhere near and spoke very freely and divisively about our situation. Except for the closed door between us, I was virtually with them and heard every word quite distinctly. Reconstructed, the gist of what she said was to the effect of: "Why is it that everything that comes to you boys, goes to Mading's mother's house? Everything, it is Man-Mading, Man-Mading, is it that Mading is so clever that he always outwits you or are you too weak to stand up to Mading?!" Apparently, Bol did not try to hush her up on the ground that she was being heard. Instead, he very gently and calmly told her that we did not share the jealousies of the women and that there was no question of Mading's mother or Bol's mother in our attitude towards our mothers; they were all our mothers. Bol was firm and unequivocally critical of Aker's attitude, but I felt that he was far too gentle and accommodating for the gravity of her wrong. So, after controlling myself for some time, I decided to open the door and intervene. Unsuspecting, absolutely shocked, but otherwise composed, Aker could not speak; I had to do the talking.

I told her that I had always considered myself son to all my father's wives, and in particular, our senior stepmothers; that I had never suspected any hostility between her and myself or my mother; that for her to talk the way she had done against me and my mother meant that there had to be a good reason; all I wanted was to know that reason.

To my surprise, Aker had nothing at all to say in defense of her position. Paradoxically, she only praised my mother and asserted that she and my mother had no hostilities or jealousies of any kind, but were indeed "friends," and that as far as she was concerned, I was a son without reservation. Her only contention was that Ayan, one of my sisters, who was taking care of our milch-cow in Abyei, had apparently refused to give Aker milk for her child. What did that have to do with my mother and me and why had she not seen it fit to report my sister to Bol and me or to me for correction? She had nothing to say. Since she did not really address herself to the issues I posed, she was not persuasive in her plea and we parted quite obviously in conflict.

I subsequently talked to my sister, Ayan, and questioned her. Of course, her version of the story was different from what Aker had said. Ayan readily saw the element of rivalry in the situation and threatened to report the matter to our mother. I told her that I wanted to get to the root of the problem myself and that it was not simply a matter of reporting to our mother, but of investigating what had antagonized Aker so much as to behave the way she had done. I told Ayan that she should leave the matter for me to discuss with Mother myself.

I did indeed discuss the matter with my mother, emphasizing to her that I was not for confrontation but for clarification and understanding. My mother was of course very offended, but she promised not to quarrel with Aker, but instead, to convene a meeting of senior wives and present the matter for open discussion and judgment. She did. Aker was blamed and made to apologize to Achok. Nyanboldit herself was reported to have defended Achok's case and strongly reprimanded Aker.

As I felt that we as sons should take the issue seriously, I reported the matter to Aker's son, Bulabek, expecting him to support me and to confront his mother as a Dinka boy is expected to do in the circumstances. He never did either of the two.

At first, I was puzzled by Bulabek's reaction, but then I realized on further reflection that he probably shared his mother's views and was indeed eventually to come into serious conflict with Father precisely because he nursed a deep grievance about his relative position in the family. Although one of the brightest members of the family and top of his class in the southern school he was attending, Bulabek seemed overtly dissatisfied with Father's treatment of him. I came to know about the extent to which relations had deteriorated between them while I was at home on vacation after my first year in the university. Bol had then left to study medicine in East Germany. Father pulled me aside shortly after my arrival, and as part of a political briefing, said that Bulabek had taken to associating with Father's adversaries and had been reported to say that the family was maintained and children educated on illegitimate means. Father sounded extremely embittered as he spoke. He said he had decided never to give Bulabek anything of the means he regarded as illegitimate. What supported Father's reports was Bulabek's close association with Deng Abot's family, where most opponents of Father always clustered and received a sympathetic hearing. We had even heard from Uncle Bona Bulabek at the university some very favorable comments about Bulabek for being a critic of Father's alleged dictatorship and financial dealings, a position Bona admired, being himself a critic of our father. Of course, I could not fan Father's anger by telling him what Bona had told us.

I was to hear Bulabek's point of view from Abdalla, then the oldest resident son. Abdalla told me of Bulabek's disenchantment with Father for failure to provide him with school fees and pocket money. In protest, Bulabek had decided to leave school and abandon education, as a result of which he had become very bitter. Abdalla proceeded to tell me of a letter he had received from Bulabek in the North, asking Abdalla to contact his mother, Aker Tiel, and to verify whether he was truly the son of Deng Majok. So, Bulabek left school, did not get employed, remained a critic whom Father never confronted, but totally discarded.

The Son Who Took a Stand Against Islamization

Another brother who had serious problems with Father was Mekki (Miyar), son of Nyanbol Deng, the sixth wife, who belonged to Nyanboldit's section. Mekki's problems with Father had their roots in the relations between his parents. Although Father was notorious for beating women and nearly every wife experienced a beating, the one he beat almost habitually was Nyanbol Deng, who was also notorious for a tough head. Whatever sympathy people had for her, Father's position was also appreciated. It was as though beating only made her more insubordinate. Unlike other women who would not only cry but submit without aggravating words, Nyanbol Deng would babble as she was beaten, which only made things worse.

The conflict between Miyar and our father was, however, more than mother-based. Miyar was once said to have lifted dates from a shop and that offended Father into scolding him in the most excruciating language, virtually repudiating him as a son and urging his sons of Miyar's age, Monyyak (Abdalla) and Monylam (Ali), to keep away from him. Miyar, who was also proud and tough-headed, grew up with a disposition for independence, largely kept to himself, and nursed a strong bitterness against his father.

Mekki was to play what in retrospect was a heroic role which provoked Father not least because it seemed to undermine his authority as the chief. As part of the recognition and respect due to us from Abyei school authorities, Bol and I were invited to attend a meeting of the school selection board which was chaired by Father and which was to admit first year pupils. The headmaster was a northern Sudanese, and as a part of the

Arabization and Islamization process that the government had embarked upon in the South, Abyei school system had been changed from the vernacular-English-Christian southern system to the Arab-Islamic system of the North. Theoretically, while Islam was favored by the authorities, the parents of the children were expected to make their choice of religion for their children. Of course, it was generally assumed that the competition was between Islam and Christianity as traditional Dinka religion was not accorded any recognition as a religion.

The new headmaster, who directed the proceedings, went beyond the usual limits of official prejudice for Islam. He informed the committee that the policy of the government was to promote Islam and that there was therefore no room for the parents of the children to choose Christianity for their pagan children who must be assumed to have become Muslims by joining the school. We were all surprised and of course offended by this discriminatory attitude, but since he claimed to have received orders from the Ministry of Education to that effect, we could not hold him responsible.

Mekki was among the crowds who blocked the windows to peek and listen. He had received his elementary and part of his intermediate education in the North and was himself a Muslim. One late afternoon, we returned from hunting to find Father and the headmaster sitting outside our house, waiting for us. From the look on Father's face, something quite serious had gone wrong. He handed me a letter to read, asking whether we knew anything about it.

I anxiously read the letter and passed it on to Bol. It was from Mekki addressed to the headmaster. He wrote of how surprised he had been by what the headmaster had said at school, and asked him where in the laws of the Sudan it was provided that all pupils in government schools had to be Muslims. It was a simple, logical, political letter which was why it was all the more disturbing to the headmaster. As he put it, before he saw the name, he had thought the letter was from a Christian missionary and could not believe it was written by one of "our sons".

We told Father that Mekki had not at all talked to us about the matter. Mekki was fetched and as soon as he came, Father exploded in anger, almost fringing on physical assault. Mekki did not withdraw, but to the contrary, continued to defend his position and to condemn the behavior of the headmaster. Father became enraged. He ordered the police to arrest Mekki and take him to prison. The headmaster intervened and pleaded with Father not to take such a drastic action. We too tried to convince Mekki that however right he was in substance, it was wrong for him to

156

address himself to the headmaster directly, bypassing not only his father, who was the responsible authority, but also his senior brothers. We urged him to apologize. But Mekki completely refused to apologize or admit any wrong-doing. We were all helpless, for Mekki would not compromise and there was no way Father would let him get away with such insubordination.

Before getting up to leave, Father said to Mekki, "I want you to leave Abyei and be out of my tribe by tomorrow." The next morning, Mekki took a lorry going to Wau, where he got employed by the northern governor, ironically promoted by his father's name. After being transferred to the North, he returned to Wau where he and cousin Lino Ayong, then headmaster of the elementary school, died in 1965 in the northern massacre of southern elite during a wedding party. Until his death, Mekki visited home on vacations, but otherwise maintained absolute independence from Father and even made financial arrangements for his mother.

The Unresolved Problem of Ongoing Marriages

A lingering controversy between us and our father was the issue of his marriage. Initially, we were prompted by a controversial case which forced Peter Michar, our schoolmate and one of Father's closest cousins, to raise against him a case which threatened his chieftainship.

Father wanted to marry Anyuat (or Nyananyuat), daughter of Achwei, daughter of Akwol, a female slave of our great grandfather, Arob Biong. Many relatives on both sides objected to the marriage on the grounds that slavery among the Dinka was an institution of adoption which affiliated the slave into the adopting family and made the slave the child of the master. This implied the application of the rules of exogamy which prohibit marriage between relatives. An exception might be made in the case of a sixth or seventh degree relationship through a principal female. Anyuat's case did not qualify for the exception. Father's argument was that adoption by slavery was different from blood relationship or affinity by marriage.

Some relatives on both sides supported the proposed marriage. But those who were opposed were more volatile. They were led by Peter Michar Allor whom Father had virtually adopted as his son. Michar turned into such a bitter enemy that he was rumored to plan assassinating our father. But it was not at all unusual for Father's favorites to become among the bitterest of his opponents. Michar became the pivot of the opposition primarily because he was educated. His case against Father did not stop at the issue of the disputed marriage. He spear-headed the grievances of many people about many issues. Members of our family feared he had our father in a knot.

Much of our conversation in the family concerned the case and the general issue of our father's marriage which had become an obsessive topic. But it was only normal for our father to occupy at least 85% of our in-the-circle conversations whether we were at home or away. Anyuat was just another refuelling point.

The case was pending as the family discussed ways of convincing our father to withdraw or speculated on the consequences of his obstinacy. Abyei court decided in favor of our father, but that was neither surprising nor consoling. It always did. Michar took the obvious road to the North to plead at a higher level. The British district commissioner, Captain Donald Rae, investigated the case in a way that intensified the family's apprehensions. Captain Rae loved the traditional ways of the Dinka and seemed to view our father's Arab cultural inclination with disfavor. He stopped a little short of finding against him and decided to take the case to an intertribal Assembly of Chiefs which met annually and which was attended by prominent personalities throughout Dinkaland. In his introductory speech, Captain Rae gave a summary of the facts, the arguments, and the decision of Abyei court, concluding that Deng Majok's position might have influenced the decision and that he had brought the case to that assembly because he trusted they would not be influenced by Deng Majok's position.

There was a division of opinion, but Father won. All the subsidiary complaints of Michar fell on deaf ears. He himself nearly got into trouble with the subtle grinding machine of Ngok legal process, but was ironically rescued by Father who quickly restored him into the position of a favored "cousin" and a close supporter.

Father's victory brought relief and happiness, but the crucial issue of his marriage and the problems pertaining to it were only fanned into an even greater potential explosion. Although we were still children, we were old enough to reason and we felt we had to talk to him. Our cousin, Justin Deng Aguer, the son of Father's sister, Awor, Bol and I asked for an appointment. Kwol was in school in the North. We spoke of the material burden of constant bridewealths, the increasing family maintenance, the suspicions as to how he made all that possible, the threat posed by the regular complaints of those victimized in one way or another by his marriages, and all the practical difficulties facing him and the family.

Father was very agreeable. He agreed with us and said that many administrators from governors to district commissioners had confided in him that they found excellent reports about him in all respects but excessive marriage. If he could only rid himself of that, he would be unmatchable.[41] He mentioned a few names of girls to whom he was already engaged and said he would complete those marriages, and then stop.

Needless to say, that intention was never realized, for if anything, his marriages accelerated over the years to the extent that he would sometimes have several brides within the same month. By then, our concerns were no longer purely political, for we were beginning to see clearly the economic implications of the family size, especially in the long run when Father would not be there as the provider.

During the last vacation of our secondary school period, Bol, Kwol, and I decided to try again. As usual, we had to make an appointment. This time, we decided to have a tea-party and to invite family elders and a selected number of tribal leaders. The party was very formal. As usual, I was asked by the brothers to introduce our case. I spoke emphasizing the changing values of our times, the importance of securing a more modern and higher standard of living for the family, and the political, social, and material strains Father's continuous marriage was exerting on the welfare of the family. We urged him to invest his wealth in agricultural schemes, shops, lorries, and better housing rather than in more wives. The arguments were known; at least they were not new, only strengthened by repetition and the seriousness of our enhanced age-level.

As I spoke, Father displayed a suspiciously calm but solemn mood. When I finished, he did not comment on my words, he simply wondered whether the others had anything to say. Kwol spoke, essentially supporting my theme. Father, still well controlled and composed, turned to Bol and said, "I have heard what Mading had to say and I have also heard Kwol's words; let me hear your words." Bol had the advantage of a last speaker, for by now it was quite obvious that Father was offended. Bol retracted a little from what we had said: "Father, it is not that we want you to abandon marriage," obviously trying to be conciliatory, "it is that we think it would be better if you would at least allow longer intervals to

---

41. It is interesting that in their responses to the questionnaire on his biography, none of the former administrators, Sudanese and British, mentioned his marriages as an administrative problem.

your marriage, so that instead of marrying every season, you let some time lapse before your next marriage."

When Father eventually spoke, he was more retaliatory than he had ever been on the subject. The thrust of his argument was that sons had no right to talk to their father about his marriage. Our right was to make claims that we were entitled to as children, to have our education provided for, to request our father to buy us commercial lorries, to open shops for trade, or to have our maintenance secured, but not to ask our father to stop marrying. Had he stopped marrying as early as we apparently would have preferred, some of us would not be there to argue on the issue of marriage. He concluded by saying that Bol's line of argument was more persuasive, that he should space his marriages more. In the future, he was not going to entertain any further discussion of the matter. That was that.

To our surprise, all the elders present, who had always supported our line and had indeed impressed upon us that it was primarily our obligation as sons to discourage our father from excessive marriage, appeared so intimidated by Father's response that their attitude was to persuade us to drop the matter. We did. Kwol and I later teased Bol about his last minute compromise. Kwol humorously declared that in the future, far from criticizing Father on the issue of marriage, he would win his favor by encouraging him to marry.

A Remarkable Marriage and its Dissolution

But Bol and I were soon to have a rare opportunity to dissolve Father's marriage to Apiny in Twichland, glamorously celebrated three years earlier. We had indeed accompanied Father on that occasion. To appreciate the import of the divorce, it is necessary to give some background on the marriage and in particular the material and emotional investment made by Father and the family.

It took place during our first vacation from Khor Taqqat and it was certainly one of the most glamorous of Father's weddings. Father went to the home of the bride-to-be in the Twich area of Chief Awich Ayuel with an impressive entourage which included several of his leading associates, a number of his junior wives, and several of us children, Bol, Kwol, cousin Deng Achwil, and me. Some were on horses, others on bulls, and many walked.

At least one hundred cows and some twenty bulls, all carefully selected, were driven by a group of young men. Apparently, the marriage was expected to be difficult to negotiate. Father was being rejected allegedly on the grounds that there was a distant blood feud between the families. But that was understood to be an excuse. The real reason was to make the girl difficult to procure and therefore to raise her value in cattle and enhance the social character of the celebration. As was to be apparent later, the girl herself and her brother were more genuinely opposed, presumably because of Father's large number of wives, but the clan and indeed the tribe were to prove more amenable to persuasion through wealth and social status. Father was known for his readiness to face any challenge of rejection with a determination that knew no limits to his material and socially ostentatious ways of persuasion. So, all this was a way of overwhelming the opposition and reinforcing the supporters.

The afternoon of our arrival in the village of the girl was one of the most dramatic expressions of Father's sense of social vanity and pride. As we emerged from the woods that concealed the open area in which the village was located, some of the riders raced their horses into the stretches of open space, encircled by the wide spreading settlements of the girl's village. As they raced, all dressed in white Jallabiyas, their turbans flying about with the reverse current, a number of gunshots were fired into the air to alert the village of our arrival. The show went on for some time before we came to a stop and selected our camping spot. Father's huge tent was quickly erected before sunfall and instead of the hosts honoring the group by slaughtering bulls, Father quickly had two bulls slaughtered not only for his group but also for the village and visitors from neighboring areas. Not content with that show, Father soon got up for a bird-hunting walk to the pools and lagoons in the area where a variety of geese and ducks assembled. Combining his hunting hobby with the intention of impressing those remote villagers with the power of the shotgun, and adding more hospitality with bird meat, this shooting walk clearly facilitated the process of winning the people to support the proposed marriage.

The following morning, more of the sport of hunting was used to provide meat for the village. Then we moved to another village where the group would be accommodated in huts and where the marriage negotiations were to be conducted. It was there that Chief Awich Ayuel and the leading personalities of his tribe called on Father, as an initial courtesy. They attended Father's assembly for the whole of that day, socializing, but saying nothing directly connected with the wedding, except perhaps to prepare the ground. He was entertained with lavish food and gallons of tea, which was considered special in those remote areas of the rural Sudan. Awich Ayuel seemed won over and a friend to count on. But Father was discreetly active in winning people: men, women, individuals, and groups. Selected persons were busy distributing the gifts of clothes and other town items which we had brought with us. But it soon became evident that our possessions would not suffice, for the circle of those to be won was rapidly enlarging. That was when Father decided to send me to a shop that was some distance away, owned by an old friend of his, Deng Kiir. Luckily, Chief Awich's clerk had come on a bicycle and I was asked to take the bicycle, hoping to be back before they had to leave. This was late morning.

I rode for what seemed to me to be a long time without any sign of the place. Then I came to a village located on an elevated spot. There I saw a lady advancing towards me. She was dressed in long elegant leather skirts trimmed with beautiful beads on all sides. She wore white metal coils on her arms and legs and was otherwise decorated with various ornamentations on her neck, ears, and head. She was clearly a woman of status by Dinka standards and despite her decorated appearance, she was not young; indeed she looked like what the Dinka would call a "mother of a girl", whose daughter could be old enough to be a bride. As I approached her, I stopped the bicycle in order to leave her the way, and as we passed one another, I said in a typical traditional fashion of respect, "Our paths are crossing, may I be excused in passing!"

She stopped and looked back to me as I passed. "Son, where are you from?"

I said I was from the Ngok Dinka.

"And whose son are you?"

I said I was the son of Deng Majok.

She said, "What you have just done has sweetened my heart very much. I used to fear that the education of children was destroying our Dinka ways. Now, you have shown me that this is not necessarily the case. May God bless you to travel in safety and peace."

I passed the village and cycled on. At one point, while in a small forest just before the open space where Dinkas usually build their villages, I asked a passerby where Deng Kiir's shop was. Surprisingly, he asked where I came from. I told him. Then he said, "You still have a very long way to go; you must cycle very fast if you are to reach before sundown." Disheartened but challenged, I exerted my strength even more and peddled as hard as I could. The wide open area beyond the woods was encircled by homesteads from which came a crowd of barking dogs converging on me. This pushed me to go even faster, looking directly ahead of me to make sure my path was not intercepted by a dog, determined to outpace them. That way, I crossed the area without looking around and was well out of danger from the village dogs. I continued to cycle on until I came to what seemed like an endless bridge, cutting through swamps of treeless savannah. By this time, I had difficulty understanding how people could have thought I would bring back the clerk's bicycle before dusk. At one point, I asked a passerby how far the shop was, and he told me it was some distance, but not too far. Then suddenly I arrived at the shop, immediately alongside the road to my left. I was so exhausted that I felt immense relief at the sight of the shop. It did not even bother me to realize that my front tire was losing air and was rapidly becoming flat. That would soon be taken care of.

I was warmly greeted and seated. Then I asked where Deng Kiir was. That was when I first got my real shock of the day. I had not only passed Deng Kiir's shop, but had gone far beyond the territory of Chief Awich Ayuel into an entirely different tribe, Awan of Chief Chan Nyal. The shop was in fact that of Chan's son, Akol, half-brother of Ajang Chan, the haughty student who had refused punishment at intermediate school and had been dismissed. Akol, too, had left school at an even younger age. Akol himself was not at the shop, having just gone to the town of Wau for a few days. I was speechless and motionless. But the people were kind and helpful. They made me tea and mended my tire, then agreed with me that I had to be heading back if I hoped to reach Deng Kiir's shop before nightfall. So I headed back. As I knew the way back, I was not as anxious, even though I was exhausted.

When I reached the area where Deng Kiir's shop was, I realized that it was the same area where the dogs had chased after me and concluded that the man I had asked in the forest nearby had misled me. Why? Perhaps he himself was not from that precise area, did not know Deng Kiir's shop, and was thinking of the shop to which I did go, as that was alongside the road, and could not be missed, while Deng Kiir's shop was farther away from the road.

I arrived at Deng Kiir's shop just before sunset and found him a gentle and kindly man. He received me warmly and was very hospitable. As one of my tires had again gone flat, he had it repaired but then he advised me to spend the night with him and leave the following morning. I insisted that I had to go back that same night as my father needed the items urgently. So he packed the items, mostly clothes, onto the bicycle and he let me leave with great reluctance. Shortly after I left, it began to shower and I almost regretted not having stayed. I could still have returned to Deng's shop, but I was quite determined to proceed on, believing that I could cycle in the rain. I soon discovered that I was wrong, for even before I went far from Deng's village, the mud frequently jammed the wheels and stopped the bicycle. I would get down, clear the mud off the wheels, give it another attempt, be forced to stop soon again, and repeat the whole process all over, a truly slow and painful operation. Again, I felt tempted to return to Deng's shop while I was still near, but I dismissed the thought as ridiculous, for I had already insisted on leaving and it would be embarrassing to admit defeat. In any case, I had to reach my father that same night. So I struggled on, mostly pushing the bicycle while I walked. Even then, I had to stop very frequently to clear the mud off the wheels.

I eventually became convinced that there was no way I could continue pushing the loaded bicycle back to my father's place. I would need someone to help me carry the load. I approached the next person I saw and offered him the job. He was at first tempted by the offer, but soon withdrew on the grounds that he had to attend to his cattle.

Struggling on by myself, I came to a village where I had met the lady. It had now been raining for some time and water had gathered on the ground. This helped wash off the mud so that the problem of getting the wheels jammed had been considerably mitigated. It was beginning to get dark when I suddenly met a group of elders almost exactly on the spot where I had met the lady. They were about four, all tall and stark naked with clothes folded and tied to their spears. As soon as they started talking to me, I realized that this was Chief Awich Ayuel with his followers. Although shocked to see them as naked as any ordinary tribesmen, I quickly decided that such things should be expected in that part of Dinkaland and felt a great relief in having encountered them, for I assumed that the least he would do would be to see me taken home to my father quite safely. It was now darkening so quickly that only the frequency of the lightning helped show the way. Otherwise, the rain, the violent thunder, and the darkness of the night were most frightening.

To my surprise, horror, and shock, Chief Awich simply inquired as to why I was so late and urged me to rush on if I hoped to reach home that night. I had not even said anything then about wanting to reach home that night. When one of his men expressed surprise that he would send me off under dreadful circumstances instead of insisting that I spend the night in his house, Chief Awich Ayuel said, "I have no room; why don't you take him yourself?" I could not believe what I was hearing the chief say. That was when I said that I did not want to be accommodated, but simply needed someone to carry my luggage and guide my way back to my father. Awich's companion again talked to him in a murmur, obviously urging him to do something about my request at least. Awich shamelessly, even loudly, responded that there were no people and directed me to a nearby cattle-byre in the hope that I might find someone to hire.

Infuriated but challenged by this unchiefly behavior, I felt my way to the cattle-byre. As I might have expected, no one was willing to undertake the task. The chief's clerk's house was nearby. When he learned that I was going back under those circumstances and that I had met Chief Awich, he showed clear indignation at the chief's attitude and tried to persuade me to stay with him until the morning. But by this time, anger had driven me into blind courage and determination to continue my way no matter what dangers lay ahead. The clerk could not help me with anyone and so he watched with astonishment as I left.

What lay ahead was miserable beyond expectation and description. So much rain had fallen that the entire ground was flooded and appeared like an endless stretch of lake, noticeable only when lightning flashed. There was no way to tell the path and although frequent lightning continued to guide me away from obvious hazards, I found myself falling into thorny bushes from time to time. On several occasions, when lightning became less frequent, I wandered into heaps of thorny barrages around the gardens and got myself completely entangled. Many times, I fell flat with the bicycle, now heavier than ever as everything was soaked to full capacity. Violent thunder continued as did occasional lightning even though the rain was ebbing. But apart from the many thorns that had pricked me all over, there was reason to fear snakes, scorpions, and of course, hyenas, lions, and leopards. More than once, I broke down and cried in utter despair. I would curse, then pray, and otherwise surrender myself to fate. The world had never, never been so cruel and lonely.

At least twice, I felt my way into a homestead, knocked on a hut, and implored to be guided and helped with the luggage. But I was told that there were no men in the hut, a clear lie I could detect. Then I came to a hut where the men made the mistake of answering but refusing on the grounds that it was too dangerous an undertaking as the area was infested with lions and other ferocious animals. Nevertheless, they did not invite me in for the night. All the prejudices we had grown up with against the Twich as inhospitable became fulfilled. I had nothing but contempt and disgust for them all, from their chief down to the people in the hut to whom I was now talking: "You Twich, I had never really known you before, but tonight, I have discovered you. I am a literate person, and I can write things to be seen and read even when I am dead. My father is Deng

Majok and you know what kind of man he is and what he can do. I am going to write down what you have done to me and how you can be found. If I die, it will be found and read. If I live, I shall tell my father all about it. In either case, you will have no way to escape and you will see with your own eyes what can become of a person who behaves to guests in such an inhuman way as you have done to me. You have your choice, either to take me to my father and be rewarded well for what you have done, or refuse and you will pay the price."

That was absolutely my last trump card. There was dead silence; then a murmur. Finally a voice said, "How much did you say you would pay?"

My answer was unequivocal: "Money is not the problem. My father will pay you all you want, I promise you. Only please take me to him."

Again they complained about the dangers on the way, the darkness, the difficulty of recognizing the way, the wild animals, and the women they were leaving behind unprotected. But, eventually, two men emerged from the hut and we got under way with better feelings towards one another. They proved to have been right about the difficulty of telling the way. Several times, we knocked on people's doors to be redirected and several times we discovered that we had been heading in the wrong direction. Several times, we heard a lion roar even though it sounded some distance away. By this time, our purpose was the same and our fate could be one. We were therefore united and we walked in solidarity.

We reached our destination long after everybody had gone to bed. The two men slept in the cattle-byre while I joined Bol, Kwol, and Deng Achwil in a hut specially allocated to us.

When I told Father the whole story the following morning, it was clear that he was deeply affected and angered by Chief Awich's attitude. My two guides were of course duly thanked and well remunerated by Father. As for Chief Awich Ayuel, although Father did not verbalize his thoughts, the consensus was that there should be some form of retaliation against him. But of course, no retaliation was appropriate or even possible in the circumstances. The only thing to do was to nurse the grievance and otherwise pretend all was well. So, when Chief Awich Ayuel came to see Father that morning, he was well received and given a good time. But if he did not recognize the hidden truth, at least behind my face, then he must have been as insensitive as he was without compassion.

The negotiations went well for Father. The marriage was discussed, agreed upon, well celebrated and concluded. On Father's insistence, we were given the bride to take back with us, thereby bypassing a few steps in the ordinarily lengthy procedure of Dinka marriage.

When word came to us shortly after our return from Twichland that Chief Awich Ayuel had been deposed and that one of his step-brothers, Ring Ayuel, had been instated in his place, I was exceedingly pleased, and further flattered by our elders that his mistreatment of me had been seen by the Spiritual Powers of our clan which had now acted in vengeance.

In Abyei, Father's wedding was again celebrated with lavish festivities augmented by the fact that the bride was accompanied by young Twich girls, entertained by young men through courtship games, singing, and dancing activities, normally associated with such occasions.

That was the marriage we dissolved three years later. Apiny had been sick and had returned home. Since her wedding days, the only time we saw her again was as she was leaving on her sick leave to her family. She then walked gingerly and looked very ill. We were indeed embarrassed not to have learned of her illness and to witness the sharp contrast between the one who had been so much sought after and the retreating one whose severe illness did not seem to have drawn much attention at home. It was no wonder, therefore, that word was later to come to Father that she did not wish to return to her marital home. Repeated messages from Father to her family did not produce any positive results. One day, Father asked me to write a letter to her chief, the successor of Awich Ayuel, to say that he should be sent his wife or have his bridewealth cattle returned. I wrote the letter which was carried by two of Father's retainers, tribal policemen. Father then said, rather casually, that I might have to go myself to demand the return of his wife or claim compensation for the bridewealth. Shortly after we sent the letter, Father went to a council meeting at the district headquarters in Rigl El Fulah. The retainers returned empty-handed, without the wife or the bridewealth cattle.

Our departure date for the final year at school was approaching; Father was still away, having taken longer than had been anticipated and we needed both school fees and pocket money. Rather than risk meeting Father on the way without sufficient money on him, we discussed and decided to undertake the mission Father had wanted me to undertake to return his wife or claim his cattle back. But instead of me alone, I persuaded Bol and cousin Osman (Koc Aguer), Justin Deng's younger brother, to come along with me. We also took with us one of Father's retainers, Abok Chol, who was aspiring to become a policeman, but was then still between categories.

We went on horseback and carried with us sufficient supplies of food and tea. Apart from a night in Ngok territory, where things went as expected, we spent a second night in a Twich village where things were not quite as they might have been in Ngokland. As we arrived at this village at dusk and the clouds seemed to threaten an imminent downpour, we decided to spend the night, if we were welcome. The initial remarks about the destruction our horses were causing to the fields indicated that we were not warmly welcome. It was soon made clear that there was no room in the area. But to proceed would be to risk a major discomfort to say the least and recalling what I had suffered three years earlier, I could not dare take the risk. Abok, who was both verbal and tactful, made it clear to them that they were being embarrassingly rude to the sons of a dangerous man, that it was in their own interest to accommodate us, otherwise they would antagonize Deng Majok, which would not be a wise thing to do. The approach was surprisingly similar to what I had successfully applied on that ill-fated trip from Deng Kiir's shop. Once they heard the name of Deng Majok, they told us that there was a hut which was not being used then and that we could have it. We told them we would use it only in the event of rain but would otherwise spend the night outdoors.

As soon as we unsaddled our horses and settled down, Abok made tea to which we invited the head of the village. This suddenly warmed up the relationship so much so that we felt quite welcome for the night. We also gave him tea, salt, and flour, commodities which were outside their local reach, which deepened the relationship even more.

Then we arrived at the house of the chief, Ring Ayuel, who proved more hospitable than his predecessor. He certainly seemed to understand and sympathize with our mission, which offered the choice of either taking back the wife of our father or claiming the return of our cattle. He began to send for the relatives of the girl and in the meantime tried to inform a few people about our mission. It soon became evident to us that there was a sharp division within the girl's family. Some, perhaps most, wanted the marriage to survive either because of their desire to maintain the relationship with Chief Deng Majok or because they saw the task of returning the cattle as quite formidable, if not impossible.

Before the court convened, we paid a visit to Apiny's family where we were shown lavish hospitality and great courtesy. Then we met with our stepmother, Apiny, herself. In her own gentle and courteous way, she was extremely frank and determined not to return to our family. She argued that there was nothing for her to return to but a circle of crowded and frustrated wives who were so subjected to silent suffering in isolation that they did not even see their stepsons. She challenged us to say how many times we had seen one another since her marriage and we could not

168

argue with her contention that we saw her again just as she was leaving for her home on illness. She said that even during her entire illness, she rarely saw her husband and certainly never saw any of her stepsons. "What kind of a family situation was that?" she asked rhetorically.

We were deeply moved by her words and felt that it would clearly be in our mutual interest to work on Father's second alternative, that we be given back our cattle. That had indeed been our motivation in undertaking the mission in the first place.

When the court convened, I opened our case, presenting the two alternatives and discreetly concealing our preference for the second choice. There was overwhelming support in court for the first alternative, that we be given our father's wife to take back with us, a trend that we could not oppose, though it was at variance with our preference. Luckily, the girl herself and her brother seemed determined beyond persuasion to end the marriage. After I stated our case, backed by statements from Bol and Koc, we turned into spectators as the family members and their public battled among themselves over the two alternatives.

Suddenly, as soon as the court realized that the girl and her brother were determined and that there was nothing they could do about that, there was a turn in the trend of thought, a surprising criticism against the idea that children could be sent to plead a case which might entail divorce. One after another of the elders spoke strongly in praise of our father and his powers of persuasion. They said he could never fail in achieving what he wanted through the power of his words and that he would certainly have succeeded in securing the return of his wife had he been there personally. They were clearly opposed to the case being argued by his sons who were not even old enough or traditional enough to have their lower teeth extracted, let alone to be initiated into manhood, the customary practices of the Dinka. This, they felt, was not only a weakness to our father's case, but indeed an insult to their tribe. There was no way they could simply decide to end the marriage and return the cattle unless and until Deng Majok himself went to declare his will in front of the Twich elders and not by sending youngsters to undertake such a sensitive task, for which they were clearly too young.

We were then reminded of the paramount value the Dinka place on cattle and the difficulty of persuading them to surrender them. Both combine to make divorce extremely difficult among the Dinka. Many relatives contribute to the bridewealth and an equally wide circle on the bride's side share in its distribution. They also contribute to what is called reversed bridewealth, about a third of the wealth paid by the groom's family, but from their own cattle. These too are shared by all those relatives who contribute to the payment of the bridewealth. In case of divorce where the marriage has produced children, the husband loses his cattle, for the marriage is deemed to have achieved its purpose. Where there are no children, and the fault or the initiative is on the part of the wife's family, then all the living cattle, the very cattle and their offspring, must be returned. Since some of these would have been disposed of in other marriages or transactions, this may threaten other divorces or contractual problems. If the fault lies with the husband, then he must wait until the woman remarries to be compensated by the new husband. On both sides, therefore, divorce was economically and socially most undesirable. That was the gist of the problem we encountered with Twich elders. They could not fathom returning the large number of cattle Deng Majok had paid and which had been widely distributed and had naturally multiplied over the years.

The hostile trend of thought was none other than a strategy to deter us away from our case, to prolong Twich possession of our cattle, and perhaps to frustrate our entire claim to their return. Because we clearly understood the purpose, we refused to be intimidated into withdrawal and we applied all the verbal skills we could command to press our case, which was in any case quite strong, for it was now the family of the girl rather than we who preferred divorce as an option, while we remained, at least on the surface, open to either of the two choices.

Chief Ring himself remained persuaded to our point of view. Eventually, he decreed that we be returned our cattle that were still in the possession of the girl's relatives and be compensated for those that were lost. Since the cattle were so many and widely dispersed among the girl's relatives, quite apart from those that had been made use of elsewhere, the process of reclaiming them would be a lengthy one that could go on for years. Since our interest was more immediately focused on procuring some cattle to sell for our school fees and pocket money, we argued that we had no time to wait as our school was opening and that we would be content with returning with any number of cattle that were easily available on the understanding that the rest would be fetched later. After intensive efforts on the side of the chief, we were able to obtain some thirty cows, many of them attractive cow-calves that had matured during the marriage, but had not yet given birth.

We rushed back home where people seemed disturbed not only by the excellent quality of the cattle we had withdrawn from Father's marriage, but even more significantly by the thought that we could have dared to break the marriage of our father in his absence. That he had asked me to present the alternatives never crossed the minds of the people, and, in any case, could not have been Father's genuine intent since he was known to be more interested in the return of his wife than of the cattle. What was worse was the reaction provoked by our selling a good number of the best cattle there were and which most Dinkas thought should have been for breeding and not for sale. The talk surrounding our adventure filled Ngokland and was rapidly moving northwards, where our father was, as we prepared to go back to school in the North. The probability was that we would meet Father on his way back, but we were too late to risk waiting for him at home. So, we left on horses, expecting to take a lorry from the Arab town of Muglad.

Throughout the adventure of divorcing Father's wife, starting from the time we had undertaken the mission, through the tough litigation we eventually won, to our controversial sale of the best of the herd, I felt a continuous strain and uncertainty about what we were doing. It was of course true and unquestionable that Father had asked me to undertake the mission and to present the two alternatives. It was equally true that I knew my father well enough to realize that he was not as interested in returning his cattle as he was in securing the return of his wife. He had never retrieved his cattle from any marriage that had failed, whether the initiative of the dissolution was his or the wife's. It was never his style to initiate divorce and his most effective punishment for any woman who would dare seek the dissolution of their marriage was to abandon taking care of her, but maintain the strings of the marriage as a restriction on her freedom. It was clear to me that what Father had meant was to exert pressure on the Twich to return his wife not his cattle. He had paid well over a hundred cows and bulls three years earlier. These had been distributed among the wide-ranging circle of the girl's relatives. Those that remained in their possession had multiplied; others had been exported off to more distant circles and would not be easy to return if traceable or to compensate for. All in all, Father knew that by giving the more difficult and heavily taxing alternative of returning his cattle, he would be sure to push the Twich public and the wider family circle into pressuring the girl and her immediate relatives to maintain the marriage and ensure the girl's return. Our objective was exactly the opposite and we knew it. By achieving that objective, we had deliberately sabotaged our father's purpose. Compounded with all that was the public reaction to what we had done.

All this gave me a deep sense of guilt which I did not explain to myself fully, let alone to others, but which made me very apprehensive about Father's reaction. The more I thought about it, the more insecure I felt, and the more frightened I became. As we proceeded, we met with people coming from the North and received news of our father's whereabouts. He would come first by car until the point where the rainy conditions would not permit further progress, after which he would continue on horses. Some of the passersby were close enough to tell us that he had heard of what we had done. While they carefully avoided saying anything that might disturb us, they clearly indicated that there was reason to be apprehensive about his reaction. One person, none other than Father's cousin, Michar Allor, who had opposed the marriage of Anyuat to Father, went as far as saying that Father had remarked, "How could the children do this to me?" That only added fuel to a situation which was already close to the ignition point.

While I was buried in my worrying thoughts, we suddenly came across Father and his party, now proceeding on horseback. We got off our horses and embraced each other very warmly, indeed unusually so. My immediate impulse on contact was one of deep relief and an unusual depth of love and affection for my father. Being anyway a convenient time to stop for the afternoon rest, he decided that we should rest together and talk before proceeding in our opposite directions. We talked about everything, frivolous and important, but all with surprising warmth, affection, and smiles – no anger of any kind whatsoever. Even when he did ask how much money we had sold the cattle for and I told him, he only remarked smilingly, "And the two of you are taking all that money by yourselves!?" We smiled back and argued that our needs were extensive. With an air of paternal concern over a prodigal child, he only added, "Send some to your brother, Ahmed," then still in jail at Nahud.

Things could not have gone better with father; I could not have been more reassured in the circumstances. Father never questioned what we had done on his marriage or on the sale of cattle and was quite the contrary, much more friendly and loving than I would ever have expected.

Unsuccessful and Successful Attempts at Mediation

While in the University of Khartoum and after Bol had left for medical studies abroad, my relations with Father involved more serious consultations over family and public affairs. I became increasingly viewed as his advisor and indeed he frequently sought my advice on political and family matters. In particular, Father felt that the increasing role of the educated class in leading or instigating opposition against him was a challenge for us, his sons, among whom I now occupied the leading position, especially as Bol was abroad. My role with respect to the educated class was a complicated and precarious one. Naturally, I shared my father's interests and concerns. To some extent, therefore, I was a party to the measures he took against his opponents. On the other hand, as an advisor, I could influence those measures to bring about constructive moderation to his reaction against his political adversaries. My influence was of course limited and depended on Father's own realization of the dangers or the benefits accruing from any line of action I might suggest. A third dimension to my role was to try to intermediate with my educated colleagues, a function which was by no means easy as the opposition often identified me with my father's position.

For instance, when I tried to reconcile Father with Ireneo Biong Bol, a cousin who had served a prison sentence after unsuccessfully accusing Father of political and civil offenses, he flatly rejected my mediation on the grounds that I was a party to the measures my father had taken against him. He said that he had seen me standing with my father, laughing together as the police were dragging him into prison.

I told Biong that if the purpose was a constructive criticism of Father, pointing out his wrongs or shortcomings, directing him in a way that would improve his leadership, even we, the sons of Deng Majok, would join in such a constructive approach. But if the objective were the overthrow of our father, whatever grievances people felt against him, then they could not expect our support.

Another attempt that failed was in a conflict with a young uncle, Manaw Kwol, Father's half-brother. The conflict between the two came as a result of Father marrying a girl with whom Manaw was in love and whom he continued to pursue even after she had been betrothed to Father. Manaw was tried by Abyei court for soliciting a married woman, was sentenced to imprisonment, and sent to the District Headquarters at Fulah to serve his term, pending his appeal to national authorities. On appeal, the judge thought that the court had been rather biased in favor of the chief and although Father had not participated in the decision, the judge decided to send the case back to him for retrial. While passing through Fulah, I had the opportunity to discuss the case with the judge. He had been a student and therefore a senior colleague in the faculty of law. The judge intimated to me that he saw no cause for punishing the man and that it was in any case rather unbecoming for Father to permit such

173

punishment against his brother over a family affair. With that background, I tried to persuade Father not to retry Manaw, hinting at what the judge had said, but only vaguely to avoid provoking him into insisting on the punishment. It was one of those rare occasions when I felt courageous and vehement with Father. Reluctantly, he agreed to forget the matter if Manaw apologized. I approached Manaw with the help of three other uncles, but he refused to apologize or to be reconciled with Father. No matter how much we tried, we failed.

Manaw then suddenly left the country and went into exile in the Congo, where I later heard from him while I was in England. Later, in the United States, a Dinka student who had been with him in the Congo was to tell me what he had heard from Ngok students about Father's autocratic leadership and my role as his right-hand political advisor and supporter.

A successful example of my efforts at mediating between Father and his opponents involved Lino Wor, Father's distant relative and the first headmaster of Abyei Elementary school who was then teaching in the South and was in Abyei on leave. Wor and Father had been very close but had drifted apart for both personal and political reasons which had to do with Father's lack of support for his candidacy in parliamentary elections. As a result, Wor became alienated and refused to be put up in our house as would have happened otherwise. The mere fact that I initiated a mediation process appeared to have helped. While a number of issues were involved, I urged them to forget the past, restore their old friendship, and resume their cooperation in the interest of the tribe. I was remarkably successful and reconciliation was achieved.

Retrospect

Looking back on the negotiation stories in the family, they mostly centered on third party mediation or bilateral dialogue. While some of the issues involved related to public matters of Father's leadership or governance, most were matters of a personal nature. In either case, there were rights and obligations of kinship in which the rules of the game or the principles of the code of conduct were well established. Mediation or bilateral dialogue created the opportunity for those rules and principles to be invoked. The rest was simply apportioning the reciprocal rights and obligations of kinship as stipulated in the rules or the code of conduct.

Since the fundamental premise was that kinship relations which have been disturbed must be restored to normalcy, the mere fact of talking things out generated a quest for consensus building and resolution of the differences. With negligible exceptions, reconciliation was the eventual outcome in all the cases of conflicts within the family. Even the cases of adultery by sons with Father's wives, which were extreme in the scale of family offenses, the matter was eventually resolved and relations normalized. Arob (Ahmed), for instance, eventually succeeded in winning his father's support in the 1965 parliamentary elections which he contested and in which he won over others, including Lino Wor, who also tried again. Even if Father's support for Ahmed had been motivated by the desire to keep power within the family rather than by a conviction that he was the best qualified, the principle of kinship solidarity prevailed over the divisive differences.

Monyyak (Abdalla) was also threatened with disaffiliation from the family for the same reason of adultery with Father's wives. He even nearly lost his right of succession for that reason. And yet, without any rituals of reconciliation, Father tacitly forgave him, left him in charge of the tribe while he was away for treatment, and although he did not pronounce himself on the ultimate issue of succession, made no hint that he objected to Abdalla as heir to the throne. And indeed Abdalla became his successor with popular support.

Even those relatives like Ireneo Biong Bol and Manaw Kwol who had rejected any reconciliation with Father, eventually normalized relations with him. As for Manaw, he returned from exile and while his rebellious disposition persisted, there was never any question about his loyalty to the leadership of the family.

A far more difficult area of tensions within the family had to do with negotiating the "sentimental" dimensions of father-son relations and the intermediary role of the mother. Talking matters out in this area was very much a bilateral affair between father and son, with the inevitable involvement of the mother. Just as individuals differed in the degree to which they initiated mediation between Father and other members of the family or kinship, so did the disposition of sons to talk it out with Father. Comparatively speaking, I probably took more initiatives in mediating or dialoguing with Father than anyone else among my brothers. Indeed, when I tell them of some of the talks with Father which I initiated, many of them find it difficult to believe that I could have been so daring.

In retrospect, I was a lot more privileged in our family than I credited my father for. There I was, son of a fourth wife, not only treated as an equal to Bol and Kwol, but indeed given reasons to believe that I had a leadership role to play in the family and the tribe. Rather than be content with that degree of recognition and respect, I suppose I was aspiring to a degree of paternal love and affection that was very much in short supply.

Judging from the experiences of the brothers, there were perhaps four types of situations and responses among Father's sons, excluding, of course, the case of Chan who was disabled by illness. The first was that of Arob whose level of success in education and employment in a position of power at a time when both were pioneering achievements, combined with unresolved grievances in father-mother relations, generated an imprudent arrogance and vindictiveness that proved fatally counterproductive.

The second was that of the obviously favored and spoiled children of Nyanbol Amor, specifically Adam and his younger brother Osman, who did not seem much motivated to improve their lot through education and ended up too dependent on Father to sustain themselves beyond his support.

Then there were those of us, of which Bol and I were prototypes, who saw education as a means not only of improving our positions, but also of winning Father's approval.

And finally, there were those for whom the gap of paternal love and affection seemed unbridgeable, either because it was genuinely too wide, which was not very likely, since Father took pride in his belief that he treated his children equitably, or because they themselves exaggerated it and allowed it to destroy their motivation for self-improvement, which was more likely the case. Both Bulabek and Miyar were bright and could have gone far with their education, had they been appropriately motivated. Instead of working to compensate for the disadvantages they felt imposed on them by Father, they thought they would retaliate by abandoning what they knew he valued – education, unwittingly imposing on themselves an even greater disadvantage.

As for Bol and me, our relationship with our father generated enough of a level of insecurity to challenge us to prove ourselves worthy, enough of a level of support to sustain our ambitions and efforts, and enough freedom to allow us to dream beyond the bounds of the tribe. Others were not fortunate enough to have the right balance.

Our fortune was also an obligation that entailed leadership responsibilities that kept us bound to the tribe and the family, no matter how far our education and professional careers took us. The fact that we were educated in the North and the South gave a special significance to the traditionally bridging role of our family. That was indeed the reason the British had given our father to persuade him to accept our going to the South for higher schooling. Paradoxically, our education in the South added to the anomaly of our position as southerners in the administrative context of the North. Indeed, it became a major contributing factor to the disintegration of the Ngok Dinka area as a bridge between North and South. Two personal experiences described in the next chapter represent illustrative pieces from the crumbling bridge between North and South.

5
Pieces from the Crumbling Bridge

Undoubtedly the most pervasive and devastating conflict in the Sudan from which our people have suffered the most has been the war between the North and the South. And while the Ngok Dinka have historically bridged and mediated North-South relations, they have also been among the most devastated by the conflict, being on the borders of hostile camps. As the war in the South intensified, the Ngok Dinka became increasingly identified with the South, which implied the crumbling of the bridge they symbolized. Two personal experiences highlighted the rudiments of these developments in the early 1960s when the war was beginning to intensify. One related to the political circumstances under which our uncle, Bona Bulabek Kwol, died in Europe and the response of the government to the repatriation of his body, and the other concerns a political confrontation I had with the government during the period of my studies in the United Kingdom, having been wrongly accused of masterminding southern opposition in Europe.

A Tragic Death and an Unsympathetic Northern Government
Bona Bulabek died the year of my second visit to Germany. My friend, Tigani El Karib, and I agreed to visit Bol and Bulabek on our way back to the Sudan. While Tigani was to follow by train, I flew with the group to

Rome, intending to proceed to Padova by train and surprise Bol and Bulabek by arriving at their hostel unexpectedly. But as I exited the transit lounge to enter Rome, I was astounded to see Bulabek in the receiving crowd. Could they have heard of my arrival through some other means? Bulabek was with his colleague, Justo Muludiang. But where was Bol? I soon learned that Bulabek had been there to see off someone who was about to take a plane to the Sudan. With Bulabek was Joseph Oduho, the co-leader of the southern movement in exile. Oduho and William Deng had just established the Sudan African Closed District National Organization, SACNO, which was later re-named the Sudan African National Union, SANU. They were then in Italy campaigning for support and finalizing the conceptual details of the organization. In this, they were aided by some southern students in Italy; foremost among whom was Bona Bulabek.

Bol and Uncle Bulabek had already made arrangements to go to Germany, purchase a Volkswagen car, and then drive through Europe into Czechoslovakia, where they hoped to visit Toby Maduot, our school classmate who was then studying medicine in Prague. Although Bulabek could not change his plans because they were connected with important matters in a program that had long been drawn up, it was decided that Bol should stay with us while Bulabek proceeded with Justo Muludiang. They left some time after Tigani's arrival and we were able to spend a few pleasant days together with Bulabek, which gave Tigani and even myself a deeper insight into Bulabek's unique attributes as a genius, an indisputable leader, and yet a man of remarkable modesty, without in any way compromising the dignity he radiated in his bearing, his self-confidence, his deliberation, and his command of language. By that time, Bulabek was entering his final year of medicine and as always in his entire educational experience, he was consistently top of his class and had already been offered a teaching position by Padova Faculty of Medicine after his graduation. He was also very popular with the people in Padova, students, professors, the clergy, and the ordinary Italians. While in effect younger than us, admittedly only by a year or two, he appeared as an elder to us, clearly deserving his status as our uncle.

We did a great many things together in the few days Bulabek spent with us, both in Padova and in Venice. Then he departed early one morning, leaving a note in which he counselled that I should go home to see the family before returning to England. I had received word while I was in Germany that I had been appointed to the faculty as a tutor and would be sent on a post-graduate scholarship to the United Kingdom to qualify fully as a lecturer. Although I was going to the Sudan, it was quite likely that the rainy season would make going home to Abyei rather impractical. Bulabek was urging me to go home whatever the difficulties. In his words, as I recall them, "You must visit your loved ones at home before returning to Europe, no matter how difficult the conditions." It was an extraordinary request considering that it was the rainy season when travelling to Abyei from Muglad, a distance of one hundred and twenty-five miles, meant walking and riding for an average of five days each way.

A few days after settling into my office at the faculty, I received a cable. Something about that cable terrified me. I had, of course, received cables on previous occasions that turned out to be purely idiosyncratic, but something about that cable told me that it bore bad news. It was from Italy. Uncle Bulabek had died in a car accident near Prague. The tragedy and the shock on me personally were and remain indescribable.

A stream of images and reflections rapidly crossed my mind: Bulabek's academic success which the Dinka explained in mythical terms as willed by his father, a spiritual leader, and now his sudden death; the picture of the man with whom we had just been, his unique attributes, a genius whose potential contribution to the family, the tribe, the South, the Sudan, indeed the world, we had felt no doubt about. And now, suddenly, he was no more. What was the logic of it all!? Why was he permitted to distinguish himself so much if it would all end up so purposelessly? Were there really a power and a reason behind all that? If so, what did it mean? I could not see Bulabek just dying and disappearing without any reason behind his death.

I did not want to attract the attention of sympathizers, for according to Bol's message, I was to contact the authorities in the Ministry of Education to arrange for the body to be transported home to the Sudan. As some days had passed since the death, the issue was of the utmost urgency. So I hurriedly contacted Santino Deng, the minister of animal resources, in the hope of cutting through red tape to have a message sent to the embassy to arrange for the transportation of the body to the Sudan. Santino Deng telephoned Ziada Arbab, the minister of education, and arranged to see him, taking me along with him.

I will never forget the manner in which Ziada Arbab welcomed us. In a cold-blooded way, smiling cynically, almost viciously, he said to Santino, "What is the matter, Brother Santino, no work in the ministry!?" At first, I could not believe my ears. Then I thought that he had perhaps not been told of the reason for our visit. But then it occurred to me that he was making the remark precisely because he knew the purpose of our visit. Even after Santino Deng had explained the reason, Ziada Arbab remained unmoved. Indeed, he became worse. First, he explained that the embassy, in fact the government, had no funds for such situations and that the burden for returning bodies home was strictly a family affair. I suppose he thought that we would be intimidated into surrendering to the official position that Bulabek be buried abroad. When we said to him that the family would pay, but that in view of the urgency of the situation we wanted the government to help on the understanding that it would be refunded later, Ziada then reached his worst: "Brother Santino," he said, "let us be frank. Our people are poor and need every bit of money we possess in order to meet the essential needs. Why would the government or for that matter the family pay some four hundred pounds just to return a dead body for burial at home!? Let us stop being sentimental and face realities. We should have him buried there and be over with the problem."

That was more or less his final word, rational-sounding, perhaps persuasive to some, but totally hypocritical, in fact racist, because we knew he could never have said that to a northern Sudanese family. In all probability, he was ignorant of the person involved, the sentiments of his people about him, and the pride and weight of his family. We left his office with more determination than ever to face the challenge to the very end. But then, we learned that the instructions had already gone from the Ministry of Education that the body be buried in Europe. Judging from the lapse of time, it must have already been buried by the time we were struggling for the authorization to bring it back home. Nevertheless, I refused to be forced into submission. So, I contacted the Czechoslovakian Embassy to enquire into the law and practice pertaining to the exhumation and exportation of human remains. They told me that it would take about three to six months after burial to exhume and that the body could then be exported under certain conditions.

Having established the principle of eventually exhuming and repatriating Bulabek's remains, I decided to leave for home immediately, despite the fact that the road had closed and I would have to travel on foot or on horseback from Muglad to Abyei. I recalled Uncle Bulabek's message that I had to visit the family before leaving for England and could not help seeing some prophecy in his words. I left Khartoum, but not before we had generated an awareness in southern circles of the treatment which the government had given a distinguished son of the South, a pivotal though little known southern leader. I recalled the role Bulabek had played in promoting William Deng and Joseph Oduho and his overall activity for the southern cause – the very reason for his going to Prague. Then I wondered whether Bulabek's accident had really been natural or had perhaps been planned. The attitude of Ziada began to raise doubts in the minds of the southerners, foremost my own, as to whether Bulabek had not indeed been killed by a hired truck driver. That was the thought I left with on my way to Abyei and that was the sparking thought I left among the southerners in Khartoum. A political movement around Bulabek's death, focusing on the return of the body, had begun as I left, infuriated and challenged by Ziada's attitude which I took to reflect the considered and concerted position of the Sudan government – the official, racist attitude of the ruling Arab North.

I left for Muglad and quickly found my way to Abyei on horseback. I had deliberately sent word ahead so that my time in Abyei would not be wasted on the devastating reaction to the news or the inertia of the mourning rituals. By the time I got to Abyei, the family had just received the news and was still in mourning, with Father still sitting on the ground according to custom. But the atmosphere had sufficiently settled down and was ripe for a serious talk about the circumstances of Bulabek's death and the challenge that the family must face. My father was most attentive to everything I had to say and his response was swift and clear. He convened a meeting of the leaders of the clan and presented the situation, discreetly insinuating some sinister reason behind Bulabek's death, but understating the political angle, and emphasizing the challenge to our dignity involved in bringing back the body. The message was very well received and cattle were quickly collected and sold. Within ten days, the required amount was collected and I was ready to return to Khartoum.

Although my visit home was prompted by Bulabek's death, it was something he had requested me to do and as it turned out, it provided a rare opportunity for a significant contact with the family that was to be my last for seven years. One outcome of the visit, apart from the fund-raising for Bulabek, was my daring to record a variety of Dinka songs, arguing that as I would be far away from home for at least two years, these songs would provide me with a useful cultural link with my people. I asked my father whether he saw any objection to my recording in the mourning circumstances. My father fully appreciated my reasons and dismissed any other considerations as secondary. I borrowed a tape recorder from an Italian missionary, but as the recorder lacked batteries, we used the generator of the local government radio communication system for electricity. That meant recording in the small office in which the generator was located. My father not only invited singers, both groups and individuals, but also attended the recording sessions himself. It was perhaps the first time the process of tape-recording had been publicly displayed among the Ngok Dinka and the response was quite enthusiastic, far more than I could possibly have anticipated. An obvious reason behind the popular interest in the recording was the interest my father demonstrated in the project. I recorded samples of virtually all forms of Dinka songs, including group songs that are professionally composed and personal songs that must be composed by the individual singer.

It was during that visit that Father talked to me about appointing a deputy from among the two senior sons at home, Kwol [Adam] and Monyyak [Abdalla]. He began by saying that he considered Bol and me as having transcended the tribal context and become sons of the Sudan. Between Kwol and Monyyak, he said that elders were arguing in favor of Monyyak on the grounds that he was a son of the first wife. He said he told them that they were both his sons. He then asked me which of the two boys I thought would be more suited for the position.

He had talked to me years earlier about his intentions to have Kwol appointed and he had indeed asked me to write a letter to the central government authorities to put the idea forward. But the issue had been dropped and we had not discussed it any more until that occasion of my departure for Europe.

Before he talked to me, I had heard much talk, especially from the women, concerning the rivalry that had already built up in the family. By then, Abdalla had not yet committed adultery with Father's wives; it was therefore a case of individual qualifications and mother's order of seniority.

My answer to him was that I had no preference to express because in a way I saw merits on both sides. Kwol was a senior son with experience and had already been designated earlier, but being from Kwol's section, I might be considered biased in expressing preference for him. On the other hand, Monyyak had considerable virtues, quite apart from being the son of the first wife, especially in his politeness and willingness to listen to advice. Although I did not tell Father, Monyyak had indeed flattered me by saying that whenever he was confronted with a talking situation, especially with Father, he would first ask himself what Mading would say and then proceed to say that. I told Father that one must tell the truth and that as far as I was concerned, the issue of mother's seniority should not be the determining factor. The choice should be for a person who was seen as possessing the qualities required for the responsibility. Should that person be Monyyak or Kwol, the criterion should be who would best serve the interests of the tribe. I concluded:

> So, I do not have a word to say in preference of any one of the two, but one thing I want to tell you personally is not to delay the decision and allow the people to drift apart on the issue. If you should delay the decision too long, people will become so divided that it may prove difficult to maintain the unity and harmony of the family. If you should quickly decide on any one of the two, yours will be the way everyone will follow.

We left it at that. He did not comment on what I said. And of course, he never did anything about it to the end.

From the time I left Khartoum, developments were already under way towards placing the issue of Bulabek in its correct political perspective. Southerners in Khartoum began to mobilize both politically and for the purposes of fund raising to ensure the repatriation of Bulabek's body. By the time I was heading back, the pressure had been sufficiently monitored and the government had been alerted to the political alarms that were potentially buried under the drive for funds. They were to act precisely on time to defuse the political bomb, not only in deciding in a cabinet meeting to exhume and return the body, but also publicizing the decision to ensure that it was heard in Abyei and throughout the South to counter any political movement that might be provoked by Ziada Arbab's initial reaction.

So, on arriving in Khartoum and confirming the news of the government's decision, I simply handed over to Santino Deng the sum of money that had been collected by the family. We agreed that it would be used for the transportation of the body, if necessary, or in any activities that might be associated with the return of the body, when that eventually materialized.

As it turned out, Bol had taken the body from Czechoslovakia to Italy and after going through the dreadful experience of opposition by the Catholic clergy that Bulabek not be buried on the church property because he had gone to a communist country, he had secured a plot in a private burial ground of a family that were Bulabek's friends, and had proceeded to bury him. The body was to be exhumed several months later and sent to Khartoum where it was buried with all the rituals and dignity of a repatriated leader. He now lies in the grounds of the war cemetery, appropriately named even for the peace-loving civilian that he was. That issue resolved, I left for England with two colleagues, Natale Olwak Akolawin, a southerner from the Shilluk, and Mohamed El Fateh, who had also been appointed on the faculty.

An Accusation of Masterminding Southern Opposition in Europe

My time in England started rather smoothly and constructively. But it would eventually develop into the second piece from the crumbling bridge at Abyei, which had historically linked the North and the South.

As a result of connections I had made in Germany, I was put in contact with an English family which introduced me to a Lady King, the widow of Sir Edwin King, who had been a Colonel in the British army. Lady King had been knighted in her own right because of distinguished humanitarian service during World War II. After her husband's death, she moved from their large mansion into a smaller house that she named, "The Little House". Apart from Flora, the maid, who came in daily, Lady King's companions were her dog, Lassie, and her cat, Ackie.

Lady King never had a child, although she loved children. She would later end her letters to me with the phrase, "The children send their love." The children were Lassie and Ackie. There was clearly a vacuum to be filled. A family bond that superseded the tenant-landlady relationship soon developed. Apart from the physical comforts of the Little House and Lady King's "motherly" care, I found East Finchley well suited to my personal likes. It was relatively quiet, clean, and greenish, more a suburb than part of London.

That tranquility was soon disturbed by a health condition that would feed into the politics of the cracking bridge and compound the crisis. I had been suffering from a chronic case of glaucoma that had gone undetected since my high school days. It was eventually diagnosed during my last year at Khartoum University when it had begun to impair my vision. Not knowing much about the disease, I had been oblivious to its implications. It was only after going through what were at first considered successful eye operations during my second visit to Germany and was told by the ophthalmologist that I had narrowly escaped blindness that I began to realize the danger that had confronted me. Soon after settling in, I went for a check-up as directed by the German doctors. The results were unexpected and shattering: the pressure was high in both eyes. I was back to the original problem; worse, I was now rather well-informed about the dangers of glaucoma and the threat of blindness associated with it. A series of tests further revealed that the pressure on the right eye could not be controlled with the drops. Another surgery was necessary.

I began to ponder a great deal on the ultimate outcome. The doctors had congratulated me for having escaped blindness with the success of the operation in Berlin. That the operation proved after all to have failed indicated that the threat of blindness was back. But what did that really mean? Would I be blind in a few years or at a later stage of my life? Or was it possible that I could delay the fate into old age? Any of these possibilities was simply dreadful. Whether the blindness was an immediate threat or an old age eventuality, it was almost equally frightening. However, time was significant if only as a matter of degree. In this respect, I had the choice between being fully informed and leaving room for doubt and perhaps hope.

I eventually decided to face the truth. On my next check-up, I told the doctor that I wanted to know the prognosis so that I could plan my life accordingly. What did he think were the odds of my getting blind and what time span was involved? His answer was the straw that broke the camel's back: "If you think you will be blind in two or three years, no, you won't. You will probably see as you do now for five years, perhaps ten. Beyond that, it is difficult to tell." I took his answer to be a license of clear vision for three years definitely, five years possibly; beyond that, unlikely, if not improbable. In posing the question, I had clearly over-estimated my ability to take the news. The focus was now on juggling with the years and giving practical significance to whatever I might choose to do.

But what would I do? Was there need to study if I could not make use of the results in any professional sense? Should I go back home and entrust myself to the unfailing care of my family? But could I possibly stand that kind of return in helplessness to a people who had always seen an immense purpose to my life? Could I conceivably live, a recipient of charitable affection and care without any meaningful contribution? Of what use was I? As I lay on my back, going home with Dinka songs that my father had helped me record, feeling a strange affinity in the sadness of Arab songs, I felt a deep fall from great heights and from the even greater heights of a future that had seemed so reachable, but now appeared clearly beyond my reach.

It was during this dismal period that Monyyak wrote to me, explaining the deterioration of his relations with Kwol, apparently in the rivalry over chieftainship. According to Monyyak, Kwol had severed himself with his company of supporters and was virtually avoiding him. I wrote to Father, telling him of what I was hearing about the situation at home, recalling my discussions with him and urging him to make a decisive move.

Father did not respond to my letter, but he sent me a letter that was to mean a great deal to me. It was delivered by a province judge who was then on an official visit to Britain. In that letter, Father explained the political situation in the tribe, the province, and the country, focusing in particular on his conflict with the new governor of Kordofan, Ali Beldo, a notorious name in South-North relations. He asked me to give special attention to the visiting judge who was his ally in the confrontation with the governor. Referring to the attitude of the governor, reported later to have said to Father that he could join his brothers in the South if he wanted, Father wrote that he now knew where he belonged, implying emphasis on his southern identity. Father concluded his letter by saying that he told me all that because he considered me the High Dam of the Dinka. He urged me to work hard in my studies as a tool for serving the interest of my people.

Of course I knew Father's expectations from our education and its relevance to the interests of our people. Nonetheless, the sentiments or views expressed in his letter came as an unexpected flattery. Bol visited me about the time I received the letter and I shared it with him. His only comment was: "Lucky you to be called the High Dam of the Dinka by Father!"

Father had often praised us, Bol and me, but never had he been so forthright about his expectations from me or the burden of responsibility he saw resting on me as a future leader of my people. That vision of my future role for my people was now at best blurred if not diminished.

A series of events began to take place that would help me reconstruct a sense of purpose and drive. I give examples of these to show not only the resilience which my past had ingrained in me and which became an asset in a situation of diminishing self-esteem, but also the precariousness and fragility of the person whom Sudan was to accuse of masterminding southern opposition activities in Western Europe. It is only by understanding the crisis I was in, the efforts I was exerting to redeem myself, and the momentum of hope that was beginning to emerge that one can fully appreciate the devastation I was to feel.

One of the people who helped me free myself from the doom psychology and discover constructive purposes to my life was a lecturer in anthropology at Oxford University. I was one day standing, talking with a group of students in the senior common room of the School of Oriental and African Studies when a man in his forties walked over and patted me on the back while I was in the middle of whatever I was saying. When I turned to him, he said in a casual manner and as though he had not interrupted our conversation, "Are you a Dinka?"

In the circumstances, the appropriate reaction might have been to be dismissive, albeit discreetly. Somehow, I was surprisingly cordial. "Yes, I am a Dinka," I responded smilingly.

"Which Dinka?" he went on asking in the same spirit.

"Dinka Ngok," I said.

"Oh! I have a rather nice photograph of your Chief," he added.

"Who!?" I asked, just to be sure.

"Deng Majok," he said.

"That's my father."

I had a glass of coke in my hand. In a manner quite consistent and which I was becoming increasingly intrigued by, he said, "Put that down and let us go to a pub for a drink." I did exactly as he commanded, smiling with surprise. We left the room without even excusing ourselves from the group. I soon learned that my companion was Godfrey Lienhardt, whose fieldwork in anthropology had been carried out among the western Dinka of Bahr el Ghazal province.

I later received a proposal from Godfrey that we jointly present a talk in the BBC Third Programme on the subject of "Man in Society", in which he had been scheduled to speak on the Nilotics. I liked the idea and quickly recalled the moving Dinka songs I had recorded with my father's assistance. How effective it would be to illustrate whatever I would say with the live voices of the Dinka singing about their religious devotion, their spiritual concept of authority, their material and aesthetic dedication to cattle, their loyalties to family ties, their pride in their Dinka ways and the worries and agonies they felt about the disintegrating impact of ill-guided change.

Godfrey liked the idea and so did the program director. Naturally, the material in the songs would be even more enriched by translating the excerpts into English to be read immediately following the voices, wherever appropriate.

The BBC program thus introduced me to the treasures of my song-collection which eventually went far beyond the pleasures of listening to the tapes. I had initially recorded the tapes for expected nostalgic reasons as a prospective link with home. Now, they were playing an educational role and evolving into a source of information on various aspects of the Dinka. I was now making use of words translated into English rather than merely listening to the sounds of Dinka songs. Godfrey soon realized that the quality and the quantity of my collection offered a significant potential and suggested that he and I work on producing a volume of Dinka poetry for the Oxford Series of African literature that he himself edited with E. E. Evans-Pritchard and W. H. Whitely. The opportunity could not have come at a better time, for even as my academic and professional future seemed dim and doomed, I could see some salvation and lasting value in the production of a volume that would embody a vital expression of an important aspect of my people's tradition. Highly motivated by this opportunity, I worked industriously on translating the songs and found solace in the process.

Another idea that germinated from my contact with Godfrey Lienhardt was his suggestion to the editors of the Stanford series on social anthropology, George and Louise Spindler, that we co-author a volume on the Dinka. The project would be delayed and eventually revived for me to carry out alone several years later. But at the time, the proposal added to revitalizing a sense of purpose or mission at a time of my greatest need.

An event which, in retrospect, also had a constructive impact on my situation was a study tour I made to Sweden in the Summer of 1963 on the invitation of a Swedish artist and writer, Percy Bucklund. It was on the Nile steamer on my second visit to Germany that I first met Percy and his wife Margarette. Percy had been to the Sudan, had traveled down the Nile to the South, and was now back guiding a group of Swedish tourists visiting the Egyptian and Nubian antiquities on which he had become an expert.

That evening, Percy asked me to join him and his wife on the deck of the steamer. He started to speak about his disenchantment with Western civilization, his discovery of the spiritual wealth of Africa, the Middle East and the Orient, and his desire, through his writings, paintings, and music, to educate the West about those spiritual and cultural values.

I was a ripe captive for Percy's ideas as I was at the brink of cultural revival, reacting to an educational process that had denied the dignity of our people's heritage in every aspect of modern life. Of course, I was excited about going to Europe, but I had begun to recognize and respect my background in a more substantive sense than personal identification with my father and family background.

My response to Percy was one of enthusiasm and the more I discussed with him the more he seemed to feel that he had tapped the African of his dream. Unbelievable! So excited was he that he not only invited me to visit Sweden, travel with him, and co-author a book on his country as viewed from the perspective of an African, but suggested that I abandon my mission to Germany so that we could immediately start our work on the project. Of course, I could not abandon the German tour, but I promised to visit Sweden on the earliest possible opportunity. My first summer vacation in England was such an opportunity.

Percy had formulated a broad-based program of extensive travel around the country, to the extreme North, visiting the Lapps, detouring into Norway, to the East into the Finnish border, to the West as far as Göteborg, to the South as far as Lund and into Denmark, with Stockholm as the base to which we returned from time to time. The program itself was varied, comprehensive, and intensive. We visited town halls, newspaper offices, academic institutions, factories, paper mills, mines, old peoples' homes, hospitals, prisons, reformatories for juvenile farms, delinquents, churches, remote villages, private homes, parks and forests. We talked to government officials, business executives, editors of provincial newspapers, journalists, writers, artists, architects, professors, students, doctors, patients, prison governors, juvenile delinquents, housewives, old people, young people, important personalities and ordinary people. We even attended meetings of spiritualists where people, including university students, became "possessed," reborn again, and witnessed spiritualists put the living in contact with dead relatives. Perhaps for my benefit, a medium even managed to have Dag Hammerskjöld, the late Swedish Secretary-General of the United Nations, address the audience. An audience with the King was even suggested, but I turned it down, more in resistance to what I saw as excessive exploitation by my host than a rejection of the opportunity.[42] We lived in youth hostels, in rented rooms, in private homes, in cabins, and sometimes at the stations. We talked intensively with the people we met and either took notes as we talked, which Percy preferred, or wrote later, which I preferred. We were continuously on the move, and constantly at work. Even social functions were part of the work. Wherever we went, we saw anyone we wanted to see and received considerable courtesy and hospitality. In most places, our visit was covered in the local press whether or not we met with the editors of the local papers. And the image of me which Percy had half seriously and half humorously promoted was that of an African Prince, which somewhat disturbed my sense of propriety but helped open doors.

---

42. I was eventually to meet the King as ambassador of my country only a few months before he died.

As our tour of Scandinavia was approaching its end, Percy suggested that we proceed to Paris, where he had made an appointment for us to meet with T.S. Elliott. By then, I felt the tour had taken too long and I also wanted to visit old friends in Germany and the Netherlands. Percy and I agreed to part and reunite in London.

I had only been back in London for a few days when Percy joined me, most excited about his meeting with T.S. Elliott to whom he had explained that the "African Prince" had had to change plans at the last minute due to unforeseen circumstances.

I kept my commitment to Percy that I would write a report on our visit. I did that with a sense not only of duty but also of purpose and pleasure since it crystallized my own views on a variety of important matters. Indeed, I wrote with considerable depth of reflection, summarizing my observations under four main themes: "The Impact of Alien Religions in Africa," "Racialism at the Meeting Point," "The Family as a Symbol of Solidarity," and "The Paradox of Contemporary Civilization." Although I did not know it at the time, these would become the basis of my first works to be published. One, "Racialism at the Meeting Point", was entered into a nationwide contest and was included in an edited volume on race relations in Britain (Tajfel & Dawson 1965). Four others were published in a series by the Hibbert Journal. Almost from the moment of its commencement to its very end, my tour of Sweden was an intensive treatment from which I emerged exhausted, dizzy, and hardly able to stand on my feet, far less distinguish between what was real, what was a dream and what was a nightmare. Yet, the experience had a cleansing cathartic effect. As I reflected on that reality, that dream, or that nightmare, I felt the strength of a new education that was relevant to the reality of my critical situation.

It was then that I became a victim to the capriciousness of the government's repressive policies in the North-South conflict. With the turn of 1963, the political situation in the southern Sudan continued to deteriorate. The southern movement abroad was intensifying its struggle. All this was reflected in the United Kingdom and to a certain extent in the relations between southerners and northerners.

My position with respect to the southern movement was a precarious one. Of course, I shared the position of all southerners against the government's southern policy, but there were significant differences. Southerners generally professed separation, either as a means to achieving less extreme goals, or as a serious political objective. I stood for a united Sudan in which the South would enjoy autonomy combined with equality in the sharing of national power and wealth. But whatever the objectives, there were different ways for attaining them and there had to be different roles for those concerned with the problem. I chose for myself the individual role of discussing, lecturing, and writing as an advocate of the southern cause to northerners and foreigners alike, but not engaging in any organized political movements. As southerners and northerners seemed to believe in a clear-cut position where one had to be either a southerner or a northerner, in favor of or against the status quo, my position was confusing to both. But I made my views known to both, hardly concealing anything about my convictions or my actions. And often, this provoked both.

This was perhaps most marked when William Deng, the southern nationalist leader and co-founder of the movement in exile, visited London, and all of us, southerners, met him. The news of his presence in London was in the British press. One day in the midst of a heated discussion with northerners, I was asked by Osman Sid Ahmed, one of the senior Sudanese colleagues, a Muslim Brother, whether I had met William Deng. I said I had. Alamin, a graduate student of history, surprised me with an emotional outburst, even calling me "a traitor". I was most surprised because Alamin had been very solicitous and friendly towards me.

That confrontation revealed to me that to most northerners in London, I was probably more dangerous than any other southerner in Britain. I was an active member of the executive committee of the Sudanese students in the United Kingdom and as always, I associated with all Sudanese, southerners and northerners alike. But to those who did not know me well, my close association with them, my open discussion of the political situation, and my frankness in voicing my views, probably made me seem particularly cunning. Indeed, although I did not realize it at the beginning, it began to dawn on me that most of the graduate students were senior government officials who had not known me before and therefore had not known my political background in both the secondary school and the university, nor my family position on provincial and national politics. Taking me simply as a southerner, they probably concluded that if I could be so critical in their face, I must be dangerously hostile behind their backs. That was precisely the gist of Alamin's accusations: that I pretended to be a close friend while I was in fact an enemy.

Although my southern colleague, Natale Olwak, was politically very active, he generally kept his distance from the northerners in so far as discussion of the southern problem was concerned and gave little evidence of his political involvement. This was of course the attitude of the southerners in general and one I had used to criticize in Khartoum University. Natale, who had been present in the heated discussion I referred to above, but had largely been silent, later expressed his surprise and even anger at my admitting to having met William Deng. He said he could not believe I would be naive enough to admit meeting a political dissident who had been sentenced to death in absentia. I told him that quite apart from my disposition to tell the truth, I could not see how northerners could expect us not to meet a southern nationalist leader who was promoting a cause we must obviously share; if they did not think we were lying by claiming not to have met William, they should disrespect us for being indifferent to the cause of our people.

Natale's own manner of handling South-North relations was demonstrated by a small incident involving Laurence Wol, a graduate of Fribourg University in Switzerland. Laurence was the editor of the southern movement's publication, "The Grass Curtain". Laurence and Natale worked very closely together on "The Grass Curtain". One time, our northern colleague, Mohamed El Fateh, visited Natale and found Laurence with him. Not wishing to be identified with Laurence as a southern activist and Laurence desirous of concealing his identity from the northerners for security reasons, they both pretended that Laurence was a Zairian who spoke only French. I felt scandalized by their own account of what they had done.

The ambivalent attitude of the southerners towards me was manifested when Bishop Mason of Bahr el Ghazal, who had been expelled with other missionaries from the South, came through London on his way to the United States to promote the southern cause. All the southerners, including my cousin, Michael Deng Abyiem, a Sudan airforce flight engineer who was on a course in Belfast and was then visiting London and putting up with me, went to meet him at the airport. I was left completely ignorant of the whole situation until cousin Michael felt morally obligated to inform me about the incident and the general attitude of the southerners towards me. When I confronted my southern colleagues on the issue, Natale was forced to explain that the problem involved the life or death of many, and that I was in dangerously close contact with northerners.

Professor Anthony Allott, pleased with my performance in African law, and with the materials I had collected on Dinka customary law, offered to sponsor me for the Ph.D. program. I wrote to the Sudan, supported by ample medical reports, arguing that I needed an extension of my course period because of the interruption imposed by eye operations for chronic glaucoma during the first year and also because of the opportunity offered by Professor Allott, that I proceed with the Ph.D. course in African law. A short time after my letter had gone, I was called into the cultural attaché's office. A letter concerning me had arrived from Khartoum, and he wanted to convey the contents to me personally. I was impressed, but surprised that Khartoum had responded so soon. The question in my mind was whether they had approved or rejected my request.

I went. The cultural attaché, Bushra Abdel Rahman, who had been our headmaster at Khor Taqqat, was remarkably detached when he conveyed the message that was to change the course of my life – I had been recalled and should return to the Sudan immediately. The letter was from the minister of education and not the University of Khartoum. That in itself was surprising, but not very much so, since the autonomy of the university had been curtailed by placing it under the minister of education, then Talat Fareed, one of the pillars of General Abboud's dictatorship. Naturally, I wanted to know why I was being recalled, but Bushra Abdel Rahman had no answer. I wanted to know many things about the meaning of the recall, whether it had been initiated by the university, whether it had something to do with my request for extension, whether the University was repudiating my appointment, whether! whether! whether! My mind was suddenly streaming with questions. But Bushra knew nothing or at least played ignorant, continuing to reveal a detachment that began to look suspicious to me, especially in view of my long association with him and my expectation that he would show interest in my future.

It then began to dawn on me that there was probably more to it than my request for extension. It was even possible that the recall was decided in ignorance of the request for extension. Might it be political? The answer seemed obvious to almost everybody, particularly southerners, except me. My political position in favor of autonomy for the South within national unity had always been considered so moderate that southerners viewed it as pro-North. My criticism against the status quo had also been so open that it could never have come to any one as a surprise. So, what could possibly have provoked the regime to consider me subversive? And how absurd that I could be suspected of subversion when one of the most active southerners, Natale, my colleague, remained completely unaffected.

Natale and the other southerners found an easy explanation in my close association and frank discussions with northerners. Although it seemed possible, especially in view of the violent discussions I had had with some northerners, it also seemed unbelievable that of all the southerners in England, the government should single me out for anti-North activities when I was the least extreme or the most moderate of them all.

Be that as it may, what was to be my response? On the one hand, it seemed quite obvious that if the reasons were political then to go back would be to risk persecution, especially as the southern problem had intensified and was driving the northerners into a political hysteria. On the other hand, to refuse to go would be to become a political refugee for the duration of the southern problem, to which there was no end in sight. And then there was the problem of my eyes. To go and risk being locked up in jail without the care I so badly needed would be certainly to accelerate blindness. But, to remain a refugee abroad would mean that even if the problem of the South was eventually solved, I would be almost certain to become blind in exile. It was a predicament for which there did not seem to be easy answers.

I decided to play delaying tactics, aimed primarily at refusing to go without saying so. First, I sent a message to the Sudan through the cultural attaché's office enquiring into the reasons for my recall. A message quickly came back saying the reasons would be given on arrival and repeating that I should proceed to the Sudan immediately. I sent another message, this time in a letter through the cultural attaché, in which I raised a series of questions about the recall: whether it had been initiated by the university or by someone else with the university's knowledge and consent, and whether it was a termination of my employment with the university and the associated scholarship. If that were the case, I should feel free to seek alternative employment and scholarship opportunities. I was trying to view the situation from the perspective of contractual relations and deliberately ignoring the political angle so that my refusal would not be interpreted as a political reaction but only as a response to the termination of the contract and its implications on my career. To my surprise, they instructed the cultural attaché to terminate all payments to me, including the scholarship and the transferred part of my salary.

Their action made their motives even more obvious. Natale and I had already begun to gather bits and pieces which substantiated our suspicion that the recall was politically motivated. But perhaps the most direct evidence I received in London was in a telephone conversation between a northern colleague and the military attaché, Muzamil Ghandour. The northern colleague had come to visit me in the Little House and learned for the first time the news of my recall and the termination of my scholarship. He insisted on calling the military attaché and although I tried to discourage him from doing so while with me, he would not be dissuaded. When I tried to leave the room to give him privacy, he insisted that I should listen to the conversation. Of course, I only heard what he said, but it was not difficult to construct what was being said on the other side and in any case, he himself told me the whole story. As soon as he heard my name, the military attaché responded with "Oh, him; I know of his hatred for northerners. He is very active against the government." My friend said to him, "Are you sure you know the person you are talking about? That cannot be Francis; in fact, he is a northerner from Kordofan. You really ought to meet him and you will see how wrong you are." The conversation went on and it seemed that the military attaché was convinced about his judgement. They ended the matter inconclusively and my friend undertook to pursue it with the military attaché whom he said was a childhood friend.

Although the political motives of my recall were obvious to all those in London, it was the letter from my colleague and friend, Tigani el Karib, which clarified the situation from within. Tigani gave me the full account of my case in Khartoum, the intelligence reports that had gone to the Sudan about me, the instructions of the minister of education to the university that I be recalled, the refusal of the vice-chancellor to act in accordance with that instruction as there were no academic grounds for doing so, and the final decision by the minister of education to recall me himself. Tigani made it clear that the whole issue was political and that I was clearly being accused of subversive activities. But he left the ultimate decision of whether to return or not to me personally and implored me not to be influenced by others in making the decision. Tigani's brother, Salah, was, ironically, the only northerner in London to advise me openly against going back and, as he was to tell me years later, found himself under heavy attack from the other northerners.

The Little House became an active meeting place between the southerners as they pondered over my predicament, showing me sympathy and solidarity, but also secretly and not so secretly cherishing the idea that I, who had always seemed so friendly and politically moderate towards the North, should be the victim of the North. Their attitude was not so much a result of ill intention towards me as it was pleasure in the lesson I was learning, and the hope that I would be provoked into becoming more militant in the struggle. With this set of ambivalent calculations, their concern over my problem did not seem to me a spontaneous gesture of brotherhood and solidarity; rather, I saw it as largely a tactical political imperative. But nonetheless, I appreciated the fact that they were after all southerners and that it was that common bond which made them particularly interested in my crisis. Whatever their ulterior motives, they were part of what united us behind the common struggle in which our differences were more in the form and the degree of our militancy against the system rather than in the essence of our struggle.

Chief Enharo of Nigeria had just been extradited back to Nigeria and was very much in the news. Although the British government was being subjected to extreme criticism for permitting extradition for alleged political crimes, a precedent had been established which could be successfully invoked by the Sudan government against me. I went to Oxford to see Godfrey's brother, Peter Lienhardt, also a lecturer in Anthropology; Godfrey was then away in Ghana, teaching for a term. Peter was of the opinion that I should of course not return. He suggested that he and I go to the foreign office to see a friend, Willis Morrison, later ambassador to Egypt. Mr. Morrison met us and was friendly and sympathetic, but understandably noncommittal. Peter and I went to see Mary Trevelyan, the foreign students' advisor, who ran The Goats Club, a popular social and intellectual international association that particularly catered to the needs of foreign students and was indeed a source of many reliable friendships for me, most among all, Trevelyan herself. As expected, we found her most sympathetic and helpful. Indeed, she impressed us by reaching for the phone and saying as she did so, "The Home Secretary is a good friend of mine. Let me give him a call." A positive conversation went on after which she put the receiver back to announce rather casually but reassuringly that all was well: "I am assured by the Home Secretary that nothing of the sort will happen to you." Even Peter, an Englishman, was most impressed with how simple it all seemed because of knowing the right people.

That issue more or less resolved, the next problem was financial support. Here again, Mary Trevelyan was to prove most helpful and effective. Even before I took any steps in that direction, she had invoked a grant request from a foundation or a fund that included Lord Euston and I later understood, Lord Twining, whose son, William, had taught me in Khartoum and had been my mentor. Before that, and on learning of my crisis, Lady King had told me to count on her continuing to provide me with room and board for as long as I needed and without worrying about payment. The grant through Mary Trevelyan came through speedily and I was able to back-pay Lady King.

My natural reaction was to publicize my case as a typical example of the injustice and political persecution prevailing in the South. This was very much the wish of my southern colleagues who in fact geared me in that direction and clearly intended to reap political fruits from it. Natale and I drafted a statement in which we gave a factual account of my recall, summarized the circumstantial evidence which indicated political motivation, and gave my reasons for refusing to return and my observations about the significance of the case as an example of what was going on in the South. We then went to see David Astor of *The Observer* and Colin Legum, the well-known commentator on African affairs, who was also with *The Observer*. The two men convinced me that it would be wiser to avoid reacting with extremism and putting myself in a position which would then be used by the government to justify their treatment of me. Instead, it would strengthen my case to react calmly and allow time to unravel the facts and expose their misjudgment. I thought it was a wise advice and a number of developments were to prove them right.

During those critical days, I spent a weekend with the family of Michael Tibbs, the last British district commissioner in our area. They lived in the village of Haselmere, in the county of Lynchmere in Surrey, a lovely countryside. That weekend, I went to church with the Tibbs on Sunday morning and was introduced to the pastor who was not only close to the Tibbs as members of his parish but held them in a special esteem as their family had been in the clerical leadership of the area for generations. During the sermon, I was astonished to hear the pastor preach a message which seemed to be directed to me personally and to give me consolation. The preacher spoke of the spiritual values of endurance, of the strength of faith to counter suffering, of the virtue in forgiving our enemies, and in the continuing hopes for God's blessing to overcome our difficulties. Even his prayer seemed clearly intended for me. I was convinced that Michael Tibbs had agreed with the pastor to hold that Sunday's sermon for my sake and to pray for me. I was deeply moved.

It was during those days that I was also invited by K.D.D. (Bill) Henderson, who had served in the Sudan civil service for a full career term during which he was a district commissioner, assistant civil secretary, lecturer in administration, editor of *Sudan Notes and Records*, and governor of Darfur province. Mr. Henderson had been district commissioner in western Kordofan when my grandfather, Kwol Arob, was still the chief. Henderson had a great admiration for my grandfather, Kwol Arob, whom he was later to describe as "a great leader and ruler of men".

I had first met Mr. Henderson in Oxford where they then lived. They had since moved from Oxford and settled in a beautiful house on lovely grounds in the tiny village of Steeple Langford, near Salisbury in Wiltshire. On hearing about my problem, Mr. Henderson went into deep reflection, pondering over the issue of whether I should return or become a refugee. It was clear that the considerations he was making were extremely difficult. On the one hand, he had known my grandfather and had held him in great esteem. He had also known my father even before he succeeded my grandfather. To see me abandon the country which my forefathers had served so loyally as leaders was something he found extremely difficult to accept. Mr. Henderson also loved the Sudan and hated to see a situation develop that would polarize the country even more and perhaps confront him with an even more critical choice of political position over the southern problem that he had felt necessary in the past. Mr. Henderson had a strong belief in the tradition of justice which the British had established in the Sudan and this provided the basis for his eventual advice.

He said I was not the kind of Sudanese who should be a political refugee and that he was prepared to write to the chief justice, Abu Ranat, whom he considered a close friend, to tell him that he knew me personally and was sure that any political accusations or suspicions against me were totally unfounded. Mr. Henderson went on to tell me about the case of Adam von Trott zu Solz, not realizing that I had met the Von Trott family in Germany and had become close friends. He recounted the story of Adam von Trott's return to Germany despite the advice of his friends in the United States and Britain, because he felt that Germany was where he belonged. I knew that Adam von Trott had returned, had worked to overthrow Hitler, had eventually been arrested, tried, and executed.

It was ironic that Henderson should invoke Adam von Trott's case at a time when Verena von Trott was perhaps one of the closest friends on whom I depended for advice and consolation during that difficult period and who often saw similarities between her father and me. It was indeed through her that I got to know the Astors, David having been a close friend of her father. Somehow, her letters invoked in me the belief that difficult situations presented a challenge and a test for the strength of one's personality.

What Mr. Henderson wanted to stress was of course not that I should go even if I were to be executed, but rather that I came from a patriotic background which he thought would be compromised by my becoming a political refugee. By pledging to clear my name with the chief justice, he eliminated the possibility of danger while emphasizing the positives of a heroic return. I was not persuaded by Mr. Henderson, although I did not say so. But his view of my family gave me an even greater conviction that we did indeed have a bridging role to play in the history of the Sudan and that I should not be driven into extremism or factionalism by anger.

It was while I was with Mr. Henderson that I met for the first time Sir James Robertson, who, as the civil secretary had been the architect of change in southern policy which abandoned the separatist trend and led to the independence of the Sudan, under a unitary system. As district commissioner of our area in the 1920s, Sir James had known both my grandfather and my father. As we discussed the developments of South-North relations since independence and especially the civil war, Sir James surprised me by saying that he felt personally responsible for the tragedy that had afflicted the country in its South-North relations, for "I should have known that the two peoples were too different to constitute a unitary state." I found myself arguing for his policy, that unity was an ideal that should be pursued and that the assumption he had made was that both sides would accommodate one another; there was no way he could have known that they would fail to do so. I doubt that Sir James has ever stated publicly what he told me privately, that he regretted his decision over the future of the Sudan.

I wrote to William Twining, my lecturer and mentor in Khartoum University, who was then dean of the Faculty of Law at Queen's University in Dublin, Northern Ireland, to inform him of my situation in the hope of receiving some advice and help. William responded promptly. He gave me the names of two professors from Yale Law School, then visiting professors at the London School of Economics, whom he said were friends. He asked me to discuss the situation with them quite frankly; he was also writing to them to introduce me and to ask them to get in touch with me. He himself would be in London by a specific date and I should telephone him on the evening of that date. We would then get together and discuss the situation further.

I received the expected call from Professors Quinton Johnstone, an American, and Robert Stevens, an Englishman with a tenured position at Yale. We met at a corner in the faculty lounge at the London School of Economics. I spoke very frankly and in detail about my eye situation, its impact on my studies, the political crisis confronting me, and my desire to proceed with graduate studies to the doctoral level.

It was Professor Johnstone who asked, "How can you be sure that the problem of your eyes will not frustrate your academic performance in the future?" I replied that my objective was to accelerate my academic advancement to achieve appropriate qualifications to be of value even if I were to lose my sight in the future. He pointed out that the prognosis of my eye situation was also a consideration, for while I was highly recommended by Professor Twining, and my academic qualifications were not in question, the required medical care and the prospects for the future had to be weighed against the value of my graduate training. Then he said in conclusion that although they were influential at Yale and their recommendations would carry weight, it was very late in the year and even those on the waiting list had been considered and a final selection made. The chances of my admission were therefore very slim but they would nevertheless do their best and keep me informed. In the meantime, he advised me to proceed with my plans as though Yale was not a viable alternative.

Nevertheless, although initially cautious and understated, Quinton Johnstone was to pursue the matter of my admission to Yale with diligence and was to become a source of unfailing support, but always with candor and a realistic, almost pessimistic, approach to problems, the type who would overstate a problem to find an appropriate solution. I received several calls from Professor Johnstone to give me up-to-date information on the chances of my going to Yale. The first gave a glimpse of hope in that I was to fill in an application form and my application would be considered at a forthcoming committee meeting. The second was more optimistic: the Committee had met and, despite all the odds against my last minute application, had approved my admission in principle, but wanted assurance that I understood the terms, especially regarding financial arrangements and medical care, and that I accepted them. Essentially, all it meant was that I would receive the amount normally granted to unmarried graduate students which Yale feared I might consider inadequate and that Yale would pay only up to some eighty per cent of the medical bills of any eye operation that I might have. The final decision of the committee would be made on receipt of my response to their conditions. Of course, I accepted their terms which implied that my admission to Yale was virtually assured.

Developments in the circles of the northern Sudanese in England seemed to indicate an increasing disapproval of the way I had been treated. In some cases, this was motivated by a genuine sense of justice, but for some, it was a pragmatic realization that the government might drive me into a more extreme opposition that could be harmful to the North, especially since I was abroad and outside the reach of the government. Hassan Omer, a law faculty member, then in Oxford, was one of those who saw my case as one gross injustice. He wrote a letter to our colleague and mutual friend, Mohamed El Fateh, in which he strongly condemned the political hysteria that was prevailing in the ruling military junta. He wrote that if I could be suspected of anti-North activities and victimized on account of that, then something was seriously amiss with the government policy in the South and that it was time for the genuinely nationalistic northerner to appreciate the dangers to national unity posed by that policy. I was moved by the letter and in a way, it was an effective reinforcement of my long held position of moderation.

More reactions were to come from the North. Sayed Mohammed El Shengetti, a prominent nationalist and a highly respected political figure in the country, the first speaker of parliament, came on a visit to England and learned about the case. He and others undertook to work towards correcting the situation. Beshir Mohammed Said, a prominent journalist and owner of the most influential *Al-Ayam* newspaper, telephoned and invited me to lunch to discuss the situation. He implored me not to react with extremism but to patiently await the results of the efforts which were being exerted by men of good will, including himself. The Sudanese Student Union in the United Kingdom, of which I was an executive committee member, met and resolved to write to the authorities to protest my recall and withdrawal of scholarship. An anti-government attitude among the northerners was clearly evolving over my case and that helped reinforce my faith in the bridging role of my political stand.

Despite this encouraging development, I was totally taken by surprise when I received a telephone call one day to learn that the military attaché, Colonel Muzamil Ghandour, was on the line. After introducing himself, he suggested that we should meet and talk about the problem, for, he said, "I believe no problem is beyond solution if there is the will and people are prepared to talk." I told him that I had nothing to hide and that I would be happy to meet with him and talk anytime he suggested. He invited me to lunch in an Indian restaurant where we had a good meal and a long talk.

I was extremely relaxed about the whole situation. Whether it was because I had gone beyond caring or because I was so sure that the truth was in my favor and that the mere fact of talking could only help uncover the truth, I cannot be sure. The military attaché told me the whole truth which unveiled him as the source of my entire problem. He said that as soon as he had suspected me for the anti-North activities, he had had me followed everywhere and full reports had been furnished to him about all I had done. He said I had gone regularly to Oxford to meet Richard Gray, the professor of history who had taught in Khartoum. (Mind you, Richard Gray lived in London and not in Oxford.) According to the military attaché, I had gone to Richard Owen, the ex-governor of Bahr el Ghazal, whose sympathies for the South were well known, presumably for the same reason. I had also visited many other places in England for probably the same reason of establishing contacts and raising funds. I had toured Sweden for the whole summer to promote the southern cause and perhaps to raise funds. I had gone to Italy at least twice to confer with the expelled Catholic missionaries and to raise funds (even though my visits had been solely to my brother Bol). I had also gone to France, Germany and other countries in Europe for the same reasons.

My activities, both in England and on the continent, had convinced them that I was masterminding the southern movement in the whole of Western Europe. He said that they had been monitoring every move I had made and had given it a political significance. He even said humorously, "If you raised your hand to scratch your head, our man following you pulled back in fear that you were about to strike!" Then he said that while he kept Khartoum closely informed, he frankly had never thought that they would act so foolishly as to order my immediate recall. "They could have waited until you returned normally and then make you account for your acts. In any case, whatever else I might have suggested they did, I would not have endorsed this stupid action, had they consulted me. As it were, they simply ordered your recall through the office of the Cultural Attaché." He went on to say that he had since been hearing a great deal of positive things about me which had begun to raise doubts in his own mind about the accuracy of the reports he had been receiving. He therefore wanted a frank discussion with me to clarify the situation, at least to himself, and to see what could be done in the circumstances to correct the situation.

I listened with absorbing interest to everything he said, not believing my ears at times, laughing at times, but clearly pleased that the whole thing was so ridiculous after all. I told the military attaché the whole story from my point of view, explaining away every area of doubt that his account had raised: my visits to Oxford to meet Lienhardt and not Gray; my cooperation with Lienhardt that took me to Oxford so frequently; the Christmas with Richard Owen, the total lack of reference to the southern problem during my stay with Owen, and my suspicion that Owen had wanted to avoid the subject because he had remembered my father's refusal to join the South so that he probably had considered me "northern" in outlook and had not wanted to embarrass me; the trip to Sweden, both in its background and its outcome; my visits to my brother in Italy; the visit to my German friends; and the detours into France and Holland. But I stressed to him my opposition to the government policy in the South, my views on the southern problem, and the approach I had chosen for myself and which entailed a frank and open discussion of the southern problem in all circles, Sudanese and foreign alike, as an individual and without involving myself in any organized political movement. I told him that since my secondary school days up to and through Khartoum University, I had never made a secret of my political stance on the southern problem and that my views were an open book to all those who came in touch with me and cared to hear them or otherwise discussed the problem with me.

Just as I had listened with great interest to his side of the story, so did he to mine. By then, we had clearly established contact and were communicating most effectively and surprisingly with considerable understanding and sympathy for each other's position. His informants were of course grossly wrong about me. They might have been sincere in their mistakes or might have felt it necessary to lie in order to justify whatever they were receiving. He himself was simply doing his duty as he thought it best and was clearly convinced about me. I too held political views that were understandable to him and if I pretended not to entertain such views, it would have been impossible for him to believe or respect me. But none of those views necessarily implied organized political movement or supported the validity of the allegations against me.

Deep into our conversation, the military attaché cited a Sudanese proverb to the effect that those who have shared a meal must no longer fight. He said he had been completely won to my side, although he had been responsible for my problem. The issue was how to undo the harm he had done. He would do his best, but he suggested that the most effective way of remedying the situation would be for him to try to arrange a meeting between me and President Abboud during his forthcoming official visit to the United Kingdom. That way, they would also test for themselves his new opinion about me.

Several days after my meeting with the military attaché, I returned to the Little House to find Lady King very worried; an officer from Scotland Yard had come, asked for me, and said he would return. None of us had the slightest idea of what the visit was about; I too joined Lady King in worrying. What on earth could it be? I knew I had not committed any offense, at least not that I was aware of. And it had been a long time since the prospects of extradition had been speculated upon and dismissed. In any case, there was now contact between me and the Sudan government;

they could not try to reconcile with me and at the same time enforce extradition. Nor could extradition be simply a matter of the police coming to tell me to leave the country. Whatever it was, Scotland Yard was a name I associated with crime and I had never expected to be sought after by an officer from Scotland Yard.

The officer came again, this time accompanied by a colleague of his. When they did not find me, they left word that I should go to see them at the headquarters – Scotland Yard. To get the matter over with, I rushed there on the earliest opportunity specified in the message. I found the whole issue both simple and perplexing. Scotland Yard was concerned about the security of the president of the Sudan during his forthcoming visit. They wanted me to assure them that I would do nothing "embarrassing to Her Majesty's government". I told them the gist of the problem with the Sudan government, that I had been wrongly suspected of engaging in an organized political movement in England, but that the officials had realized their misjudgment and were working to correct the situation. In any case, I told them to be assured that I would do nothing against the president of the Sudan, far less embarrass Her Majesty's government.

They did not do anything beyond that relaxed conversation and verbal assurance. But I left both relieved and disturbed, relieved that the matter was after all nothing serious, but disturbed that Scotland Yard would check on me and interrogate me as though I were a potential assassin or criminal. The whole thing seemed absurd and painful, but I decided to dismiss it.

My initial suspicion of southerners as finding some political advantage in my crisis was confirmed when Laurence Wol, clearly speaking on behalf of the southerners and in the presence of Natale, requested me to lead a demonstration which was being organized against President Abboud by the East African students.

According to Laurence, since most southern students were government officials on graduate courses, for them to join the demonstration would be risking dismissal and the withdrawal of their scholarships. As for Laurence himself, since he was permitted into England under the pretext of being a student who would not engage in political activities, for him to join the demonstrations would also be to risk expulsion from Britain and endanger his covert activities in promotion of the southern cause. I was therefore the only one who had nothing to lose, for I had already refused to obey orders from Khartoum, had lost my scholarship in consequence, and had chosen to be a political refugee.

I was outraged at the attempt to exploit my difficulties unscrupulously and in total disregard of the principles involved in my political stand, which were very well known to the southern Sudanese. I restated the obvious, that they were grossly mistaken if they thought I could deviate from my objectives and act out of tune with my character because I had been victimized by the Sudan government. My response simply opened the door for a heated and angry discussion of my whole attitude towards the southern problem, with Laurence making incriminating arguments and I becoming even more enraged. Laurence dismissed my pledge to Scotland Yard by stating dogmatically that they had no right to require such a pledge, that any student was entitled to exercise his political rights of peaceful demonstration. Yet, he maintained that he was in Britain on a student permit and that engaging in political demonstrations might lead to his expulsion.

Natale on the other hand sat through the discussion, quiet, solemn, head bent down, occasionally biting his lips, obviously very uncomfortable with the whole situation, because he had probably given each one of us a reason to believe that he might be on our side. He avoided taking a position, but made it rather obvious that Laurence should not expect me to do what I did not want to do, thereby hoping to give the impression to me that he appreciated my point of view and to Laurence that I was not committed to play such a role.

We parted that day after having decided to lay the subject aside and turning to something else about which we could smile. But our differences had clearly sharpened and seemed impossible to bridge not because I disagreed with whatever they were doing in the interest of the South but because I felt they were totally incapable of seeing my point of view or appreciating my role in the struggle. I resigned myself to the confidence of my own convictions and loyalty for the South and dismissed them as people who could not reach the depth of my perception, which was in itself the result of a long chain of experiences, some due to the geopolitical location of my family and tribe between South and North, some being the outcome of personal experiences in southern, and northern, academic institutions, and some being the result of my own personality. Reinforced with that faith in my individuality and my undoubted commitment to the ultimate interest of our people as I saw it, I remained very much at peace with my line of approach even though I deeply regretted our failure to communicate and appreciate each other's position.

About a week before the president came, I was once again visited by officers from Scotland Yard and I soon discovered that all the other southerners in London had also been contacted. Essentially, they let us know that our names had been furnished by the Sudan Embassy as among the people who posed a potential threat to the president during his visit. They talked to us individually and requested us to sign an undertaking that we would neither harm the president nor act in any manner that was politically hostile during his visit. What we did before or after was not really their concern; they were simply keen on the visit not to be negatively affected by anything we might do. The same embassy which was trying to arrange a meeting between me and the president was giving my name as one of the people who posed a potential threat to the president's security. How paradoxical!

President Abboud came and the appointment for me to meet him was made. I received the word to that effect from Muzamil Ghandour, the military attaché, who received me and escorted me to Talat Fareed, the minister of education, who would then introduce me to the president after the initial discussion of the situation. Talat greeted me very warmly and offered me a cup of tea. We were then alone in the room. As we sipped tea, we engaged in an informal friendly conversation about matters not related to my problem. They had just been to China on an official visit and I asked him how they had found China. Talat spoke most praisingly of China, the organization, the spirit of the people, their hard work, their enthusiasm, and the progress they had made. At one point, he remarked, "If that is communism, then we ought to welcome communism."

Now feeling relaxed and almost uninhibited with him, I said spontaneously, "But did you think the people were free?"

"Free?" he shot back at me. "What do they need freedom for when they are so happy!" I must have just laughed. Then he made a remark, which like the one he had just made, was typical of him: "You seem like such a nice person, how could you do what you did?"

I laughed and could not help saying, "What did I do, Mr. Minister?"

"I mean your activities against the government!"

The knowledge that I had acquired from Muzamil about the suspicions and accusations against me gave me the upper hand. I told Talat what I had told Muzamil, with the advantage of rehearsal and repetition. I emphasized the fact that my position on the government policy on the South was not a secret and that I would be delighted to make it known to whomever cared to know. Then I went on to draw a distinction between my own views on the government policy, my own way of making my views known, and the allegations of involvement in an organized political movement. While emphasizing that I was not a member of any organized movement, I also stressed that I was not in agreement with the policy of the government over the South, but that this was very different from leading an organized opposition movement abroad.

From the start, Talat seemed quite conciliatory towards me. I knew a great deal of that had to do with whatever Muzamil had said to correct the picture, but the chemistry of our interaction was also helpful. With conviction and seeming faith in the justice system, Talat still argued that I should have gone to the Sudan, defended myself against the accusations, and returned free to pursue my studies. He said that as a military man, what had offended him the most was my disregard to orders; that had angered him even more than the subversive activities which I had been reported to have engaged in.

Talat then summarized his position. He said he could see in me and in my words that I was an honest man. He believed that I had been wrongly accused of subversion and anti-government activities. His main problem was how to convince his colleagues about me in the first place and persuade them to withdraw a decision which had been reached in the council of ministers. But he said all that would simply be a matter of procedure and time. Then he said the president wanted to see me. As a word of advice, he asked me not to get into the unnecessary details of saying I did not agree with their southern policy. "All that you need to say is that you did not do what you are alleged to have done."

So, he got up to join President Abboud and then sent word for me to go to the president. President Abboud received me very warmly while Talat explained that I was the southern student who had been alleged to have led anti-government activities in Europe. It seemed to take a little while before the case crystallized in Abboud's mind. That is when he said to Talat, "Do you know that he is the son of our brother, Chief Deng Majok!? In fact, just before I left, his father sent me a telegram asking me to look into the case of his son when I came to England. Until then, I had not been aware that the student about whom we had talked was Deng Majok's son. Now that I see him, it is so clear that he is his father's son, both from his looks and from the way he speaks. Sit down, my son!"

Abboud then offered me something to drink and proceeded with a flow of nice sentiments and a humane air that truly typified the qualities of a Sudanese elderly statesman.

Talat proceeded to summarize his own findings about the case and the fact that I had been misjudged, adding his own impression that he did not think I had done what I had been accused of having done.

The president, displaying a degree of cordial impatience with the explanation, said, almost interrupting Talat, "His father is a great patriot. He is one of the leaders of the Sudan most committed to national unity and to the service of the country. Even if his son had done the things he is said to have done, for the sake of his father, let us forget it all. It is clear that he is his father's son. Even the way he smiles is his father's."

After a brief exchange of polite, friendly, and patriotic remarks on all sides, the president gave us permission to leave, saying "Go with your uncle Talat to work out the details. All is well! Let us forget the past. Just discuss the details with Talat as your uncle, not as the Minister."

That was of course not my first time to meet President Abboud, for, as will be recalled, we had met during our study tour in Germany when he had also displayed considerable warmth and had been lavish in his praise of my father. Now that I saw him even more closely, I could easily see that there was a great deal to the generally held view that his dictatorship did not reflect his personality as much as it was a reflection of the personalities of a number of his subordinate clique, who were the effective dictators under his umbrella.

After the president's return to the Sudan, I received a letter from my father saying that he had met the president after his visit to London, that he had been promised that all charges against me would be dropped on account of my father's loyalty to the country, that I must promise him not to engage in any political activity, that I should watch his own steps at home and follow suit, and that I should pass the message on to Bol to do the same. He asked me to write to him at the earliest possible opportunity to assure him that I was acting in line with his directives.

It was very rare for my father to write to his sons. In fact, I don't remember ever receiving a letter from him before the one that called me the High Dam of the Dinka. This was the second, and like the first, it touched me enormously, not so much for what it said, as for the mere fact that it had been written and sent. Nevertheless, it angered me because I felt betrayed by the president or whoever had transmitted the message to my father. I had been of the opinion that the government had realized its misjudgment of me and that it was correcting itself by undoing all that had been done on the wrong premise. Now, I was being told that I had in effect been "pardoned" on account of my father. I realized, however, that President Abboud must have said something courteous to my father about their change of position. To me he had said that the matter should be dismissed even if I had done what I was said to have done. To my father he had probably said that I had done what I was supposed to have done but had been forgiven on account of my father. One made me innocent, the other made me guilty but pardoned. I felt reasonably sure that the president did not fully realize the distinction and that in both cases he had acted in good faith. But I felt the difference to be very significant. Anyway I never responded to my father's letter.

Word eventually came from Khartoum giving the final signal for the restoration of my status and approving resumption of my monthly entitlements with back payments to be fully effected, which Talat Fareed, with characteristic humor had called forced saving. As soon as I received the money, I repaid all the grant money I had received through the help of Mary Trevelyan and got a very appreciative response from the foundation.

It was at that point that my brother Bol visited me. I invited the military attaché, Muzawil Ghandour, for dinner at the Little House. Muzawil was so liberal in his attitude toward the southern problem and the military regime that it was difficult to believe he had been responsible for my problems. In projecting a positive fortune, he argued that even if we ruled out any revolution of change, the present leaders would eventually die out and the future would be with *us*, the younger generation, about whom he was more optimistic. Bol later told me that either he was a clever manipulator or he was genuinely liberal. Bol vacillated between being suspicious and trustful.

Now that the situation with the Sudan government was fully normalized, the alternatives in front of me seemed considerably improved but by no means simple. I could pursue my original request for extension, even leading to a doctoral program, and decide to remain in London instead of proceeding to Yale. Going to Yale for me was a new horizon fraught with risks, some foreseeable, others still part of the mystery about the United States. If Khartoum were to approve my request for continuation in London, it would be morally wrong and indeed disloyal to disregard my commitment to them and proceed to Yale. Yet, there was something exciting about adventuring new horizons and despite all that I had heard about racial problems in the United States and my long-held prejudices on account of that, I had come to know a number of Americans both in Khartoum and abroad who had influenced my view of their country very positively. Indeed, fears of racial prejudice among the Americans had ceased to be a matter of concern to me. So, I found the prospect of going to Yale to be quite appealing.

To clear my conscience, I wrote to Khartoum once more suggesting three alternatives: to grant an extension for both Master's and doctoral degrees in London, or to grant me study leave with my salary to continue graduate studies on the Yale scholarship, or to grant me leave without pay, salary or scholarship, which essentially meant honoring our employment commitment with one another and retaining my seniority.

I received a letter rejecting my request and explaining that I would have to relinquish my position on the Faculty if I wanted to proceed for graduate studies at Yale. I could then reapply after completing my studies and my application would be considered on its merits as a new application. I decided to proceed to Yale, implicitly opting for the last alternative, but without responding to Khartoum University in writing. The tone of Khartoum's response and indeed the substance of Father's message indicated that while the government had compromised its position, there were probably still lingering assumptions about my political stance that left something of a rift between them, including the university, and me.

I was later told by the dean of the law school on a visit to Yale that the denial of my request was not a decision taken by the faculty or the university administration, but rather by some junior administrator. He urged me to return once my studies were over at Yale. And yet, when I wrote to the university as I was about to complete my graduate program, recalling the history of my case, and indicating my willingness to return, I received a form letter normally addressed for foreign applicants, informing me about the country, the terms of service, and the hopes of the Sudanese authorities that I would join the university and enjoy "our beloved country." Whoever sent that letter clearly thought of me as a foreigner, placing me clearly in the cracks of the identity crisis from which the country was suffering. Those who sought my services and to whom I felt greater loyalty than my own national university included the University of Singapore, where my former British lecturer in Khartoum University was dean of the faculty, and the Human Rights Department of the United Nations Secretariat in New York. Attracted by the neutrality and the universality of the role of the international civil servant, in particular in an area close to my concerns, I chose the service of the United Nations.

There can be little doubt that the insensitivity with which Ziada Arbab, representing the government, initially reacted to Uncle Bona's death revealed a vacuum of moral responsibility which was symptomatic of the identity crisis the country was suffering from. Likewise, the capriciousness of the measures taken against me by the government at a time when my greatest preoccupation was not with politics but the impending threat of blindness with which I had just been confronted gave the conflict between North and South an almost zero-sum character. On the other hand, it also revealed to me that there were significant exceptions to be considered. For one thing, a number of northerners stood by me, even though some might have been motivated by the pragmatics of containing me to minimize any potential danger I posed. After all, it was a northerner, a friend, who conveyed to me the most reliable information on the thinking in Khartoum, perhaps taking some risk in doing so. As for the southerners, although they naturally sympathized with me and gave me emotional support, some of them, perhaps even the majority, saw my plight as an opportunity for pressuring me to be more active in their movement and to take a leading activist role against the government, since I had nothing to lose.

In a way, the event paradoxically confirmed the bridging perspective which had become deeply entrenched in our anomalous position at the North-South border which our family, and in particular, our father represented. My commitment to dialogue and the principles of unity under appropriate conditions remained unshaken. Indeed, in the United Nations, I maintained close contact with the Sudanese mission and became close friends with the two permanent representatives, Fakhreddine Mohamed and Mansour Khalid, who served during my period in the secretariat. With both men, and indeed with a wide array of concerned Sudanese on both sides, I maintained intensive consultations aimed at ending the war through a settlement that would reconcile between the northern demand for the preservation of unity and the southern quest for self-determination. Such a compromise in my view could be achieved only through autonomy, not as the ideal, but as a framework that would facilitate a gradual process of national integration in the long run. My commitment to the framework of unity was not a dogmatic glorification of the principle, desirable as unity is, but a pragmatic recognition of the African and indeed international commitment to the preservation of colonial borders. It was an exercise in the art of the possible. Our people were, however, to experience more hardship in the coils of the civil war before the Addis Ababa Agreement would bring some relief through regional autonomy for the South.

6
Coils of the Civil War

While the battlefield in the South has been ablaze, conflict in the Ngok area has been less openly violent, but more insidiously penetrating. As a result, North-South, Arab-Dinka, and intra-Dinka conflicts have all become inextricably intertwined. By the same token, roles of leadership, such as negotiating, mediation, and peacemaking at various levels, and the countervailing, conflict-generating intrigues of the spoilers, have been equally cross-sectional and intercommunal. In all of this, the descendants of Deng Majok, being heirs to a historical responsibility of leadership in the area, have both confronted the challenge of providing protection for their people and suffered from the self-destructive contradictions of the power struggle within the family, compounded by the intrigues of self-seeking and unscrupulous alliances across the lines of conflict.

My personal role, played with varying degrees of success and failure, has been to pursue the objectives and the principles of leadership as passed down to our generation, and adapt them to the prevailing conditions in the country. This meant taking initiatives for which I had no formally assigned mandate, whether by election or by appointment. Quite the contrary, I often did so against the desires or wishes of people who saw advantage in the conflict I sought to resolve.

Deng Majok's Successor Installed Amid Escalating Conflict

The challenge intensified immediately on Father's death and it had to do with succession. As was expected, the competition was between Abdalla, the third son of the first wife, Nyanboldit, and Adam, the first son of the second wife, Nyanbol Amor. It will be recalled that several years earlier, Father and I had discussed the issue of which of the two he should appoint as his deputy and therefore successor, but he never did anything about the matter. Indeed, he resisted naming a deputy, far less a successor, until his death.

During the last days of his terminal illness and as we were about to take him to Cairo for further medical investigations, I tried to broach the issue of succession with him rather delicately. I told him that as he was going to Cairo and no one knew how long his treatment might take, perhaps he should name one of his sons to whom he could entrust the leadership of the tribe in his absence. He looked at me suspiciously, as though he read through my thoughts. "When I left the tribe," he responded in measured tone, "did I not leave someone in charge!? What is different now?"

I saw his apprehensions and decided to withdraw in the interest of his hope for survival. Building on his comment, however, I concluded that if Abdalla were the one we thought suitable for the responsibility, as Bol and I were inclined, then we could construe Father's response as a blessing for him.

The last days of Father's illness and eventual death were quite traumatic for Bol and me. We had gone back to Khartoum where we learned that he was suffering from terminal cancer. We nevertheless took him to Cairo, partly to be seen as doing our best for him, but also in the hope that a second opinion might be more promising. The day he died, we went to see him. It was a few hours before he died. There was a retiring look in his glowing eyes, a sense of surrender and submission to the inevitable that he must have ultimately realized was at hand. He was lying back gazing at us with his penetrating eyes now deep in the sockets of his otherwise skeletal head. All three of us, Bol, his clerk, Achier, and I were standing around his bed. Suddenly, as though to make his very last move in life, Father pulled himself up, wrapped his arms around my neck, and pulled me towards him. Achier immediately intervened and disentangled his arms from around my neck, saying, "The doctor said that you should lie still." Father fell back and lay motionless on his back, still eyeing us intensely.

216

I was deeply saddened by that. It was admittedly a frightening moment, but that he was pulled away from me was to torment me for years and still does. Bol tried to belittle the significance of the event by saying that it was only a dying man's behavior, but I have secretly always wondered what my father was thinking when he did that and whether he wanted to convey something he could not.

Uncle Ngor had no doubt about the significance of the incident: "There was something important which he wanted to pass on to you. His mind was thinking about major things and it is most significant that he wanted to pull you towards his heart."

Both Ngor and I knew secretly what that important thing on Father's mind must have been, for, to the extent that he was still conscious and aware, he had to have been concerned about what would happen to his family and the tribe after his death. And I fully realized that being the son of the fourth wife or not, much of the responsibility would descend on me personally. Even as Father was still not yet on the death-list, Uncle Arob alerted me to be mentally prepared, for should my father die, it was to me the tribe would look for protection. I felt sure that what Father had wanted to say to me had something to do with that responsibility.

Tragically, however, Father never made a dying declaration or will; his only wish was that should he die, he must be buried in his tribe. He anticipated that people might say that the rainy conditions would not permit taking his body home, but argued that he was not one to be buried anywhere. He elaborated immodestly that he was a man who should not only be buried in his tribal home, but on whom a tomb should be erected.[43] In making the argument, he invoked his image to both the North and the South.

With the help of Bona Malwal, a dynamic young Dinka politician, with whom Father shared mutual admiration, and the intercession of Joseph Garang, the minister for southern affairs, President Nimeiri instructed that the body be flown to Abyei by military plane. We were therefore able to fulfill Father's only dying wish under the conditions of the rainy season when transportation was almost impossible and at the peak of the North-South civil war.

---

43. It is interesting that in her review of my book, *The Man Called Deng Majok* (Deng 1986), Sharon Hutchinson questioned the author's preservation of Deng Majok's treatment of women without an explicit condemnation, but added that was perhaps the tomb Father had requested to be erected in his honor.

Abdalla was at home; Adam was in the North. Tradition has it that the successor must be installed as the dead chief is lowered into the grave. Discussions about succession ensued as the grave was being prepared. Uncle Deng Makuei tried to reclaim the leadership as having been wrongfully usurped from him by Deng Majok, but was booed by the assembly of elders and the public. During his last days, Father had sought my legal opinion on whether Deng Makuei could claim the chieftainship after his death. I had told him that the issue had been settled and that leadership would pass on to his descendants without any controversy. I was glad that my opinion on this issue had been vindicated. The tribe united behind Abdalla, and because we thought he was the right man, we agreed with the tribe on his succession.

Abdalla's major problem was that he was suspected by the security forces of cooperation with the local rebel leaders of the southern Sudan Liberation Movement and its military wing, the Anya-Nya. Father had played a delicate role of balancing between his official role as the government representative in the area and his discreet dealings with the rebels to keep them at bay. Abdalla was trying to fit himself into his father's shoes which, considering his youth and inexperience, were far too big for him.

In the absence of Deng Majok, the commanding officer, Captain Ali Sid Ahmed, had terrorized the people, tortured many, and killed a number, including members of our family. Among those tortured was aunt Awor Kwol, whose son, Osman Koc Aguer, was one of the local rebel leaders. His partner in the leadership was another cousin, Justin Deng, the son of Uncle Biong Mading.

The extent to which the Ngok had become disenchanted was brought home to us by our great Uncle Mahdi Arob, so named because he was born the year our great-grandfather, Arob Biong, his father, visited the Mahdi. He was now an old man of nearly ninety. While the burial rites were underway, and the crowd of mourners mingled with the security forces, we were told that Mahdi wanted to see us. We sat apart with several soldiers standing by observing us. Mahdi asked us whether we were in touch with the British administrators who had been in the Sudan. When we answered in the affirmative, he seemed elated. "When they were leaving," he recalled, "they came and met with us here under the court tree. And they said to us that although they were leaving, they would keep a close watch on developments in the Sudan. If we failed to get along, they would be back. Would you go and tell them that we have failed to get along?"

218

Mahdi was particularly baffled by the fact that our family which had been the link between North and South was now targeted by the Arabs. And indeed, because of the dual leadership role of the family within the government and among the rebels, the officer was particularly suspicious of the members of the family. On arrival, we learned that one of our uncles, Anyiel Kwol, had just been killed by the security forces. Our people were so afraid for our own security that they wanted us to be guarded by tribal warriors in the official guest house where we chose to stay, our home being a public mourning place. The local administrator, Hereika Izzeldin, an Arab chief's son whom we had known from earlier times, also wanted us to stay with him. Captain Ali, having received instructions from Khartoum to ensure our security, suggested that we put up in his house, which he thought would ease his task. It was also apparent that he wanted to have a close watch on our activities. Reflecting quickly, we decided to stay with him.

That afternoon, as he went to play volleyball with his men, Ali threw a pistol at me in the bed saying, "Have this; here, you need it." This underscored the fear under which all were laboring. The commander obviously gave us the pistol to protect us against our own people who had tried to convince us to have the tribal warriors guard us against him and his men.

As I had a cold and was exceedingly tired, I fell asleep as soon as we went to bed. Bol, on the other hand, could not sleep. He kept waking me up to draw my attention to the commotion that was going on around the house, with people audibly coming in and going out; their murmuring voices indicating that something serious was amiss.

Early the next morning, as Ali joined us for tea, we decided to have a frank talk with him. We told him of the news we had learned on our arrival about the death of our uncle, Anyiel, and the commotion we had heard at night. We said that we realized the precariousness of the security situation in the area and wanted to know about the state of affairs and what we could do to be of assistance.

Ali clearly appreciated our candor in raising the issue. He in turn was equally candid. He told us that it was he himself who had shot Anyiel, that he was sure he had been a rebel and the contact man of the rebel leaders, and that he had provided them with medicines and other supplies. He explained that after having arrested Anyiel, he had gone with him to his house where they had found medical supplies that had clearly been intended for the rebels and that he had also found a uniform with badges that indicated his rank in the rebel movement. He said that Anyiel had tried to run away, which was when he had then shot him.

As for the activities of the night before, he confirmed that he had had the town and, in particular, our home, cordoned because he had learned that our cousins, the local rebel leaders, might come at night to pay their last respects to their late uncle. His instructions had been that if they came, they be shot dead on the spot. But they had not come as expected. He also explained to us that Abdalla himself was suspected of cooperation with the rebels. That was not only reflected in the security records from his predecessor, but was also confirmed by his own intelligence reports. According to him, Abdalla's position was known to the security authorities in the province headquarters. He would therefore have to be very careful to correct that image, if he were to be effective as chief.

The story of Anyiel's death as we later learned was in sharp contrast to Ali's version. A Nuba soldier who had been involved in the incident told us that after Anyiel was arrested and tortured, he was escorted to his house by the officer and several soldiers. Ali found some medicines which Anyiel explained he had received from a relative in Khartoum for a sick relative. The officer had accused him of lying and threatened to kill him. Anyiel, with extraordinary serenity, told the officer that he was not afraid of death and that if he killed him, he would be accountable to the government for justice and if not, eventually to God. Captain Ali, provoked by that comment, took his pistol and shot him in the head at close range. Anyiel died instantly. The officer then ordered his soldiers to shoot in the air and later reported to the police that Anyiel had tried to run away and had been killed in flight. At the time we were speaking with the officer, we did not know the details of Anyiel's death, except that he himself had killed him.

We told Ali that Anyiel had been a very dear uncle to us and that his death was a tragic personal loss. However, the most important thing for us was how to transcend our own grief over the dead and seek ways in which we could best protect the living. Our father who had been responsible for the area was dead and we, as his senior sons, had to assume his role in the tribe. We then proceeded to discuss the overall situation and how we might cooperate to improve matters.

We agreed on an approach whereby we would hold a public meeting with the people to discuss the general security situation very candidly after which we would design appropriate strategies for action.
Captain Ali suggested that in order to encourage the people to speak their minds freely, neither he nor his men should attend the meeting. I argued

that precisely because we wanted to foster openness and cooperation between them and the people, they should attend the meeting, but Commander Ali insisted and we eventually accepted his point of view.

At the meeting I spoke very sternly to the people. Emphasizing the state of insecurity which we had found, I told them that the death of our father did not mean that there was a vacuum of leadership, that among the Dinka a man who had left behind grown up children continued to live and participate through his descendants, that we fully realized our responsibility to our people as the successors of our father and that we intended to discharge that responsibility. I urged them to speak their minds and tell us the truth as they saw it so that together with them and the security forces, we could seek ways of alleviating the crisis of insecurity in the area. Bol followed and spoke along the same lines.

Elders began to speak their minds, highlighting the problem of informants who lived off telling lies and reporting innocent people to security forces, to be arrested, tortured, or killed. To them, that was the real source of insecurity in the area, not the alleged threat by the rebels.

Amidst this candor, one of our younger brothers, Osman Mijak, spoke to tell us that he thought it unwise to encourage the people to speak their minds, that whatever the officer had said to us, his informants were there in the meeting and that anyone who said anything against them or the security forces would almost certainly be reported and would suffer the consequences. We ourselves would soon leave and there would be no one to protect those innocent victims. He therefore urged the people to refrain from speaking their minds. He also raised the issue of Anyiel's death and said that when the road opened, he intended to seek justice from the central government. He hoped that when we returned to Khartoum, we would help them pursue that case with the authorities. He said he spoke the way he did because he did not care what would happen to him, but that he did not want the people to follow his example. Osman sat down with a roaring applause from the crowd.

An Arab trader, Mohammed Ali Beshir, who had lived long in the area and had married a Dinka, followed Osman, speaking in a metaphor. Abyei, he said, was like a ship adrift at sea without a captain. From beneath the waters, strange monsters would emerge, extend their deadly arms into the ship and snatch the people one by one. That way, people were being eliminated. He saw us as the captains who could take charge and guide the ship safely ashore. He too received a loud applause.

In the end, I made concluding comments in which we highlighted the importance of unifying the channels of communication and cooperation with the security authorities through the legitimate leadership of the tribe. Those who sought to enrich themselves at the expense of the innocent must be made accountable to the ancestral spirits whose ultimate power was embodied in human conscience and deep sentiments of right and wrong which even evildoers must sooner or later feel as human beings. God and the ancestral spirits had their ways of sanctioning their divine code. Punishment would eventually fall on those who brought harm on the innocent. We certainly intended to have the channels of evil deeds closed to those people.

In retrospect, perhaps we seemed rather arrogant, appearing not only sure of what was right and wrong, but as events would prove, too assured of the understanding we felt we had established with the commander of the security forces.

After the meeting we went home with a number of elders to appraise the situation. One of them was Omda Achwil Bulabek, the chief of Abyor sub-tribe. Speaking to the other elders, Achwil commented on the way I had spoken, seeing it as a reflection of my father. Listening to me speak, could people say Deng Majok had not reproduced himself? He posed a rhetorical question. To my embarrassment he went on to say that my education had clearly enhanced the qualities of my father in me and made me excel over him in my ability to articulate the cause. This was reminiscent of the way Father saw himself and was seen by his supporters in a favorable comparison with his father, which represented a departure from the traditional Dinka way in which the forebears are always deemed superior in performance.

One of the known informants of Ali Sid Ahmed was Matet Ayom, chief (sheikh) of one of Alei sections, a cunning and shrewd man with whom Father had maintained an ambivalent relationship of friendship and adversity. Arabized, sophisticated, and very articulate in both Dinka and Arabic, Matet had been one of the prominent members of Father's court, whom we observed as we grew up. With time, and as he entered into conflict with Father, he became known to be unscrupulously ambitious and self-seeking. Father would have him imprisoned for a variety of reasons, but as soon as he was out, they would be reconciled and would resume their close friendship. Father had kept him on a tight leash to contain him. Without Deng Majok to check him, Matet and his clique now terrorized the family and the tribe with a vindictive vengeance for his old grievances. Although we were somewhat aware of his role, Father having alluded to it during his last days, Matet appeared to be so much in the grip of the security forces that it would have been futile to try to disengage them. The best course of action was to win the commander of the security forces.

Subsequent to the meeting, we wrote a powerful letter to our rebel cousins, drawing their attention to the magnitude of the crisis in the area, how Father's death had created a vacuum of leadership that needed to be filled, urging them to balance between their value in the movement and their responsibilities as leaders whose role was urgently required at home. We informed them of the overtures the government was making toward peace and reconciliation, the offer of general amnesty and the opportunity which was open to them to make a constructive contribution to the tribe. We implored them to choose between two options: joining the local leadership in their efforts for peace and security in the area or moving their forces further South, away from the helpless people of Abyei on the very sensitive borders between the North and the South. If they did not heed our advice, we would have no option but to urge our people to cooperate with the security forces for their own protection.

Initially, Captain Ali opposed any contact with the rebels which he argued would be treasonable. But we impressed upon him the higher call of duty, the conciliatory policies of the central government and the imperative of being creative in their implementation at the local level. He eventually succumbed.

It was difficult to find anyone who was prepared to be our messenger to the rebels. Understandably, they feared that they would subsequently fall victim to the security forces. For what it was worth, we eventually persuaded the officer to give them his assurance that they would not risk any retaliation from the security forces.

There was also the question of where to locate the rebel leaders since they were constantly on the move and no one would acknowledge knowing their whereabouts. The officer's informants told him that they had been spotted in an area where someone had accommodated them and slaughtered a bull for them the previous night. The officer dispatched his men to go to arrest the man who had offered the rebels hospitality.

We went to our family home to continue our informal consultation with elders after learning from Captain Ali about his pursuit of the rebel host. There we found my maternal uncle, Ngor Mijok, to whom I had been very close since childhood. He had heard of our arrival and had come to see us. As Bol and I stood talking with him some distance from everyone, Uncle Ngor intimated to us that he had just entertained "the boys" in his home.

"Which boys?" I asked.

"The men of the forest," he said, using the Dinka word for rebels.

"Get into the car immediately," I said, as I gestured to Bol that we should return to the officer urgently.

"Where are we going?" Uncle Ngor anxiously queried.

"Do not ask questions; let's just go!" I responded.

Once in the car, I told him that the security forces were looking for him, that if they apprehended him before we acted, it might be too late, and that I wanted to introduce him to the officer myself so that he would explain his situation in my presence. Without much discussion, I wanted him to tell the officer that he had been confronted with a difficult situation in which he had had no choice but to accommodate the rebels and offer them hospitality and that as soon as he had heard of our arrival in Abyei, he had decided to come to report to us. I would do the rest in explaining the situation.

There was nothing really contrived in that approach since those were essentially the facts of the situation. Indeed, Uncle Ngor was to present them even more forcefully in his own words than I had prepared him.

"Here is the man your people are looking for," I told Captain Ali in a casual manner. I then asked Uncle Ngor to tell his own story, while I interpreted. Ali could not believe what he was hearing.

"Do you realize that my men are right now looking for you?" Ali restated the facts. "How could you accommodate the rebels? Don't you know that it is a crime that could lead to your death?"

Ngor only elaborated his theme of helplessness and cooperation for survival. "They carried guns and all I had were spears, how could I disregard their demand for accommodation and food? I would be a dead man. Can I say which death is worse or better, death in their hands or death in your hands? When God willed that my nephews should come in such an opportune moment, I rushed to Abyei to explain my position in the hope that they might be able to explain it to the security authorities."
Ngor did much of the talking; I was only an interpreter. So convincing was he that the only thing Captain Ali could say was: "If my people had found you there, you would probably be a dead man or you would languish in jail for many years. You are a very lucky man to have been brought to us by your nephews."

"It is not luck," Uncle Ngor retorted. "It is just that God knows the truth."

Not to be outwitted, Captain Ali reacted with, "You are also a very clever man." Ali then offered to let him go on condition that he move to Abyei and join the ranks of his informants.

That was when I stepped in and explained to Ali that my uncle was a respected elder and that whatever he himself thought of his informants, they were not highly regarded by the society. He could not expect my uncle to be one of them. Ali did not press the point, although he still advised Ngor to move to Abyei to avoid being caught between the rebels and the security forces. I thought that was wise counsel and supported it. Little did I know that Ali had planted a seed that would later haunt my uncle and perhaps me.

Issues with Regard to Family Unity

In addition to the security situation of the tribe, we were busy managing the affairs of the family of which the future of Father's numerous wives, especially the young ones, and the unity of the family behind Abdalla's leadership were the most urgent. On the first issue, I argued in front of a family council comprising our brothers, cousins, and Uncle Arob, that we must part with the custom of the levirate, whereby the young widows of a dead man are inherited by his older sons and other relatives to continue to have children in his name. My reasons were two-fold. First, Father's excessive marriage, which we all acknowledged had inflicted injustices on the women, had been his greatest weakness for which we had criticized him. To force the women to continue in that marriage after his death was unconscionable. Second, we had to be practical and to realize that maintaining that vast family and educating the children would be a daunting task which we would not be able to afford. Unlike Father, who had varied sources of income, the only source for most of us would be at best salaries which could only sustain each person's own nuclear family. I therefore argued that we should give any woman who wanted to leave permission to do so without demanding our cattle from her family. Any man that would marry a woman who had chosen to leave would be recognized as her lawful husband and father of the children they would beget together. We on our part would remain committed to Father's own biological children, whether their mothers remained at home or chose to leave.

Those women who chose to remain in the family and be inherited according to the custom of levirate must be given full freedom to choose the men they wanted to live with. Instead of having sons inherit the women in their section, I suggested that we widen the circle of eligible relatives to go beyond the Deng family to include members of the lineage of Kwol Arob. Once inherited, the children a woman produced with her

225

chosen partner would be regarded as their own, and not as the legal children of Deng Majok. Their biological father would have to assume full responsibility for the woman and her children, including their maintenance and their education. We would remain responsible only for those children who were begotten by Father.

My proposals were met first with silence, then a nervous laughter, followed by a uniform rejection. The theme of the rejection was that Father had successfully maintained his wives and children and had kept the family largely united and in harmony. For precisely the same reason that he was much criticized for his marriages, it was important for his honor that we as his children should keep the family united the way he left it. Not only did they oppose freeing the women to leave if they wanted, they objected to opening up the circle of those entitled to inherit, insisting that it be limited to the descendants of Nyanaghar, Father's mother.

It was then that Bol chose to come to my defense, but argued in a way that proved counterproductive. "Children should not be born like chickens without planning for their future," he said. "There are in fact parts of the world where they castrate men to control birth and limit the number of children a family can have." Uncle Arob, who had listened to the debate with silent indignation, now chose to intervene. "You people better stop talking," he said, addressing Bol and me. "You talk like people who have been too long where they castrate men." He received a sympathetic laughter which indicated that we were hopelessly outvoted.

Later, in a meeting with Father's wives, I repeated only the theme of giving the women the choice to leave, if they wanted, and otherwise emphasized the importance of family unity among those who remained and our determination to honor our father's name by discharging our responsibilities as his sons and preserving the unity and integrity of family. One after another, the junior wives to whom our offer applied argued against our position. If they did not leave their husband while he was alive, how could they possibly think of leaving him after his death, they reasoned. The implication was that wronging a man after death would inflict a more deadly curse than wronging him while alive. We learned the lesson that tradition, unreasonable as it may seem from an external perspective, has an intrinsic logic that is not easy to challenge.

On the issue of support for Abdalla, the family was solidly united with the exception of Adam who insisted that he should have been the successor. He could not believe that Father had died without mentioning him as his successor. And he kept questioning me as though we were hiding the facts. When he realized that there was no hidden truth, he pleaded the democratic process, arguing that while he understood why Abdalla, who was at home, had been installed to leave no gap of leadership, the matter should ultimately be resolved through elections, which he somehow expected to win. No amount of talk could persuade Adam otherwise.

As a member of his section, I held private discussions with him in which I tried desperately to persuade him that if he were to accept and cooperate with Abdalla, we could try to have him appointed as deputy chief and that by his seniority of age and experience combined with his other qualities, his own influence in the tribe could be formidable. He could both be a positive influence on Abdalla and a leader in his own right. But Adam was either so confident about his prospects through elections or was aware of Abdalla's precarious standing with the security authorities at Abyei and in the Province headquarters and their contrastingly favorable view of him that he could not be swayed. On the contrary, he tried to persuade me to convey to the authorities his claim for chieftainship and demand that the matter be put to the vote.

Although Adam's brothers, Ali and Osman, stood united with the family behind Abdalla, his sisters, Abul and Achai-Jur, and presumably at least some of the women in their section, backed him. The sisters were particularly critical of my stance, accusing me of being blindly committed to the unity of the family against my own interest, which of course they identified with our section of the family.

Ironically, apart from Bol and Abdalla himself, who knew and trusted what I was doing, the section of Nyanboldit viewed my activities, in particular the private meetings with Adam and his sisters, with deep suspicion. They could not believe that I was fully committed to Abdalla and suspected that I was perhaps engaged in some secret plot in favor of Adam. Once, Adau came passing by as I stood in the evening with Abul and Achai-Jur, pleading with them passionately to support Abdalla. After stopping, presumably to identify us and to let us know that she was aware, Adau apologized for intruding and left grudgingly. My own sisters, Awor and Ayan, who were conducting their own intelligence, kept feeding me with the suspicious rumors that were going on about my role. Although I was fully aware of those suspicions, I decided not to be bothered as there were far more important things to do than invest valuable time in clearing the rumors.

Difficult Commanding Officers

The security situation continued to be our main preoccupation. Although we first received encouraging signals from our rebel cousins, their final response was negative. We therefore embarked on our alternative course of action by which we planned to develop a common front between the security authorities and the traditional leadership of the tribe to cooperate for the security of the area.

When the day for the final public gathering came and as people assembled under the tree and we were about to join them, one brother entered our room gasping for breath from having been running and announced that our brother, Osman, who had been outspoken in the first gathering, had been arrested and taken to the military as opposed to the police station. That was regarded as a certain road to torture and possibly death. As we waited for the officer to join us for lunch, Captain Ali was interrogating Osman in his office next to the room where we sat, secretly wondering whether or not to storm into his office.

Captain Ali eventually emerged smiling and urged us to start eating, as though nothing had happened.

"Aren't you going to tell us?" I broke the ice.

"Tell you what?" he dared to ask back.

"What about Osman?" I said in a matter of fact manner.

"Oh, Osman!" he remarked and went to explain that he had been arrested and was being interrogated by the police. What he, Osman, had done was extremely dangerous, not only for the security of Abyei area, but indeed for that of the Sudan.

"What has he done?" we queried.

"You obviously know what he has done," Ali responded.

We were rapidly losing our patience. "Ali, please tell us what Osman has been arrested for."

"What did he say at the public meeting!?"Ali asked rhetorically.

We felt somewhat relieved since we knew that nothing Osman had said could have been that serious.

I then repeated what Osman had said, urging people not to speak their minds. That did not satisfy Ali. He wanted more. Then I recalled Osman saying that he would pursue the case of his uncle, Anyiel Kwol. Ali suddenly looked more interested in my account. And when I added Osman's appeal to us to help them, Ali jumped in and said, "You see, you know. He asked you to help!"

"Of course he asked us to help pursue the case of Uncle Anyiel." And with sarcasm, I added, "And what did you think he meant, help them with arms?"

To my astonishment, Ali laughed and said, "You clever man; you know that is exactly what he said."

According to him, Osman had said that he planned to take up arms against the government and called on us to procure weapons for them in the United States.

The whole story was so absurd that we told Ali to release Osman at once, if that were all he had against him. But he insisted that all four of the informants he had planted in our meeting had reported the same thing independently. He had to believe them, or else his entire intelligence system would be undermined.

Overlooking the fact that he had dishonored our agreement with him, we said that we did not care how many of his informants had reported to him; they were all lying. It was their word against our word and we could not believe that he would trust their word above ours.

Ali argued that the matter was now in the hands of the police and that we should leave it to them to investigate the case. I reminded him that I was a lawyer by training and that no one could be arrested without a prima facie case. Osman was absolutely innocent of the allegation which we knew for a fact to be a fabrication. Besides, by his accepting that fabrication as a source of danger to Abyei and the country, he was including us as potential accomplices to the alleged plot. Unless he released Osman forthwith, we would conclude that the reports about his use of unreliable informants to victimize innocent people were accurate. We would simply not confront our people and urge them to cooperate with perpetrators of such a clear abuse of power. Instead, we would immediately terminate all our efforts and leave to report to the authorities in the central government what we had witnessed and leave it to the government to decide on a course of action. Our anger was beyond control. We knew anything could happen to us, that we were now clearly part of the danger Ali saw, probably to himself more than it was against the country, and that gave immediacy to his worries about the implications of what we might do that could endanger his own future.

Presumably because he knew the truth and that the real threat was personal rather than national, he began to modify his position. At first he suggested that he would persuade the police to release Osman so that we could overcome the embarrassment of going to the meeting with our brother under arrest. We ruled that out as a deception which we could not entertain both in our own conscience and in our appearance to the people. Grudgingly, Captain Ali eventually agreed to release Osman, but not before he revealed his true state of mind; Osman was impudent and deserved punishment, but was fortunate we were there to protect him, he said.

We learned later that Mohammed Ali Beshir, the Arab trader who had also spoken critically, had also been interrogated by the security forces and released.

That issue resolved, the assembly went as planned. But after I had made our concluding comments on the new plan for cooperation, Ali got up and ended the meeting on a threatening note against anyone who would dare do anything that would endanger the security of the area, no matter what his social standing or leadership position in the tribe. Clearly, his words made the meeting end on a very sour note.

In subsequent discussions with tribal elders, they recalled how Deng Majok's word had always been final on such occasions and how no government authority, civilian or military, would have dared say a word after his concluding remarks. They all reflected a spirit of helplessness and despair. They also felt that the month we had spent in Abyei had provided some protection for the people and worried about the repercussions of our departure.

Five years later, in a discussion of the worsening crisis in the area, Marieu Ajak, one of the elders who had talked to me at that time, recalled:

The day your father Deng died, when you came with Bol, ... I called you aside and ... said, "Mading, now that you have come, the few people who have survived, it is you who have made them survive. While you are here, whenever a person is arrested, you bring him out. Now that you will leave, our front has broken down. Now that you will leave, will our tribe not spoil? Will the land ever be good again?"...

What I told you, if it were not that people forget words, you would recall. I said, "One day, you will come to respect this area only as a graveyard and not as a country with people. Our people will finish. We are too delicately poised on the borders, the borders of the South and the North. This will destroy us. The tribe of your father will turn into a graveyard. I want you to be the chief. You should remain here. They will shy away from you, but they will not fear Monyyak [Abdalla]" (Deng 1980:290-291).

That evening, Captain Ali intimated to us that twelve people, including several members of our family, would be arrested the following morning, the day of our planned departure. He wanted to assure us that it would only be a demonstration to show the people that no one, including members of the leading family, was immune from the authority of the security forces. He wanted us to be sure that they would be safe and would be released shortly afterwards. When their arrests took place as planned, and people came running to us in a panic, all we could do was tell them that we had known about the arrests, that they were not to worry, for they would be safe and secure. We left feeling somewhat helpless and determined to present the situation to provincial and national authorities for some remedy from above.

We travelled in a convoy of military trucks with soldiers who were being transferred. One of them was the Nuba soldier who told us about the circumstances under which Uncle Anyiel had been murdered by the officer. He said he would be prepared to testify in front of any commission of inquiry that might be established to investigate the case. He also intimated to us after we had reached northern towns that Captain Ali had been so afraid of any report we might present to the central authorities that he had considered contriving a situation where the rebels might be alleged to have attacked the convoy and we would be eliminated under the guise that we were killed in an exchange of fire between the troops and the rebels. It was never made clear to us as to how and why that idea was eventually dropped.

Bol and I differed on the approach we should adopt in our report. He thought that we should unequivocally condemn Captain Ali and his men. My idea was, however, that we should report dispassionately with an attempt to see his point of view as a young frightened officer who was trying to do his duty as he saw it. Our recommendations for the future should be to address a common problem, not a vindictive desire for vengeance. Bol felt strongly about his stance and although I myself wrote the final report to the national authorities, his view more or less prevailed. Even more than the strength of his argument, I was pushed to that position by the biased response of the province authorities.

Although our verbal report to the province security committee tried to be evenhanded and appreciative of the different points of view, it was obvious to us that the authorities were not happy about Abdalla's succession, seemed to favor Adam, and were transparently skeptical of our findings and conclusions. One of them, the representative of the attorney general in the province, was my junior colleague from the Faculty of Law. With obvious ambivalence, the province commissioner thanked us in the end, saying that as sons of late Chief Deng Majok our perspective on the situation was of course important and would be given due consideration, but that we should recognize that there were also other points of view from the area. We were outraged. I told them that we were not just sons of Deng Majok, that by virtue of our professional standing, we carried national and international responsibilities that transcended our local background, and that it was with that sense of responsibility that we had reported to them and intended to report to national authorities.

That cold reception and response convinced me that there were no prospects for justice in the province headquarters. As a result, the report I wrote subsequently was more condemning of the Captain and his superiors in the province headquarters than I had initially intended. After analyzing the situation, we recommended the removal of the young officer and his men, his replacement with a more experienced officer and a new contingent of soldiers, the confirmation of Abdalla as the chief with administrative and judicial powers, and an investigation into the circumstances of Anyiel's death.

Our written report was supplemented by oral briefings to key personalities in Khartoum, including Abel Alier, one of the two southern ministers in the central government, and through him the minister of the interior and the chief of national security. The central government authorities clearly took our observations and recommendations seriously. In a meeting with the minister of the interior, he telephoned the chief of security to tell him of our report and to urge that they consider our recommendations seriously. As an officer in the human rights division of the United States, he said, how would it look to the international community if my views on the human rights situation in the area which I had personally witnessed were disregarded.

In response to our reports, Abdalla was confirmed as paramount chief and given judicial powers, the commanding officer and his men were transferred, and a commission of inquiry was established to investigate Anyiel's death and other incidents of alleged brutalities in the area.

The New Chief Killed in a Massacre

Mohammed El Basha, the successor to Ali Sid Ahmed as commander of the security forces, a member of the neighboring Arab tribe who was

232

immersed in local ethnic politics, proved to be worse for the Dinka. A series of confrontations between him and Abdalla about the way he treated innocent people accused of cooperation with the rebels, confiscated their cattle, and sold them, accompanied by physical threats against the chief, resulted in a massacre involving Abdalla, his older sibling brother, Lino (Chan), Abujabar (Bulabek), the son of Aker Tiel from their section of the family, and three uncles, under circumstances that left no doubt that the security forces were responsible. Indeed, eyewitnesses identified the assassins as the commanding officer and six of his men. The official report of the officer to the province headquarters and to Khartoum was that they had been killed by the rebels.[44] This happened at the time the May regime of Jaafar Nimeiri was ambivalently trying to win the South with the promise of regional autonomy, the implementation of which was being impeded by his communist partners, among them the minister of state for southern affairs, Joseph Garang. Under the title, "How Six Sudanese Died: A Family Massacre," Michael Wolfers (1970) wrote of these murders in *The Times* of London, October 19, 1970.

> Mr. Joseph Garang, the Minister in the Sudanese revolutionary government responsible for southern Sudan, has just announced a year's extension of the amnesty for southerners who have been engaged in secessionist activity but wish to return to their own country ... [I]t requires a considerable act of confidence and faith for a southerner to return to territory still garrisoned and administered by northern troops and officials.
>
> The growth of their confidence may be seriously damaged by some information on the recent killing of six members of one of the leading Dinka families (one of the main tribes in Sudan), including the paramount chief of the

---

44. Citing official District reports, Abdelbasit Saeed (1982:177) wrote of the incident: "Abdallah ... was murdered, together with three of his uncles and his two immediate lawful successors ... in an ambush by the South Sudanese Anya-Nya forces in late 1970." Needless to say, there was absolutely no reason for the Anya-Nya forces to commit the murder. In any case, blaming atrocities committed by government forces against the rebels was a common practice. Indeed, the author was informed by a senior military officer that the investigation into Chief Abdalla's death established the case against the security forces, but that there was disagreement within the military on action to be taken. Some, including himself, felt that it was good for the image of the army that action be taken against those responsible. But the dominant view was that such action would demoralize the security forces. In the end, even the report was not published.

Ngok Dinka. The critical point about these events is that they take place in a family which has traditionally favoured cooperation between north and south, and at Abyei in Kordofan Province, not on the southern borders of the country, but in the borderland between northerners and southerners. Kordofan is geographically in the north, but the Ngok Dinka are a part of the complex of southern tribes.

The paramount chief, Abdalla Deng, was elected only a year ago on the death of his father. It is alleged that last month he was killed, with two brothers and three uncles, by seven Sudanese Government soldiers. He was then 27. His grandfather, Chief Kuol Arop, had sought cooperation with the Anglo-Egyptian Government in Sudan, and his father, Chief Deng Kuol Arop, had cooperated with the Sudanese Government.

The following report of the circumstances of Chief Abdalla's death has been prepared by his relatives:

"In all, six were killed and these are Abdalla Deng, Bulabek Deng Kuol, Lino Chan Deng Kuol, Arop Mahdi Arop, Thuc Col Gueny, and Kiir Jal, as they were just having a walk on the evening of September 17, 1970. Eyewitnesses say that they were shot by a group of about seven soldiers which included the local commanding officer, Mohammed El Basha.

"The immediate cause which resulted in the killing in cold blood of these people was that during August or early September, Mohammed El Basha, with a number of his followers, following a false report of an Anyanya (southern rebel army) cattle camp at Dokura, went to Dokura where they found a camp and killed four persons from Tuic. As usual, they took away the cattle of those killed, in all amounting to 150 cows. Mohammed El Basha wanted to sell these cows as is the normal practice, but he could not do so without the local (chief's) court approval.

"Thus he came to the court and Abdalla told him that those who had been killed were not rebels but law-abiding citizens, and consequently he saw that there was no reason why those cattle should be sold and told him that he was referring the case to the resident magistrate. As a result of this, Mohammed El Basha became serious and threatened Abdalla to the effect that this was his last time to come to his court and if anything at all happened, the first bullet that he would fire would be for Abdalla.

"With this threat, Abdalla wrote to the Provincial Commissioner at El Obeid reporting the incident and actually asked for the Province Security Committee to visit Abyei to see for themselves what was going on. However, a few days after the quarrel, specifically on September 17, Mohammed El Basha and six other soldiers ambushed Abdalla and those killed with him and opened fire on them. All six died on the spot."

The family point out that the Tuic Dinka, four of whose men were killed in the cattle raid, by tradition come from the South to graze their cattle at Abyei. The Ngok Dinka, believing in the good faith of the Sudanese central government, look to the northern administrators in the provincial capital for protection of law and order. Documentary evidence supports this. Two of Chief Abdalla's brothers living abroad have once before had to rely on provincial administrators after an alleged murder by Sudanese soldiers. They are Dr. Francis Deng, with law degrees from Khartoum and Yale Universities, who is now a senior official of the Human Rights Division of the United Nations in New York, and Dr. Zakaria Bol Deng, with medical degrees from Padua and Bologna Universities, who is a senior house physician at Waddon Hospital, Croydon, Surrey ...

Chief Abdalla's family are now seeking public enquiry into the killings this September. Dr. Bol Deng said that ... he and his brother still believe in the intentions of the central government, but argue that the test is whether the government will control the army on the ground. Their initial hopes for the new government which took power nearly 18 months ago are now tinged with skepticism.

The initial response of the government was quite positive. Major Abul Gassim Mohamed Ibrahim, one of the strongmen of the May Revolution, was dispatched to Abyei to appraise the situation, express the government's condolence to the family, and otherwise moderate the political climate. Beyond that, the government conducted an investigation which, according to reliable sources, placed the responsibility on the commanding officer. The issue then was whether publishing the report and admitting responsibility would tarnish the image of the security forces in an undesirable way or promote the integrity of government justice. Opinions were sharply divided on the issue, but the bottom line was that the report of the committee was never made public. Those who wanted to cover up the crime prevailed.

Increasing Disunity in the Family and the Clan

The appointment of Adam by the security forces to succeed as chief, along with his known ambition for the position, raised suspicion of some involvement on his part in the conspiracy to assassinate his brothers. This suspicion was later reinforced by the attitude Adam displayed to the investigation committee, for although the evidence was presented in secret, it was commonly believed that he had testified in favor of the security forces. Since the testimony was given under oath sworn upon the Sacred Spears, those who swore to opposing positions were ritually considered to be engaged in a blood feud and had to sever all ties, not eat or drink in each other's homes, and to all intents and purposes, regard themselves as enemies. Adam was thus severed from the family and isolated. Even his sibling brothers, Ali (Monylam) and Osman (Mijak) stood with the family against their brother. Only his mother, sisters, and the junior wives of his father whom he had inherited under the levirate system remained on his side.

Under the leadership of Abdalla's mother, Nyanboldit, most members of the family emigrated to the North, allegedly to avoid any further atrocities which the security forces might commit in alliance with Adam. That a woman could lead such a radical response which threatened to tear the clan apart indicated the degree to which things had fallen apart and the total loss of leadership on the part of the male members of the family, and, indeed, the clan.

The family was so divided that if anyone from the mainstream family was seen even exchanging greetings with anyone from Adam's side, that was a ground for ostracism. It was a devastating feud, far worse than the conflict between Deng Majok and Deng Makuei following the death of grandfather Kwol Arob.

236

Some time after receiving word of the family massacre, I went to the Sudan on my way to Gabon on a UN mission. As the time available to me then was short, I decided to return by way of the Sudan and see what I could do to address the problem of disunity in the family.

On my return, I consulted some elders from other Dinka tribes who happened to be in Khartoum on the Dinka customs relating to such feuds and the appropriateness of my initiating a process of reconciliation within the family. I was encouraged by the elders to go ahead, emphasizing that in a situation involving an external threat, internal differences must be submerged or transcended to forge a collective stand against the common threat.

Having listened to the evidence against Adam, I concluded that his ambitions must have carried him too far to the extent of welcoming Abdalla's confrontation with the security forces and even hoping that it would result in Abdalla's deposition so that he, Adam, would then ascend to the throne he had always assumed to be his rightful entitlement. But I was not persuaded that he had conspired to have his brother assassinated. By imputing conspiracy to him, the family was compounding its own tragedy with the internal divisions. There was, in my opinion, no justified ground for inflicting such a devastating disunity on the family, especially since it was being exploited by the enemies of the family to undermine its leadership role in the tribe.

Naturally, the tribe had become divided behind the two factions of the family, with most of the Dinka backing the mainstream position without scrutinizing it and the opposition groups led by Matet Ayom siding with Adam. Since the opposition was favored by the security forces, their stand with Adam was merely a tactic for undermining the leadership of the family. Reconciling and reunifying the family would circumvent their machinations.

Armed with that message, I went to El Obeid, the capital city of Kordofan, where the family was congested into a few rented houses. Leading the discussions with me on the other side were Nyanboldit and Uncle Arob Kwol. As soon as I opened the topic of reconciliation, Nyanboldit seemed shocked that I would even entertain the idea. Tears streamed down her eyes and the other women began to cry. Even Uncle Arob, whom I had hoped would take my side, identified his position with them. It became clear that the feud was far from ripe for resolution. So I left, a definite failure.

My realizing that the conflict was not resolvable at that point was in part dictated by the amount of time available to me. Clearly, the feud was an abnormal state of affairs which, judging from the customary Dinka response, could not be allowed to prevail for long. Sooner or later, someone would have to intervene to make peace and reconcile the family. In the prevailing conditions, however, no one seemed placed to do that. And although I was handicapped by distance, the task would eventually fall on me.

The enemies of the family apparently realized that and despite my absence and distance away, I became a target. Some 14 years later in a tape recorded conversation, Uncle Ngor would give me a graphic insight into what had transpired after our fateful month at home in the aftermath of Father's death and how Matet Ayom, the leader of the security apparatus among the Dinka, tried to recruit him as an informant with me as their enemy number one. Ngor apparently led Matet to believe that he himself had reason to ally with them against me and the Deng Majok family. The interview with Ngor, conducted in the presence of my mother, gives a remarkable insight into the complexities and intrigues of a society that had been infiltrated and had lost its autonomy.

After we had narrowly rescued him from the security forces in Abyei, Ngor left the area for El Obeid for treatment from some ailment. While he was there, the massacre in our family took place. Ngor decided to go back against the advice of his sister, my mother, whose message he received on the way at the last leg of his journey on foot, since it was during the rainy season and there was no transport between Muglad and Abyei. He arrived and stopped in his home where he had entertained the rebels a year earlier. There, he received word that he was wanted in Abyei by Matet Ayom. Ngor first went to Achwil Bulabek, the chief of his sub-tribe, Abyor.

> Achwil said to me, "Come, let's go to Matet." I said, "Very well." We went. Achwil said to Matet, "Ngor has come!"
>
> Matet called me in and said, "Ngor, what do you have in your heart that made you run back home from treatment during the rainy season!?"
>
> I said, "It is because I heard that our area was destroyed and I had left my children alone at home."
>
> He said, "No man can match your courage, coming back into this destruction ... I would like to have a meeting with you this evening here in my house."
>
> I said, "Very well! ..."

We spent the day. Then, in the evening, we met again, I, Matet himself, Achwil and Patal. We were four.

He then said, "Achwil, if it should turn out that you are misleading me, you will have committed a serious offense. I have no desire to cooperate with the people of Abyor. A man from Abyor may seem very well versed and reliable, but one day, he will suddenly break away and go into the forest [as a rebel]. Even you Achwil, I do not yet trust you fully."

Patal spoke and said, "Shame on you Matet! How can you express such doubt about Ngor Mijok, when he has come all this way to see you!? Let us say what we need to tell him."

Patal then turned to me and said, "Ngor, we are going to register you!"[45]

I said, "Register me for what!?"

He said, "We will register you to be a spokesman!"

I said, "To speak as a Chief, a leader of my people!?"

He said, "To help report the words that flow around."

I said, "But there are two kinds of words that flow around. And please do not hide anything from me any more. Let us be absolutely frank with one another. Would you want me to speak as a leader or as an informant for the Government?"

Patal said, "Those who are important to the Government as leaders are those who inform the Government about what goes on. And you, Ngor, if God has brought you back and we have brought you to meet with Matet, then he will no longer disrespect what Achwil and I say. But if you should allow yourself to be disrespected by Matet, that will be your own affair. We will leave you alone with Matet. Say everything that is in your heart and let it be recorded on paper. Matet will take it to the commander of the security forces."

Matet then intervened and said, "Ngor, I am not going to hide it from you. If you accept to work with us, then you will have to spend the night with me here in my house

---

45. A euphemism for recruiting him as a security agent or informant.

and you and I will talk at night. And I will see to it that
sleeping arrangements are made accordingly."

Ngor, now realizing that he was being recruited as an informant of
the security forces and fearful of the consequences if he should openly
reject the offer, decided to lead them on, appearing to be fully in line with
them.

I said, "I have no more left in my heart to say. If I had
any reservations, I would not have come this far."

Matet then said to Achwil, "Please tell Ngor about the
nature of our work."

Achwil said, "Ngor, it is our clan [Pajok] which is
destroying our tribe. When they see a man speak for the
good of the tribe, they label him a spy. Even I, whom
Deng Majok left as a leader, I am now labelled as a spy.
And yet, had I not struggled on behalf of my tribe and
united my words with Matet and Patal, our section,
Abyor, would have been destroyed. There would be no
fires burning in Abyor today. What I want is for a
gentleman like yourself to unite his words with me and
we unite our words with Matet.

"The family of your brother-in-law, Deng Majok, seems
to believe that there is such a thing as independent
chieftainship. There is no such a thing. What the
Government wants is someone who will serve its
interests. So, son of my tribe, I ask you to follow me from
your heart and not merely from your tongue. I want you
to be written down as an informant and we will present
you to the commander of the security forces." That was
the huge man called Mohammed [El Basha] who used to
beat the people.[46] Achwil said, "We will have you write
down your words with them."

I said to them, "If what you want me to write down are
the words that concern the Anyanya [the rebel army], then
I will have to tell you that I cannot do that. I must be
honest with you, Brother-in-Law, Achwil!"

---

46. The man who succeeded Ali Sid Ahmed and who was responsible for the family
massacre.

Matet said, "You are right about that. But what about the words of your sub-tribe, Abyor!? And what about the words of the family of your sister!? It is the family of your sister which misleads the tribe. Abyor do not want to share leadership with anyone else. Even your large lineage of Maluk, which, as Achwil tell us, is the largest in Abyor, is excluded from leadership. What good is there in a person like you if you cannot plead the case of your own clan!?"

Ngor now spoke against Abyor and the clan of Deng Majok with a tone of grievance that sounded, and might in fact have been, sincere and therefore convincing to Matet and his associates, as a ground for his cooperation with them.

I said, "You have touched on my real grievance with our tribe and with the family of my sister. This is why I do not agree with their words. I now isolate myself to go my own way precisely because I resent the way they do things. And if anyone can help me check them, I will happily add my voice to those who criticize them and say, 'What you are doing is wrong.'"

Matet said, "That is all I wanted from you."

Turning to Achwil and Patal, he said, "Gentlemen, we will have to segregate ourselves for the night. I am going to tell my wife that I have a guest to share the hut with me."

Then we went to his hut. A large lamp was taken into the hut. The floor of the hut was expensively carpeted. Papers lay spread out all over the room. I don't know what was written on them.

The conversation that took place between Ngor and Matet that night and which Ngor recounted to me with surprising candor and vividness, is astonishing, even in the mere fact that it took place. It is particularly intriguing that this is the same man who had always called me "the Fox," who had flattered me for being in the image of my father, and who would later urge me to realize the responsibility which Father's death had imposed on me for the protection of our people. In that very fact lay his bitterness against me as a political enemy. Ngor's account continues:

As we sat down, he said, "Ngor, tomorrow, you will take an oath. We are going to speak tonight, but your final word will be said on oath tomorrow before the commander so that he holds no doubt about you. But let me tell you what is in my mind and my heart.

Who do you think is the source of all the troubles which are making us suffer as much as you see!? It all comes from the family of your own mother. It is Mading, the son of your sister, who is fully responsible for our suffering. So, let me tell you quite frankly that the only person I am after is none other than your sister's son, Mading. Mading believes that he is so educated that he excels over everyone else with ideas. But he does not know the words of the Government. If I were to decide to turn the heart of the Government against him, although he thinks he is clever, the Government would follow him until it catches him. But I did not want to do that because I did not believe that he would touch on people like me, Matet. I thought that he would treat all people as equals, the way his father used to equate between people. So, let me tell you, son of our tribe, I am not going to advise you to counsel your sister's son any more. I have gone beyond that. If you have truly joined me as you now seem to have done, what I am going to tell you is that I am going to show him something he will see with his own eyes. If there is anything you object to in your heart, then I should tell you that words should not be heard indirectly through gossip; that complicates relationships and makes conflicts far worse. So, let me know your thinking right now. If you should say that you disagree with me, then I may not have to reach for Mading. You and I will have to resolve that issue before I think of reaching Mading. The conflict would be between you and me.

Matet was now explicit in his threat to Ngor, should he hesitate in cooperating fully with him and against me. Ngor saw no option but to continue his performance in misleading Matet to believe that he had indeed found an ally with his own reasons for working against the family of Deng Majok, and, in particular, Mading:

242

I said, "You have just introduced a subject of great interest to me. I have a deep grievance in my heart which I have never voiced because I did not know how to go about finding a remedy. Why do you think I keep away from Abyei? It is because of Mading. I deeply disapprove of the way he does things.

You know that I was a child among my sisters. My sisters' marriages did not bring the rewards I had hoped for. You know how Deng Majok treated me when I was after my wives!?"

He said, "Yes, I do!"

I said, "Well, people like you, Matet, took his side. You made it seem as though an ordinary person could not voice any grievance against a chief. Now that my sister's son has extended the problem to you and you have brought me close to work against them, you may find that I am more effective against them than you who should be my leader. You are from another sub-tribe [Alei] and I am from Abyor. I know how Abyor does things and you have no way of knowing. And forget Mading; I know him extremely well. After all, he is virtually my mother's child. Even if I wanted to go to him where he is abroad, he would welcome me. If he comes and I tell him that I want to see him, he will always meet with me!"

He said, "Yes, he would surely meet you."

I said, "However, I know that there are areas in which you are more knowledgeable than me. All I need is for you to reinforce me with your knowledge to be better prepared to do what we want to do." At that point, we both laughed.

He adjusted himself in the seat and appeared more relaxed. He seemed to think that if I could have said what I said, then we were truly together in our plans.

Reassured by Ngor's willingness, indeed enthusiasm to cooperate with them, Matet felt comfortable enough to delve into the details of how they planned to pursue their objective:

"What I now want from you is to help me get Mading."

I said, "How do you think I can help you, should it be by my going after him or our bringing him here!?"

He said, "What we will do is that I will take you on a visit with me to the Province Headquarters [in El Obeid]. I will introduce you to them as an elder to whom Mading feels very close. That will make the leaders of Kordofan take your words very seriously. And when you hear people speak about going after someone, it does not mean that they will run after him and as soon as they see him, shoot to kill him. What is meant is that people follow him and try to understand how he speaks or does his things.

Ngor, to tell you the truth, I have found Mading, the son of your sister, too formidable for me alone. I have tried to get him, but I have not succeeded. What I want to do now is to bring you close to the heart of the Government and have you tell the Government all about Mading and how he does things. Even though you do not write, I want you to keep everything about Mading in your heart and mind and we will have it all written down and shown to the Government. The day he will come into clashes with the Government is not for us to say now. It will come by itself. And it will come from the words you say.

Ngor, if the son of your sister ultimately subdues me and it becomes impossible for me to get him, it is because something will have removed me from this land, but as long as I am alive and in this land, I will get him however long it might take me."

For some reason, Ngor not only challenged Matet by questioning his resolve, but also by asking him to confide in him more than Achwil, the chief of Abyor. Since he was only leading Matet on, Ngor probably did not want the information to be leaked to Abyor who might believe it and thereby tarnish his own image among his people.

I said to him, "Matet, you speak with anger against my sister's son, Mading, but believe me, my feelings towards him are far worse than yours. What I am in fact afraid of is that you may be leading me astray and then let me down. I fear that you may betray some of our secrets to people like Achwil Bulabek. Somehow, I do not trust Achwil. First of all, he is rather timid and may easily get frightened by Abyor. Besides, he is a member of Pajok clan and his loyalties may be to his clan rather than to his alliance with us. He may go and brag to someone, "I have found Ngor to be the man through whom we can get Mading." That person may go and speak to members of Pajok clan and our secret may become exposed. I really would not want Mading to hear my name associated with what you and I are now planning."

He said, "My dear friend, Ngor, you have now proved yourself to be truly the son of Mijok Duor. If you have expressed doubts about Achwil, then you are truly the son of Mijok. I am also afraid of Achwil myself. He is a coward. He is joining us not out of conviction, but because he is fearful that I might hurt him. That is why he is sticking his neck out. It is merely because he is afraid.

Now that you have joined me, what I will do is to push him further away and I will let you occupy his seat. You will sit facing one another and you will find that you will be the person to whom he will turn for advice."

Finally, Ngor's wit seemed to have achieved its secret objective, namely to appear to be the one committed to getting his nephew and thereby detracting Matet from being preoccupied with the matter, supposedly leaving it for Ngor himself to pursue. Evidently, Matet could not be that naive, but Ngor at least satisfied his conscience in the belief that he was in fact protecting his nephew: "I will now ask you to forget all about getting Mading. Occupy yourself with other matters and leave the issue of Mading to me. I will take care of that. Should he come, he will certainly get in touch with me and I will meet with him. He tells me everything. I do not know exactly how we shall eventually get him, but I am at least sure of his feelings for me as an uncle who is very close to him."

At that point in the interview, my mother, who had been listening most intensely, intervened and said, "I think you people better stop talking about this. I cannot stand it any more." But I disagreed with her and urged Ngor to continue, stressing that I wanted to know the facts. Ngor agreed with me. "These are the facts, and even though they reveal an ugly picture, that is the truth. Since we have started it, we might as well finish it."

But most of what Ngor had to say beyond that did not add much to the intrigues in the area. They met the officer and the terms of the position were explained to him. They included a financial arrangement and a supply of such commodities as tea, sugar, and other food supplies. Ngor then left on the understanding that the formalities of the recruitment, including the oath of service, would be finalized later. That was when Ngor went to one of his trusted clansmen to inform him that he was leaving the tribe and to explain his reasons. Ngor said that he had now understood why Matet had always been accused of lack of heart. He said he could not imagine what man and woman could have begotten Matet. How could he possibly believe that he could win his cooperation against his closest nephew, Mading? What could anyone give him that would substitute for the value of Mading?

That night, he went back to his area, took his cattle and family, and left for the South. There, he ran into the rebels and went through more trials, getting almost killed, but eventually he was saved by a local rebel leader who had been my schoolmate, and was well disposed to Ngor as my uncle. Ngor only returned to the area with the end of the war. And he gave me the account of his encounter with Matet and the Abyei security apparatus at a time when I was actively engaged in negotiations with national security to free the leaders of Abyei who had been arrested and were in detention, an operation in which Matet had been fully involved. Ironically, they included Achwil Bulabek and Patal Biliu, who had then separated from Matet and had been welcomed back by their people, as a result of another mediation effort I had undertaken earlier. Initially, that reconciliation had included Matet, whose comings and goings between the Dinka and the Arabs were to continue according to the dynamics of the situation.

Indeed, Matet would remain the single most influential security agent, a source of terror and pervasive insecurity in the area, and the principal obstacle to the unity of the family and the tribe. He and I would have a series of confrontations, ranging from shrewd diplomacy to open hostility. In retrospect, he was right to see me as his principal and most formidable adversary in our family. The only difference was that while he saw me as a personal enemy, I felt no personal animosity toward him; I saw him only as a menace and indeed a source of grave danger to the security and stability of the Ngok Dinka.

7

Quest for Ngok Autonomy

The Ngok Inclined, and Pressurized, to Join the South

Matet Ayom's intrigues with the security forces as evidenced by our own findings and the account of Ngor Mijok, and the fact that the Dinka themselves were not able to end the feud within the family of Deng Majok which had become a source of disunity to the tribe, were symptomatic of the loss of the tribal autonomy which Father had zealously protected. The result was that Ngok power structures and processes had been infiltrated by Arab tribal and governmental agents, operating through Dinka cronies against the welfare of the community as a whole. The cohesiveness of the Dinka cultural values for conflict management and resolution were being replaced by gossip, rumor-mongering, and intrigues that profoundly shattered the Dinka sense of security. Restoring the unity of the family and the tribe had become imperative and I could not relegate that responsibility to anyone else. For reasons of gender, education, and profile in public service, the Ngok Dinka looked to me for protection. The Addis Ababa Agreement of 1972 had ended the war between the North and the South by granting the South regional autonomy. Following the peace accord, I had joined the government as ambassador, first to the Scandinavian countries and then to the United States of America. That added to my obligation and leverage in the service of my local community, even from abroad. In due course, I would get even closer in the position of state minister for foreign affairs.

The status of the Ngok Dinka had been discussed in the Addis Ababa talks with southerners (initially alerted by me during my return visit from my U.N. mission to Gabon where a preparatory committee on the talks was in full operation), claiming the Ngok area as part of the South, while northerners asserted that it was northern. It was agreed at the Addis Ababa talks that the issue would be decided by the Ngok Dinka in a referendum. This compromise was seen by the Ngok Dinka as a betrayal by the South and a northern scheme for continuing Arab domination of the area.

Their view was soon confirmed to me when I went back to the Sudan to assume my new role as ambassador to Scandinavia. I travelled to the South and held extensive discussions with leaders at both the national and regional levels, and in particular with Abel Alier, the regional president who had negotiated the Addis Ababa Agreement. It became quite obvious that the central government did not intend to hold the agreed upon referendum, nor did the South intend to confront the central government on the issue.

Meanwhile the Ngok, having identified themselves, and become identified, with the South during the civil war, and nursing the bitterness of dreadful experiences, began to agitate for joining the South. The educated were particularly vocal on the point. To make things worse, the Ngok were not provided with the repatriation, resettlement and rehabilitation services given to the post-war South, even though the area had also been devastated by civil war. In their bitterness, they accused the South of having sacrificed them. Bulabek Malith articulated the sentiment of the Ngok thus: "We fought together ... [the Arabs] burned down all our villages, including cattle-byres ... Even grain, they burned ... [T]hey did that ... because they ... knew we had joined our people. But when the settlement was reached, it was as though the Abyei people were sacrificed for peace ... We had had people die in the forest; we had had people die at home while we were supposed to be in the North ... What makes us remain in the North?" (Deng 1980:284-285)

The strategy of the Arabs was to claim Ngokland as belonging to Kordofan, the implication being that if people wanted to join the South, they had to move physically and leave the land. Since other areas of the Dinka had been affiliated to Kordofan and subsequently severed and affiliated to the South, such claim of land ownership could not be justified on purely administrative grounds. The authorities therefore revised the history of occupation of the land to give the Homr Arabs prior claim to ownership, even though historical evidence abundantly contradicted their claim. The Commissioner of southern Kordofan, Mahmoud Haseeb, an

Arabized and Islamized Nuba known for a pan-Arabist ideological bent, summarized the history of contact between the two groups in present-day Abyei district in a passage quoted in the study conducted by Abdelbasit Saeed: "This area is a territory of Kurdufan [sic] which had been uninhabited until the beginning of the 17th century when the Misiriyya Arabs from the north and the Dinka from the south met here ... The two groups have mutual and vested interests in peaceful cooperation so as to share grazing land and available water resources offered by this generous environment for their pastoral nomadic existence" (Saeed 1982:210-211).

The same study quotes the passage from Henderson which confirms the Ngok accounts of their prior settlement even in the areas now occupied by the Baggara who came in subsequently. The critical point in Henderson's account is that the Baggara Arabs first came in contact with the Ngok section of Thorjok Alei who were still farthest North in the Muglad or Denga area "one generation" after the mainstream Ngok had settled not only where they are now but in the fertile northeast area called Ngol [which Henderson spells as Gnol] under the leadership of Kwoldit. That the Ngok were originally farther north than where they now are is further substantiated by the fact that Kwoldit's grandson, Allor, Deng Majok's great-great grandfather, "subsequently moved South to Korreita" (Henderson 1939:58).

And indeed, Abdelbasit Saeed cites a document of unidentified source which states that "The Missiriya groups of the Sudan have their origin in the Missiriya tribe which inhabits – until today – French Equatorial Africa (Tchad). They have their origin in the Juhaina Arab tribes [who] entered the River Shari basin in 1650 where they encountered Beigi tribes, fought against them, and continued their migration eastwards until they reached the site known today as Al Muglad" (Saeed 1982:121). Later, "The Humr [sic] moved southward and after several battles with the Ngok Dinka in Bahr al-Arab to the South established a *modus operandi* between the various sections of the two groups" (Saeed 1982:122).

Notwithstanding the documented history of Dinka and Arab early migration and settlement, Arab sources, including provincial reports, assert that the Arabs predated the Dinka as settlers not only in the present-day Arab areas, but also in the heartland of Ngok territory. This tendency is clearly new and has been fostered by the rise of pro-South nationalism among the Ngok and the fear of the Arabs that if Ngokland were affiliated to the South, their seasonal access to the land in search of pastures and water would be hampered. This is precisely why their claims to the land are now being made without any attention to objective facts. Abdelbasit, for instance, wrote: "The Humr ... believe that it was *Nazir* Ali Al Gulla of the Humur (appointed in 1905) who first permitted the Ngok – at the request of Nazir Arob Biong ... to cross Khor Abu Nafiesa to the North and settle at a place later to be named Sultan Arob" (Saeed 1982:163-164). He also refers to Babo's claim made at the peace conference in March 1966, to the effect that "it was his father, Nazir Nimir Ali Julla who ... permitted the Ngok in 1939 to move even farther North into a place known as Ragaba Zarga" (Saeed 1982:164). He does not, however, register the response of either the Dinka themselves or the arbitrators, presumably because they were omitted from the official district records.

The reaction of the Baggara Arabs and the authorities of Kordofan to the Ngok demand to join the South demonstrates that the fears of the Ngok leaders that their hospitality to the Arabs would be reversed to turn them into "guests" was justified. Joining the South had become the equivalent of the southern call for "federation" in the 1950s and 1960s, which was seen as synonymous with separation and had to be suppressed in the same way the southern movement had been suppressed. Although killing had stopped, the methods used in fighting this alleged separatism were quite similar to those prevailing in the South during the southern struggle for recognition. Educated Ngok were exiled or subjected to annoyance or provocation. In the words of Marieu Ajak: "The educated had already been picked and sent away. Each [one] would come and it would be said, 'This boy can read; send him away ... If you leave him here, he will be able to read what is in the books and he will understand the accusations. Let all the educated be moved!' That was why all our boys were sent away. Only we, the ignorant, remained. And the [opportunists] became the educated because they spoke Arabic" (Deng 1980:336).[47] The Ngok Dinka were confronted with a dilemma not much different from the one faced by the South: should they press for joining the South, which was clearly not going to be allowed, or seek alternatives within the North?

Government suppression of the Ngok aspiration to join the South directly interfered with the local autonomy of the people within Kordofan which had given their leaders a privileged position in comparison with their counterparts in both the North and the South. With this privileged position gone, being in the North was perceived as an anomaly that imposed considerable disadvantages on the Dinka. This in turn intensified

---

47. For a reaction from the South, see Deng 1980:92-93, 219-220.

their active political move to disaffiliate themselves from the North. But the more they acted in that direction through pressures on both the regional and the central governments, the more they were repressed by the local authorities in Kordofan and the more the confrontation and the conflict escalated. And in this respect, the southern regional government was powerless.

An Initiative Towards National Integration

After reflecting on the impasse or the dilemma, I came to the conclusion that instead of leaving the fate of the Ngok Dinka to an agreement between the North and the South, it would be more practical to adopt an approach that would take the initiative to the Ngok Dinka themselves as the focus of concern. I therefore wrote a policy paper entitled, "A Proposed Plan for the Development of Abyei as a Model for National Integration", in which I made a case for empowering the area to play its historical role as a bridge between North and South and a model for national unity and integration. I argued that the Ngok demand for joining the South was a reaction to the on-going policies of Arab domination in the area in contrast to southern autonomy and the fact that they did not benefit from the programs of post-war resettlement, rehabilitation, and development, even though they had suffered from the war with the rest of the South. By giving them a micro-autonomy which would recruit local people in administration, the police, education, and other services in the area and a program of economic, social, and cultural development that would build on the distinctive features of the area as a border region between North and South, the Ngok Dinka could be reconciled to their role as southerners in a northern province. Northerners and southerners could meet and interact in a positively harmonious climate with people committed to facilitating and promoting national unity and integration. That way, the people of Abyei could benefit locally and yet serve a national purpose, that would justify the national attention their autonomy and development would receive.

My paper began with an assessment of the autonomy solution to the southern problem and its long-term implications for the unity and integration of the country. It stated:

> There is still an unresolved fear on the part of some
> Sudanese that autonomy is a degree of separation and
> may be a step in the direction of greater separation ...
> Quite the contrary, ... autonomy is a safety-valve which

251

guarantees harmonious interaction between citizens in their process towards national integration ... Where the strains of a power-struggle and the threats of outside domination are removed, and the freedom of social intercourse is guaranteed and promoted, symbols of identification may be accepted or rejected on the basis of their own appeal or strength and not on the basis of prejudice. The issue for the Sudan ... is finding out and formulating those symbols which would tend to unite rather than divide. With these symbols to guide development, with autonomy to ensure the security of those whose support is vital, with free interaction between the various parts of the country, and with calculated action at all levels to maximize the net outcome, there is every reason to believe, indeed expect, that there would emerge a genuine consciousness of the wider Sudan as a basis for a common national identification and integration.

The report then proceeded to review the context of the Abyei area to make the case that it is a microcosm of the Sudan in much the same way that the Sudan was a microcosm of Africa. The unsettled situation in Abyei area was highlighted to explain the impact which the Addis Ababa accord was having on the Ngok who felt left out of the settlement although they had suffered in the war as much as their compatriots in the South. After arguing that it would be a mistake to dismiss as unrepresentative the educated youth of Abyei who spoke for their people, the report enumerated the basic issues which had to be addressed if the situation were to be eased and the area made a positive symbol and model of national unity and integration:

First, the Abyei people still felt oppressed, dominated and deprived of an equitable share in their local power. That was not due to any national policies from Khartoum, but to the still lingering 'colonial' mentality and attitude of the administrators, officials, and security forces in the area and to some extent, in the district and the province.

Second, the Abyei people felt that nobody cared about their suffering from displacement, hunger and disease resulting from the southern problem. Instead of being privileged as the prototype for national unity, they were ignored and abandoned as insignificant and worthless.

Third, they believed that while development schemes were being planned and implemented in the South, they remained caught up in the South-North gulf not only unable to play their bridging role effectively but, worse, left backward, suffering, and without prospects for self-improvement.

The solutions I proposed emanated from the analysis, based on the assumption that it was necessary for Abyei people to feel that they had a share in their local power rather than remain dominated by what they conceived as an outsider, that they received equal attention for relief, resettlement and rehabilitation, and that they were not left behind on the path of development. I therefore proposed:

First, that a form of local control be implemented by the appointment and transfer of Abyei sons and daughters to significant positions in the area, and in particular in the fields of administration, police and education. I suggested that Abyei be upgraded to a local council and a district, responsible to the Province authorities, but with a special protective eye from Khartoum that would enhance their sense of autonomy and security from the local, often biased, administrators who symbolized external domination and oppression. I also suggested that the educational institutions of Abyei be upgraded with syllabi welding both the educational system of the South, which was vernacular-based on the elementary level, and that of the North, which was Arabic-based. That would alleviate the fear of the Abyei people that their distinctive cultural character was being disregarded while that of the South is being developed. At the same time, it would allow for the marriage of the two cultural contexts – southern and northern – and indeed enrich the Abyei people from that mixture. In case it was argued that the Abyei population was too small for those services, I suggested that the area's importance for the national interest warranted special attention even if it became necessary to fill the population gap by admitting pupils from both the South and the North to facilitate integration. The graduates of Abyei could then proceed to the South and the North for higher education.

Second, that the issue of relief, resettlement and rehabilitation be regarded as a matter of emergency. Maximum results would be attained if the measures in that respect were coordinated with the other administrative proposals.

Third, that the question of mid and long-term development of the area be addressed. If Abyei were to play the important role of model for national unity and integration, its people had to be made to see the advantages of that role through special and intensive measures of accelerated social and economic development. Such a program should encourage the Dinka to integrate and mix with their northern compatriots in the area on the basis of equality, brotherhood, and mutual share of the advantages of nationally guided, but locally managed development. It was a fact that some of the local Arabs fully identified their interests with those of the Dinka and were therefore integrated members of the community.

The report concluded:

> Abyei has always been a model of Sudanese national unity even though this fact is little known ... [The Ngok Dinka's] past identification with their Northern compatriots [was] founded on mutual respect, an equitable control over their own local power, and their realization of common interests in their wider association with their Northern neighbours. With the granting of autonomy to the South, with the implementation of relief, resettlement and rehabilitation measures, and with prospects for extensive social and economic development, the South now feels a sense of solidarity with the North as it has never felt before. Abyei needs something similar on a much smaller scale; charging local boys with administrative responsibilities in the area, availing the area of a relief, resettlement and rehabilitation programme, and implementing a scheme of development which could build on local potentials with minimum capital demands. But the stakes, as well as the potential advantages of Abyei, go beyond the local level: Abyei should be made a model of guided ... change towards the long-term goal of cross-cultural diffusion and national integration.

The Proposal Rejected and Chieftainship Abolished

The proposal was well received by the central government under the influence of the ministers of local government, Dr. Jaafar Mohamed Ali Bakheit, and of foreign affairs, Dr. Mansour Khalid, who, being scholars and the most influential personalities at the time, found the idea intellectually intriguing and politically attractive.

Persuaded by these ministers, President Nimeiri went to Abyei in December 1972 to announce the new policy. I was supposed to accompany him, but as that conflicted with the urgent need to open the embassy in Sweden, I felt obliged to give the national interest priority over my local area. Although I did not go, I tried to pass my message to the local leaders through Bona Malwal, then deputy minister of information in the central government. But, although Bona himself accompanied the president to Abyei, and, according to him, tried to moderate the position of the Dinka, there appears to have been a breakdown in communication, for according to the local leaders, my policy line was never explained to the people the way it was intended. Since they were not prepared for the policy, the Ngok people, in particular the educated class, responded to the president's announcement with hostility.

Their spokesman, cousin Ring Arob, with an impressive command of Arabic, articulated the differences between the Ngok Dinka and the northerners, and what their people shared with the South. Apparently, the tone was so offensive that the President was outraged, declared that he had not come to Abyei to divide the country, rejected the hospitality of the people, and decided to hold back some of the things he had planned to do for the area. But he was eventually persuaded by Bona Malwal to be magnanimous, agreed to accept their hospitality, and promised an autonomous status in Kordofan, with a special central Government interest in the development of the area.

The President was also confronted with complaints against Adam Deng, especially his heavy drinking. Since the leftist revolution of Nimeiri was antagonistic to tribal chiefs and had in fact dissolved native administration in the more developed North, excepting the Ngok area as culturally southern, the complaint against Adam prompted Nimeiri to dismiss him summarily and declare chieftainship abolished. The Ngok Dinka were stunned. A system which they believed had been part of their social order since time immemorial and which they considered indispensable had suddenly been abolished with a casual pronouncement by the president.

In the place of the chief, people's courts were instituted which were dominated by the opponents of the family, foremost among whom was Matet Ayom, who now saw himself as the new chief. But their system of justice was essentially one of unscrupulous vindictiveness against the traditional leaders. In the name of their newly found "democratic" rule of the people, they became scandalously oppressive to the people, especially those who owed allegiance or loyalty to the old leadership. Calls for the restoration of chieftainship and the installation of one of Deng Majok's sons began to pour on me, urging that I intercede with the president to reverse his decision.

The Issues of Development and Integration Taken up Again

Meanwhile, after pausing for a while to let the dust settle, in the wake of the turbulent and clearly unsuccessful visit of the president, I began to urge the influential ministers of local government and foreign affairs to press for the implementation of the policy of developing the area as a symbol of national unity and integration. Dr. Bakheit responded very positively. A ministerial committee comprised of some of the leading ministers in the economic and service sectors was formed to formulate and oversee a development strategy for Abyei. Although I was then ambassador to Scandinavia, I was appointed member of the committee. The area was elevated to a sub-province level and a senior administrator (a northerner) was appointed to head the administration, assisted by nine local government officers, one for each sub-tribe (also all northerners).

While that was a major move in the implementation of the policy of development in the area, it did not involve the recruitment of the local people, which I regarded as the essential element in the micro-autonomy I had proposed. I therefore continued to urge Minister Bakheit to Dinkanize the administration of the area, and proposed as deputy commissioner for the area Justin Deng Aguer, who had studied law and economics in France and was serving in the South. My efforts eventually bore fruit and Justin Deng was seconded to head the administration in the area. A number of Ngok policemen and teachers were transferred to the area from the South. At my initiative, the Harvard Institute for International Development (HIID) was invited to assist in designing an integrated development program in the area with funding from the United States Agency for International Development (USAID). Toward the end of 1975, HIID sent a two-man team of Lester Gordon, the Director of the Institute, and Stephen Joseph, Director of their International Health Programme, to Abyei in January 1976. The team prepared a report on their preliminary view of the development plan. The report stressed three points: the physical isolation of the area, and hence the urgent need for action on transport and communications; the complex administration with its cumbersome decision-making machinery, and the need for simplification, especially in budgeting, for fast and effective planning and implementation of development projects; and finally, the almost complete absence of basic information necessary to development.

The team considered the last point so essential to any plan of development that they recommended the establishment of a development research centre in the area, to be jointly staffed by Harvard and counterparts in the Sudan, such as the National Research Council, or the Development Studies Centre of the University of Khartoum. The Harvard contribution would be phased out over a period of time. As well as research, the Centre could implement immediate projects, to convince the then disillusioned people that the Government was in earnest about its declared policy. The longer-term programme would be confined to coordinating research with practical implementation. The envisaged strategy of development aimed at maximum use of the human resources available in the area, and the contextualization of development to minimize social disruption and disintegration, and was to be a model capable of being applied to other parts of the Sudan, Africa, and indeed the developing world. In addition to USAID, the European Community also assisted with the funding.

These efforts at implementing government policy towards Abyei became more institutionalized when in November 1976, and with the personal involvement of Professor Abdalla Ahmed Abdalla, the Minister of Agriculture, Food and Natural Resources, the ministry was invited to take part in meetings and field trips undertaken by representatives of various organizations, financing groups and planning institutes, to investigate and exchange views on the possibilities for coordination of international and local approaches for the development of southern Kordofan. David C. Cole, Associate Director of HIID, represented the Institute. As a follow-up to the report of the first team, and as a consequence of Cole's participation in the November discussions, it was agreed that a group of consultants, headed by him, was to visit the area in January 1977 and exchange views with the various executive branches so as to draw up both short and long-term development plans for the area.

With the support of Dr. Mansour Khalid, who had become assistant to the president for coordination and foreign affairs, we got President Nimeiri to reiterate the policy on Abyei at the National Unity Day in Kadugli on March 1, 1977, solemnly pledging his personal responsibility for the development of the Abyei area. Placing it in the context of the overall development of southern Kordofan, President Nimeiri stated:

> I would like development in this rich province to be an
> overall and integrated development. I direct the Ministry
> of Finance, Planning and National Economy and the
> People's Executive Council of the Province to co-operate

in the setting up of a comprehensive plan for the development of the province by promoting the traditional sector, indicating the contributions of the four economic sectors, and the share of the local development and self-help in this effort which we want to be an example to be emulated by all provinces. If this is what we want for your province, I want the area of Abyei – where the great Dinka and Missiriya tribes meet and co-exist – to be an example of the interaction of cultures. Abyei is to the Sudan exactly what the Sudan is to Africa. This project will be implemented under my personal supervision in cooperation with all the institutions of the state, universities and international organizations (Deng 1986:264).

Shortly after the President's statement, which spotlighted Abyei to the whole nation, the second team from HIID arrived, headed by David Cole and with the membership of Richard Cash, Public Health Specialist, William Huntington, Anthropologist in the School of Social Studies, John Villaume, Education Specialist, and John Thomas, Agricultural Specialist. They were later joined by Henk Slottower, Agricultural Adviser for the Development Fund of the European Economic Community, and a five man team of Sudanese counterparts, with the Agriculturalist, Sadiq Kabbashi, a northerner as their team leader.

After extensive travels and consultations in the area, the team prepared a detailed and comprehensive report which was presented to an inter-ministerial and inter-departmental meeting, chaired by Husayn Idris, Minister of State for Agriculture, Food and Natural Resources, and attended by representatives from USAID and the Development Fund of the European Economic Community. The report focussed on five principal areas which, according to the team, the people of Abyei saw as needing improvement. These included increasing agricultural production to self-sufficiency and varying production for a better diet; increasing water supply for people and livestock during the dry season; improving communications by road and radio; expanding education from the limited basic level to one that would approach national standards and also meet local needs for relevance and cultural continuity; and extending health services to cover more fully the needs of the scattered rural populations. The Harvard plan was formally adopted by the meeting, which also elaborated a programme for short and long-term development of the area, and established a technical committee or secretariat to finalize the plans and follow up their execution. USAID became the principal funder.[48]

Family Reconciliation and Restored Chieftainship

But without the traditional institution of chieftainship, even these measures could not ensure the security and stability of the area. Complaints on this issue continued to pour on me from the tribe. It became imperative that I approach the issue of restoring chieftainship with the minister of local government, Dr. Bakheit. I was then ambassador in Washington, D.C., but back in the Sudan on a mission.

Persuaded by my argument, Dr. Bakheit sought and obtained the approval of the president for the restoration of chieftainship among the Ngok Dinka and the appointment of one of Deng Majok's sons as paramount chief. The stipulated condition was that I should unite the family and the tribe. This meant ending the blood feud in the family. Despite the rebuff I had received from the family two years earlier, I felt that the circumstances were ripe for another attempt. Besides, the stakes involved were very high.

My first task was to try to persuade Bol, who was now practicing medicine in northern Italy, to support the initiative. Bol was the sibling brother of Abdalla and Chan, and as I have already noted, the third brother who was massacred with them, Bulabek, was also from their section of the family. Bol was extremely bitter towards Adam. But his support for reconciliation was crucial to any prospects of success.

Bol had initially agreed to join me on my trip to the Sudan, but had declined the last minute. Despite the return of peace to the country and my own involvement in the government, he remained suspicious and politically noncommittal. His last minute refusal to go back indicated a degree of uncertainty about his own security.

I arranged for the Ministry of Foreign Affairs to send a message to Bol through our embassy in Rome saying that his immediate presence concerning the situation in Abyei was required and that a return air ticket was waiting for him at the embassy. He was expected to arrive by a specified flight and date. The message was signed "Kharjiya," the Arabic code for the Ministry of Foreign Affairs.

---

48. Abyei Integrated Rural Development project is cited by Mansour Khalid (1989:88) as one of the major projects funded by USAID in the Sudan in the 1970s.

I was not sure Bol would actually come as directed and therefore did not go to meet him at the airport. Surprising us by turning up in Bona Malwal's house, he announced dramatically, though jokingly, that he demanded knowing why his presence was required and that he was prepared to take the next flight back if he were not persuaded.

The task of convincing Bol began immediately. It was not easy, for he could not stomach the idea of reconciling with Adam. It was a bitterness that was not amenable to rational arguments. But the pragmatic case for reconciliation, especially the prospect of restoring chieftainship, was too compelling for Bol to obstruct.

The government arranged for us to fly to El Obeid, where we were joined by the governor of the province, Salah Ahmed Bukhari, and his chief of security, and together flew to Abyei to embark on our formidable task.

Shortly after we landed, we went to pay respects to our father's grave and to greet those members of the family, mostly women and children, who had not been in the receiving crowds at the airport. Uncle Arob, with whom I had discussed the prospects of reconciliation in El Obeid two years earlier, was there to receive us and to conduct the ritual blessings before we could enter the compound. A lamb was held down as we stepped over it before it was slaughtered in sacrifice, while Arob uttered a prayer of thanksgiving to God and the ancestral spirits. With a crowd of people gathered around us, he said in his prayers that he had not been worried by the abolition of chieftaincy because he trusted that it would sooner or later return to us. It was not something our clan had usurped from anyone else; it was a responsibility God had bestowed upon us in the Byre of Creation. Even if someone found it lost in the forest and tried to pick it up, it would burn his hands and he would be forced to hand it back to us.

As soon as the welcoming rituals were over, I pulled Uncle Arob aside and told him that he must never ever again say the sort of thing he had just said. Times were changing and democracy was the principle behind the revolution. The kind of thing he had said was precisely what the revolution was against and could be used by the enemies of the family to fan hostility with the regime. Uncle Arob got the point and responded accordingly.

We already knew that among the key leaders of the opposition who had been installed in positions of authority and were waging a vindictive war against our clan, and in particular the Deng family, were Matet Ayom and Zachariah Atem, the medical assistant in charge of health services in the area.

Much has already been said of Matet Ayom as a veteran politician with whom Father had maintained an ambivalent relationship, alternating from being a close friend and companion to being imprisoned for various offenses. Zachariah Atem had grown up with us, living in our house while at school and for all intents and purposes, virtually adopted by our family. His shift from being a beneficiary of Deng Majok and an adopted member of the family to an embittered enemy was something we never understood or investigated.

As the account of Uncle Ngor indicated, working closely with them were Achwil Bulabek, the chief of Abyor, our sub-tribe, Father's uncle who had been his right-hand man in the struggle for power within the family, and Patal Biliu, a sectional chief from Anyiel sub-tribe, who had also been one of Father's close associates. Again, what had turned these men against Deng Majok was a mystery, except perhaps the hardness of times, ambitions for power, and the rewards of working with the security forces, as contrasted with the risks of confrontation with them.

During his last days, Father had spoken to us about these men as he worried about the state of affairs in the tribe and what would happen to his people if he should not survive the illness. Clearly, Matet Ayom was their ring leader and Father knew how far he could go in his unscrupulous ambition, vindictiveness, and exploitation of situations. Father did not have any clear guidance for us in reflecting on the destructive role of these individuals, only to draw our attention to the situation.

In addition to being the judges in the newly instituted people's courts, they virtually established themselves as the ultimate tribal authority in all matters and did not disguise their determination to use their power with a vengeance, often bragging about the reversals in tribal hierarchy. They maintained a very close relationship with the security forces, had their enemies arrested and detained on allegations of some anti-Arab and anti-government activity that was nearly always contrived or fabricated to conceal very personal and selfish motives, and conspicuously enriched themselves from security bribes and misappropriation of the cattle of people accused of some wrongs or misdeeds.

The day of our arrival in Abyei, I asked Matet Ayom for a private meeting with me. I began the meeting by explaining to him that my childhood memory about our people and their dignity derived largely from the noblemen I had observed in Father's court and that he was among those who had made a lasting impression on me. In that, I was being sincere, for Matet had been a very impressive man. I proceeded to say that although I had heard a great deal about what was going on in the tribe, I did not want to come to any conclusion before I heard from him. That was why I decided to speak to him before I talked to anyone else about the state of affairs in the tribe. I wanted him to brief me fully about the situation, what the problems were, what his explanation was, and what he saw as the solutions.

Matet was clearly taken by surprise. He prefaced his remarks by saying that he would speak to me very candidly. When he heard that we were coming, he said he convened a meeting with his close associates and told them that the son of Deng Majok who was coming, by which he meant me, was the closest to his father's ways. He would be certain to think of moves that would surprise them. He therefore warned them to be on the alert to counter any moves I might make. The fact that I would call him to discuss the situation with him before talking to others was precisely the kind of surprise moves he had anticipated and feared.

And indeed, despite his ambivalence, Matet had a great deal of praise for his enemy-friend, our father, and the way he had managed the affairs of the tribe. Deng Majok, he said, brought noblemen from all over the tribe to broaden the basis of his leadership. He contrasted all that with the way the family had narrowed its leadership base after Deng Majok's death and how the behavior of those responsible had eroded the unity of the tribe behind our leadership. He particularly focused on what he saw as the arrogance of power which was antithetic to the principles of the revolution.

Matet then illustrated his case with the way Justin Deng was handling the situation. Apparently, Justin, in a spirit of overconfidence and characteristic straightforwardness, had confronted Matet and his clique, particularly Achwil Bulabek and Patal Biliu, with a threat the moment he assumed his administrative responsibilities. He had said to them that he knew they had been living on the blood of innocent people and had amassed wealth in the process. He warned them that those days were over and that he would see to it that justice prevailed.

From that day on, the elders, among the proudest and most capable administrators in the area, resolved to undermine the authority of Justin Deng with the security forces and the Arabs. Their objective was to make him fail, to frustrate the autonomy I had been striving to achieve for the area, and to return full control to Arab administrators from whom they stood to benefit.

His complaint to Ngor about my role which I only learned about many years later indicated that he held me responsible for the manner in which the basis of leadership had been narrowed to exclude him. And considering that during our visit following Father's death, I had endeavored to undermine the power of the informants, of which he was the leader, his antagonism against me as their number one enemy was understandable. What he did not and perhaps could not appreciate was that I was for the security and welfare of the tribe, not the monopoly of power by our family and our sub-tribe, Abyor, which was evidently his preoccupation. My talk with him must have alleviated some of his concerns about me personally. But since he had always considered me a fox in a very ambivalent sense of the word, Matet realized that he was negotiating with a difficult adversary in a situation that was no longer so favorable to him. He therefore had to be shrewd and practical.

The lesson Matet wanted to convey to me from his account was that if I wanted to unite the tribe, I should check the arrogance of power in our family and make them open up to the democratic changes in the country. Nonetheless, he conceded that he was not opposed to the leadership role of the family, only the way that leadership was being displayed by individual members. Arrogance of power was of course antithetic to traditional notions of leadership among the Dinka and although our clan believed themselves chosen by God to rule, the manner of their leadership could not be described as arrogant. I certainly did not and would not support that notion of leadership. In principle, there was nothing in what Matet said, including his criticism of Justin Deng, that I could disagree with. Judging from the way we had come with the government authority behind us, Matet realized that the tide was turning and wanted to make the best of the situation over which he was losing control. He and I had therefore established a base for forging ahead with tribal reconciliation.

That evening, we met with Justin Deng, the nine local government administrators (still all northerners), and the security authorities to assess the situation and plan our moves. Their reports confirmed that the tribe was yearning for the return of chieftainship and the appointment of one of Deng Majok's sons as the paramount chief. We agreed that we would verify that fact by consulting with the chiefs of all the nine sub-tribes the following day. It was also agreed that the task of reconciling and reuniting the family would be left to us, the family leaders, although the governor would be available to reinforce our efforts. Once the unity of the family was achieved, we would then work on reconciliation at the tribal level. In effect, efforts at both levels would be concurrently conducted.

For several days, we talked endlessly day and night with individuals privately, smaller groups, and large numbers according to the issue and the context. First, we had to bring on board the senior members of the clan, on top of which were Uncles Deng Makuei, Arob Kwol, and several of their half brothers. Then we zeroed in on the conflict within the Deng Majok family in which Nyanboldit, her daughter Adau, and members of their section were the most difficult to persuade. For the same reason, Bol's role was absolutely vital. Beginning with a mild support for reconciliation, Bol felt challenged by their hard line and asserted his leadership in support of our stand.

Adam's side of the family was, in contrast, quite amenable. Of course, they had no apologies to make for no one ever admitted to Adam having had a hand in the assassination plot, but their tone was inherently apologetic about the whole tragedy and the disunity of the family.

As we moved toward a consensus, there was never an explicit concession on the part of Nyanboldit and the hardliners; only a softening of position in the face of the unified pressure on them to concede. The final episode was for us to assert the need for unity with a mild resistance from the opposition and an implicit understanding that reconciliation and reunification provided the common ground.

The last issue to be resolved and without which reconciliation could not have been possible, was that the Sacred Spears which had been forcefully seized by the security forces from Abdalla's family and handed over to Adam (a tragic replay of the Deng Majok-Deng Makuei crisis), had to be returned to the section of Nyanboldit. Adam and his side of the family conceded.

News of the family reconciliation was received with a sigh of relief and jubilation by the tribe. It made overall tribal reconciliation much easier. But not before an exhaustive discussion with key individuals, groups, and finally the public in the general assembly. In one of the most crucial all-night meetings in which the process had led to a private confrontation between representatives of the clan and the opposition, Zachariah Atem once again raised the issue of the arrogance of power the clan was continuously accused of by the opposition. "If you really want to unite this tribe," he said in words almost identical to those of Matet, "then you must make your clan abandon the claim that they are born leaders and that the power to lead this tribe was bestowed upon them by God at Creation."

Uncle Arob was at the meeting and of course I thought back to my first discussion of the same issue with him following his prayers and the rituals of our reception. Then, to my surprise, Arob unwittingly betrayed the confidentiality of my advice to him by responding to Zachariah Atem, "Do not worry, we have already been warned."

When Matet bragged that apart from the late Chief Deng Majok himself, there was no one in the tribe who could beat him on his ability to articulate his case, Arob retorted, "Matet, no one has ever questioned your ability with words; what I don't know is the state of your heart." And in Dinka usage, the functions of the heart and the mind are fused, so that what Arob had in mind was not just compassion, but also judgment and prudence.

In the public meeting, Matet Ayom, Achwil Bulabek, and Patal Biliu all recounted with impressive candor and eloquence how they had looked forward to the assumption of administrative control of the area by someone who was not only a son of the area, but a kinsman, only to be rebuffed and rejected by Justin Deng. It was anger that had driven them to the enemy. Even Justin saw their point and appropriately apologized. In those confessions lay the foundation for reunification.

In the meeting with the governor, the security chief, Justin Deng, his administrators, and the chiefs of the sub-tribes, it was agreed that Ali Deng, Adam's younger sibling brother, who was the late Abdalla's age-mate, and who was then a police officer, would be chosen the next chief.

The following day, a public meeting was held to announce the family settlement and the tribal accord. Rituals of peace and reconciliation were held at both levels. It was unquestionably the most moving event of my life. The first was the tribal reconciliation ceremony in which Deng Makuei was called upon to bless the tribe as the spiritual leader of the leading clan. He spoke of how conflicts and animosities had soiled the ground on which the people walked, the food they ate, the air they breathed, the beds they slept on, and the words they spoke. He prayed to the ancestors and to God to heed the call for peace and reconciliation, to cleanse the ground on which people walked, to purify the food they ate and the air they breathed, to clean the sheets on which they slept, and to bless their tongues to speak words of peace, unity, and harmony. In the typical fashion of the Dinka in which what is wished is willed, Deng Makuei, raising his voice, becoming virtually possessed to the point where he looked almost physically transformed, cried out, "I have rejected the word of quarrel and I call on you spirits in the sky above and you ancestors in the earth below to bring peace into our hearts, let our people breathe the cool air of health and security, let the food in their bellies settle well and let them sleep in tranquility. I speak not as a chief or anybody's master, but as your eldest son among your children."

These quotes are a crude recollection of the spiritually charged words uttered by Deng Makuei and which almost literally brought tears to the eyes of his audience, including myself. Although I had been and would continue to be involved in mediation efforts in the tribe and in the country, that was for me a most gratifying moment of accomplishment.

The other aspect, almost equally moving, was the process by which the Sacred Spears were taken by a group of elders, singing the oldest hymns of the clan, from Adam's hut, circling around the village several times and taking them to the hut of Amel Yual, the head wife of Nyanboldit's section in Abyei.

Meanwhile, the tribe was jubilant with joyous festivities. Bulls were slaughtered, food prepared in plenty, and everywhere there was singing and dancing. It was a moment of true consensus and positive harmony.

8
Arabs and Dinkas at War

Suspicions, Perceptions and Antagonism

The Dinka were now united and harmonious, but relations between them and their neighboring Missiriya Arab tribes were deteriorating and threatening the Ngok with a relapse into disunity. Ngok-Homr relations had already been strained by the North-South war and had involved bloody confrontation in the mid-1960s. With the Addis Ababa settlement, tension was once more raised by the issue of whether the Ngok Dinka should be annexed to the South or remain in Kordofan province. For the Missiriya Arabs, more than the preservation of unity, the area was of vital importance to them as a source of dry season pastures and water. But they also enjoyed a hegemonic dominance in the province which they did not want to abandon. And of course, the provincial authorities in Kordofan who shared this view saw Abyei as their domain. The North-South politics, which were dominated by the division between those who were labelled separatist and suppressed by the authorities and those considered unionists who were thereby favored by the system, now focused on Abyei.

Although my alternative policy of developing the Abyei area as an autonomous bridge, a model of unity and national integration, was meant to alleviate this tension, it had the opposite effect. Dinka southern nationalists, including Zachariah Bol Deng, saw it as a betrayal of the cause. The Arabs saw it as a clever ploy to southernize the administration of the area as a first step toward its eventual annexation to the South.

They saw the appointment of Justin Deng Aguer, whose identity many of them confused with his cousin, Justin Deng Biong, one of the rebel leaders in the area during the civil war, as a clear affirmation of their suspicion. Some of them knew that the other rebel leader, Osman Koc Aguer, who had been killed in the war, was Justin Deng Aguer's younger brother, and that too did not reassure them. The Arabs also saw the proposed development of the area as a preferential treatment which favored the Dinka over the Arabs. The fact that the project had been initiated at the center was also seen by the provincial authorities as an imposition by the central government on the regional government with undue influence from me.

What was more, Justin reinvigorated the Dinka sense of identity, encouraged their social and cultural activities, utilized their traditional institutions to mobilize self-help labor in building schools and other public utilities and to encourage constructive competition in agricultural productivity and other development activities in the area. The provincial authorities saw all that as an attempt to reassert Dinka identity against Arabism.

The more the Arabs suspected Justin Deng as hostile to them, the more they cultivated Dinka supporters against him. And since the Arabs, both the tribes and the provincial authorities working together, had the power and the material means to use the stick and carrot strategy for winning supporters, they soon succeeded in recapturing their old allies, Matet Ayom, Achwil Bulabek, Patal Biliu, and Zachariah Atem. Justin Deng also reacted against them with a vengeance by suspending the three tribal leaders from their administrative positions, accusing them of undermining his authority and frustrating the administration of the area.

Ironically, the Arabs took from the Abyei policy the rationale I had used to persuade the authorities, namely the mutual interest in making the area a model of unity and integration, attributed that part of the policy to the president and the minister of local government, and sought to exploit it as a ground for claiming Ngok Dinka territory as a common property on which the Arabs too had a legitimate claim. That way, they turned a policy which was meant to benefit the Dinka into a justification for their usurping Dinka land. And indeed, Arab ambitions over the land would escalate from demanding equal access to claiming that they were indeed the original owners of the territory to which they had welcomed the Dinka as guests. In this, they enjoyed the sympathy, if not the open support, of the provincial authorities.

Ambassador Salah Ahmed Bukhari had been replaced as governor by Mahmoud Haseeb, a senior military officer, who, though a Nuba and therefore not an Arab, was a hardcore Arab nationalist and a frontliner in the pursuit of Arab interests in the area. Haseeb soon identified Justin Deng as the enemy of the Arabs in particular and of Kordofan in general in the Dinka area. He strove to undermine his authority in various ways, including over-ruling his suspension of the tribal administrators as beyond his powers.

Tension Increased by the Choice of a New Chief

Meanwhile, the selection of a paramount chief had also taken a turn that the Arabs and the provincial authorities disapproved of. A much younger brother, Kwol Adol, from Nyanboldit's section, was favored by the Dinka over Ali whom they opposed on the ground that he was Adam's sibling brother and also as too soft in confrontation with the Arabs. The objection to Ali had surfaced during our reconciliation talks, but only through whispers and rumors. Amidst the jubilation of reconciliation, I had been approached by Adau, Bol's sister, soon followed by a cousin, Arob Allor-Maker, both saying the same thing: If I really wanted the unity of the family and the tribe, then I should not make Ali, the brother of Adam, the chief. While Arob Allor merely argued that the choice be left entirely to the tribe, according to Adau, I should look for someone from the section of Nyanboldit to succeed, no matter how young. And indeed, while the section of the second wife, Nyanbol Amor, had senior sons, Nyanboldit's section had lost its senior sons in the massacre and had only high school children among its oldest sons.

My insistence on Ali was one of principle. Ali had stood with the family against his own sibling brother, was not only the oldest of the brothers at home, but by virtue of his experience in the police force, was professionally more qualified on security matters than the other brothers. To punish him for whatever wrong his brother had committed, which he had stood against, was grossly unfair. Besides, the reconciliation we had just achieved meant that we had transcended the conflict. It should, therefore, no longer be used against anyone, including Adam himself, let alone a brother who had opposed him. I knew that I was not successful with the hardliners, but I felt I was right and stood firm on my ground.

I later learned that after our return to our respective posts abroad, Bol had written to Justin Deng restating his position against Ali. He said that we had not carefully considered the matter as time had been too short, that the Arabs had maneuvered in favor of Ali, and that his impression was that his choice would be against the will of the people. Bol obviously wanted one of the younger brothers from their section of the family to be chosen. More specifically, he favored Kwol Adol. As he later put it to me, jokingly but seriously, Nyanboldit's section had suffered much and needed to be compensated.

Shortly after the reconciliation, I returned from my post as ambassador to the United States to be minister of state for foreign affairs, where I continued to follow even more closely the developments in the tribe. I also succeeded eventually in persuading Bol to return to the Sudan. We agreed that while I should remain in the central government and protect the interests of our people there, he should go to the South to practice his medicine and look after the interests of our people in the southern context. He was appointed to the regional Ministry of Health in the South. At Nimeiri's initiative, I went on an informal, fact-finding visit to Abyei following the January 1977 unity celebration in Kadugli in which the president had restated his policy on the area. I asked Bol to join me. That visit gave us the opportunity to witness the excellent work Justin had done in restoring a sense of confidence and security in the Dinka, but we also realized the growing gulf between him and the Arabs. The nine Arab administrators had now been withdrawn, but had not been replaced with Dinka administrators as I had proposed. Justin therefore operated singlehandedly in an environment of Arab hostility. The Dinka teachers and policemen who had been transferred to the area from the South were becoming demoralized, viewed with hostility and left stagnant without promotion or benefits. Clearly, Kordofan authorities were antagonistic to the autonomy and development of the area.

It was then that Justin advised me to change my position in favor of Ali and to endorse Kwol Adol. In his view, the people wanted Kwol and if I were to insist on Ali, I might be accused of a bias for a member of my section of the family. Besides, he argued less persuasively, Ali still retained his position as a police officer while Kwol had left his school to assume family responsibilities. I decided that perhaps Justin Deng, being the man on the ground, knew best, so I accepted his advice. And as soon as we were back in Kordofan, we approached the chief justice to expedite conferring judicial powers on Kwol Adol.

My task now was how to persuade Ali to give up his own ambitions for chieftainship and to support Kwol Adol. That proved to be a formidable task. Ali wanted the matter to be decided by elections. It was virtually a repeat of the experience with his brother, Adam. I even offered him my civil service retirement benefits to invest in a trucking business, arguing that with a sound financial base, added to his age and experience, he could be an influential leader behind the authority of his younger brother, Kwol Adol, which also sounded like an echo from my discussions with Adam years back. I combined that with the threat of opposing his candidacy if he should insist on his claim. After long, extensive and intensive discussions, I eventually succeeded in persuading Ali to surrender.

Ironically, just as my efforts at persuading Adam were not believed by some members of the family, especially from the section of Nyanboldit, my change of position in favor of Kwol Adol and efforts at persuading Ali to give up his claim were also suspect. Once, in a meeting with the brothers in my office in the Ministry of Foreign Affairs, I withdrew with Ali into another room in order to have a candid and tough talk with him, which crystallized the carrot and stick tactic that eventually worked. That was interpreted by the brothers who were at the meeting as suspicious, for why would I need to speak to Ali alone, unless there was something I did not want them to hear, and which they assumed must be in favor of Ali and against the united family position. But throughout that entire episode, Kwol Adol himself maintained an impressively serene, positive, and deferential attitude that did not reflect competitiveness, resentment, or suspicion, which contributed to my genuine change of mind in favor of his leadership.

But the appointment of Kwol as chief would become one of the things Kordofan authorities would hold against Justin Deng. Complaints against him began to pour on me. The commissioner, Mahmoud Haseeb, began to persuade me about the need to have him transferred elsewhere in Kordofan. In his effort to persuade me that his disapproval of Justin Deng was not anti-Dinka, Haseeb, the non-Arab, pan-Arabist, pointed at his own color of skin, saying, "Look at this color. If I should leave my position as governor, your people will fall victims of the Arabs." Unwittingly, Mahmoud Haseeb had admitted that race was a major factor and that the Dinka were vulnerable in the racial politics of Kordofan.

A Tragic Tribal War

It was not long before the brewing tensions between the Arabs and the Dinka exploded in violence. One incident after another escalated into a bloody tribal war in which the security forces working in cooperation with the *marahleen,* an armed mobile force that moved with the Arab

271

pastoralists for their protection, sided with the Arabs. Several hundred people lost their lives on both sides.

One event was particularly tragic not only because of its brutality, but also because among the victims was an individual of great promise to the area and the country. That incident calls for the elaboration of the developments that led to the tragic incident. As I reflected on the situation and considered Haseeb's position on Justin Deng, it became obvious to me that while Justin was doing exactly what I had expected of him, he had somehow become a symbol of the Arab-Dinka animosity. There was no way we could persuade the Arabs to have confidence in him. And yet, mutual trust by both Dinka and Arabs was necessary on that sensitive border. Reluctantly, I began to give in to the position of the governor on Justin, but I persuaded him that if Justin were to be transferred, he should be replaced by a Dinka who would be hopefully more acceptable to both sides. That was agreed.

In looking around for Justin's substitute, my choice fell on Mark Mijak Abiem, a former local government officer who was preparing for a Ph.D. in History in London University and had just returned to the Sudan to do a two-year field work on the relations between the Missiriya Arabs and the Ngok Dinka. I thought that his presence and his area of research provided us with a rare opportunity. As someone who had been educated entirely in the North and had been trained and employed as a local government administrator, the Arabs could not question his credentials and qualifications for the job. Mark had indeed started his education as a Muslim convert and although he later converted to Christianity he was well versed in Islam, fluent in Arabic, and culturally at home in northern society. Apart from our need for him, I thought that Mark might be in an even better position to have access to information in that leadership role than he would in a private scholarly capacity. I was convinced that by accepting the assignment, he would strike two birds with one stone.

Mark was not grabbed by the idea. I had to preach the cause in an attempt to persuade him. And even then, the most I got from him was a promise to think about it and be back to me within a day or two. As he was on his way to Abyei, his decision would determine whether he would go as the new governor for the area or as a mere research scholar in the field. I was eagerly waiting for Mark's final response when I heard the tragic news that he had decided against my offer, had left for Abyei almost ahead of his time, and, together with eighty other Dinkas, had been ambushed by the Arabs on the Muglad-Abyei road, and brutally murdered. It was a tragedy that echoed up to London. His supervisor,

272

Professor Richard Gray of the School of Oriental and African Studies, whom I had known while teaching in Khartoum University, wrote me a letter of condolence which conveyed their own grief. He said Mark had been one of the very best foreign students they had ever had. In his words, his death was not only a loss to the family and the country, but also to Africa and the world. That promise was destroyed in a blind and senseless tribal feud.

I went to a family memorial gathering in the home of Mark's older brother, Michael Deng Abiem. As I sat amidst the gathered crowd, their younger brother, Raphael Tiglei, then a student of law in Khartoum University, a dynamic young man whose revolutionary zeal had prompted him to join the southern Sudan Liberation Movement in the 1955-72 war at the remarkable age of nine, got up, asked for everybody's attention and called on me to answer a question: "As an advocate of the Ngok Dinka and the Missiriya Arabs remaining together in Kordofan, instead of letting the Ngok join their kith and kin in the South, what can you now say in the light of the violence prevailing in the area?"

It was of course a very unfair context in which to raise the question, but I had to respond and I did so by telling the whole truth: my initial attempt to have the definition of the South include the Ngok area, the clever referendum clause by which the negotiators at Addis Ababa had evaded the issue, my conclusion that the North and the South were not going to confront each other on the case of Abyei, and my decision to place the matter in the hands of the people of the area by making the best of a bad situation. The autonomy and the development of the area which I had proposed was my attempt to remedy a situation that was otherwise beyond our control. The tragedy of violence which Mark's death represented at its worst did not in any way invalidate the prudence and pragmatism of my approach. On the contrary, it underscored what I had feared and tried to remedy. I don't think I won applause, but I felt sure I had passed the test.

Talks in Various Contexts

The first vice-president, General Mohamed El Baghir, who was then acting president, as Nimeiri was out of the country, convened a meeting of the National Security Committee of which he was the chairman. General El Baghir had served in the South during the war and had been a leading member of the government delegation in the Addis Ababa talks. He understood the South very well and was highly respected by southerners.

General El Baghir invited me, ostensibly as acting minister of foreign affairs, since the senior minister was abroad. But as that was the first and only time I sat on the security committee, I realized that Baghir's real reason was my concern and familiarity with the situation. It was obvious from the start that some people did not understand my presence, which must have prompted the chairman to highlight my position as acting minister of foreign affairs.

Called upon by the chairman to brief the committee from my own perspective, I stressed the grievances of the people of Abyei, criticized the policies of the regional authorities and in particular their resistance to the implementation of the central government policy of autonomy and development in the area. I also highlighted what the Dinka saw as the partiality of the security forces in favor of the Arabs. In my view, there was need for the central government to be more assertive in ensuring justice for the Dinka and in implementing the policy of autonomy for the area.

After a lengthy discussion in which several members, though not the chairman, seemed critical of my allegations against the provincial authorities and the security forces, it was decided that a delegation be sent to the area comprised of the political overseer, Mamoun Awad Abu Zeid, and the commissioner of the province, Mahmoud Haseeb, the Nuba Arab nationalist. I explained that those people would not be seen by the Dinka as neutral. On the contrary, they were perceived as partial in favor of the Arabs. Some members strongly objected to my accusing national leaders of tribal partiality and argued that whatever the Dinka perception, the government must assert its authority and responsibility. I remained firm on my position, arguing that we would be burying our heads in the sand if we pretended otherwise.

After a heated argument, Vice-President El Baghir announced that he would himself go to the area. Several people protested that it was not advisable from a security point of view, but he insisted that he would go as soon as the president returned from his trip abroad, which would only be in a few days.

General El Baghir asked me to accompany him. As Bol happened to be in Khartoum, having just arrived from the South, he also joined us. We flew by helicopter. After brief stops at the oil fields in Muglad and Bantiu, we landed in Abyei, met with the local security committee to assess the situation, and then called for a public meeting to listen to the people. Emotions were extremely high and the Dinka most explicit in their expression of anger. The theme was the same: unprovoked aggression by the Arabs and the partiality of the security forces behind them. One spokesman went as far as saying that the government and the Arabs were one and the same thing. "We will face the Arabs knowing that you, the Government, are fighting with them against us." There was absolutely no fear in the way they stated their case.

The vice-president listened very patiently, but when it was his turn to speak, he was stern in his response, arguing that the army was by its composition, training, and deployment, a national institution which could not be allied to any faction. He had allowed them to say what they said simply because he understood their pain and bitterness, but they must dismiss those thoughts and trust in the neutrality of the army and the government to see to it that peace was restored and justice ensured.

At the Abyei meeting, Bol and I refrained from talking. Perhaps for the first time in our involvement in the affairs of the tribe, we sat in a public gathering without saying a word. That in itself underscored the degree of our anger and the people knew it. On the other hand, we met privately with the chiefs to discuss the situation. In that meeting, Matet Ayom, who was now back in solidarity with his people, asked me why I had proposed the alternative policy for Abyei instead of working for joining the Ngok to the South. Did that objective prove too difficult for me to accomplish? Even then, his motives were probably cynical, for Matet was never unequivocal in his stance.

At Muglad, we met with Arab leaders and elders in the house of their paramount chief, Babo Nimir. The Arabs seemed obsessed with what they saw as the separatist trend in the Dinka area for which they held Justin Deng responsible. Everything was misconstrued to make the policy of autonomy and development in Abyei an anti-Arab strategy, masterminded by some unnamed individual in the central government using Justin as a tool. I was, needless to say, that individual.

Baghir spoke about the need for peace and security in the area and the higher goal of Arabs and Dinka living together as they had done in history.

It was obvious that I was expected to speak. Whereas in Abyei I was too angry to speak without sounding too partial and adding to the bitterness of the Dinka, in Muglad I felt propelled to explain the grievances of the Dinka to the Arabs and to plead the case for the historical role of Abyei as a bridge in North-South relations, which, I argued, could only be done on the basis of mutual accommodation and respect. I explained the genesis of the policy for the development of Abyei as a model for national unity and integration, how the project had been

275

meant to serve the common good of the Dinka and the Arabs, and how it had been grossly misunderstood as a separatist ploy that aimed not only at eventually annexing the area to the South, but also at benefitting only the Dinka with development. I defended Justin Deng as a man who was dedicated to the implementation of the policy as presented to him. I urged the assembled Arabs to question themselves seriously whether they thought the Ngok Dinka could voluntarily choose to remain in the North in an unequal status with the Arabs, feeling dominated and repressed, while their fellow Dinka in the South were masters of their own situation, with special benefits for rehabilitation and development from the central government. If they wanted the Ngok to favor unity with the Arabs, they had to give them reason for doing so. Domination was not the answer.

Most of the Arab speakers recalled the cordial ties that had prevailed between the Missiriya and the Dinka, the good old days of Arob Biong, Kwol Arob, and Deng (Majok) Kwol, but contrasted that era with the prevailing climate of hostilities. For the deterioration in relations, they blamed the young men who, as Nazir Babo Nimir had predicted at Deng Majok's death, had been educated mostly in Christian missionary schools in the South, and favored joining the South. Babo Nimir conceded that the people of Abyei deserved at least as much right as the South to govern themselves, but should the Dinka insist on joining the South, he argued, the Missiriya would not want to be separated from them and would prefer to go with them to the South.

As we sat with Arab chiefs and elders in Babo's sitting room, I spoke informally of how I thought the Arabs and the Dinka were divided only by myths of identity that did not reflect the reality of their racial mix. I asked Babo Nimir: "Uncle Nazir (Chief), you have been to Saudi Arabia and other parts of the Arab world, what do the people there look like?" He said, using colloquial Arabic, "*Wallahi hommor!*" (By God, they are white!) I said, "Well, look around and see the color of all the Arabs assembled here, where do you think this dark color came from, is it not from the people you consider racially different from you? There is more in common between you people than you realize." My comment was greeted with roaring laughter.

On my return to Khartoum, I learned that parts of my speech in Muglad had been broadcast by Radio Omdurman. Southerners, in particular the Ngok Dinka who felt extremely embittered, were outraged by my conciliatory tone. In one gathering, a southerner was reported as having remarked on hearing me talk, "Someone should advise Mading; he is going to get himself assassinated."

General El Baghir and I were in full agreement in our assessment of the Dinka-Arab conflict. As far as he was concerned, he said he would find it fully challenging and fulfilling to be given sole responsibility for the case. If he could ensure peace and cooperation between those tribes, he would have served a major national purpose. Baghir also tried to convince me that an assignment to devote my time to that challenge, working with him, would be a greater national service than the work of a state minister for foreign affairs. The vice-president was totally sold on the national interest involved in the Abyei situation and the enormous challenge of managing those strong and highly conflictual tribal sentiments.

To my profound disappointment, I learned one day shortly afterward that General Baghir had been relieved of all his duties. That was of course a euphemism for resignation and I soon got to know the whole truth from Baghir himself. He could not continue to work in an atmosphere in which the whims of one man dictated the national course of events and decision making. He had had enough with being Nimeiri's vice-president. But he told me that the only thing he regretted about the manner in which he had resigned was not to have requested a special assignment to continue with his conflict resolution efforts in the Dinka-Arab conflict. He repeated that he would have found that a challenge to which he would have happily devoted his energies and urged me to consider it a primary obligation in the service of the nation.

A Difficult but Successful Peace Conference

As was characteristic of intertribal wars, the government eventually organized a peace conference with tribal chiefs from different parts of the country as mediators (*ajaweed*). It was to be held in Kadugli, the headquarters of the newly established region of southern Kordofan. Abdel Rahman Abdalla, the minister of public service and administrative reform, an intellectual and a highly experienced administrator, was asked to chair the conference. I was asked to assist him.

As soon as we arrived in Kadugli, I asked the governor, Mahmoud Haseeb, about the composition of the Dinka delegation. From what he said, it was obvious that Matet Ayom, Achwil Bulabek, and Patal Biliu were not in the delegation. I immediately concluded that they had been excluded because of their links with the Arabs and that their exclusion was going to be a source of on-going disunity which the Arabs would exploit; it could indeed undermine Dinka-Arab reconciliation. I asked the governor whether it was too late to bring them to the talks. He said that he had just sent a helicopter to bring Justin Deng and that if he could send a message immediately, it might arrive before he left. But he hastened to inform me that the Dinka did not want them in their delegation. At the same time, he intimated, the Arabs wanted them as their witnesses. My fears were confirmed.

I decided on a course of action that would bring them immediately while leaving open the issue of whether they could join the delegation. I would have to discuss the latter issue with the Dinka delegation. My message to Justin Deng was that I wanted to interview those elders in connection with a research project I was working on. No mention was made of the peace talks.

Meanwhile, I went to see the Dinka delegation, talking first to Deng Makuei, and then to other key individuals and finally to the entire delegation, trying to persuade them that it was strategically and tactically wrong for them to exclude those individuals. After all, they had the knowledge and the professional experience to be among their best spokesmen and, if antagonized, could be their worst enemies to the advantage of the Arabs. Deng Makuei agreed and gave me his blessing, but he had a bad cold and was too ill to assist in persuading the others. His son, Hassan (Arob), one of the first to be educated in the area, together with Ahmed Deng Majok (also Arob), disagreed with his father. He could not see how they could be accepted by the people as their spokesmen. Kwol Adol, our young brother who had become the chief, saw things the same way. All in all, the Dinka did not want to have anything to do with those people and the news that I had arranged for them to come was greeted with hostility. I continued to argue my case with conviction and determination. One by one, the tide turned in favor of admitting the renegades back into the delegation.

Ironically, when the chairman of the conference, the governor and I went to have preliminary talks with the Arab delegation, their demand was that the three chiefs together with Zachariah Atem, who had been left behind, be brought to the conference because they were their principal witnesses among the Dinka. I later learned that the Arabs had indeed planned to transport those men to Kadugli through their own means. Obviously, they were not aware that I was at that very moment striving to let them attend as members of the Dinka delegation. I told the Arabs that their objective should not be to get a few Dinkas to side with them against their own people, but rather to make peace and be reconciled with the Dinka as a whole. The more united the Dinka were in their agreement with them, the more reliable the peace agreement would be. The governor supported my position and added that as the Arabs could not imagine the Dinka questioning the composition of the Arab delegation, they had no right to question the composition of the Dinka delegation. The Arabs eventually conceded that point.

When the renegade group arrived and I confronted them with the problem and how it had been resolved, the issue suddenly became one of how they could change their frame of mind which had been set to oppose their own people. It was quite obvious that they were tormented by the dilemma that confronted them. They seemed pleased to have been accepted back by their people, but disturbed by having to shift positions, especially against the more powerful Arab adversaries. Achwil Bulabek conveyed the personal anguish they felt when he asked me whether there was anything legally wrong with one changing one's testimony. He said the Arabs had made them take oath to testify against the Dinka. But he intended to explain that they had done so because of anger, having been rejected by their own people. Now that they had been accepted back, he had no reason to be vindictive against his people. Was there anything wrong with that? I assured him that I saw nothing morally or legally wrong with that. Certainly, no legal action could be taken against them.

I also seized the opportunity to interview the three men among others for the biography of my father. I interviewed Matet Ayom on the eve of the conference. His perspective on the situation went beyond Deng Majok and included words of advice for me:

> Mading, why I used to call you "The Fox" is for the same reason you have now fulfilled your leadership position so well. And a country survives because of the arm of the Chief. It is in the hands of the Chief that a country survives. And a country survives through the son of the Chief. When our people used to walk on foot, the man who would lead the way at night would be the son of a Chief. Even if he be a small boy, it is he who must take the lead. He leads the way and when people sleep, he sleeps in the center. And the following morning, when people take to the way again, he takes the lead. There is no one else to whom you can entrust the tribe. Your father is no longer there at home. It is you, Mading, who now occupies the place of your father, Deng Majok. If things do not go well, it will be because of you. So, you better abandon the relaxation you enjoyed when your father was

alive. Today, the responsibility of the tribe has been bequeathed to you. The strong words you say today only Deng Majok is able to say them.

It is ironic that the person who was preaching to me about the responsibilities of leadership in the Dinka context was the same person who had conspired and tried to recruit my Uncle Ngor to incriminate me and put me in a deadly collision with the government. Even more ironic, he was praising my father, the very man who had inspired me to assume the leadership responsibility he was now determined to undermine:

> Tomorrow, when you listen to speeches, you will be disappointed by the words of many. If it were during the time of Deng Majok, he would determine in advance the people who should speak, the people whose words would reflect the truth. Now, the country is taken over by children. But there is always one person who is known as the seat of the country. And that is you. You are the front line and you are the seat on which the tribe rests. And you are the carriage into which the people will load their belongings. And you are the dish in which the food will be served. So, do your best. Deng Majok is no longer alive. And Deng is not going to return from death. Each person goes with his own fame and leaves the suffering behind for the remaining generations to face. Then the successor develops his own fame again, by the way he faces those problems. So, you will develop your fame as your father developed his.
>
> ... Your manner of speaking is that of your father, Deng Majok: Your manner of speech by which you handle problems calmly, listen carefully to the view point of another person, and adjust your words to accommodate the truth as you see it. In you, we find something of the qualities of Deng Majok.

I reciprocated Matet's compliments and advice with words of appreciation that were both sincere and intended to influence his performance at the conference. It should be remembered that the intrigues and conspiracy Uncle Ngor told me about many years later were not known to me then, although I was fully aware of the security game Matet had been playing for years. My words in his praise were therefore both sincere and constructively or pragmatically calculated:

Uncle, your words are truly important. Even the words of advice with which you ended your words are very important to me. Sometimes, one almost despairs when one hears the many words that are being uttered by the youth there, people who speak from anger without even seeing the realities of the country. And these are people who will not have listened to the words of their elders at home. Yet, they make themselves experts on the problems of the tribe while remaining isolated far away. They say things which hurt the people at home. Their words, when heard by the people here or there, lead to the ill-treatment of our people there. So, I almost despair sometimes and say that if people have suddenly appeared who say they know the affairs of the tribe better, and they believe they can save the tribe, then why not withdraw and leave to them the affairs of the land? But then when I think of it, and I see our people who are suffering at home, and I listen to the voices of the people, especially now that I am near enough to the people so that I can hear their voices, then I feel that if I were to withdraw, I would have abandoned my people to disaster.

Your words are valid. People like you are truly dear to one's eyes and one's heart. Even when you were quarrelling with my father so that your quarrel was heard, and people would say that you were the person who wanted to destroy the Chieftainship of Deng Majok, my respect for you and my pleasure at seeing you as a nobleman of our tribe which had started very early in my childhood continued. This is despite the fact that I have done nothing for you to indicate to the people that you are a person whom I have always admired. What I do though is whenever I come home and I hear complaints about you, the words of the people do not convince me. Whatever I hear said, my heart still tends to recall the good things of the past even though I might not have done anything to you personally to be pointed at that Mading has done this or that for Matet. The good things one sees in a person and wishes that the Dinka would continue to respect, that is certainly there. So, your words are truly important and I have heard them.

I felt pleased with the decision I had taken to ensure their attendance. And indeed, in the negotiations that followed, Matet Ayom and Achwil Bulabek, who were both excellent orators, and having been tutored and influenced by their late friend, Deng Majok, were among the most experienced in Dinka-Arab relations, proved to be by far the most effective spokesmen for the Dinka.

During the talks, I moved in four circles which were diametrically opposed and in which my message had to be custom tailored. There was my inner circle with the chairman of the conference and the governor of Kordofan, probably the most straightforward and the easiest, although it also involved continuous discussions and interpretation of the various moves of the different groups which we had to monitor. The main challenge of my close association with both men was to make them appreciate the justice of the Dinka cause, while also mindful of Arab concerns. Since the chairman was a fair-minded person and the Dinka were obviously the underdogs, that task was not at all difficult. And yet, his sympathy for the Dinka was rather exceptional among northern authorities. The governor too was sympathetic to the Dinka cause, but hostile to Dinka leadership and bent on winning and maintaining Arab political support; he was therefore quite torn and ambivalent, but with a pro-Arab profile.

There were the two opposing delegations with whom I tried to keep equally close contact so as not to be accused of bias for the Dinka. Nevertheless, the Arabs assumed that as a Dinka I naturally had the interest of my people foremost in my mind. They were of course right, but what they did not realize was that I was also trying hard to look at the situation from their point of view and arguing their case with the Dinka where I thought it justified. This, the Dinka delegation resented. On the other hand, whenever the Arabs took an unreasonable stand, I found myself free to argue with them, which reinforced their suspicion of a pro-Dinka bias.

At one point, the Dinka walked out of the talks and it fell mostly on me to try to persuade them to return. At another point, the Arabs, invoking the 1965 precedent referred to earlier between the Ngok Dinka and the Missiriya Arabs, argued against the payment of the conventional blood wealth, *dia*. In their view, the precedent required that everything be forgiven and forgotten. They offered instead a ridiculously small sum of fifteen hundred Sudanese pounds per person for what they called an appeasement fee. Since many more Dinkas than Arabs had been killed, this outraged the Dinka. I was equally outraged. For the first time, I threatened to pull out of the mediation role. With pressure from the chairman, the commissioner, and the *ajaweed* (the tribal mediators), the Arabs eventually agreed to increase the amount considerably, estimated in cattle terms at fifteen head per person, as opposed to the usual thirty head for *dia*.

It was suggested by the *ajaweed* that in the future, the parties should revert back to the conventional payment of the *dia*. The Dinka refused and insisted that if the payment of *dia* was dispensed with on that occasion because of the alleged precedent, then that practice should be maintained in future cases. The obvious implication was that the Dinka intended to avenge and expected to inflict more casualties on the Arabs than they would suffer. In a heated, almost violent confrontation with the Dinka delegation, I tried to impress upon them that it was self-defeating to convey that impression, not only because it revealed an aggressive intent, but also because it alerts the Arabs to be prepared. In any case, it was grossly naive to assume that the Arabs would suffer more casualties in the future, since past experience showed the contrary and since the Arabs were far better armed than the Dinka. At one point, a hot-headed young man said to me, "Why do you always have to step between us and the Arabs? Why don't you allow us to confront one another?" At the same time, one Arab remarked in the conference that if it were not because of their respect for the government, they would have demanded that "that Dinka," be removed from the podium of chairmanship.

Almost equally problematic was my relationship with the *ajaweed*, the tribal mediators. Seeing me move between the parties and maintaining a close association with the chairman and the governor, these mediators seemed to feel that their role was being usurped. They even complained to the chairman that they felt redundant and threatened to withdraw from the conference. The chairman, the governor, and I applied our greatest powers of persuasion to restore their confidence in the process.

All in all, the process was an extremely frustrating uphill struggle, day and night, for two weeks, several days beyond the allotted time. But in the end, it was an astonishing success. In addition to the reconciliation of the parties, clear principles were agreed upon for regulating the movements of the Arabs into Dinkaland in their seasonal search for pastures and water. Procedures for preventing, managing, and resolving future conflicts, including periodic peace conferences, were also established. Elements of the original policy for the administration and development of Abyei area were reiterated and reaffirmed.

It was only in the final speeches that I realized how much my role was appreciated by both sides. What was more, the spirit of reconciliation that emerged and all the words of exaltation for the role played by everyone seemed very sincere. I left Kadugli feeling that we had made significant progress towards the search for peace, security, and stability on that turbulent and highly sensitive border area between the North and the South.

9

Encroachment on National Security

Deepening Hostility in a Wider area

Although the Dinka and the Missiriya were reconciled, the North-South dimensions of the conflict persisted and continued to threaten the peace and security of the area and eventually the country. The Ngok Dinka intellectuals in the South had organized themselves politically under the leadership of Zachariah Bol Deng and had played an important role in the regional changes of government. In the process, Bol had become appointed first as a deputy speaker of the regional assembly and then as regional minister of health. As soon as he joined the government, he became aware of the sensitivities of the Abyei case in North-South relations and although he succeeded in having the regional assembly adopt a resolution calling for the implementation of the stipulated referendum, he had moderated his position, at least in institutional politics.

Toward the end of 1979, I took leave of the president to go abroad to attend to the eye problem which I had neglected with the pressures of national responsibilities. The president first tried to persuade me to obtain any amount of care I needed abroad while retaining my position in the government. On my insistence, he eventually asked me to take a diplomatic assignment abroad, while retaining the status of state minister. I went as ambassador to Canada.

I had been gone for only a short time when news began to reach me that the political situation in Abyei had flared up again, over the issue of joining the South, that the family was being accused of masterminding the pro-South nationalist movement, that as a result, the authority of Chief Kwol Adol was being seriously undermined and that the unity wing of the opportunists was again having the upper hand. While I was in Khartoum in the central government and known to hold views that saw an important national role in the Ngok Dinka presence in Kordofan, at least a faction of the family could still be said to identify with the North. Now that the family leadership inside the country, with the strong support of the politically active youth, was conspicuously identified with the South, the shift was almost total. Fearful that Abyei's annexation to the South would mean losing a most valuable land, the Arabs, tribal groups, provincial authorities, and security forces, all united in their harassment of the Ngok Dinka. As I noted earlier, even the policy of developing Abyei as a model of national unity and integration was misconstrued as a shrewd strategy formulated by the president and his minister of local government to entitle the Arabs to claim an equal right of access to Ngokland as a common border territory. With that interpretation of the policy, the Arabs could not credit a Dinka as the author of the policy.

The situation continued to deteriorate rapidly, as the security forces working with the Arabs and their Dinka cronies continued to tighten their grip on the tribe at large. In reaction, a group of young Dinka warriors, led by former Anya-Nya soldiers, were recruited, trained in guerrilla warfare, appropriately armed with clandestine assistance from the South and sent back to the area to confront the *marahleen*, the Arab tribal militia. They began with reprisals against those who were notorious as informants to the Arab security forces, capturing individuals among them, some of whom they handed over to the provincial authorities in the southern province of Bahr el Ghazal, where they were detained as trouble-makers.

The rebels inevitably clashed with the Missiriya, inflicting heavy casualties on the Arabs. The security forces intervened and under their protection, enabled the Arabs to stage a massive attack on the civilian Dinka population in the winter of 1980. With a vengeance, they fell on Dinka villages, burning houses, destroying the crops, looting the livestock, killing at random, and forcing masses of the people to flee southward to camp in open shelters under trees.

Minyiel Rou, a traditional poet, commemorated the events with a song, pleading for justice from the central government. Since the plea was all in vain, he projects the last resort of the Ngok as pleading their case with God:

Fire continued to blaze [as our houses burned],
And our cattle were driven away;
But we had no one to hear our case.
We called and called,
But no one asked what we were calling about;
We cried and cried,
But no one asked why we were crying.
We talked and talked,
But no one asked what we were saying.
God, it was you who gave the Dinka the cow,
And you gave the Arabs their wealth in money,
The Arabs have consumed their wealth,
They have gone to capture our herds,
And there is no one to whom we can take our case:
Our cattle have been captured,
Our children have been captured,
And our villages have been burnt down;
We are now clustering under trees like birds.

The Call to Intervene

Written and tape recorded messages reached me in Canada, detailing the catastrophe that had befallen the area. Letters signed by chiefs and elders and from individual relatives and concerned members of the tribe urged me to intercede with the central government to save the situation.

I responded to both the family members and the elders of the tribe in letters addressed to them collectively expressing a degree of bitterness, that the policy line I had proposed for the area had not received the appreciation and support it deserved from the Ngok people. I argued that there was nothing else I could do and that those on the ground must now assume responsibility and develop their own policies and strategies. I urged our younger brothers that conditions of change in Africa forced leaders to assume responsibility at a young age and that they should rise to the challenge of leadership and not consider themselves below age. The mantle had been passed on to them.

But of course I could not disassociate myself from the problems back home, nor could I stop tormenting myself with the thought of what to do. What compounded my frustration was the fact that I was working on my father's biography, translating and transcribing extensive interviews with family members, tribal elders, leaders from neighboring northern and southern tribes, and central government officials, Sudanese and British, who had known him. Those interviews revealed to me the wisdom of our ancestors in exercising leadership at the crossroads, which in turn confirmed my perspective about the unique role of the area in the country. The elders I had interviewed also placed on me personally much of the responsibility for ensuring the protection of our people.

Ironically, the words of Matet Ayom about my responsibilities to the tribe were among the most moving. But there were many others. The elder, Bulabek Mijak, for instance, had these words to say:

> You know, Mading, as we talk to you today, a man's heart will cool down because you have been found. The pains of the past will cool down because, if people have talked to you, then people hope that you can do something. You are a man who is educated and who has been made a leader. People may respect you. We cannot be sure, but that is why we tell you the words of our tribe and the things that have been disturbing us in this country. The way our people are being killed in their homes deeply pains our hearts. You have seen some of it and we have seen much more. When you went home, that was the beginning of destruction. It worsened after you were gone. You only heard the rest of it with your ears (Deng 1980:278).

Marieu Ajak reflected on the situation and reported on a conversation he had had with Chief Pagwot Deng of Bongo sub-tribe whom I had interviewed earlier:

> Today, we are very pleased. If we have now met with you, all the bad things have passed. Pagwot went and told me one thing. He said, "You, Marieu, you disbelieve everything. Even if a man brings a true word, you disbelieve him. This is what Mading said."
>
> I said, "Have you met?"
>
> He said, "Yes, we have met."
>
> And I said, "What did he say?"
>
> He said, "Mading said, 'Our young men all swarm in anger without arranging their words well.' He said, 'In my heart, joining the South or the North is not a good

choice. Our area has always been a border-home. If we were to follow what I have thought out, I would like us to be on the borders, not to be considered part of the South nor fully part of the North. The Arabs will shy away from us. We shall be the people to put the country in order. The area of Abyei will develop in a way free from jealousies. If it were left to me, I say that our area should remain separate. I want to write that down. But the young men of our area begin to complain that I have sold the country away. So I have given up the case!'"

I said, "Pagwot, what you are now saying to me, if Mading were here, I would have said, 'Do not listen to the words of your age-mates. Do not let your mind be confused. Do not abandon your word. Write it down and show it to the leaders of the Sudan. We are the people of the borders. Nothing is bigger. The land extending to the South down to Agarland, down to Kiecland, down to the land of the Black Jur, and further down to the southern end of the country, your grandfather, Arob Biong, was the man who controlled the whole country. In the generation of my father, were not people like my father captured and enslaved to the point where their cheeks were scarred? If his mother had not rescued him from captivity, would we ourselves not be the Arabs of today? It was Arob Biong who brought peace into this land so that anyone who escaped could return to his home and not be forced back into slavery. That was how my father returned and remained in Dinkaland. The land was one!' So, as I see it, Mading should not abandon his word. He should remain and not give heed to what other people say and give up. If he should abandon the tribe, it will be spoiled; it will be spoiled by those people. If he should say, 'I shall leave the tribe to you to do with it whatever you want,' the tribe will spoil ...

"So, when my heart was on Mading, I said, 'I believe you will be the person who will bring our tribe back to order', it was the truth my heart hit. I am only sad that I shall not be able to meet him. I would tell him, 'Son of my brother, hold to your plan. Do not listen to the words of your age-mates. Do not allow them to confuse your words by saying, 'We are going to the South.' Your words are the goodness of the land. The land is full of jealousies. If it is the Arab, he will not permit any goodness for the area. He will say, 'These young men who are flocking to the area are going to take the area away.' ..."

He said, "I like what Mading said."

I said, "It is a pity he is far. If he were near, I would say, 'Hold on to it. Do not listen to the words of the children; they are people spoiling the land. Keep writing it down and say, "We are different; we are the people of the borders. We shall be southerners here. That is how they will treat us well."' They will treat us well out of jealousy. The relationship of people who have had a feud is like food which has not yet been tasted. Now, the Arab unites the opportunists. It will take us a long time to repair their damage. The Arabs say, 'These are the people who have kept the people with us.' Their hands will stretch to hold the food given them by the Arab.

"If one travels and happens to find Mading, he should be told not to abandon his word. We are separate and we are Northerners. That is how Arob Biong left us; that is how Kwol left us; and Deng too recently left us there. We are people of the borders. The Nuer come to our land; the Twic come to our land; the Ruweng come to our land; the Rek come to our land; the Arabs come to our land. We are suited to our situation as the people of the borders. If peace were to cease, our country would be the battlefield because it is the border. So Mading's word is my word. It is only that he is far away."

So, what we should now say is that what you are doing is correct. Write it down; write it down, it is the truth (Deng 1980:291-293).

Chief Biong Mijak, the sheikh of the leading section of Abyor and Father's cousin, held to Nimeiri's promise of a special status for the Ngok Dinka between North and South:

So, my son, why Pagwot said that we today cannot unite with the people called the Arabs, but that we will also not unite with the people called the southerners, that we should remain separate, was because of words said by President Nimeiry. When he heard our people saying that they wanted to join the South and then remain with the North in the one Sudan, that is when Nimeiry spoke and said, "You will not do it that way. You will remain with your own ways. You will not be part of the South and you will not be part of the North." But all that was covered up as soon as he left. It is being pricked by the politicians to this day (Deng 1980:279).

I pondered over the situation: the efforts I had made, the opposition of the modern elite that had confronted me in the area, the voices of elders telling me that I was right in my original policy and should persist, and my increasing conviction that we were out of options. I felt I had no choice but to keep trying. The opportunity arose for me to go back to the Sudan to attend a conference of ambassadors.

A Presidential, but Abortive, High Level Committee

Shortly after my arrival, I received a hand-delivered letter from a cousin at home, Uncle Arob's eldest son, Hassan Deng. In it, he briefly described the situation of harassment and insecurity in the tribe and ended by saying that the people were relieved when they heard that I had returned to the country. They were confident that together with the president, we would bring relief to the area. The letter was short, but succinct and powerful.

I soon sought and obtained an appointment with the president. In the meeting, I explained what I had been hearing from home and gave my own analysis and evaluation of the situation, highlighting the degree of oppression and degradation which the people of Abyei felt in their relations with both their Arab neighbors and the regional government of Kordofan. Then I pulled out the letter and asked him to read it.

Nimeiri was moved. After an expressive silence, he remarked, almost talking to himself, "I will not tolerate any Sudanese being treated with indignity." Then he went on to say with remarkable candor that he had never been comfortable with the government policy toward our family. That was the first explicit admission that there had indeed been an official policy to erode the authority of our family. Dr. Jaafar Mohamed Ali Bakheit, the minister of local government, had made hints to me about the experiments of the revolution in instituting popular democracy; but

291

nothing had been said to indicate that what the family was suffering from was the implementation of high policy at the local level.

Nimeiri then said to me, "We can go on for the rest of the day discussing the problem. The question is what should be done." He then asked whether I thought it would be useful for him to set up a high level committee to investigate the situation and recommend to him an appropriate course of action. I strongly supported the idea, explaining that it would at least assure the people of Abyei that the president was concerned about their plight. We immediately started on composing the committee. Nimeiri wanted me to be a member.

The committee, which was to be chaired by Sheikh Beshir, the president's adviser on decentralization and formerly under-secretary of the Ministry of Local Government, was expanded in the course of time and eventually included Dafalla El Raddi, the deputy chief justice, Martin Majier, the southern regional minister of legal affairs and local government, Chief Babo Nimir of the Missiriya tribe, Sheikh Sarour Ramli, a tribal leader and a prominent national figure, whose role in the South-North politics went back to the Juba conference of 1947, a southern member of the national assembly, a representative of the national security, and later, Daldoum El Khatim, from the Nuba mountains who was a regional minister for cabinet affairs in Kordofan, and Bokur El Hag Ajbar, former local government executive officer in the area and son of the Missiriya El Zuruq Nazir, El Haj Ajbar.

Before the formation of the committee was announced, I communicated the developments to a group of Ngok Dinka students, mostly brothers and cousins, who had come to discuss the situation with me. To my surprise, they argued that I would be exposing myself to criticism among the Ngok Dinka who held me responsible for the area continuing to be in the North. My intercession would be seen as yet another scheme from me that would again complicate and perhaps compromise the Dinka demand for joining the South. They advised me to leave the situation to run its course, wherever it would lead.

Although they were only teenagers, so convinced were they and so surprised was I that I decided to go back to the president and cancel the initiative. Since it was after the office hours, I went all over town looking for the president's legal advisor, Dr. Yusuf Mikhail, who had been given the task of drafting the presidential decree. Yusuf could not believe that I would succumb so easily to the views of students. He argued that he and others had tried earlier to persuade the president to intervene, but had not succeeded. The fact that I had moved the president to act the way he had done was a great accomplishment. We had to seize the opportunity and move swiftly. Any second thought would be damaging to the cause of a people who were desperate for central government intervention. His words reassured me that I had done the only thing I could have done in the circumstances.

Even at this critical moment, the people of Abyei were hopelessly divided between the victimized population and the informants who were busy reporting on the activities of the local rebels. During the early days of my return to the Sudan, a delegation led by Matet Ayom arrived from Abyei. This group had been organized by the administration and security authorities of Kordofan to take their complaints to the central government authorities, alleging that the rebel activities in the area were being orchestrated by the southern regional government. They even cited an instance in which Zachariah Bol Deng was reported to have visited people who had been seized by the Ngok rebels and taken to Gogrial District where they were detained. As minister of health, Bol had visited the prison accompanied by the governor of the province, Aldo Ajou Deng, and had allegedly called the detainees traitors who deserved what they got. This was a serious allegation, for while the regional government was understandably sympathetic to the cause of the Ngok Dinka, it could not be seen to support rebel activities.

Before the committee could begin its work, I flew to the South to consult with the regional government and leaders of the Ngok community there. In sharp contrast with the reaction of the young men in Khartoum, I received a very warm welcome and a strong endorsement from Abel Alier's government and the Ngok community under the leadership of Zachariah Bol Deng. They had all felt helpless and found the idea of the committee a way of breaking the impasse.

I also briefed Alier and Bol about the allegations of support for the local rebels and in particular Bol's supposed encounter with the detained informants. The news was quite disturbing to Alier who could never have condoned such behavior from his minister or officials. The event clearly signalled a warning that the situation in Abyei was most precarious and called for great caution and prudence from the responsible authorities.

The work of the committee soon turned into a highly divisive North-South political confrontation, which inexorably led to the fundamental question of whether Abyei should belong to the South or the North, an issue which went beyond what President Nimeiri and I had envisaged in agreeing on the formation of the committee. Daldoum El Khatim, the Kordofan minister, was by far the most prejudiced against the Dinka. His role alone almost assured the committee of failure.[49] Nevertheless, the committee did its job thoroughly, investigated with individuals and groups in Khartoum, visited the Abyei area, conducted field tours of the devastated areas and the displaced people under trees, and held hearings in Abyei with both the Dinka and the Arabs. The tenseness of the security situation in Abyei became abundantly clear.

A delegation comprising members of the Ngok community in the South which had been sent by the regional authorities to assess the emergency needs of the situation and report back on what the regional government could do to help had just arrived and had been immediately arrested by the local authorities. But they were allowed to testify in front of the committee.

Dinka informants who were cooperating with the security authorities expressed complaints about the local rebel activities, in particular the seizure of people suspected of cooperation with the authorities, for which they blamed the sons of Deng Majok and the Ngok community in the South. They shrewdly did not refer to Bol's role as they wanted to focus attention on me in order to discredit and undermine my efforts. Matet Ayom, who had again reverted back to the leadership of the opposition against the Deng family, dramatized the situation by claiming that they could not speak freely in front of me, in fear of the reprisals from the rebels whom he described as my army in the forest. He asked the committee how I could be both a representative of the government and the leader of that army in the forest which was terrorizing and capturing people. I did not myself respond to him, but the chairman ruled him out of order, stating that my role in the leadership of the country and loyalty to the nation were unquestionable. Notwithstanding this fact it was even rumored by the Arabs and their Dinka allies that I was sending arms from Canada and the United States in collaboration with the Harvard Institute for International Development.

---

49. Daldoum El Khatim, a Nuba lawyer and politician who saw his prospects in cooperating with the Arabs, told me later that he could not understand why the Dinka were so resistant to assimilating themselves into the Arab-Islamic mold. He proudly explained that he was married to an Arab woman and that the majority of those who had voted for him were Arabs. Why did the Dinka not want to assimilate the way the Nuba did? Of course, he had prejudged the Nuba future, for as the country would tragically realize, the Nuba would become increasingly involved in the civil war on the side of the South as Africans.

Perhaps the most dramatic indication of the unscrupulousness with which the Arabs manipulated the situation was when the representative of the joint Dinka-Arab constituency in the National Assembly, himself an Arab, read a statement signed by Dinka chiefs, but written in classical Arabic, declaring that the land occupied by the Ngok Dinka was Arab land which the Dinka had settled as an act of hospitality by the Arabs. When I requested that the statement be translated into Dinka, Matet Ayom spontaneously cried out loud in Arabic that the document should not be translated. I was of course certain that those who had signed did not know the contents of the document. With his motives so evident, the chairman of the committee authorized its translation. Once they knew what they had signed, the Dinka chiefs, one by one, disassociated themselves from it. "We cannot unite through cleverness," declared Omda Pagwot, the oldest of the chiefs.

After the meeting, I approached Matet Ayom with a controlled rage, and said rather lightheartedly but in earnest, "Uncle Matet, has the land become truly destroyed so that even people like you can speak the way you did?" Without any change in his demeanor, Matet responded, "Mading, the land is destroyed." I could only laugh sympathetically at his self-deprecating candor.

The committee presented a number of alternative solutions to the president, ranging from holding the referendum provided for in the Addis Ababa Agreement to the establishment of a separate administrative arrangement for the Ngok Dinka within Kordofan.

When the report was formally presented to him, Nimeiri lavishly praised the committee members, claiming that he had pondered over how best to acknowledge their contribution, whether with financial rewards or awards of honor. He pledged to study the report carefully before making a decision. Even then, it was obvious to those who knew him well, particularly to me, that the president had already been swayed to the Kordofan point of view and would not take any decision to alleviate the Ngok situation. Nevertheless, he said to me that he would give the people of Abyei the right to decide their future, but that he would have to wait for a more opportune timing. The ambivalence of our cooperation was revealed when he said to me, "You go back to your post and rest assured that I will take the decision at the right time. If I did so now, people will say Francis Deng has become the president." President Nimeiri never took the decision he promised.

Escalating Rebel Activities

A few months later, Matet Ayom and his new bride were shot to death in the middle of the night by unidentified assassins. His family together with the security forces attributed the incident to the local rebels whom they suspected were inspired, if not led, by the Deng Majok family. Shortly after Matet's assassination, an armed group swarmed the Deng Majok family quarters late one evening, shelling indiscriminately, and although people escaped by crawling into the corn fields around the houses, the attackers succeeded in killing one man, the son of Uncle Arob, a teacher at Abyei elementary school. Internecine violence was spiralling.

It was under those circumstances that Michael Deng, whose Dinka name was Miokol, one of the leading sons of Deng Majok in the area, defected and joined the rebels. He had already been tipped that he was among the most wanted by the security forces. His defection was perhaps the most prominent event in a series of developments that would eventually explode into a full-scale resumption of North-South hostilities.

Although he was educated in the Arabic system of the North, Miokol had resisted conversion into Islam, probably as a political protest against the northern agenda of assimilation. Instead, he converted to Christianity and adopted the name Michael.

After leaving school at Father's death, as many of his generation in the family did, Michael was employed by the local council as a clerk. He was later elected as the secretary of the Sudan Socialist Union in the "basic" unit and as the representative of the area to the central committee, a capacity which made him bear the brunt of Ngok confrontation with the opportunists, the Arabs and Kordofan authorities.

By that time, Anya-Nya II, the fore-runner of the SPLM/SPLA, was beginning to form in dispersed areas of Bahr el Ghazal and had started with sporadic acts of violence. Their attacks were still being publicly played down by the security authorities as isolated cases that did not indicate a trend toward a wide-scale rebellion in the South. And yet, the authorities knew that groups from the Ngok area were beginning to take to the bush with arms procured for them by the Ngok community in the South and were active in the adjacent areas, particularly in Bahr el Ghazal. The activities of these groups became a source of increasing concern to the authorities of Kordofan, but were still not regarded by the central government as of any national significance. However, the developments in the Abyei situation following the armed attack on the Deng Majok family soon raised the profiles of the rebels.

After joining the rebels, Michael became not only the leader of the Ngok group, but also one of the leaders of the rapidly growing guerrilla force in the Dinka region of Bahr el Ghazal. By now, the Ngok movement had established itself as Abyei Liberation Front.[50] Soon, the name of Michael became synonymous with the gradual, but inexorable, resumption of hostilities in the South. The national dimension of the mounting crises heightened when the rebels attacked Ariat station on the Wau railroad on January 18, 1983, "killing twelve Northern Sudanese merchants" (Niblock 1987:288). The chain of violence that subsequently spread over the South-North borders perpetuated by Anya-Nya II, was blamed on the Ngok Dinka, under the supposed leadership of Deng Majok's sons, of whom Michael had become the hero or the villain, depending on the point of view involved.

Of course, the activities of the Abyei rebel group constituted a minor part of the Anya-Nya II movement that was now beginning to mushroom in Upper Nile and Bahr el Ghazal and that would form the first major part of the movement with which the SPLM/SPLA first cooperated, then came into armed conflict over the objectives of the renewed southern struggle. Anya-Nya II wanted separation from the North, while the SPLA espoused the liberation of the whole country and the establishment of a new democratic and secular state. At this early juncture, however, with the authorities still playing down the nascent rebellion in Bahr el Ghazal, the tendency of the authorities in the South and Kordofan was to place the responsibility solely on the Ngok, and more specifically, the Deng Majok family.

The national security authorities reacted swiftly. Massive arrests of Ngok leaders, including tribal chiefs and intellectuals, (North and South educated, Muslims and Christians alike), several of them sons of Deng Majok (among them Zachariah Bol, who had since left the regional government and had been practicing medicine privately in Khartoum, and Kwol Adol, the young newly appointed chief), took place across the country, some in Abyei itself, others in Bantiu, El Fashir, El Obeid, Juba, Kadugli, Khartoum, and Wau. The elders included Achwil Bulabek and Patal Biliu, who, since the Kadugli peace conference, had become fully identified with their people, unlike Matet Ayom, who had drifted back into alliance with the Arabs.

---

50. See Johnson & Prunier 1993:127.

An Extended Mediation Process with Short-Lived Success

Again, I found myself back in the Sudan to attend the national congress of the Sudan Socialist Union held in the spring of 1983 (several months before the Bor and Fashalla incidents that led to John Garang's defection and the eventual formation of the SPLM/SPLA).

In their reports to the congress, the governors of the southern and Kordofan regions, James Tumbora and Mahmoud Haseeb, attributed the rising tide of violence in the South to the Ngok Dinka, and more specifically the family of Deng Majok, the charge being that the revolution threatened them with loss of the monopoly of power over the tribe. Being the only member of the Deng family in the congress, faces turned to me as the family was being publicly attacked. I wrote a note to the vice-president, Omer Mohamed El Tayeb, who was chairing the meeting, wondering whether I should remain silent or respond, and he wrote back advising me not to react.

It should be mentioned in this context that the government of James Tumbora was collaborating with Joseph Lagu who, as vice-president of the Republic, was known to be working for the redivision of the South, allegedly to free the Equatorians from Dinka domination. Their position against the Ngok Dinka was also an attempt to explain away the problems brewing in the South.

Even as the authorities were playing down the rebellion in the South, the situation in that part of the country was rapidly deteriorating under the impending threat of redivision of the southern region and the overall interference of the center in regional affairs. At about the same time, Abyei leaders were arrested, a number of prominent southerners, among them the speaker and deputy speaker of the regional assembly and several former ministers in Abel Alier's government, were also arrested on the grounds that they were planning a rebellion in the South. The resumption of a full-fledged civil war seemed imminent.

Joseph Lagu welcomed me in his office shortly after my return to explain the prevailing situation and to impress upon me that many of my friends and acquaintances in the southern leadership were suspected of involvement in the unfolding security situation in the South and that the arrested Ngok leaders were facing serious charges. He explained that the authorities had a positive view of me, but his advice to me was to avoid getting involved and indeed to leave the country as soon as the congress was over. Whether he was genuinely concerned about my safety or was afraid that I might play a role that might favor his enemies in the eyes of the central government, I could not be sure, but I suspected the latter.

I could not see how I could remain aloof and indeed represent the country abroad when leading members of my family and the tribe were in detention. I also thought that it would be too parochial to be concerned about Abyei alone without also thinking about the situation that was unfolding in the South and which in fact was intertwined with the political developments in the Ngok Dinka area. After informal consultations with a wide variety of individuals, I decided to embark on a mediation effort aimed at alleviating the deteriorating situations in both the South and Abyei. On the South, I proposed the establishment of a mediation committee under the chairmanship of the former first vice-president, General Mohamed El Baghir, who had participated in the Addis Ababa negotiations of 1972 and for whom southerners generally had high regard. The objective would be to help southern leaders to explore a common ground on the divisive issue of the redivision. I mobilized the support of prominent northern individuals, among them two influential ambassadors who had been chiefs of national security, Mirghani Suleiman and Ali Nimeiri.

The idea was endorsed by the southern leaders, among them Abel Alier, Bona Malwal, and eventually, even Joseph Lagu himself. Ambassador William Kontos of the United States, who was keenly interested in the situation, followed my activities very closely and gave me his full support. Indeed, at one point, when the government seemed to waiver in its acceptance of the idea, Ambassador Kontos told me that he was prepared to tell the president that his government supported the initiative and would want it to be taken seriously. I discreetly discouraged the ambassador from discussing the matter with the president, since that might be viewed as interference and harden the government position. So popular did the initiative become in diplomatic circles that it was reported to me at diplomatic receptions by ambassadors who did not realize that it had originated from me.

Initially, both the vice-president and the president also welcomed the idea. But when El Baghir, who had accepted the assignment, wanted to see the president to assure himself of what was expected from the exercise, he was never given the appointment. That convinced him that the mediation initiative was not really supported by the president. And in retrospect, he was right, for the president would obviously not have welcomed an initiative that might have united the South and probably aborted his plans to divide the region into three antagonistic factions.

The Abyei initiative envisaged a mediation process between the Ngok leadership and the authorities of Kordofan, led by Fadhalla Hamad, the deputy governor, since the new governor, El Fateh Bushara, was on a visit to the United States. The idea was first explored with the vice-president, whose response initially seemed supportive, but said that he would first seek the president's approval. I waited so long for the approval that I began to doubt whether the president and his vice-president were at all interested. Suddenly, I received an enthusiastic call from the vice-president who wanted to see me immediately. Explaining that he had received the president's approval, he showed me a handwritten note from Nimeiri, lavishly complimenting me and expressing the view that I would not do anything harmful to the national interest. Omer Mohamed El Tayeb proceeded to pour on me his own lavish praise, calling me a "wise man", a quality he considered a special gift from God. I could not help recalling Ibrahim Mohamed Zein's words in which he attributed Father's qualities to a special gift from God.

With the green light from the president and the vice-president a mediation commenced that was to last several months, the objective of which was to reconcile the national security authorities and the rulers of Kordofan on the one hand and the detained leaders of Abyei and their followers on the other hand.

Ironically there was also a strong opposition to the initiative among the Dinka. I was informed that the chiefs of the sub-tribes and other elders had sent me a signed letter which the bearer had lost with his stolen bag in which they urged me to keep out of the situation, allegedly because they were afraid for my own safety. In Khartoum itself, views were sharply divided. Some supported my efforts, but many opposed them. Several family members argued that any mediation might result in a compromise on principles and should be avoided. I disregarded all that and moved ahead with my plans.

The authorities of Kordofan with the support of the national security leaders at first wanted the family of Deng Majok to secure the surrender of Michael, which, of course, I persuaded them, could not be done. I explained to the authorities that their best option was to cultivate the cooperation of those who were still within the system in order to consolidate peace and security in the area. That could be their most effective weapon against the rebels, including Michael himself.

Even as I was making progress in my negotiations with the authorities, they continued to make stalemates which, at least on the face, seemed to undermine my efforts. After visiting the South, General Omer

Mohamed El Tayeb, who was also in charge of national security, again put the responsibility for the rebellion on the Ngok and went as far as declaring to the nation through the media of public information that the detainees would be charged of, and tried for, treason. Even at this late hour, the national security authorities were either unaware of the seriousness of the situation in the South or were deliberately playing it down for security reasons and using the Ngok Dinka as the scapegoat, especially as they were seen as not posing a serious threat to the system. By acknowledging their rebellion and crushing it, the incident could provide an effective deterrence to the more potentially dangerous rebellion brewing in other areas of the South.

In a statement to the Arabic daily, *Al-Ayam* of March 21, 1983, El Tayeb offered this report about the security situation in the South:

> Rumors typically rely on some degree of truth around which they can build a coherent fiction. I do not deny that there are groups of rebels engaged in skirmishes with our Armed Forces, but I am not unduly apprehensive about our situation. After all, at one time, the entire South was in rebellion and our Armed Forces were fighting to maintain the unity and integrity of the nation. At present we are fighting isolated groups which are small in numbers. In fact, from our tour throughout the southern provinces we witnessed a high degree of peace and stability in the provinces of Equatoria region, and parts of Upper Nile ... However, I cannot deny that skirmishes continue between the two sides ... The Armed Forces cannot adopt the tactics of the rebels such as hiding in the bush, ambushing non-combatants, and plundering and confiscating people's property.
>
> This does not mean, by any measure, that the rebels have the upper hand. I want to assure you that they represent only a minority of the local population – many of whom come from Abyei and want to secede from Kordofan. I met with 9 sub-tribal chiefs [Omdas] from the area and of those 9, 7 were opposed to secession. The two that favored seceding from Kordofan were followers of Deng Majok and his sons, extremists like Dr. Zachariah and Michael, who is in the bush. When they realized that we [the Central Government] paid them little attention, they formed a group of about 39 people and

began to collect weapons from outside sources. It was not long before they began their campaign of plundering the area. In fact, they were responsible for the incident at Ariat. At present we have Dr. Zachariah in custody and will charge him before a court of law because he, more than anyone else, was behind what happened. One of the reasons for this is that Dr. Zachariah's position as regional Minister under the last government enabled him to relocate most of the residents of Abyei to Bahr al-Ghazal. Recently I learned of a bizarre development, that he and his supporters sent 25,000 Sudanese pounds to the relocated residents of Abyei to live presumably on the grounds that the latter are refugees. I cannot understand how a person can live as a refugee in his own country. This is a very dangerous practice. Nevertheless, we in the Central Government have the means and the capability with which to deal with practices that disrupt the security of the country.

I decided to ignore the statement as part of the psychological warfare aimed at intimidating the Ngok to cease their hostilities. It probably had the opposite effect as it hardened the stance of the Ngok. Indeed, winning the cooperation of the detainees was to prove extremely difficult. Zachariah Bol himself was ambivalent about the process, at times hopeful but at times despondent and despairing, but appreciative of my attempts. After the vice-president's statement, he asked me to stop the mediation effort and focus on getting him a good defense lawyer. The process itself was remarkable. Every morning, the detainees were brought from prisons and detention homes around the three towns for the meetings which were held at the security headquarters under conditions of comfort and relative freedom, without any harassment, intimidation, or undue influence, only to be returned to their confinement at the end of the meetings.

During the first session with two senior security officers present, I asked the group which language we should use. Bol immediately suggested that we should use Dinka since some of the elders did not understand Arabic. His real intentions were quite transparent, for he did not want the security officers to be fully in the picture. For the same reason, I immediately disagreed with him and suggested that anyone could speak any language, Dinka, English, or Arabic, but that if people spoke Dinka, it should be translated into Arabic so that all those present could follow. The most senior of the officers felt somewhat embarrassed and announced that he would leave in a few minutes. As the discussions progressed and everyone opened up, the officer not only stayed for the entire duration of the talks, but would say in the end that it had been the best course in political science he had ever had.

And indeed, although the Dinka were initially suspicious about the presence of the security officers in the discussion, they took an increasing interest in their attendance and were concerned whenever the recording officer was not taking notes. They were clearly satisfied that their point of view was getting to the top through the security channels. It was obvious that they felt they were having a sympathetic hearing from the security authorities. There was of course no doubt that they objectively had a convincing case and felt assured of the third party moderating role that the central government had always played in their relations with the Homr Arabs.

The gist of my message to the detainees was to explain the nature of the ongoing struggle over the area, the threat which Abyei's potential annexation to the South posed for the pastoral Arab tribes of Kordofan for which the area was a source of water and pasture, and the extent to which the Kordofan regional and central governments were naturally aligned with Arab tribes, while the South was too weak and lacking in political will to make a difference. I explained to them that the historical position taken by the leaders of the tribe to remain under the jurisdiction of Kordofan had been a strategic move to circumvent confrontation over the land. If the Arabs were forced by Ngok political association with the South, they could falsify history to claim the land, as they had already done, instead of the gratitude which they had historically shown to Ngok leaders for being given access to water and grazing lands. And however absurd their claim to the land, they were likely to receive the support of the authorities at the regional and the central government levels who identified with them more than they did with the Dinka. The message was pessimistic and pragmatic.

On their part, the Dinka rehashed in great detail the history of mistreatment, oppression and subjugation which they had received from the authorities of Kordofan aligning themselves with the Missiriya Arabs. They invoked their legal right under the Addis Ababa Agreement to determine their status between the North and the South. I told them that their approach, while understandable, missed the real issue. It assumed a situation of objective justice where there was none, partiality where the judge was inherently an interested party. The best they could expect was the old formula for the autonomous development of their area within Kordofan. I therefore urged them to endorse the main elements of the president's policy over Abyei, which had been designed to include effective control over local affairs by the people of Abyei and the provision of services and a nationally sponsored development program in the area.

Some were receptive to my approach, while others, including Bol, maintained a hard line. Bol was particularly tormented by the statement of the vice-president accusing him of treason. His statement was a painful combination of elaborate self-defense and assertion of a political stance for the record. I listened with mixed feelings of sympathy and impatience that I could eventually not control. Interrupting Bol gently, I said we were not in a court of law nor was I there to debate the legal issues of their arrest as I did not know precisely what they were alleged to have done or what they would be charged with. My sole objective in the exercise was to explore with them what we ourselves could do to remove what I saw as the underlying causes of the conflict and thereby diffuse the situation, turning their arrest into an opportunity for finding workable solutions to the problems of the area.

After seemingly endless discussions from early morning to late afternoon for weeks on end, an agreement was eventually reached that secured their release in a remarkable manner that seemingly transformed hostility into cordiality. Before finalizing the agreement, one of them remarked that if they gave in on their political demand for the referendum on joining the South, it was because they had no alternative way of pursuing their rights. I agreed with that formulation. They all laughed at my humility. We now stood on the same ground.

The plan of action, which was agreed upon with the authorities of Kordofan and sanctioned by the central government, promised special administrative status for Abyei in Kordofan, with increased autonomy, services, and development activities. It was in essence an agreement to reactivate the implementation of the initial policy on Abyei without touching on the sensitive issue of the referendum provided for by the Addis Ababa Agreement of 1972.

The sons of Deng Majok and the Ngok Leadership issued two statements. The statement of Deng Majok's sons said:

> We, the undersigned sons of Deng Majok, hereby
> reaffirm our commitment to the noble principles which
> our late father and our forefathers before him pursued for
> centuries within the framework of Kordofan to advance

the cause of peace and unity as a link between the southern and the northern parts of the country.

Some of us have recently felt themselves driven to the call of separating the area of Abyei from Kordofan and joining it to the southern Region in the hope of ensuring participation in the government of the country on equal footing with fellow countrymen in that region. We have now learned that one of us has even taken up arms in pursuance of this objective and with most regrettable consequences to the peace and security of our people.

While we recognize the frustrations which have led to this sad development, we remain unequivocally opposed to this destructive means of attempting a solution to the problem of Abyei.

We also declare that our objective in the area has always been to secure for our people the dignity of equal partnership in the government of their country. To promote this objective in line with the ideals which our forebears have always spearheaded in the area, we have resolved to work within the framework of Kordofan and in full cooperation with our brothers and sisters in that region for the common good of all our people in the region (Deng 1986:266).

The declaration of the Ngok leadership was similar in essence, although it did not, understandably, attribute the bridging role of Ngok history to any individual or family:

We, the assembled sons of Abyei, have been watching with profound sorrow and anguish the recent developments in our area and the general threat to the security of innocent people in the area. We are also deeply concerned that these developments have had the effect of reversing the historical image of our area as a vital link between the southern and northern parts of our country. Rather than the symbol of national unity and integration which it has been for centuries, our area is now seen as a point of confrontation and animosity and a threat to peace and unity, the most precious achievements of the May Revolution.

We have always considered it absolutely essential that the call for joining the South be conducted peacefully and in accordance with the constitution and the laws of the country. While we therefore recognize the frustrations of the political tensions and conflicts which have recently prompted some people in the area to resort to violent means, we totally oppose the use of violence as a means of solving the problem of Abyei.

We would also want to emphasize that we have always regarded the call for joining the South as a means and not an end in itself. The main objective has always been to secure for the people of Abyei the enjoyment of full rights of citizenship as free and equal partners in the government of their country. We therefore declare ourselves willing and ready to work within the framework of Kordofan as long as opportunities for the enjoyment of full rights of citizenship are offered to our people on equal footing with the rest of the people in the region.

We have also concluded that the policies and principles declared by His Excellency the President of the Republic for the administration and development of Abyei area as a symbol of national unity and integration constitute a sound basis for the realization of the common interests in the area. We hope to achieve this in accordance with such programmes as may be agreed upon with the authorities of Kordofan in a spirit of cooperation and mutual understanding (Deng 1986:267).

The agreement was celebrated in the North as though it were a second Addis Ababa Agreement. The luncheon I had secretly organized in anticipation of their release was attended by a hundred and fifty spontaneous guests. And for days to follow, various social functions were organized by the Dinka and the Arabs of the area together, and all were glamorously covered by the national media.

The news was, however, ambivalently received in the South and among the "opportunists" of the Ngok Dinka and the leaders of Kordofan, in particular the governor who had been away when the agreement was negotiated and concluded. Whether because he had not been part of it or because he was trying to gain political advantage with the Arabs in his region, El Fateh Bushara seemed almost antagonistic to the accord. In reaction to his attitude, I confronted him in front of his accompanying ministers and assembly members, arguing that he, as the head of the regional government, had more to be appreciative about than the national leadership, that he should be grateful to those who had made it possible, and that his attitude was a clear demonstration of what the Ngok Dinka objected to in the government of Kordofan. As far as I was concerned, I had done my utmost and would henceforth wash my hands and let the responsibility fall on him.

The governor seemed startled by my attack and from that moment on tried to win my appreciation for his delicate position. He explained that the people we considered opportunists were his political allies and that together with the Arabs, they had enabled him to win the elections. Indeed, the political faction with which we identified had not voted for him. Since he found the climate in Khartoum favorable to the Deng family, he wanted to assure the other side that they were not alone in the cold and that they still had his support. That way, he could then work to build bridges in order to consolidate on the regional level what we had achieved on the national level. Together, we held a public meeting with the Ngok leaders and the public in which he tried to moderate his position and win approval of his idea to move the whole process to the region and broaden support for the reconciliation.

The Arabs and their Dinka allies in the area immediately sent a delegation to Khartoum, their objective being to oppose the agreement just reached. Against the advice of many who thought that my life might be in danger, I decided to visit the delegation and perhaps have a dialogue with them. When I was escorted to the hotel lounge where many of them sat watching television, all but one got up to greet me, Arabs and Dinka alike. The one who did not rise remained conspicuously focused on the television screen, clearly avoiding me. Realizing what was going on, I went around him greeting people and also conspicuously avoiding him. I learned later that he was Matet Ayom's son. Since he somehow held our family responsible for the death of his father, a blood feud was presumed to exist between us. Shaking hands was therefore out of the question. My discussions with the group were more a courtesy report and an explanation of what I had tried to do than an exchange of views, even though some of them spoke reservedly, but courteously.

After consultations with the national security authorities, the groups all agreed to go back to Kordofan and broaden the reconciliation process in the region. I decided it was time for me to go back to my post, especially as our embassy in Canada was one of the twenty-one missions abroad that was to be closed for austerity reasons.

Before leaving, Izekial Kodi, one of the prominent southern politicians and Bol's political ally, invited Bol and me to a dinner which was attended by Arthur Akuien, another politician and ally. To my utter surprise, Izekial asked me why I had taken such bold initiatives on Abyei, including proposing an alternative policy to joining the South and now mediating the release of detainees: Did the people of Abyei elect or mandate me to speak on their behalf? Was it my education or my status as the chief's son that made me feel entitled to take such initiatives and speak on behalf of the people of Abyei? He was of course critical of what I had done. I was infuriated by his discourtesy and rudeness, considering that I was a dinner guest. Being his guest did not, however, inhibit me from paying him back in kind. I told him that if his idea of leadership was that people should give one a job or else one did not feel obligated to protect the interest of one's people as one saw it, then my own notion differed from his. I said I did not need to be elected or given a pertinent job for me to care for my people. If he wanted to attribute that to my being son of a chief or to my education, that was his business and I would not shy away from either reason. Both Bol and Akuien came to my defense.

And yet, as I reflect back, Izekial's harsh criticism evokes in me one major flaw with most of my initiatives, whether with respect to Abyei or the South. They were undertaken through individual contacts and relationships in a non-democratic political climate. By their very nature, they had to be conducted discreetly and sometimes secretly so that the rationale behind what one was doing was never made explicit enough for the public to understand. Well-motivated and carefully thought out initiatives were thereby exposed to misinterpretations which assumed self-serving objectives, especially since they ran against the emotionalism of populist politics. As a result, these initiatives often failed to win popular support. I have not the slightest doubt in my mind that if I had fully argued my case for the alternative policy of developing Abyei as a model of national unity and integration, I would have won popular support. Indeed, the views of the elders I interviewed or with whom I held private talks confirm my confidence in this respect. The same applies to the reasons behind my initiative for the release of the detainees and the arguments I made for their adjustment of political stance. But if I had exposed my reasons publicly, they would have appeared to the North as shrewd and pragmatic, divested of the national idealism that inspired the kind of support and enthusiasm they received. I would have been even more labelled than I was by some northerners as a "clever" operator in the primary interest of my people and not for the mutual benefit of the Arabs with the Dinka, and of the nation as a whole. Perhaps that too might have been a realistic argument with which to win genuine support, but it also presupposes an atmosphere of openness and democratic dialogue which was lacking in the political system. I consider this as one of the major lessons I learned from these experiences.

The understanding that was reached in April 1983 between the authorities of Kordofan and elements from the Ngok Dinka brought back only a small patch of calm in what had become a sea of turbulence that would soon engulf the whole South in a second wave of civil war.

As the resolution of the Abyei situation was still being celebrated, Bona Malwal, a prominent southern leader, was arrested. Even Abel Alier was feared to be under the threat of imminent arrest. Then, suddenly, President Nimeiri announced the division of the South into three regions. Shortly afterwards, the Bor and Fashalla crises that triggered the full rebellion of the units which would form the nucleus of the SPLM/SPLA under the leadership of John Garang de Mabior took place. The South was back in arms.

III

EXTERNAL RELATIONS

10
Reaching Out Abroad

If conflict management or resolution is a method of negotiating human relations which is conditioned or at least significantly influenced by culture and personality, then handling personal relations abroad requires the added responsibility of bridging among individuals, groups, and cultural attitudes. It is in essence a form of diplomacy, if the individuals involved are conscious of their representative capacity. And it is an even more precarious diplomacy because it lacks the aura and the paraphernalia of diplomatic representation. It is to these personal encounters that the Dinka apply the saying: "A gentleman of one tribe does not know a gentleman of another tribe." This calls for a deliberate effort at reaching out, which requires more than self-introduction. While identification can help remedy mutual ignorance, it also poses its own risks of bragging and self-promotion that can be counterproductive. A typical example was my interchange with an oriental taxi driver to whom my explaining who I was in the hope of making him trust me only confirmed how much of a storyteller I was. The farther apart and alien to one another the groups represented by the interactive individuals, the more difficult it is to bridge the gap.

What the credibility gap between strangers in foreign encounters requires is a cross-cultural dialogue. This is triggered by the mere fact of the encounter, but it is not enough to come in contact; the challenge requires a meaningful and constructive communication that elucidates the different perspectives involved and helps facilitate mutual understanding.

The episodes covered in this chapter are selected from the two countries where personal experiences have had a profound impact on me, Germany, the first foreign country I visited when I was in my early twenties, and the United States where I have lived for many years, both in the representative capacity of ambassador and as a private individual.

Establishing Communication in a Rural German Town

As explained in the introductory chapter, when I was in the University of Khartoum, I was one of the founders of a program of study tours with German students, through which we lived with families, worked in factories to acquaint ourselves with conditions in different parts of the country, and studied German in the Goethe Institut. During our first visit on this program, twelve students, nine male and three female, went to Germany, where after an initial work period, they were divided into two groups to study German in the Goethe Institut for one month, followed by a tour of the country. I was sent to the small town of Zell-im-Wiesenthal in the Black Forest, where I was probably the first black man to be seen by the local population.

The level of curiosity, mixed with fear and prejudice, was astounding. Whenever I got out of the hotel to go to work or for my frequent walks, I was literally bombarded by a crowd of children from the nearby school, running after me and shouting, both in fear and excitement. If I stopped to talk to them, they ran away from me; if I ignored them and walked on, they ran after me, encroaching so close that there was no way to ignore them. What compounded the significance of their reaction was that adults too would suddenly lay eyes on me, stop in shock with hands on their mouths, and perhaps betray a withdrawal reaction that was different from the children's in that it was only slightly more inhibited. Otherwise, the adults, particularly the aged, saw me as strange and peculiar as did their children.

After a while, this got on my nerves and I would no longer tolerate it. I decided to enter the school and ask for the director. I was shown into the director's office amidst crowds of following and screaming children. When I got to Herr Böhler, the director, there was the problem of the language of communication as he did not know enough English and would not expose the little he knew. So, one of the teachers, Fräulein Passens, was fetched to interpret. As I discovered eventually, apart from the Fessmanns, my hosts, and the local doctor and his wife, Fräulein Passens was the only other person I knew who spoke English at Zell.

I gave them the gist of my experience with the children, how much I had tried to dispel their fears by approaching them in a friendly manner, how they had refused to respond to my gestures, how they would run after me when I proceeded and away from me when I approached. I told them that there was a limit to what any human being could tolerate and that I was not there as an animal in a zoo but a human being with feelings and sentiments. I said I was keen to cultivate relations with the children, but, instead, received only insult and an unwillingness to learn on the part of the children. I said that where I came from, the school was the institution which cultivated manners in the pupils and was therefore the example for proper conduct in society. I was therefore surprised to find that school was an example of the opposite in that society. I ended by appealing to them to do something about the problem.

Herr Böhler, whom I later learned came from one of the prominent families of Zell, was enraged by the behavior of his pupils. He said in a language I well understood even before interpretation, "They will be punished!" And judging from his demeanor, he meant it. Fräulein Passens was purely an interpreter, but she reflected an enthusiastic agreement with my point of view and with the director's reaction. I argued against the director's declared intention to punish the children. I said that since they were afraid of me, punishing them would only add to their fears. All I wanted was to make them understand that I was a human being, that what they were doing was offensive to me, and that I would not harm them as they feared. The director promised me to look into the matter and to inform me of the action they would take.

A few days later, I received an invitation, through Herr Fessmann, to give a talk to the school in English to be interpreted by Fräulein Passens. I accepted. The talk was well attended and I gave a general survey of the Sudan, giving some emphasis on the aspects I thought children might appreciate, but without being simplistic. The pupils asked a number of questions that showed a determined interest. The occasion was a clear success.

The next day, as I was having my late afternoon walk, a lady came out of her house and tried to gesture me into the house. As I looked somewhat confused, she rushed back into her house and re-emerged with her husband and photos of their children, indicating that they had talked about me and gesturing her invitation for me to stop for tea. I was also invited for dinner by the director and became a close friend of their teenage daughters and a son in medical school at Basel in Switzerland.

From that time on, not only would the children approach me on the road with a "Good morning", but many would come to shake hands and even follow me to my room, just chit-chatting, feeling proud that the little English they had learned had opened up channels of communication with this otherwise total stranger.

Enduring and Confronting Biased Hatred in an American Residential Area

The incident in the United States occurred during my third year at Yale Law School as a graduate student. I was in the process of completing my doctoral dissertation. I had met and become friends with Etna Castle who lived with her family in a New Haven suburb that was predominantly, if not exclusively, white.

As the Castles were about to go on holiday, they asked me to house-sit for them. This was an opportunity to accommodate a fellow Dinka, Ambrose Ahang, and his American wife, Mary, with their baby boy who were about to visit me from Indiana on their way to the Sudan. My time in the Castle's house was to confront me with the most blatant racial hatred I was ever to encounter in the many years I spent in the United States.

Next to the Castles was an Italian-American family of a musician. Their house was elegant and their lawn well maintained. They had small children who initially seemed very pleasant. As soon as we moved into the house, the children would come over and engage in a curious but friendly conversation. For instance, they approached Mary and wanted to know how it happened that her baby was black while she was white. She explained that his father was black.

Another day, they approached me in the morning, while I was in my long white Sudanese robe, the jallabiya. "Excuse me," one of them said politely, "are you a human being or an angel?" I smiled and told them I was a human being. "A male or a female?" she asked. I said I was a male. Our conversation was all in a matter-of-fact manner, which added so much to the purity and innocence of their curiosity.

But all that innocent exploration suddenly stopped and we could not explain the development other than as a result of the attitude of the father, a rather heavy man of medium height in his late forties or early fifties, who was often seen in the garden, looking fierce and hostile, or heard shouting loudly and angrily at someone, perhaps the children, perhaps his wife. He clearly seemed obnoxious, even without speaking; he was much worse when we heard him reproach the children for coming to our side. In front of us and in a voice loud enough for us to hear, he said to them never to come to us again: "Communists should be shot at, not talked to." It sounded so strange that we never even took it to be seriously aimed at us, although that seemed quite obvious. The children suddenly stopped coming or talking to us, even when they were within talking distance. They would approach our side, come close, but rather than talk, merely gaze with a combination of curiosity and fear.

But more was to come, even after Ambrose and Mary were gone. If anyone visited me and went into the driveway, my neighbor would stand alertly, observing the car. With the slightest touch of the edge of his lawn, he would scream, telling the person to get off his lawn. If the person visiting happened to park his or her car on the street, my neighbor would telephone the police that there was a strange car in the neighborhood, supposedly alerting them to a possible burglary. If I had people in the house for a party or a small get together, he would telephone the police to say we were too noisy and a nuisance to the neighborhood.

In all of these situations, the police would come, find the situation to be different from what they had been told, apologize, and leave. The same situation would be repeated again and again and again. The police would apologize and leave; others would come, and yet others would come. There did not seem to be any coordination between the different policemen who came or they were agreed to use the pattern of being a nuisance to me and my friends, and yet acting surprised and apologetic. Somehow, I believed them when they apologized and I only took it to be an issue of organization and coordination or more appropriately, the lack of those.

As though all that was not enough, my neighbor telephoned frequently only to hang up on me or maintain a dreadful silence when I answered the call, with only his heavy, hateful breathing reaching my ears.

I went to the police station to complain, but not only did I receive no help, I was frustrated by the lengthy, time-consuming formalities, with a dismissive, almost rude, attitude from the police who made me feel as though I was wasting their time for nothing. In the end, I was told that nothing could be done, although I could of course file a complaint that no one could tell as to how long it would take or where it would eventually lead to. Even though a Ph.D. student of law, I felt helpless because I realized there was a lot more involved than law.

I considered talking to the man, but all my friends, nearly all whites, strongly ruled out the idea. They said he was a bigot and that talking to him would only expose me to an even more painful experience without resolving anything. So I just suffered at the hands of the man. Some friends advised me to leave the house, but I refused to do so because I had committed myself to the Castles that I would take care of their house. Besides, I could not accept such moral defeat. In fact, I could not make myself believe that what was happening was truly on racial grounds, for I could not believe someone who did not know me could hate me so much simply because I was of a different race. I was itching to explore the real reasons in case there was something else of which I was unaware and which could be corrected. But there was a clear unanimous position from all my friends, not to venture.

Despite the racial hatred I was confronting from the neighbor, and the insensitive, even inhumane treatment from the police, I felt no bitterness on racial grounds beyond the anger I felt towards the individuals involved. I had difficulty accepting even the blatantly racist attitude of my neighbor as an instance of racism. I took it more as a case of an individual person who was so bitter, hostile, and cruel even to his own family, the racial expression of his hostility being only an aspect. Now that I think back, I was really free of racial bitterness or animosity, and ironically, that was what gave me the strength to fight and survive the most miserable treatment I had ever and would ever experience.

The Castles came and I moved back to my apartment, feeling a sense of remorse at my failure to dig deeper into the situation with their neighbor. Of course, I explained the situation to them and all they could say was that they had never had anything to do with him and that they had always heard him loud and hostile to his own family. They shared the attitude of all my other friends that it was not worth discussing the matter with him because one would not get anywhere with his kind of attitude.

A few days after I had moved back to my apartment, I came to visit the Castles, riding a bicycle they had lent me. As I passed through the driveway towards the garage in the back of the house, I saw the neighbor sitting in the garden all alone. It was a beautiful sunny day. As I walked back to the house from the garage, I felt an impulse to talk to him, despite all advice to the contrary. I walked towards him. Standing in front of him, I said, "I would like to have a word with you, may I?"

"What do you want?" he said in a voice and manner that clearly indicated that I was not welcome.

I decided to persist, "It will take some time, would you mind if I sit?"

"Sit down," he conceded with disdain.

"Would you please tell me what wrong I did to you to deserve the way you treated me."

He immediately became defensive: "If you think I am prejudiced, you are mistaken. If you go into my house, you will see many pictures of black musicians hanging on my wall. Some of them are very good friends of mine." He then went on to explain what he had against me. "But I object to one thing, and that is marriage between the races. Aren't you people proud of your own race? I am a good Catholic and I believe in God and respect God's creation. God created man in different races and it is not right for man to change what God has created. I am an Italian and I am proud to be Italian and Catholic. I perform for rich Jews and Protestants, but as soon as I finish my performance, I go back to my people, the Catholics, the Italian Americans."

Hearing him talk made me feel a sense of relief that I was dealing with a case of dogmatism that posed no significant moral or intellectual threat to my position. Indeed, his extremism placed me in an advantaged position to render help rather than defend myself. So I relaxed and interacted with him in an almost patronizing fashion.

"You, of course, know that I am not married, don't you?" I said with an almost frivolous sense of detail.

"I know you are not married," he explained, "but you accommodated a man who is married to a white girl. That to me means that you approve of mixed marriages."

My response was more substantive, although even more patronizing: "You say you are a Catholic and a strong believer. I am also a Catholic and one of the principles I remember the Bible advocates is giving accommodation to the needy. Are you telling me that your objection to mixed marriages is so important that it overrides other Christian principles, such as providing accommodation to those in need?"

"Don't tell me that your friend was destitute," he said, "I know about you both. You are a law student, working for your doctorate and he is a graduate from Indiana and a university professor. He was not a destitute needing your accommodation."

"But all the same, the Christian faith teaches us to observe many principles of behavior towards our fellow human beings. Is the issue of mixed marriages so important to you that it outweighs all those moral principles concerning responsibilities towards neighbors and fellow human beings?"

319

"Look, I told you that I consider races to be God's creation and we should not mess around with God's work."

"I had an uncle," I said, recalling Bona Bulabek. "He was a genius; always top of his class, even after jumping grades. He was about to graduate from a famous Italian medical school, Padova, when he died in a car accident. He always maintained that one should marry from one's own people. Although he was very westernized and had spent many years abroad, he always insisted that he would go back and marry from amongst his people."

"That uncle of yours would certainly have been my friend," he interjected.

"In fact, he is no exception," I went on. "Most of my people feel exactly the same way. Indeed, most people throughout the world feel the same way. It is a small minority that does otherwise. Mixed marriages are an extremely small exception, compared to the overwhelming preference for marriage within the group. So, you are absolutely right that people should marry within their groups, because that is the norm."

Having established a base of agreement, I then introduced my own line of thought: "But my disagreement with you stems from the fact that the norm reflects a situation where people were somewhat isolated from one another and the chances of meeting and marrying across the border were not only limited, but they also threatened the individual with separation and isolation from his or her group. This situation is now changing rapidly. People are mixing intensively across all kinds of barriers. And when individuals meet in this mixing, there is no way of controlling their feelings. Love knows no boundaries, especially when people are able to know and understand one another across those boundaries. It doesn't mean that it is easy or that it is preferable; it is just a fact of our changing world that mixed marriages will continue to increase as contact between races continues to expand."

My words did not of course register significantly to him, but he listened rather attentively and patiently.

"That is your opinion; I certainly do not share it and pray to God that our world does not get off the track that way."

I resumed my lecture: "You see, unless you approach future realities with flexibility, you are bound to clash with them and could harm yourself. There are certain developments that we can only predict, but cannot control. To stand against an inexorable current would be only to drown yourself. Take, for instance, what you were telling your children, that communists should only be shot at and not talked to. You were

320

calling us communists simply because we are black. When your children grow up, they will certainly realize that being black does not necessarily make one a communist. What do you think they will feel about what you had taught them? You will be discredited."

On this issue, he had a strong, unwavering point of view, which he put in the form of a rhetorical question: "Are you telling me that the civil rights movement in this country is not infiltrated by communists?"

"I am not telling you that, nor do I know enough about your civil rights situation to judge. What I am telling you is that I am not a communist and, indeed, I believe that if the communists were to take over in our two countries, the United States and the Sudan, I would probably be more negatively affected than you would be, if only because of my family position in the present system."

By now, although we were not agreed on anything, we were arguing quite amicably and with hardly any hostility towards one another, only a realization that we genuinely disagreed.

"Let me go back to the question of the importance you attach to mixed marriages as compared with other principles of human relations. Do you know that every time you called the police, they came and apologized when they discovered the truth? Was that in itself not enough to convince you that you were being hard on me for reasons that were unfounded, at least to the police?"

Again, he seemed certain about his position: "If you think they are on your side, you are wrong. There are many phoney liberals who go about giving the Blacks the wrong impression that they support them, but I know them and how hypocritical they are – I will tell you, all those policemen will not admit to you their feelings, but they not only share my point of view, some are even more angry than I am. Don't let them fool you by their apologies. It is just a put-on."

He was now speaking in a manner that almost made him seem sympathetic to me for being so naive about such a strong hatred toward my racial group. Perhaps he felt that if I were that naive, I could not be all that bad, and certainly could not be a communist. He even seemed friendly.

"Let me introduce you to my family," he said as he called his wife and children. After meeting them, he asked me whether I would want to have a cup of tea or coffee. By now, we had been talking for over an hour and I felt I should not stay any longer. So I thanked them and excused myself, but only after some concluding remarks from me:

"I would like to ask of you one big favor."

"Sure, what?"

"Next time you find yourself in a similar situation with anybody, would you allow contact and exchange of views rather than cut him off and display hostility towards him! At least you will give him and yourself the opportunity of learning each other's point of view and you may find that he can be convinced to your point of view or you may see some sense in his point of view. In either case, you will have promoted understanding and reduced tension and animosity."

He did not commit himself, but he did not dismiss the point either. We seemed to agree without words on this last point and although we had disagreed on all other points, a spirit of mutual understanding and a degree of respect for each other's point of view had evolved between us. I still realized he was a bigot; he probably still saw me as one of those intellectual dreamers. But we shook hands warmly and smilingly as we parted. I left feeling very proud that I had resisted the unanimous advice against talking to him. My faith in the values of my society, which had propelled me to do so, was rejuvenated.

A Rewarding Visit to an Antagonistic American

The second incident occurred in Woodstock, New York, where we own a house. After leaving government, we used the house as our regular residence for some years. One day, as we drove to the railroad station in Rheinbeck to meet an old friend from New Haven, a child psychiatrist, my wife, an American, who was driving her father's car, got into a minor accident with a man who was backing from his garage onto the road at a dangerous corner.

Irrespective of who was right or wrong, my wife informed the man that as it was her father's car and he was very strict about procedures, she thought they should exchange relevant information on their insurance policies. My wife was simply being correct without any intention to sue, especially as the damage to our car was very slight. The man, however, read her request for insurance documents as evidence of her intention to sue. He turned from being friendly and apologetic to being hostile and haughty. Producing a call card, which he virtually threw at my wife, he said that he was an attorney and could be reached at the address on the card. My attempt to talk to him to sort the misunderstanding out was rebuffed in a rude manner, as he got back to his car and drove off insultingly.

I was more offended by his manner than by the accident, especially by his implied assumption that he could intimidate us with his professional title as an attorney. We drove to the station with me fuming with anger. I told my wife and our friend that I intended to go back to the man and clear the situation. Both of them disagreed with me, since they saw in the man's behavior a personality trait that they did not think would be amenable to a meaningful dialogue.

As soon as we were back in the house, I decided to go to the man. He lived only a few minutes walk from our house. As we were expecting other guests for dinner, my wife and our visiting friend did not think it wise for me to get myself into a potentially even more upsetting situation. I persisted and went against their advice. One of my sons wanted to come with me, but I thought it better to keep the children out of the uncertainties. I therefore went alone.

I was glad to see the man's car back and the house lit. I rang the doorbell and heard a man approach. When he opened the door and saw me, he surprisingly welcomed me very warmly and immediately started apologizing for his behavior. He said he had been wondering how he could find the opportunity to make up for his conduct. With that apology, not much explanation was required on either side. We simply proceeded to exchange conciliatory explanations from our perspectives. I told him that all my wife had wanted was a formality that she knew her father would expect. I had wanted a friendly interchange to explain her position. He on his part admitted to anticipating a lawsuit and had reacted to that prospect.

We then proceeded to talk about our occupations and interests and discovered much in common. Far from being a practicing attorney, he was more of an artist who had taken interest in writing and illustrating children's books. He was very interested in my writings on the Dinka and in particular those relating to culture, such as songs and folktales.

I would have invited him to dinner, had I not known that he was expecting a friend with whom he had an engagement for the evening. I returned home a much happier person, not only because I had turned an enemy into a friend, but perhaps more importantly, because I felt that my approach had been vindicated.

The Effectiveness of Talking it Out in Most, But Not All, Cases

I have given these examples as illustrations of a pattern of conflict management or resolution techniques which I believe reflected values and principles of human interaction that have guided my behavior from childhood. In that sense, they may be said to be culturally specific, at least in origin. But I also believe that they are capable of universal application to human relations in cross-cultural situations. The fact that in these examples, and many more could be given, a degree of communication and mutual understanding was developed to bridge the gap to a functional degree does indeed confirm the potential for application in cross-cultural situations.

Although I believe that my inclination toward talking as a means of trying to resolve conflicts or differences has more often than not succeeded, I have encountered a number of failures, some of them dramatic and painful. Virtually all the instances that come to mind were in cross-cultural situations, more specifically involving interracial encounters abroad.

In 1962, I visited Sweden on a study tour with a Swedish writer who was planning to write a book about his country and sought my input as an African. Although most of my experiences in Sweden involved positive discrimination in my favor, as an "exotic" African, I encountered some racial prejudices. In one case, my friend and I went into a crowded night club. One man deliberately pushed me out of his way in a hostile and rude manner. As I did not speak Swedish, I asked my friend to interpret as I approached the man for explanation. Why did he push me, I asked. The answer I got was, "I hate foreigners!" I was more intrigued than offended: "Why?" I asked. "Nothing personal; I just hate foreigners." I tried to engage him in a discussion, but he was totally disinterested. All he made sure I understood was that he had nothing against me personally; his position was one of principle against all foreigners. As someone later commented, "foreigners" was probably a racially loaded euphemism.

Another incident occurred in the United States. We were vacationing in Vail, Colorado, where my wife and I attended one of the Stanley Foundation's annual conferences on the United Nations of the future, accommodated at The Lodge at Vail. At the pool, we took a canopy and a table we thought to be free until an elderly woman came to pick up her belongings that were lying near by. Realizing that she must have occupied that place earlier, we apologized to her and offered to leave, but all she did was to look at us with hostility and leave without uttering a word in response. She went and sat in a chair without protection from the sun. Thinking that she might not have heard us, I went to her and repeated our apology and offer to leave. But she would not even acknowledge my presence. I left feeling defeated and suffering the agony of total failure.

In yet another incident, this time in Washington, D.C., I took a cab from the Watergate Hotel, where I had visited a friend. It was Sunday and I was informally dressed in a sweater. After going some distance, the taxi driver, an African, ran out of gas. He suggested that I take another cab and gestured the one immediately behind us. Although he did not want to be paid, I wanted to give him a tip and reached out for my wallet, only to discover that I had forgotten it at home.

The next cab was driven by an Asian man. The question he immediately asked me was why the other driver had kicked me out of his cab. I explained to him that he had run out of gas. He looked up the fare from the chart and asked me to pay in advance. I asked him why I had to, explaining that I had never before been asked to pay for a taxi in advance. He insisted that I should pay or leave his cab.

Of course, I had no wallet and no money to pay him. But as it had begun to rain, I also did not want to get out of his car. I chose to negotiate the situation by telling him the truth about my wallet. I assured him that I would compensate him well when we got home. It seemed that what I said merely confirmed his suspicion. He now asked me to leave his cab. I pleaded with him, providing whatever evidence I thought might help to establish my identity and trustworthiness, but nothing would persuade him to change his mind. I urged him to trust a stranger for once and see whether or not his trust would be rewarded. He said he had trusted too many times before and had been the victim of his trust. He did not want to have any other experiments with trust. In desperation, I tried to use my titles, both at Brookings and as former ambassador and foreign minister of my country. That was the final straw: "You are a good story-teller. Get out of my cab." I had no choice but to get out, slamming the door as hard as I could, almost wishing it were on his face. I saw how tempting committing a crime could be in the face of such humiliation.

How does one explain such dramatic failure to talk it out? One way of looking at it is that we come with preconceptions about the gulf separating us from the identity group represented by the stranger we encounter and that for some reason we do not consider it worth our while to try to bridge that gap. But why do some people prove impervious to the human dimension even when explicitly asserted? Is it something within the resisting personality or in the behavior of the person resisted? And is such behavior a universal phenomenon or cultural conditioning? For me personally the real frustration is when the urge to talk it out meets with no response, except for wordless hostility.

11
Diplomacy of Mediation

One of the principles that guided me in my foreign service, as stated at the outset, was that diplomacy is ultimately an art of managing human relations. The degree to which this principle is consciously felt and observed obviously differs with the individual and his or her particular context, including cultural conditioning and family upbringing. Some individuals insulate themselves from this personal responsibility by placing impersonal notions of representation between them and their official role. Others more readily discharge their tasks with a strong sense of personal responsibility. I belong to this second category. Another principle that guided me in my diplomatic representation was that foreign policy is largely a reflection of domestic policy and values. Not only do domestic interests and needs dictate what is sought abroad from whom and how, but the values and principles that are postulated and followed domestically should provide the basis for external linkages, alliances, and partnerships. Again, some people may draw a distinction between what is desirable for the domestic constituency – the nationals – and the outside world for whom there is no commensurate responsibility. My personal bias is that what is viewed as desirable for one's own people ought to be, as a matter of principle, desirable for others.

These differences are not merely theoretical; they can and do confront diplomats with concrete choices. In my tour of duty, I often came across ambassadors who were reluctant to take moves, which seemed to me clearly within their mandates because they claimed that they needed instructions from their governments. And there is of course the debate about the degree to which fundamental human rights are universal or culturally relative, an artificial debate used only by those with a vested interest in protecting themselves against international scrutiny.

An Ambassador of a Country with a Conciliatory Internal Agreement

When I joined Sudan's foreign service, what persuaded me to give in and accept the position of ambassador to the Scandinavian countries, the fourth offer I received within a year (after the positions of deputy head of mission to London, province judge, and deputy minister of foreign affairs), was the end of the civil war in the Sudan through a peacefully negotiated settlement that granted the South regional autonomy within the framework of national unity. For me, the attraction of my diplomatic undertaking was that I had a positive page in my country's contemporary history to display to the well-intentioned world as a basis for winning their support and cooperation in a wide variety of areas – relief and rehabilitation, development, and the pursuit of the common ideals of regional and international peace.

Only those with bad intentions who did not share those positive values would fail to see merit in such a goal. Just as much as I had resisted government service during the war because I did not want to be used against my people, I now saw my assignment abroad as a service to both my country and my people at home. That was indeed the essence of what I conveyed to the president and the minister of foreign affairs as my understanding of my assignment and for which I received an explicit endorsement before I embarked on my diplomatic mission to Scandinavia. And that was the principle that guided me in all my other diplomatic postings, both abroad as ambassador and at home as minister of state for foreign affairs. And once I felt that the domestic policies had shifted so much that I could no longer represent my country with conviction and dedication, I left, cordially but decisively.

In the wake of the Addis Ababa Agreement, Sudan's foreign policy, as I saw and reflected on it, became one of conciliation and peacemaking, not as ends in themselves, but as methods of addressing the underlying causes of conflict in a mutually satisfying way. In this chapter, I will focus on selected aspects of Sudan's foreign policy: support for the Camp David Accords, relations with Ethiopia, the problem of Western Sahara, the

OAU handling of the Tanzania-Uganda war of 1978, and our establishment of diplomatic relations with South Korea. I have chosen these not as exhaustive cases linking Sudan's domestic context with its diplomacy, but as examples of situations in which I was personally involved and tried to apply the values and principles I regarded as internally rooted, but globally pertinent. And indeed, the agreement created a climate of Arab-African reconciliation that turned the Sudan into a strong advocate of peaceful resolution of conflicts. With that domestic accomplishment as a basis for its foreign policy, Sudan became acknowledged as a moderating factor in the Arab and African circles and an ally of the western world for whom peaceful settlements of disputes was a high diplomatic priority.

Perhaps for the first time in its modern history, Sudan took a major step forward in realizing what had always been a promising potential – reconciling its internal differences, bridging between Africa and the Middle East, and offering the world a model of peace and stability that was internationally applauded. In support of this achievement, the international community responded promptly and generously in assisting the Sudan with the emergency phase of relief, resettlement and rehabilitation and undertook to support the longer-term challenge of development. For the first time, the pluralism of the internal identity configuration and their linkage to the outside world came together in a manner that promised mutual benefit to the Sudan and its partners in the international community.

For the Sudan, it also provided an opportunity for reshaping its external relations to build on these features to generate and sustain international cooperation in the long-term challenge of development and nation building. These objectives were indeed consciously fostered almost as an ideology, at least a strategy, which effectively replaced the war psychology of seventeen years and captured the imagination of the nation. Projecting the Sudan as an advocate of peaceful resolution of conflicts and a force for moderation in the region was seen in conjunction with the potential of the country as an ideal context for international partnership in development.

Influencing Sudan's Qualified Support for the Camp David Accords

For me, more than any other policy issue, the Camp David Accords provided the Sudan with a golden opportunity to translate the principles of the Addis Ababa Agreement – a negotiated and mediated resolution of conflict – into an effective tool for regional and international peace and security.

President Nimeiri was on his way to the United States when the Camp David Accords were concluded and signed. He had sent me ahead to Washington to prepare for the visit. Ambassador Omer Saleh Eissa and I prepared a note to brief the president about the Camp David Accords. On arrival in Washington, Nimeiri expected to be confronted with the question of whether he supported or opposed the accords. His vice-president, Rasheed El Tahir, who was also the minister of foreign affairs, formerly a leader of the Muslim Brothers and a known Pan-Arabist, together with the president's press advisor, Mohamed Mahjoub, also a Pan-Arabist, recommended rejection of the accords, and even drafted a press statement to that effect. It was obvious from the president's tough talk with the Egyptian ambassador, Ashraf Ghorbal, at the Blair House shortly after his arrival. The president was very critical of Sadat's unilateral decision without consultations with his Arab colleagues. His critical state of mind was perhaps the result of discussions with his advisers during the journey.

That night after everyone had left except Ambassador Eissa and myself, President Nimeiri showed us the press statement, which Rasheed El Tahir and Mohamed Mahjoub had drafted. Omer Saleh Eissa and I read it and responded immediately. In our view, for President Nimeiri to openly reject what was in effect the most important accomplishment of his host would be a discourtesy that could be very damaging to the fragile U.S.-Sudan relations. After all, the reason the Sudan enjoyed the admiration and support of the western world and in particular the United States was largely because of the peaceful manner the war in the South had been resolved through negotiations and how that had made the country a force for moderation and peacemaking in the region. To reject the Camp David Accords would be to contradict the principles, which had served the cause of Sudan's foreign policy so effectively. We urged the president to at least defer judgement, to explain that he had just heard of the accords, that he would instruct his institutions back home to study the situation and make recommendations, and that he would then take his decision in the light of those studies after his return to the country. That was the line Nimeiri took in his response to the press and to President Carter's request for support in their official talks.

By way of a background to his personal stakes in the decision to support the accords, it should be stressed that in the western world in general and in the United States in particular, Nimeiri was seen as the man whose wisdom, humanity and courage were the driving force behind Sudan's remarkable achievements. That message was voiced everywhere the president went: by President Carter himself; Vice-President Mondale; Senator Dick Clark, chairman of the Senate Sub-Committee on Africa; Congressman Clement Zablocki, chairman of the House Sub-Committee on Africa; federal government officials; state authorities; business leaders; university authorities; the press; and virtually by everyone who had any involvement with the Sudan. It was particularly gratifying for me to be hearing Americans say back to us the very words I had fed into their system in my efforts to promote bilateral relations.

Senator Dick Clark stated in his remarks at a luncheon for the president: "Sudan now stands as a model of reconciliation showing that political solutions are possible for the kinds of internal problems that confront many other nations. Muslim and Christian, Arab and African, are all accommodated in the Sudanese system. President Nimeiri serves as an inspiration for all nations striving to overcome ethnic, racial or religions divisions that can be so destructive ... Both in bringing peace to his country and in pursuing an active role in world affairs, President Nimeiri has made his nation a vital bridge of communication spanning the world's cultures."

Congressman Zablocki had this to say to and about President Nimeiri: "Your courageous efforts to end the civil war in your country have born fruit; your agreement last month with members of the opposition in your country has furthered the process of national reconciliation. You have, in addition, made your constitution a living document, emphasizing respect for human rights, democracy and an independent judiciary."

On the occasion of granting President Nimeiri an honorary doctorate of law, Thomas Melady, president of Sacred Heart University had this to say about the man:

> We honor a chief of state and a leader whose special qualities we wish to proclaim as virtues that can be a model for our young people. At a time when many of our students note the lack of courageous leadership in the world today, we have here a man of clear courage.
>
> He is an architect of peace for he has established within his country the structure of peace. There can be no other greater title than ... *Leader for peace* ...

> History gives us the privilege only on rare occasions to stand with an architect of peace; to associate with a man of vision whose goal has been the well-being of his people.
>
> His leadership has been recognized by peoples throughout the world ... His passion for reconciliation that has been so successful within his own country has also brought nations together in constructive dialogue.
>
> An architect of peace; a leader of vision working for economic development; a chief of state recognized for his ability to conciliate.

President Carter, in his meeting with President Nimeiri, stressed the peace role of the Sudan as a ground for his special appeal to President Nimeiri to support the Camp David Accords. The same appeal was later made by Vice-President Mondale and by representatives of the Senate and House Foreign Relations Committee. The appeal reflected both a request and an expression of a positive expectation based on the achievements and reputation of the Sudan, crowned with an emphasis on the importance of President Nimeiri's support. President Sadat had been confident of a constructive evaluation by the Sudan and had added to the preparation of an already fertile ground for the rising American expectations in the crucial role the Sudan could play in the promotion of the results of Camp David.

Back in the Sudan, Nimeiri had to confront the critical question of whether he would support or oppose the Camp David Accords. He had postponed the decision for his institutions to study the situation and make recommendations. The studies of virtually all the institutions, the Army, the National Security Agency, the Socialist Union, the National Assembly, and the Ministry of Foreign Affairs had all been for the Sudan standing in solidarity with the rejectionist position of the Arab world.

Nimeiri was torn and tormented by the decision he had to make. One night, I was awakened around 1 a.m. and informed that the president wanted me at his residence. With him was the minister of information, Ali Shommo. They had been preparing a statement on Camp David. My task was to assist in finalizing the text and translating it into English. It was clearly an ambivalent and ambiguous statement in which the special relationship between Egypt and the Sudan was underscored as providing a basis for Sudan's support of Egypt, the U.S. efforts over the Camp David Accords were acclaimed, the shortcomings of the accords were highlighted, the need for a comprehensive settlement was emphasized, and the importance of Arab unity was proclaimed. It was clearly an attempt to appear in the same breath to be supportive of Egypt, express strong reservations on the agreement, and stand behind Arab solidarity. The ambivalence of Sudan's position at that time was to be spotlighted by Nimeiri about a year later, when in a conversation with the Algerian president, he said in self-defense against Arab condemnation for Sudan's support of the Camp David Accords, "We were the first to come out in condemnation of the Camp David Accords." It took me some time to understand what the president must have had in mind. In a way, the statement was Nimeiri's way of testing the water to help him determine the best course of action. It did, however, signal, at least to me, that he was not comfortable with the reports.

I intimated to the president shortly after our statement that I disagreed with the position taken by the studies, which included that of my own ministry. Nimeiri asked me to prepare an independent study and make my own evaluation and recommendations for him to consider. He wanted my report to be strictly confidential; if I needed the help of anyone in the ministry, it should be someone in whom I had full confidence. I confided in a young diplomat to assist with research and in my under-secretary to read an early draft. None of them was fully aware of the purpose of the exercise. I wrote my report in English and submitted it to the minister for presidential affairs, Dr. Baha El Din Idris, who had it translated into Arabic. From Baha El Din I learned that the president was going to use the Arabic translation verbatim in his policy statement to the politburo of the Sudan Socialist Union. Shortly after the Politburo meeting, the president also used the same report verbatim in his televised monthly Face the Nation program of December 11, 1978.

The original report began with a critique of the study of the Ministry of Foreign Affairs as a basis for making alternative proposals, but since all the studies were almost identical in content, the president's statement referred to "the studies" instead of singling out that of the Ministry of Foreign Affairs.

Of course, neither the president's statement nor my original report on which it was based used domestic reconciliation as the sole basis for supporting the Camp David Accords. Quite the contrary, there was much in the Middle East situation which justified support. The report and the statement began by posing a number of probing questions. After four successive wars in which the Arab cause had suffered more losses than gains, and considering the imperatives of the international situation, was negotiated peace not preferable to war as a means of achieving Arab objectives? If so, was it possible for the Arabs to achieve a negotiated settlement on the basis of predetermined principles that permitted no compromise or concession? Was a collective and uncompromising commitment to the details of the Arab strategy and to the achievement of all Arab objectives at one instance a realistic approach to a negotiated settlement? In view of the fact that the deterioration of the Arab position since 1948 had resulted in the pluralization of Arab demands, was it not understandable for the most affected Arab parties to aim at obtaining the achievable objectives soonest possible as steps in the direction of the ultimate goals? Should it prove to be more in the interest of those with remote objectives to stand in the way of those with more achievable objectives, then did that in itself not imply a divergence or at least diversification of interests that could understandably lead to differences in the strategies of the respective parties?

On the basis of these rhetorical questions the president then laid out the grounds for his critique of the accords, the Arab response as reflected in all the institutional studies, and the respective positions of the ideological camps, particularly the two super powers, the United States of America and the Soviet Union. For our present purposes, it is worth reproducing in some details the statement's position on the particular role the Sudan was expected to play and should play as "a natural outcome of Sudan's domestic, regional and international orientation towards the cause of peace and peaceful ways of settling disputes, an orientation for which the Sudan ... has become known to the outside world". The domestic rationale of the policy was therefore not the substantive content of the policy, but rather an added catalyst. On the other hand, the pertinent question that poses itself is whether this catalyst, which made it possible for Sudan's policy-makers to see the situation differently from other Arabs, could have been possible without the internal dynamics and the contribution of those to whom those dynamics were of pivotal importance.

The position taken by the studies was based on the argument that Sudan, as an Arab country, should follow the collective Arab stand. The reasons given for this contrasted sharply with the reasons that based support for the Camp David Accords on domestic perspectives. According to the institutional studies: Sudan had an unwavering commitment to the Arab objectives and strategies agreed upon in the summits of Algiers and Rabat; Sudan was under an obligation on account of its chairmanship of the Arab Solidarity Committee and the great efforts exerted for the restoration of a united Arab front; Sudan's declared position for the cause of liberation and especially with the president as chairman of the Organization of African Unity rendered it responsible for following up the implementation of its decisions; Sudan was committed to the instruments of the Revolution and of international institutions as well as international agreements and treaties; Sudan was also committed to the service of national and regional interests through such arrangements as the program of integration with Egypt and economic cooperation with other Arab countries.

Building on these principles and considerations, the studies concluded with a negative evaluation of Camp David. They argued that while the Sudan had initially supported Sadat's initiative in the hope that it might be an alternative avenue to the objectives of the Arabs, the initiative had proved a failure and had led to a dangerous division in the Arab world. The role of the Sudan was therefore to work for the restoration of Arab unity and collective effort as the only guarantee for the achievement of Arab objectives. The studies acknowledged Camp David as a genuine effort for peace but concluded that its results did not achieve even the minimum requirements of the Arab demands, a fact which accounted for its rejection by the majority of Arab countries, thus leading to the exclusion of Egypt from the Arab cause, a development which had deprived the Arab struggle of an element vital to the achievement of Arab objectives. The studies recommended an Arab summit to redefine new strategies, which would effectively meet the challenge of the situation.

While the studies considered impractical the suggestion of Iraq that the Sudan and Saudi Arabia mediate to bring President Sadat back to the Arab line of approach, they supported the Jordanian suggestion that the Sudan should persuade Sadat to postpone the signing of a peace agreement with Israel to some time after the Baghdad Summit conference. The studies thus conformed very closely to the Arab line of approach and viewed the special role of the Sudan largely from the collective angle of the Arab strategy.

My report on which President Nimeiri based his policy statement saw the role of the Sudan from a perspective different from the one pursued in the other studies. It stated that Sudan had a more complex and positive role than the standard role of the collective Arab strategy. That role emanated from Sudan's internal situation, dynamics and achievements, especially in the harmonization of diversities through the creative instrumentality of negotiation, conciliation, and accommodation. Those achievements had not only transformed Sudan's domestic situation into one of peace, unity, and constructive preoccupation with development, but had also conditioned the country to play an active role for peace and stability in the region. Sudan was able to move in African, Arab, and other international circles and to play the long postulated role of linkage in a more effective way than had been possible when it had been torn apart by racial, cultural, religious, and political tensions and conflicts. So effective and internationally recognized had the constructive and stabilizing role of the Sudan become that it was often voiced by government and business leaders around the world as a moral, economic, and strategic ground for increasing assistance and development cooperation in the Sudan. The president added his own words, paraphrasing the original report where references to his personal role and the way he was perceived abroad were too embarrassing for him to use verbatim:

> It is from this premise that we decide our policies and not as a result of being led by the collective Arab stand. Instead we should take the lead. We should not be too rigid. We should not freeze our positions. I urge all our citizens to read the magazines and newspapers that are published abroad in order to appreciate the image of the Sudan abroad. Sudan is this nation, which has succeeded to solve the problems of national unity and has planned for social and economic development. Sudan has gone further to assist brothers and neighbours to solve their own national problems. This is the Sudan we want to take a strong and courageous stand, a Sudan which reflects and decides on its own national grounds and not on the basis of foreign positions.

With respect to the positions of the super powers, the statement, now reverting to the original report, unequivocally endorsed the role the United States was playing to find a solution to the Middle East conflict: "Considering that the crucial choice with respect to Camp David is either support for peaceful alternatives to the conflict or the perpetuation and likely intensification of the military confrontation, there is little doubt that the United States of America is more committed to the former while the Soviet Union backs the latter."

The statement went on to say, "Both as a matter of commitment to principles and as a matter of gaining more appreciation of Sudan's constructive role in the area and therefore winning support for this role, we should take a position that reflects the reality of our situation, a reality for which we should be prepared to sacrifice, if need be, knowing that in the long run, moderation, conciliation, and constructive efforts will prevail."

Sudan's support for the Camp David Accords was not without qualifications or reservations. Both my report and the president's statement made it clear that while following the line of support for the positives of Camp David, the Sudan must continue to criticize the negative aspects constructively and work to improve the peace process that had been set in motion. The United States in particular should be made to realize the full responsibility it had assumed for peace in the Middle East and that unless Israel showed a considerable spirit of cooperation or was made to be more positively responsive, the reaction of the extremists would be justified and the cause of peace retarded to the detriment not only of the parties to the conflict, but also of the United States.

Rather than a case of talking it out, my role in influencing Sudan's policy on Camp David was essentially one of translating my orientation toward a negotiated or mediated settlement in favor of the peace process brokered by the president of the United States. This should not be understood as a blind commitment to the process, which did not consider the justice of the end result. As my report indicated, I saw the accords as a means of reversing the downward trend that wars had inflicted on the Palestinian and the general Arab cause since 1948. Whatever the shortcomings, it promised more for the Arabs than the persistent state of war with Israel.

Futile Attempts to Improve Sudan's Relations with Ethiopia

Bilateral relations between Ethiopia and the Sudan was one of the negotiation situations which occupied me during my term in office. My main objective was to work for the improvement of relations, which were adversely affected by Sudan's support for the various Ethiopian, and in particular, Eritrean liberation movements for which the Sudan provided a pivotal base.

My first encounter with bilateral problems with Ethiopia occurred shortly after I was appointed minister of state and I went to Ethiopia for the OAU ministerial meeting. There I received a coded message with instructions to deliver it to the Ethiopian head of state. Ethiopia had violated Sudan's air space and had bombed villages on the Sudanese side, inflicting casualties. The message was an ultimatum comprising several demands, ranging from an immediate cessation of all violations to compensation for the victims of the bombing. Both the terms and the tone of the ultimatum indicated that the two countries were at the brink of armed hostilities.

Although our relations with Ethiopia were tense, I had been very well received by the government and had taken that as an indication of Ethiopia's desire to improve relations. What had just happened therefore came as a total surprise to me. I immediately requested and obtained an appointment with the head of state, Tefere Benti. Sitting with him were other members of the military junta, "the Derg", that had overthrown Emperor Haile Selassie, including Mengistu Haile Mariam, who would later execute Tefere Benti and emerge as the ruthless leader of the revolution.

The challenge I put to myself was how to transmit the substance of the message without conveying the antagonistic tone that would only have added fuel to the fire. Rather than read from the document containing my instructions, as I had seen ambassadors of major powers do, I decided not even to reveal the document and to present the same points in my own way, which was far more conciliatory or at least polite than what I had been instructed to convey, but without concealing the facts.

The Ethiopian head of state responded in a spirit of conciliation. He reaffirmed his government's desire to improve relations, explained that there were rebel activities on the borders emanating from the Sudan, but asserted that it was not their policy to cross Sudan's borders, although it was possible that local commanders might overzealously or perhaps inadvertently do so in the course of fighting. He promised to have investigations immediately carried out and to inform us of the results. Meanwhile, he deeply regretted any injury that might have been inflicted on innocent persons and was prepared to discuss with the Sudan appropriate remedies once the facts had been ascertained. The meeting could not have gone better and I could not see how a literal transmission of the original message could have accomplished the same result.

The second and main encounter with Ethiopia was in the OAU ministerial committee chaired by Nigeria to mediate in the conflict between the two countries. I was chosen to head the Sudanese negotiation team. The first meeting was held in Freetown, Sierra Leone, whose president, Siake Stevens, was then the chairman of the organization. That gave Sierra Leone's foreign minister, Abdullahi Conte, a leading role on the committee. Abdullahi was perhaps the youngest minister of foreign affairs in the organization. A lawyer, he both flattered and aged me by saying that my first book, *Tradition and Modernization: A Challenge for*

Law Among the Dinka, had been required reading during his post-graduate studies in England. He and I became friends and worked very closely in the council of ministers.

At the Freetown meeting, my counterpart on the Ethiopian side was Colonel Felaka, the minister of foreign affairs. The case we made and which provided the parameters of the committee's mediation was that Ethiopia's internal problems in Eritrea had overflowed over the borders into the Sudan. It had ceased to be a purely internal affair. Sudan, therefore, had an interest in the resolution of the Eritrean problem. While we traced the history of the problem to reinforce the argument that the Eritrean cause was internationally recognized by the United Nations and that Ethiopia had abused the trusteeship mandate given it by the U.N. by converting the initial federal arrangement into coerced or connived unity, our focus was on practical ways of remedying the situation, offering to intercede and mediate in the conflict. The principles we offered for our cooperation in the search for a solution was that Ethiopia had to recognize that Eritrea had a legitimate cause and Sudan had to respect the integrity of Ethiopian unity in some form. To convince them about the sincerity of our intentions, I recalled the role Ethiopia had played in brokering the Addis Ababa Agreement that had ended Sudan's seventeen-year war. How could we work for the division of a country that had helped us preserve our own unity? On the contrary, we owed it to Ethiopia to help her find a workable solution within the broad framework of unity. We even saw our experience in the South and the model of autonomy as a useful guide, though by no means a prescription.

In sharp contrast to our moderation, Ethiopia's position was a dogmatic assertion of the old principles of sovereignty and non-interference in the internal affairs of others. They were keen to normalize relations with the Sudan, but without any reference to Eritrea or Ethiopia's internal affairs. We clearly emerged as more practical, flexible, and reasonable. With pressure from the committee members, the Ethiopian delegation was persuaded to accept a formula, which tried to reconcile recognizing the Eritrean cause with respect for Ethiopian sovereignty and territorial integrity and a mediatory role for the Sudan under the overall rubric of the OAU mediation committee.

To create a conducive climate, both sides undertook to stop their media campaign against each other, Sudan was to stop providing the Eritreans with radio facilities, the airlines were to resume flights between the two capitals, and ministerial committees were to begin their discussions of bilateral matters.

As we flew back to the Sudan, I thought that in the light of the OAU bias against changing the national borders inherited from colonialism, we had accomplished for the Eritreans the maximum possible within the OAU system. Indeed, as I would admit to President Isias Afwerki years later, despite my conviction about the legitimacy of their cause, I did not believe at the time that Eritrean independence could be realized. Although my northern colleagues always argued that the case of Eritrea was different from that of the South, I thought that the Addis Ababa model, with all flaws I saw in it, had something to offer Eritrea.

As the situation was then, we returned home feeling euphoric about the degree to which we had advanced the Eritrean cause within the OAU. At the same time, I emphasized to the delegation and in my press comments that seeing the outcome in terms of victory over the other side was wrong and that the true significance of our success lay in the fact that both sides gave and took to facilitate exploring the common ground. But inevitably, as is always the case with national perspectives, the media played up our side of the story and made it seem as though we had outwitted our adversaries and scored major points.

President Nimeiri himself was pleased with the results of the meeting. He instructed me to brief African and Arab heads of missions and to also explain the situation to the representatives of the Eritrean movements in Khartoum. In addition, he and I met jointly with the Eritrean leadership, including Isias Afwerki, to brief them about the agreement and some of the constraints we would have to place on their activities in accordance with the agreement. The Eritreans reacted to our briefing with a remarkable combination of courtesy, appreciation, and total dismissal. The future of Eritrea could only be determined by the Eritreans themselves, they argued. While they appreciated our efforts, they wanted us to know that we could not in any way negotiate on their behalf.

Their concerns were echoed in many circles in Khartoum, including the chief of our national security, Abdel Wahab, and the vice-president and minister of foreign affairs, Rasheed El Tahir, both of whom asked me rhetorically what the Eritreans had gained from the agreement with Ethiopia. Others emphasized that the Ethiopians could never be trusted and that I had been naive to believe that they were sincere in their dealings. I could not believe the depth of mistrust that prevailed within the leadership. As I strove to explain the results of the meeting, I felt that it was almost more difficult to convince my colleagues than it had been to promote our position in the mediation committee.

Two themes began to emerge about Ethiopian-Sudanese relations and the Eritrean factor in those relations. One was the depth of suspicion against the Ethiopians, which was underscored by an argument Nimeiri often gave whenever the differences between the Ethiopians and the Sudanese were discussed. According to him, Sudanese live in an open space in which one can see far ahead and feel secure and trusting of the environment. In contrast, the Ethiopians live in a mountainous region where you cannot see far ahead and must of necessity be suspicious of what lies behind the mountains. The other factor which I realized then but became increasingly more aware of was that the Eritreans had succeeded in building a constituency that penetrated all relevant Sudanese institutions, including and perhaps in particular the security apparatus. This was in addition to their effective international outreach, especially in the Arab world. As Nimeiri later said to Mengistu, he could not disregard the Eritrean point of view, even if he wanted, for there was no way he could do so with impunity.

If I felt humbled by the cold response my heroic efforts and results in the OAU mediation committee received at home, my Ethiopian counterpart apparently had an even more chilling reception at home. Indeed, in the follow-up meeting we had in Tanzania under the leadership of Abdullahi Conte, the leadership of the Ethiopian delegation had been shifted from Felaka to his deputy foreign minister, Dawit Wolde Giorgis, later to become the deputy chief of the Ethiopian Relief and Rehabilitation Commission (RRC), a position from which he eventually defected. Dawit Giorgis was said to be very close to Mengistu. That meeting did not go very far as the Ethiopian delegation sought to undo all that had been done, reverting to the position that all they were mandated to do was to discuss bilateral relations and nothing more.

Privately, however, I persuaded the leader of the Ethiopian delegation of our intentions in support of the unity of Ethiopia, but that they also had to be practical and recognize that the cause of the Eritrean people must be addressed and workable solutions found. We could only help them in the search for solutions if they would recognize the problem and the mutual interest in cooperating to solve it. Denying it or insisting on the dogma of noninterference would neither solve their internal problems nor advance our bilateral relations. I again recalled the role Ethiopia had played in facilitating the Addis Ababa Agreement and our sincere commitment to helping Ethiopia find a solution within the framework of unity.

Wolde Giorgis, who seemed persuaded by my sincerity, intimated to me that he thought a meeting between me and Mengistu would go a long way in facilitating understanding between the two countries. He also informed me that Mengistu felt slighted by the fact that I had visited many countries in Central and Eastern Africa, delivering personal invitations from Nimeiri to the heads of states to attend the OAU summit to be held that year (1978) in Khartoum, and that I had not included Ethiopia on my itinerary. I immediately jumped at that and told him that the reason I had not visited Addis Ababa was because I could not be sure to be received by President Mengistu and that if that could be arranged beforehand to avoid any embarrassment, I saw no problem at all in delivering the invitation to President Mengistu from President Nimeiri. Wolde Giorgis undertook to make the necessary arrangements and to inform me within days of our return to our respective capitals. That was the main outcome of the follow-up meeting.

Another positive by-product of the meeting was my persuading Abdullahi Conte that the only other avenue open for a potentially positive move would be for the president of Sierra Leone, Siake Stevens, to invite Mengistu and Nimeiri to Freetown. I felt that if they met, they would be able to sort out their differences. Conte undertook to look into the prospects.

Back in Khartoum, my briefing was less promising than my report after the first meeting. I did not of course inform the president about the possibility of an invitation from Mengistu, since I could not count on it and did not want to add insult to the mutual grievances between us. Nor did I mention the prospects of the invitation by President Siake Stevens of Sierra Leone, since that was a secret plot with Minister Conte.

Suddenly, and almost unexpectedly, the invitations from Ethiopia came. It was from President Mengistu personally and it requested that I be mandated to discuss bilateral relations. Mengistu was travelling in the provinces, but he promised to come back for our meeting as soon as dates were agreed. The invitation could not have been more felicitous.

Pleased by that development, I called to see the president urgently and was immediately granted an appointment. As I spoke, Nimeiri looked at me dispassionately, but with indications of disguised scrutiny. When I had finished, he said to me, "You really do not know these people." He then went on with his thesis about how the Ethiopians were a devious people whose word should never be taken on face value. He then informed me that the first vice-president, Abul Gassim Mohamed Ibrahim, had conveyed to the Ethiopians his wish to visit Ethiopia to discuss bilateral relations, that Ethiopia had initially welcomed the visit, and said they would inform the vice-president of a convenient date. We were therefore waiting for their information on the dates. According to Nimeiri, their inviting me was clearly a way of trying to undermine the visit of the vice-president.

I felt obliged to explain to the president the background of the invitation, focusing on the fact that Mengistu had felt excluded from the invitations of President Nimeiri as the incoming chairman of the OAU, and that I had assured his representative of an invitation once I was sure that Mengistu would receive me. Nimeiri was unequivocal in his response. "Why should I extend him a personal invitation?" he asked rhetorically. "He is not my friend." He then went on to explain that the summit was open to all heads of state and did not depend on personal invitations from the host country. His extending personal invitations was only to exert greater pressure on those he personally wanted to see come to Khartoum. Mengistu was free to come or not as he pleased, but Nimeiri did not feel a personal interest in urging him to attend.

I tried to argue that once he sent invitations to some heads of state he created an expectation that all those expected to attend would be invited. Besides, I argued that we had an interest in resolving our bilateral differences, which should justify extending him an invitation. "Do you really think you are going to convince me to change my mind?" he remarked in a decisive tone. He then virtually ordered me to excuse myself from the visit. "Say you have other pressing commitments."

I was barely back in my office when the "secret" phone rang. It was the president. He said he had reconsidered his position and had decided that I should not bother to respond to Mengistu's invitation. "Just as he has ignored the vice-president's request to visit Ethiopia, you ignore his invitation."

After we hung up, I wondered what to do. I was sure it was wrong to ignore Mengistu's invitation, but I also did not feel comfortable about disobeying my president. In the end, I decided that as long as Nimeiri did not know what I had done, I could do the right thing by politely excusing myself from the visit without doing any harm, except perhaps denying President Nimeiri the opportunity of using my silence to send a message to Mengistu, an objective I did not believe balanced the impoliteness of not responding.

At the OAU summit, Ethiopia was represented by the foreign minister. In the delegation was Berhane Dinka, one of the diplomats who had been in our negotiations and whose features betrayed a resemblance with his name – Dinka. When the report of the mediation committee was presented, Nimeiri had very harsh words for Ethiopia which were responded to in equally harsh terms by Berhane Dinka. As head of the African Department in the Ministry of Foreign Affairs, Dinka was far too junior to be Nimeiri's counterpart. More importantly, both Nimeiri's and Dinka's statements did not address the substance of the negotiations that had taken place under the auspices of the mediation committee.

I indicated to President Nimeiri that I wanted to speak. He approved without equivocation. In my statement, I presented the main themes of the arguments that had been presented to the committee and the formula that had been adopted to try to reconcile the conflicting realities of the situation: the Eritrean cause, its impact on the Sudan, the need for preserving the unity of Ethiopia, and the case for Ethiopia-Sudan cooperation in seeking a peaceful settlement of the problem. I believe I succeeded in presenting a balanced and dispassionate account that accommodated all points of view in line with the formula, which the committee had worked out. The response to my statement was overwhelmingly supportive. The Nigerian foreign minister wrote me a note to the effect that as chairman of the committee he bore testimony to the effect that all I had said was true. Notes from several other foreign ministers, among them Abdullahi Conte and Cecil Dennis, were lavishly laudatory about the validity and effectiveness of my statement.

The Ethiopian diplomat, Dinka, responded to my statement by saying that he was pleased to hear the minister of state of Sudan speak so positively about Ethiopian unity, but he wanted to know whether my statement signified a change of policy or differences of positions between the president and his minister. I immediately asked for the floor on a point of order and posed a question: "If, as I said, we are trying to help our Ethiopian brothers to preserve the unity of their house, is it becoming of them to respond by trying to tear our house apart?! Of course, my president and I are not in disagreement." My statement was met with laughter and applause.

It was then that President Nyerere in his elder's wisdom suggested that in the light of the statements made and the clarification I had just given, the matter should be left to the efforts of the OAU mediation committee, under the chairmanship of Nigeria.

The invitation from President Siake Stevens eventually came and although I never indicated that I had plotted with Abdullahi Conte on the idea, I urged President Nimeiri to accept. A great deal of expectation had been generated around the meeting. I too felt reasonably optimistic that once the two leaders met, their differences could be resolved.

As we waited for Mengistu to arrive at the meeting point, Nimeiri and I consulted on how they should greet one another and we spontaneously agreed that he should be as natural as possible. When they met, that was translated into an embrace, which increased our optimism about its success.

The main talks were conducted in private between Mengistu, accompanied by his ambassador in Khartoum, Yelma, and Nimeiri, accompanied by me. President Siake Stevens did not attend and there was no third party mediator. The two presidents spoke their native languages, Amharic and Arabic, while we translated into English.

Nimeiri was at his best that I had ever seen – cordial, rational, constructive, and flexible. Mengistu was the exact opposite – solemn, dogmatic, unimaginative, and inflexible. Occasionally, he opened up with a smile that was deceptively charming and seemingly humane, but that would soon be replaced by the cold, relentless assertion of an unchanging position.

With remarkable candor, Nimeiri tried to persuade Mengistu that from his own experience, there was no way he could defeat a guerrilla army, that behind the determination of the Eritrean movement was a cause which must be addressed, that Sudan had no choice but to support that cause, and that he would endanger his own security at home and in the Arab world if he did otherwise, and that all he wanted was for Mengistu to help him to be helpful to Ethiopia in its quest for peace, security, and stability. That was the gist of Nimeiri's position. Mengistu on the other hand focused exclusively on the need to discuss bilateral relations without any reference to Eritrea, except as a source of refugees, that Sudan had to disengage from rendering any support to the rebel movements, and that preserving the unity of Ethiopia was a sacred duty, which he was not free even to discuss. He stressed several times that he had not been mandated to discuss with Nimeiri the Eritrean problem. About four hours of intense talks went into these basic positions without any give and take. The talks proved to be an absolute failure in which Nimeiri had little if any share.

Once it was clear that the talks had failed, Nimeiri's attitude shifted to the opposite extreme. No effort by the host country or by us, the ministers, could control the damage or put a positive face on the diplomatic fiasco. Nimeiri wanted the meeting declared to be the total failure it was. The host country on the other hand struggled to find a formula that might leave some window open. Abdullahi Conte arranged a meeting between me and the Ethiopian foreign minister who had not attended the bilateral discussions between the presidents. Conte tried to recapture the elements of the mediation committee's report, but agreed to have the Eritrean problem euphemistically described as a "refugee problem". The parties could then discuss the political issues within that formula. The Ethiopian foreign minister saw in it some room for maneuvering to try to retrieve the situation. I undertook to discuss the matter with the president. Before I could do so, Minister Conte drafted a document on those principles which he wanted the parties to sign. When Nimeiri saw it, he was outraged and would have nothing to do with it. The Ethiopian foreign minister, who had presumably sold the idea to his president as a concluded agreement, felt betrayed. The failure was now not only at the top, but had filtered down and poisoned relations between the two delegations. Diplomatic niceties were replaced by foul language as infuriated ministers exchanged incriminating assertions and allegations. It was the ugliest confrontation in my diplomatic experience.

To my surprise, some people in our delegation were delighted with the failure of the talks. Mohamed Mahjoub, the pan-Arabist press advisor to the president, was outspoken about it. He wondered why I was so keen on improving relations with Ethiopia, what did Sudan stand to gain from that. He implied and even made it explicit that by maintaining a state of adversity with Ethiopia, Sudan stood to gain from the Western and Arab enemies of Mengistu's regime. In a lighthearted way, he indeed painted the failure of the talks as a diplomatic coup for the Sudan since it would heighten the profile of the conflict with Mengistu and win more security support from the anti-Communist camp.

Clearly, my own orientation was to push for dialogue and a negotiated resolution of the conflict, but I did not intend to promote a settlement that would maintain the status quo with its repression of the rights of the Eritrean people. Quite the contrary, I wanted our cooperation with Eritrea to promote a just solution of the Eritrean problem within a broad framework of Ethiopian unity, which I presumed was what Africa and the world would accept. In the light of the Eritreans' own commitment to independence and the changing post-cold war international climate, my calculations were obviously wrong.

Talking Towards a Consensual Outcome with Regard to Western Sahara

The case of Western Sahara was more clearly focused on talking it out, aiming at developing a consensus. But it was also one in which I felt caught in conflict between applying the principles of a moderated, peacefully negotiated settlement in which the parties give and take without a winner-take-all and a loser-give-all scenario and the more polarized position of the OAU behind the parties to the conflict.

I had just assumed my responsibility in the ministry when I was asked to lead our delegation to the council of ministers in Addis Ababa and found myself the chairman of the political committee. And although the session was ordinarily administrative and financial, a cluster of political issues, among them Djibouti's independence, the situation in the Comoro Islands, and the toughest of all, Western Sahara, emerged as pressing problems. My committee room was jammed and spectators standing outside blocked all the windows. I was clearly in a hot chair.

The specific issue involved on the item of Western Sahara was whether or not the Polisario should be recognized as the legitimate and sole representative of the Saharawi people in their struggle for self-determination. Positions were sharply drawn on this issue. Algeria, represented by its trade minister, Yaker, advocated the cause of the Polisario. Among the Africans, his closest ally was the foreign minister of Benin, whom I had known in Washington as his country's ambassador and who was therefore an old acquaintance. Opposing them were the foreign ministers of Morocco and Mauritania. For Morocco, not only was Western Sahara part of Morocco but the people had indeed exercised their right to self-determination in favor of loyalty to the king. King Hassan's claim had been dramatized by his Green March in November 1975. As I would eventually find out, the OAU membership was almost equally divided behind these two positions. One would favor Polisario as the leader of an independence movement for the Saharawi people; the other saw Western Sahara as a part of Morocco.

Sudan was allied with Morocco. King Hassan and President Nimeiri maintained a close relationship that consolidated that alliance. I was well aware of that. But I also saw my position and the challenge it prescribed as different. Both as an individual and as representative of a country that advocated reconciliation and assumed a regional role of bridge building, I did not want the chair to be responsible for the disunity of the OAU on the issue.

Because Algeria was the toughliner, supported by Benin, I deliberately developed and maintained conspicuously friendly relations with their two ministers in the hope of influencing them to moderate their positions and thereby bridge between them and the other party. Since the policy of my government was closely allied with their position, I decided that my interaction with the delegates of Morocco and Mauritania should be correct, but not conspicuously close. Somehow, and in retrospect mistakenly, I assumed that they knew the problem was how to contain the radicals. On the contrary, my conspicuous appearance with their adversaries gave them the impression that I was siding with them. And perhaps the minister of Algeria and Benin also thought the same thing, and felt sure that they had won the support of the chair.

Eventually, it was proposed that the issue of whether or not the Polisario should be recognized be put to the vote as the controversy seemed unresolvable by consensus. The assistant secretary-general for political affairs, Peter Onu from Nigeria, also urged me to go to the vote. I opposed the idea for two main reasons. First, I believed in the value of consensus. Second, I knew how divided the OAU was on the issue and I did not want to aggravate that division. I called for a brief recess for consultations.

I spoke with the chairman of the council of ministers, Cecil Dennis, the minister of foreign affairs of Liberia, and persuaded him that it was too risky to put the issue to the vote and that I would prefer to submit the report of the committee for discussion by the plenary in the hope that conciliatory ideas might be found at that level. Cecil Dennis was fully supportive of my line of thought.

I told the committee that the issue we were considering was far too important and sensitive for us to resolve by the vote, that I believed consensus was important to preserving the unity of our organization and that since we could not reach a consensus, I preferred that we merely report to the plenary to determine whatever course of action it deemed appropriate. We then proceeded to draft the report describing the various positions presented to the committee and the level of support they received.

When the report came for adoption, delegates began to raise questions as to whether "some", "many", or "several" held one point of view or another. I suggested that we resolve the issue by giving the precise numbers of those who spoke in favor of or against a particular point of view. As the numbers were also contested, it was suggested that rather than give the numbers only, we should specify the names of the delegations. It eventually became a form of a roll-call vote without calling it a vote as positions were being reflected without a decision reached.

Significantly, when it went to specifying the names of delegations that took specific positions, a process of criss-crossing as delegations corrected their recorded positions eventually ended up with an equal number of those in favor and those opposed, with abstentions and absentees. That was the report we took to the plenary.

Cecil Dennis suggested that the item be placed last on the agenda of the plenary to allow maximum time for consultations and maneuvers. As a result of his tactic, the item on Western Sahara came up at about 6:00 a.m. in a council that had sat all night to complete its work. The debate featured an attack on me by the delegates of Morocco and Mauritania who alleged that I had been partial to the Algerian position. But a number of delegates came to my defense, with much applause from the council. All that was left for me to say was that I did not think it fit to defend myself and that others had done it better for me. I received a loud applause.

Fortuitous circumstances added to our efforts. The Polisario had just declared independence and formed a government in exile, thereby implying an exercise of the right of self-determination. In summing up the situation, Cecil Dennis applied his legal genius in a remarkable way. As his first point, he stated that self-determination was a right guaranteed to all peoples. He won applause on that point. The people of Western Sahara were entitled to the right of self-determination. He also won applause on that point. In fact they had exercised their right of self-determination. Here he was speaking from both sides. For the Moroccans, they had long exercised their right in favor of unity, and for Algeria the Polisario had just exercised that right by declaring independence and forming a government. So, both sides applauded. Recognition of a government, Cecil Dennis proceeded, was a sovereign right of every government, not the responsibility of the OAU. The applause was even louder. Declaring that he would request the chairman of the political committee (me) to draft a resolution to that affect, he ended the meeting, the audience, now almost euphoric at the miraculous resolution of what had seemed to be an intractable conflict. I declined the responsibility of drafting the resolution, which then fell on the Secretariat.

Of course, in the long run terms, the conflict was far from resolved, but for now, the unity of the OAU seemed to have survived the crisis and all sides felt as though they had won. To my surprise, the Moroccans and the Mauritanians were the first to congratulate me. Embracing me, the minister of Morocco thanked me profusely. When I told him that I did not understand what he was thanking me for in view of what he had just said in the meeting, he explained that he knew all along what I was doing, but he had to perform the way he had done. My only comment was, "At my expense?" We laughed, realizing the game that was being played.

News of the outcome was then transmitted by the international media to the distorted effect that the OAU had recognized the Polisario and its declaration of independence. To my knowledge, despite daily briefings to the press by the secretariat, I do not think we even shared with the media the delicate negotiations and considerations that went on in that sensitive and difficult session.

When I reported to President Nimeiri, who seemed pleased with the manner in which we had managed the situation, he intimated to me that he had received a telephone call from King Hassan, informing him that I was acting against the policy of my country and imploring Nimeiri to give me explicit instructions. Nimeiri told me that he laughed at the thought that the King believed he understood what I was doing better than my president. He said he had simply responded by telling the King that he knew me and trusted my judgement. The matter ended there until Nimeiri himself spoke to me about it.

In 1978, Adam Kojo became the secretary-general of the OAU in a difficult election in Khartoum in which the organization was sharply divided. Several ballots were cast to no avail. It had to take President Nimeiri and myself as hosts to lobby the heads of state in an all-night meeting to obtain a vote in his favor. His approach to the issue of Western Sahara proved to be dramatically different from the line we had followed. Almost as though Peter Onu, assistant secretary-general for political affairs, had eventually had his way, the matter was put to the vote. The Polisario won, but Morocco withdrew from the organization with a sizeable following from member votes; the organization became sharply divided almost to a dysfunctional degree. That division also accounted for Adam Kojo's failure to win reelection for a second term.

Reversing an OAU Chairman's Withdrawal from a Crucial Summit

My commitment to the principles of talking it out and forging a consensus was severely tested by a crisis that occurred during Nimeiri's 1978-79 chairmanship of the OAU which would have ended in his withdrawal from the summit had I not endeavored against all odds and mobilized the support of other heads of state to prevent him from leaving. Some background on the developments is necessary to appreciate the situation.

As chairman of the OAU, Nimeiri confronted a number of trying situations from all corners of the continent, but perhaps one of the most challenging episodes was the war between Tanzania and Uganda. President Nimeiri, who had now acquired the reputation of a peacemaker, decided to embark on a shuttle diplomacy in the region. I accompanied him on that mission.

We first flew to Uganda to find President Idi Amin euphoric about the victories of his forces in their invasion of Tanzania. Nimeiri did not preach peace with Amin; he mostly focused on learning the facts about the war situation. But he did of course speak of a cease-fire and negotiating peace. Amin was not averse to peacemaking between him and Julius Nyerere, for one of his known motives in the fight was the quest for recognition by Nyerere who was not only accommodating the man Amin had overthrown, Milton Obote, but had no respect for Amin personally. Indeed, Amin justified his invasion as retaliation against repeated incursions by Obote's forces across the Tanzanian borders. Mediation by Nimeiri, if successful, would establish his legitimacy with Nyerere, whom Amin paradoxically admired as a revered elder and from whom he yearned for approval.

The meeting with Nyerere contrasted sharply as he was extremely angry and bitter. Nimeiri's rather dispassionate and nonjudgmental quest for peace only caused Nyerere's moral outrage. Nimeiri wanted to speak Arabic to be translated by me into English, but I suggested that it would make the atmosphere less formal and more relaxed if he spoke English. I had met Nyerere on several occasions before and knew that his style was to conduct serious business in a relaxed and intimate atmosphere without diplomatic formalities. Since he knew that Nimeiri spoke English, injecting interpretation into the talks would give it an air of formality that I thought unnecessary and potentially counterproductive.

A certain amount of tension, however, seemed to exist between the two men. Nimeiri seemed to begrudge Nyerere's superior profile as both intellectual and statesman, which he saw as generating in him a flair of snobbery and arrogance. On his part, while generally courteous to fellow heads of state and admiring of Nimeiri's peace achievement in the Sudan, President Nyerere had a thinly disguised contempt for military rulers and suffered them only as a diplomatic imperative. These inherent tensions seemed to flare up in the discussions over the Tanzanian-Ugandan conflict.

Nimeiri was more assertive in advocating peace without condemnation of either party. Both seemed outrageous to Nyerere. But the more Nyerere took Amin's responsibility for granted, the more Nimeiri seemed propelled to be defensive of Amin and the more Nyerere's outrage intensified. The crucial point of conflict was that Nyerere wanted Nimeiri, as the current chairman of the OAU, to come out with a strong condemnation of Amin's aggression, a move Nimeiri resisted as incompatible with his mediation role. Nyerere was so vocal and eloquent in his moral outrage and Nimeiri so disadvantaged by language deficiency that I regretted having persuaded him to speak English. I could not resist injecting myself into the discussion in an attempt to moderate the situation, a role that neither of them seemed uncomfortable with.

At one point, Nimeiri rather unwittingly insinuated that there might be a regional bias against Amin as a Muslim. Surprisingly, Nyerere responded very calmly. "Mr. President," he began in a lowered voice, "do you know that my commander-in-chief is a Muslim and I did not know this until only a few days ago? This does not at all matter with us."

Nyerere of course had the sympathy and support of many countries in the region and from the international community. While I was on an official visit to the United Kingdom, David Owen, the foreign secretary, told me in no uncertain terms that they were prepared to support Nyerere fully in his military efforts to do away with Idi Amin. And indeed, it was the combined force of foreign supporters that enabled Tanzania to stage a counterattack on Idi Amin, strike a deadly blow on his regime, and instate a regime of their own choice in Uganda.

All this provided a background for the show-down that was to take place in the OAU summit in Monrovia, Liberia in 1979. The confrontation was between those who wanted Amin's invasion of Tanzania condemned and Nyerere's counterinvasion justified, and those who saw the invasion of Uganda and the overthrow of the Amin regime a foreign intervention that created a dangerous precedent that must not be condoned. Nimeiri was one of those who strongly espoused the latter position. The assembly became sharply divided behind those two positions and feelings were high on both sides. While some people saw the newly instated government in Uganda as a puppet of Tanzania and looked upon it with contempt, others saw Amin as a monster for whom support was morally indefensible. As chairman of the OAU, Nimeiri was seen as personally responsible for the failure to condemn Amin and the sympathy he now received in the wake of his overthrow by Tanzanian forces.

The criticism against Amin and his supporters, among whom Nimeiri was seen as the principal culprit, was reflected in the local press, which in turn outraged Nimeiri. Unable to fathom the notion of a free press, Nimeiri took the attitude of the local press to have been condoned, if not engineered by the host government and he took that as a personal insult. He walked out of the meeting, determined to leave as soon as his plane could come to fetch him. He gave instructions to that effect.

As Nimeiri sat fuming with anger in one of the lounges in the conference center, I went to President Talbert, the host, briefed him about Nimeiri's anger and decision to leave, and urged him to do something. Talbert immediately decided to go to Nimeiri. I attended their talk. Talbert went out of his way not only to explain the freedom of the press in his country, but also to apologize and ask for understanding. He particularly pleaded with Nimeiri not to leave. But it was as though salt was added to the injury. There was not even a tone of courtesy in President Nimeiri's reaction to Talbert's plea. In fact, he seemed to hold Talbert personally responsible for the attack in the press. Talbert left defeated but hoping that Nimeiri would reconsider.

I told Rasheed El Tahir, vice-president and minister of foreign affairs, that as chairman of the OAU, Nimeiri must not be allowed to leave the summit, but Rasheed argued that nothing could be done. "You know the president," he said. "Once he has made up his mind, no one can persuade him otherwise." The president's press adviser, Mohamed Mahjoub, shared Rasheed's pessimistic assessment. Nor did they really seem to share my concern about the damage Nimeiri's withdrawal would cause the OAU and Sudan's position in the organization.

Desperate for help, I went to the president of Nigeria, General Olusegun Obasanjo, explained the situation and urged him to intervene. With surprising calm, General Obasanjo said to me not to worry, "We will not let him go." He said to me that he would call on President Nimeiri sometime that evening. But it was getting late and Nimeiri was scheduled to leave very early in the morning, around 6 a.m. When Obasanjo did not come until about eleven in the night, I began to panic and went to his foreign minister at the summit meeting. The minister promised to call President Obasanjo to remind him. Word came back that General Obasanjo would keep his promise. I went to President Nimeiri and waited. Naturally, he had no idea what I was plotting. Nor did he know as far as I could tell that Obasanjo was going to visit him.

Until midnight, Obasanjo had not yet come. I was not concerned about Nimeiri going to bed, for he hardly ever did so before the early hours of the morning and then only slept for three to at most four hours. But I had no way of knowing Obasanjo's habits and I began to despair that my plans had failed. I was just beginning to resign myself to the fact that Nimeiri would indeed leave and the issue now was how to manage and minimize the damage his withdrawal would cause.

Suddenly, Obasanjo appeared and, without apologies for butting in, indicated that he wanted to talk to President Nimeiri. We all withdrew to give them privacy, but as we sat within hearing distance, I directed my ears to get some sense of the discussion. I was delighted to sense that while Nimeiri was persistent about leaving, Obasanjo was adamant that he must not leave. Toward the end, I heard Nimeiri say, "But I have already given instructions for the plane to come and my people will be expecting me to return tomorrow." Obasanjo responded by saying, "You don't mean to tell me that there is somebody else in charge to whom you are responsible?!" They laughed and the meeting ended on a lighthearted conversation.

The following morning, Nimeiri not only attended the meeting but also made an impressive contribution. On the theme of human rights, he spoke passionately, urging all governments to promote the protection of human rights, to end internal conflicts by addressing their just causes, to open doors for their refugees to return to their countries, to empty their prisons of political detainees, and to give every citizen the access to the full rights of citizenship and the principles of human dignity. It was a spontaneous statement that had not been written or prepared and Nimeiri delivered it with the force of conviction because it reflected his own accomplishments at home. When he had finished speaking, I received a note from the secretary-general to the effect that these powerful and historic words must not be allowed to fade away. We should incorporate them in a draft resolution and mobilize a number of delegations, including Nigeria and Sierra Leone, to speak in support of it. When the resolution was introduced, however, the first to speak was Benin followed by a number of antagonists, arguing that it was a utopian declaration of ideals that could not be substantiated or realized. They challenged if any government could pledge in earnest to implement the objectives stated in the resolution. More moderate voices argued that since Senegal had presented a document on the promotion of human rights (which would eventually culminate in the OAU Charter of Human and People's Rights) it would be redundant to embark on a parallel initiative. Not a single delegation spoke in support of the draft resolution.

The fact that Nimeiri had stayed and made such an effective contribution to the summit was, however, indisputable. And that could not have been possible without General Obasanjo's intervention, in turn the result of my personal plea which Nimeiri never heard about. Had I conformed to the normal course of decision instead of following my personal instincts and judgment, I would not have dared to go beyond the word of the vice-president who was my senior minister and he would of course not have questioned the president. Fortunately, we have no way of knowing what harm Nimeiri's withdrawal, anger at the OAU, and possible exchange of acrimonious statements would have done to the organization and to the regional interests of the Sudan.

What is particularly noteworthy is that the episode demonstrated the importance of several factors: the role of the individual and personal attributes in diplomacy; the link between domestic principles as perceived by individuals in shaping perspectives on foreign policy; the significance of human relations with all the individual sensitivities and vulnerabilities involved, in state matters that are otherwise of collective concern; the risks for all which those individual sensitivities and vulnerabilities entail; and the positive potential derivable from a more constructive utilization of individual initiatives energies and goal orientation.

The Impromptu Establishment of Diplomatic Relations with South Korea

The issue of relations with South Korea was a particularly dramatic and problematic test to my diplomatic initiatives and conciliation. President Nimeiri had told me that he wanted me to visit South Korea as part of a process of promoting bilateral relations. Although South Korea had a trade representative in Khartoum, Sudan had diplomatic relations only with North Korea. My proposed visit was envisaged as a first step aimed at exploring the prospects for establishing diplomatic relations. The senior minister, Dr. Mansour Khalid, who was opposed to the establishment of diplomatic relations and the idea of my visiting, undertook to discuss the matter with the president. His account of their discussion was that they had agreed to send our ambassador in Tokyo on an exploratory visit to Seoul after which the issue of my visit would be reconsidered in the light of his report. I called the trade representative of South Korea in Khartoum and conveyed the message to him. I then included an account of my meeting with him in our daily report to the president. Meanwhile, Dr. Khalid had left for the General Assembly in New York.

The following morning, I received a telephone call from President Nimeiri who was fuming with anger. He said that the account of what I had conveyed to the South Korean representative did not reflect his position. Since he had asked me to go to Seoul as his personal envoy, how could I pass that responsibility to a man he described as "your ambassador whom I don't even know?" If I did not want to undertake the mission, then I should forget it and he would look for someone else to send. I tried to tell the president that I had merely reflected what I had been told, but he did not want to listen. As he was terminating the interchange, I pleaded with him, "Mr. President, let me try to explain!" He responded with, "I don't want any explanation" and slammed down the receiver.[51]

It was Thursday and Friday was the Muslim day of rest. I wondered whether I should rush over to the palace to confront the president, but decided that he was probably too angry to reason. As far as I was concerned, if the president had withdrawn his confidence to the point of hanging up on me and looking for his own man to send, then what was the point in my continuing as his minister? I was prepared to resign, but only after making him know the facts.

Saturday morning was to be the day of the president's meeting with new ambassadors to receive their letters of credence, a ceremony which he usually wanted me to attend, even when the senior minister was in town. I decided to seize the occasion and went to the president before the scheduled time.

---

51. In his account of the incident, Dr. Khalid reports that he simply told the president his objection to the visit which he claims was extended to him, and that I was instructed to go instead after his departure for New York:

> Invitations were extended by the Seoul government to several Ministers, including myself. My response was that while technical Ministers could visit Seoul to discuss specific projects, the Foreign Minister should not go there before recognition. Nimeiri insisted and I persisted. He acquiesced only to wait for my departure to the UN for the General Assembly meeting.
>
> No sooner had I left for New York than he instructed the State Minister for Foreign Affairs, Dr. Francis Deng, to undertake the trip. Dr. Deng called me in New York and I advised him to tell the President that my argument still stood and that the visit was untimely. The US Congress and administration (President Carter) were then launching a vehement attack on the Seoul regime for abuse of human rights and corruption. These were the friends and overlords of the Seoul government. Two days later it was all over the wires, the visit of the Sudanese Foreign Minister to Seoul. Nimeiri forced Deng to undertake the mission (Khalid 1985:340-341).

The president received me with a warmth and friendliness that did not reveal any of the anger he had conveyed earlier. I immediately went to the point by stating that I owed him an explanation. "About what?" he asked, to my surprise. "About the issue of my visit to South Korea!" I explained. "Oh, that!" he remarked and quickly restated his point of view, vehemently, but not angrily. I then explained the situation from my perspective, emphasizing that if I had known that he still wanted me to visit, I would of course not have said what I had said to the South Korean representative. I had merely reflected what I had been told by the senior minister, Mansour Khalid, to be their agreement. How could he believe that I would disregard his instructions and continue to be his minister? I told him that by hanging up on me and saying he would send someone else, I felt virtually dismissed. Unless he still wanted me to go, in which case I would of course go, I was prepared to resign. He said that he of course still wanted me to go.

I visited South Korea accompanied by my wife. We were given a red carpet reception at the airport, a guard of honor, and the highest level of diplomatic courtesy throughout the visit. On arrival at the hotel, I was given documents relating to the program; they included the draft of an agreement that the foreign minister and I were to sign on the third day, establishing diplomatic relations between our two countries. I was dumbfounded since I had understood the purpose of my visit to be exploratory, to prepare the ground toward an eventual establishment of diplomatic relations. There I was, suddenly confronted with what I knew to be a highly controversial issue at home.

How should I react? I considered telling my hosts the truth, but decided that doing so would dampen their spirit and seriously undermine the positive purpose of the visit. And yet, I could not pretend that I was mandated to establish diplomatic relations. After pondering over the issue, I decided not to say anything to the South Koreans. Instead, I telephoned the ambassador in Tokyo and asked him to send an urgent message to the president informing him that I was scheduled to sign the establishment of diplomatic relations by a specified date and would do so unless I received instructions to the contrary. I knew the president would probably not object to the move, but I also knew that the minister of foreign affairs was vehemently opposed and behind him was the official position of the ministry. And since the ministry was the institution that advised the president on foreign affairs, there was no way of knowing what the outcome would be. I therefore waited anxiously as the scheduled time approached. Even when I did not receive any response, I could not count on the silence as tacit approval; it was probably more an indication of the slow process by which my message had presumably gone through the channels of communication and decision-making.

The signing went as planned and the visit proceeded smoothly. But international reactions to the establishment of diplomatic relations began to reach us in Seoul. Apparently, Mansour Khalid was asked in New York whether the establishment of diplomatic relations with South Korea reflected a change of Sudan's policy toward South and North Korea. Dr. Khalid reaffirmed that Sudan's policy had not changed, that relations with South Korea were merely commercial, and that the establishment of diplomatic relations did not affect our political stance. The South Koreans, disturbed by this statement, sought an explanation from me. I told them that they would be expecting too much if they thought that our having established diplomatic ties would immediately make every spokesman of the Sudan everywhere reflect the new policy in its letter and spirit. Dr. Khalid was reflecting an element of the old policy to maintain some continuity in the circles in which he moved. I had just signed a document containing our new policy. They should allow time for that policy to become known and reflected in pertinent circles. They seemed satisfied with my explanation.

Back in the Sudan, I would later learn that the diplomats in the Ministry of Foreign Affairs were rather disturbed by the establishment of diplomatic relations which they took not as a lone initiative by me, confronted with difficult choices, but as yet more evidence of the presidency, working with his palace advisors, making foreign policy decisions above the ministry as the specialized institution. The president himself, as I had expected, was pleased with the action I had taken, and no reference was ever made to the fact that I had not been authorized to do what I had done. My initiative was also vindicated by the fact that our bilateral relations flourished very prominently and South Korea soon became one of the most active countries in Sudan's development.

These two illustrations from bilateral relations with Ethiopia and South Korea are degrees of the way personal interactions and attitudes impact on intergroup dynamics. Certainly, not all Sudanese diplomats would have reacted the way I did in South Korea. Many might have said the truth and asked for time to seek instructions. And perhaps the Koreans would have understood and appreciated the situation. But that too would only have pushed the problem back to Khartoum and no decision would have been reached without serious disagreement. So my objective of facilitating harmonious relations could in retrospect be defended from a variety of perspectives, not merely to foster a cooperative climate for my visit.

Needless to say, to emphasize the role of human relations in situations involving groups is not to underrate the significance of the group or the collectivity, especially in matters of state policy. It is only to underscore that even within a corporate entity, a tribe, or a nation, there are individuals with values and perspectives whose specific approach and mannerism could be critical to the outcome. And since individual and collective perspectives and interests are interwoven, they cannot be dichotomized and evaluated in exclusive terms.

IV

COMMENTARY

12

Themes from the Stories

The objective of the project, which has resulted in this volume, was to record negotiating stories from my experience which stood out in my memory as significant events. Since this was an objective I had entertained but repressed, once I was persuaded to pursue it, recollections began to unfold and the stories flowed. This does not mean that I have tried to be exhaustive. Quite the contrary, I have been selective, although the process of selection and in some cases the manner of presentation have not been easy because of the personal nature of the material.

If negotiation and conflict resolution or management are, as I contend, aspects of everyday conduct of human relations, then they cannot be treated as isolated events. The context which produces the conflicts and the circumstances leading to initiatives aimed at resolving or containing them become pertinent. That is perhaps what makes these episodes and negotiation efforts not so much cases, but stories. In an attempt to reproduce the events in their context, I have recounted these episodes as aspects of interconnected developments and not as isolated events.

Overview on the Themes

In my view, several themes from these accounts substantiate the thesis of negotiations and conflict resolution as management of human relations. One is that these situations involve identifiable actors, individuals, groups, and states or nations. As groups and nations are ultimately represented by individuals, the individual becomes the central unit of analysis. In turn, individuals are never out of a social context, in which the family and the intimate circle of friends and associates are among the most pivotal in influence. The influence exerted by these circles is not idiosyncratic but a part of a system of values and institutions passed down through various channels of communication and education, both formal and informal. In this system, a person's status in the social unit and the community at large determines the role he or she is expected to play. The functions involved in such a role may be explicitly prescribed or voluntarily assumed as part of social consciousness and responsiveness to the real or perceived needs of the community. The techniques available to the responding individual may also be part of the heritage of the community or the product of personal creativity and inventiveness, enriched by experience and other sources of knowledge.

While the individual may of course choose to ignore or undertake the prescribed or presumed responsibilities, the potential for responsiveness is inherent in the cumulative effect of social conditioning and engineering. The difference between those who are born to bear such responsibilities, those who are trained to assume them, and those whose ambition or social consciousness drives them to take the initiative of leadership may well depend on other variables.

It is obvious from the negotiating stories within the Dinka context and in the relations between Dinka and their Arab neighbors and government agents that Deng Majok, my father, was highly motivated by two rather contradictory factors, his own self-perception as the one entitled even by traditional standards to assume leadership and his drive to prove himself against his father's preference for another son that he was indeed the best qualified for that role. Toward this end, he strove throughout his life, not only to excel beyond any doubt and by a wide array of criteria, but also to extend his connections into the neighboring tribes and the central government in order to win allies who would support his claim to leadership. In the process, he did a great deal of service to his people, their neighbors, and the government. On the other hand, his half-brother, Deng Makuei, the preferred son, took his entitlement so much for granted that he did little, if anything, to improve his lot. What was intended to be an assured qualification by traditional yardstick proved inadequate in the new context. Inheritance of a status or a role alone does not, therefore, guarantee the delivery of the goods and may, quite the contrary, induce complacency and incompetence.

In our own generation in a family of over two hundred wives with several hundred sons and daughters, where gender favored sons over their older sisters, a similar process was to take place. Although our father sought to correct his father's injustice against him by claiming to treat his own children equitably, a traditional seniority system combined with unavoidable preferential sentiments for certain wives and children dictated that some were more favored than others. Again, the degree to which sons performed and distinguished themselves depended on an interplay of factors. Some sought to improve their lot against what they saw as the disadvantages of the traditional order and its seniority system by making use of the opportunities open to them in the modern context such as education and government employment. I would place Bol and myself in this category. Arob (Ahmed) also falls in this category, but in his case, although he was the first to be educated and assume a position of government responsibility, he ended up in a conflict with Father, which was interpreted as an attempt to avenge what he saw as Father's mistreatment of his mother. Others allowed themselves to be debilitated and destroyed by their bitterness against what they saw as gross inequalities. Bulabek (Abujabar) and Miyar (Mekki) fell into this category. And yet others, among whom Kwol (Adam) and his brother Mijak (Osman) were prominent examples, overindulged in their privileged positions, lost incentive for self-improvement, and atrophied or disintegrated. What made for individual differences in going the one or the other way was also the result of varied factors, including the influence of the mother and her side of the family.

Even when the individual succeeds in enhancing his personal position, there is still the question of what that success signifies in terms of the leadership contribution to the community. As sons of the paramount chief, we were essentially raised to serve our people as leaders. Here again, the variables at work include such factors as the encouragement and support of the maternal relatives. That had been the case with Father and that was also the case with me. Although a son of the fourth wife, again like Father, I was supposedly born in answer to prayers, in my case by my maternal grandfather and his clan leaders, that their daughter bear a son for a firstborn. And my grandfather had a clear view of what he hoped for and which he explained in terms of leadership aspirations for his grandson, building on the legacy of both paternal and maternal branches of the family. My maternal relatives did not stop at that; they discreetly, but effectively, geared me toward that end and reinforced in me the attributes of leadership. The ability to articulate societal values and to intercede and mediate in conflicts is among the most important attributes of leadership in Dinka society and was indeed one of the pivotal assets that won Father his victory against his father and half-brother.

In the modern context of the state system, the effectiveness of Dinka values and institutionalized practices now depends on the degree to which they are harmonized with the interests of more powerful outside actors, Arab neighbors and the Arab-dominated government. Since the interests of these two sets of people are often in conflict, individuals with less sanguine objectives intrigue to promote their own interests, sometimes in the name of noble sounding principles of change for the better. This trend, initially pioneered by Deng Majok in his struggle for power against his father and half-brother, but which he was able to contain through his control over contacts and the flow of information between his people and the outside world, went out of control following his death. In retrospect, Father indeed opened a pandora's box that led to the invasion of the Dinka political and social order and has fundamentally undermined the cohesiveness, the integrity, and the autonomy of the Dinka system. Much of my own efforts in conflict management have been invested in trying to minimize the damage caused by this breakdown in the system, its values, and its institutional structures and processes.

In doing that, I have tried to equip myself with the tools of both tradition and modernity, a combination that also characterized the manner in which Father carried out his campaign for power and the conduct of his leadership. In our generation, the shift was more decidedly in the direction of modernity, the aspect of Father's personality and leadership that seemed to predominate in the end. In my own case, partly due to the influence of my maternal relatives and my own early inclination, I took a keen interest in traditional Dinka culture, norms, and patterns of behavior, which I pursued in my studies of Dinka law, religion, oral history, folklore, and biographies of prominent traditional leaders.

In tune with the operating assumption that negotiation and conflict resolution are aspects of managing human relations, I have tried to follow the normative code of Dinka society, not in isolation, but in a dynamic process that links tradition with transition and modernity. Since the effectiveness of the efforts in one context depends on the dynamics of the linkage with other levels, this requires an awareness of the structures, processes, interests, and potentials for cooperation across the dividing line. The prospects for peace and reconciliation become contingent on harmonizing and reconciling the pivotal elements at all levels of the interactive process. By the very nature of the situation, the normative and operational principles at work have to be flexible and dynamic enough to incorporate the perspectives and expectations of the principal parties involved in the negotiation process, some of which are politically motivated, culturally conditioned, or personally driven.

Even within the one country, the pluralism of the modern nation-state dictates sensitivity to the cross-cultural perspectives involved. In my experience, one of the most conspicuous incongruities of the Dinka situation in the modern context is the extent to which "talking it out," which is very time consuming, runs against the perspectives of modern national leaders who drop in with a limited time at their disposal, listen with unease and impatience if talks go beyond a certain time frame, and not infrequently interrupt the speakers and disruptively bring an end to the discussions. It was indeed an aspect of such intolerance that drove the local commander in Abyei, Ali Sid Ahmed, to abruptly end an inconclusive discussion that was meant to foster a consensus for cooperation between the local leadership and the security forces, much to the dismay of the Dinka. But even Dinkas who have become acculturated to the modern Western-oriented sense of time and its utility reflect intolerance to the traditional manner of discussions. Bol several times displayed this characteristic, which the Dinka humorously and forgivingly dismissed as part of the foreign influence on him.

These underlying principles and considerations need to be factored into a culturally sensitive appreciation of the negotiating stories included in this volume whether they relate to individuals and groups within the domestic framework of the family, the tribe, and the nation, or pertain to external relations, both diplomatic and personal.

These negotiating stories involve three sets of relations: interpersonal, intergroup, and interstate or international. The dynamics in these situations vary considerably. Interpersonal relations, domestic or external, are simpler and more definable; they are therefore easier to understand and manage than intergroup situations, which are more complex and involve the perspectives of numerous representatives with diverse motivations. Interstate situations, whether bilateral, regional, or international, are even more complex, institutionalized and impersonal in their motivational and operational dynamics. Of course, the human factor is involved in all three, although more pronounced in interpersonal relations and less conspicuous in intergroup and interstate situations.

By definition, internal conflict management or resolution efforts must be seen within a framework of interlocking layers of domestic jurisdiction, ultimately dominated by state power and sovereignty. This interconnection in part explains the complex mixture of successes and failures in the experiences covered in this collection. The successes are reflected in the fact that in most cases, some agreements were reached and the conflicting parties appeared to reconcile their differences and enter into a new relationship of peace and harmony. The failures, often more glaring than the successes, meant a resumption of hostilities, resulting in a great deal of bloodshed. How can this contradiction be explained?

Success has to do with the mutual need for one another, acceptance of fundamental values and rules to govern the relationship, and the overall sense that there is more to gain than lose in ending the hostilities. In an autonomous context this was reaffirmed, sanctioned, and consolidated by the realization that there were no alternatives to what the system provided. On the other hand, much of the failure in the cases with which I was involved resulted from a negation of the bases for reconciliation due to the interconnectedness of diverse contexts and the impact of dependency on the part of one of the parties on external actors to change the balance of power and the mutual interest involved in the original framework of the agreement. Often, the dynamics are such that the external actor has more power and a greater leverage and therefore is more attractive as an ally. And if the external individual authority or actor is less interested in peace because he is more remote and therefore less harmed by conflict, or has other objectives that are fundamentally incompatible with those of one or both of the parties concerned, then destabilizing the situation becomes a strategy for weakening the adversary. This is particularly true of those situations where there is no agreement on a fundamental national or subnational framework for forging a common identity and a collective sense of purpose.

It must not, however, be assumed that the next layer up is always a source of complication and inevitable failure of agreements. On the contrary, an outside higher authority can be a source of impartiality and just solutions. Failure to reach a solution within the family can be remedied by a clan head or subtribal chief. Ultimately, in serious conflicts, resort can be had to the highest authority in the tribe, the paramount chief. In relations between tribes, the government, both local and central, can be an arbiter for fairness and cooperation.

In the layers of interaction and potential or actual conflicts, the higher controlling authority can therefore be a source of aggravation or a force for peace and reconciliation. In Dinka-Arab relations, for example, the colonial period of British rule ended slave raids and fostered cooperative relations by enforcing an evenhanded system of law and order. The independence period has largely, though not entirely, been one of government partiality in favor of the Arabs, which has inevitably resulted in an imbalance of power relations and the diminishing of the incentive for cooperation on the side of the Arabs.

Negotiating Family Conflicts

Let me now illustrate more specifically with the cases covered in this account, beginning with tensions in the family feud. Among the Dinka, family feuds must be quickly resolved because members must live together in close proximity. The alternative is for families to break up and the disaffected members to move away and eventually establish a separate branch of the clan that may retain the name and continue to observe the rules of exogamy prohibiting marriage between clan members, but otherwise lose contact with the original section. In a way, that was what Nyanboldit, the first wife who had lost her sons in the family massacre allegedly carried out by the security forces in conspiracy with their competing half-brother, Adam, sought to do by moving the family to the North. However, their move was anomalous not only because the largest faction of the family was the one disaffected, but also because they moved into what was in effect the enemy territory, since the government was perceived as the force behind Adam and the security forces, the actual assassins. Their move could therefore not be sustained. Indeed, it was more a symbolic demonstration of their grievance than a genuine migration. For the same reason, it called for an urgent intervention, even though, as I soon realized, mediation efforts had to wait for an opportune time.

Usually, mediation is not requested by the conflicting parties, especially in such extreme cases as a blood feud. The initiative is immediately taken by the elders or chiefs of the unit concerned. Being the senior son of the family holding a public office, and also having the advantage of being removed from the scene of alignments, placed on me the responsibility to initiate reconciliation. In the division of the family, I was classified in Adam's section, but I had established my impartiality, not only in my attitude toward the various sections since my childhood, but especially by having stood for Abdalla in the dispute over succession. Although one never succeeded entirely in overcoming the divisions, I was for the most part supposed, as indeed all sons were expected, to have transcended factionalism, which women were seen as more inclined to than the men for whom the unity of the agnatic kin should be paramount.

369

Given its position in the tribe, its size and potential for internal conflicts, our family was expected to, and in fact did, live up to the moral ideals of the Dinka Society, especially those pertaining to unity and harmony and peaceful resolution of conflicts. They were also united by a common destiny, especially in their confrontation with outsiders. It was therefore important to reconcile individual differences in order to reaffirm the common purpose and interest of the family, then threatened by tribal and national politics. It was in that context that several conflicts, especially between Father and sons, were contained.

In a polygynous society, and certainly in our unprecedentedly large family in which the father dominated as head of both the family and the tribe, relations centered around the interconnected father-mother-child relations. And since the system is inequitably structured on the bases of descent, gender and age, in which one's status in the distributive system depended both on the stratification dictated by these factors and father's favors, competition and jealousy were prominent, if repressed, aspects of family life. By the same token, unity and harmony were most emphasized. Indeed, the emphasis on unity and harmony can be said to be commensurate to the potentials for conflict.

The examples of tensions or conflicts in this collection may give the impression that relations with Father and among the wives and the children were predominantly adversarial. In reality, the perceptions of the family members as revealed in the biography of Deng Majok reflect an opposite emphasis on the unity and harmony of the family. This may in large measure be the result of positive thinking about family relations, in itself part of the normative code, but judging from the potential grounds of conflict inherent in the polygynous structures and inequities, the degree of consensus and harmony is striking.

A predominant aspect of the system that may at least in part account for unity and harmony is that problems are never allowed to fester undetected and unresolved. The openness and intensity of social interaction makes privacy and therefore secrets virtually impossible. Every personal problem is likely to be a matter of concern to relatives. And once they are in the picture, the instinctive reaction is to do something about the situation. The problem of an individual soon becomes a matter of concern to all.

Talking it out is a striking feature of managing human relations in the family. The examples included in this volume indicate that no problem is too personal or private to be openly discussed. What could be more personal or private than women expressing secret desires that merely reflected wishful thinking? As for secret affairs in the family, a suspicious conduct was enough to have women pressured into confessing. And once the facts were exposed, the issue became a matter for open discussion. Invariably, such discussion eventually entailed more than a confrontation between the opposing parties; third party mediation was nearly always indispensable.

The initiative for mediation can come either from one of the parties to a brewing or active conflict or from a concerned third party. And rarely do family conflicts remain unresolved, once they have been open to discussion. It is true that memory may linger on to be reactivated by other incidents of conflict, but episodes nearly always end in a reconciliation. It is in this sense that the cultural bias is to regard peaceful coexistence and interaction the norm and conflict the exception or the abnormal state of affairs.

What is noteworthy about the incidents covered in the chapter on tensions in the family is that they took place and were resolved within the framework of the autonomy of the family, largely because they were indeed personal and private. By the same token, they did not lend themselves to the intrigues of intergroup relations in the political and social structures of the tribe or the country. Although Mekki's confrontation with his father over the headmaster's policy of forced Islamization in the school, which led Mekki to leave the tribe, had a political dimension, it was treated as a matter between father and son. That was why the headmaster disagreed with Father about having Mekki arrested and detained. He personally also realized that such detention would have reflected more Father's anger with his son than the commission of a criminal offense. And while Ahmed's adultery with his father's wives led to a family feud that would deny him Father's protection against politically motivated criminal charges, the conflict between him and his father was recognized as a family affair. Although adultery is a crime in the Sudan, framing criminal charges against Arob and later Abdalla for the same offence was never contemplated. Because these family conflicts were not complicated by the involvement of external actors, the normative principles involved were well established and it was therefore relatively easy to achieve a consensus on how to resolve or manage conflicts.

Even with respect to the more serious blood feud in the family in which Adam was alleged to have conspired with the security forces to have his brother, Abdalla, and other family members assassinated, all that was required was a healing period, persuasive skills, and exhaustive

371

discussions to explore the common ground, reshape people's understanding of the facts, narrow perceptions of the differences (not to explain them away, but to see them as far less serious than had been fanned by bitterness), and encourage appropriate apologies and atonement for whatever wrongful conduct had occurred. In essence then, although everyone's perspective had to be catered for, which is always time consuming, family feuds, though painful and bitter, are more compelling to resolve or manage than those between strangers.

To the extent that intra-family conflicts do not involve factionalism between groups but merely between individuals, the stakes involved in offending an individual are not as severe and pressures can be exerted on the person in the wrong with greater force and less diplomacy. Of course, the status of the individuals is critically important in determining the method of approach. Sons are more likely to be reprimanded in a conflict with their father even if the latter may be more to blame. This is not to say that a father in the wrong is protected by his status, but rather that he is treated with reverence. To a certain extent these principles also applied to the tribe as a fictionally extended family that was reinforced and sustained by a network of kinship ties. Under normal circumstances the treatment of conflicts at the tribal level would also be in accordance with the tribal code and within the framework of tribal autonomy.

Intra-State Conflicts

The single most important factor that has linked the various levels from family through the tribe to the national level has been the involvement of the central government, with the North-South conflict as the main driving force. This involvement and linkages of levels or contexts of participation have fundamentally undermined the autonomy of the family and the tribe and the normative code applicable to their contexts. The configuration of this conflict is further complicated by the fact that while the lines of confrontation are clearly drawn, the dynamics of participation by individuals and groups cut across these levels and weave them together.

In the chapter, "Pieces from the Crumbling Bridge", the death of Bona Bulabek in Europe and the initial refusal of the government to assist in the repatriation of his body to the Sudan which was assumed to be politically motivated, generated a reaction that cut through the various levels and motivated his family, the tribe, and the South to take action. The issue was not that Bona was politically innocent of whatever the government was assumed to hold against him, for he was indeed a political leader, rather it was that the position taken by the government was seen as a dimension of the North-South conflict which called for action. Whether or not that perception was justified did not make the situation any less conflictual or polarizing. The fact that the government eventually backed down indicated that the minister responsible might not have been initially aware of the political dimension and that once the potential danger of southern reaction became obvious, the need to avert the crisis became imperative.

Even more blatant as a case of political persecution was the government's action against me under the suspicion that I was masterminding the southern movement in Europe at a time when I was absorbed in a health crisis under the threat of blindness. Again, the shock waves penetrated the various levels, back to the family, prompting my father to intervene directly with the president. Quite apart from the capriciousness of the government action and the element of injustice involved, a pertinent issue was the pervasiveness of the conflict and the linkage of individual involvement across various levels, from family through the national context to the international arena. The most crucial dimension of that linkage is the involvement of the government in tribal and even family affairs as their political and military interests dictate.

The chapter, "Coils of the Civil War", reflects the most blatant infiltration of the government in tribal and even family affairs, with the alignments of the North-South conflict as the rallying points. This has had a profound effect on the traditional methods of conflict resolution or management. And because the various contexts are now interwoven, even the traditional means of seeking refuge outside the family or the tribe in cases involving a blood feud or a major rift have lost their value or effectiveness. The interconnection of contexts, the ability of individuals to operate across various levels, and the extended reach of the government authority locally and globally were underscored by Matet Ayom who bragged to my Uncle Ngor that in collaboration with the government they would eventually clamp down on me, wherever I was, inside the country or abroad.

As Matet's attempt to recruit my maternal uncle against me and the alignments in the family feud both indicate, government infiltration and the intrigues by individuals threatened the traditional cohesiveness, unity, and solidarity of the family. The situation at the tribal level was even more susceptible. Since the relations among sections of the tribe, whether represented by individuals or groups, are less bonded and the interests involved more diverse, conflicts at that level can be expected to be more difficult to manage or resolve than family disputes. What is really at stake are not specific grievances that could be isolated and redressed, but long-standing rivalries over power. External alignments under those circumstances become imperative.

Since it was more difficult for those whose families had no traditional legitimacy to voice claims or ambitions for power, whatever outside support they could muster, individual aspirants at the tribal level also sought opportunities through alliances with members of the leading families. Internal conflicts within those families provided the opportunity for linking and manipulating for influence. Enemies of our family were therefore quick to seize on Adam's rivalry for power against Abdalla as a ground for alliance with him, not necessarily because they believed he was better qualified for leadership, but as a means of dividing and weakening the family and acquiring access to power. In that vein, they labored hard to impede any possible reconciliation within the family.

That was why Adam persisted in his quest for power, deluding himself into believing that if the matter were put to the vote, he would win. That view simply echoed what his manipulators among the political adversaries of the family impressed upon him for their own reasons. Adam's vanity took it literally so much so that even after the reconciliation agreement, those individuals continued to operate on his behalf and he himself kept vacillating between his commitment to his family and his conspiracy with the opportunists. When they lost on Adam, they shifted their position behind Ali, Adam's sibling brother. Matet Ayom and his allies even tried to influence me by invoking Kwol Adol's youth and inexperience. Matet even flattered me by arguing that if I wanted Ali to become the chief, he was confident that I was capable of doing it so discreetly that it would not even be known that I had done it, as though that was the main constraint.

Historically, when the head chief provided the only viable and fruitful link between the tribes, the Arabs saw advantage in cooperating with his family. But once Ngok autonomy had been exposed and weakened, especially after the death of Deng Majok, and the family became perceived as providing leadership for those who aspired to join the South, Arab loyalty to the friendship with the family dissipated, if only in the short and medium terms. Their alliance shifted to those favoring Ngok identification with the North for purely opportunistic reasons. When those opportunists saw the family and the tribe united behind Kwol Adol, they sought the influence of the Arabs and the central government to undermine his governmental authority and tried to intimidate the tribe into backing their own candidate in the family and their newly acquired positions in government.

The family feud had thus become extended into a feud between factions of the tribe, and then externalized even more through linkages with outside actors, whose interests and agendas were adverse to those of the tribe. This clearly accounts for the degree to which Matet Ayom and his clique would be repeatedly reconciled with their people and would persistently fall back into alliance with the Arabs against the mainstream position of the tribe. Matet was a man torn apart by antagonistic contexts, interests, and nationalistic objectives or ideologies, all of which he strove to manipulate to his own personal advantage.

To complicate the picture even more, the perspectives of the provincial and national authorities were ambivalently poised between aligning with the Arabs as people with whom they shared racial, cultural and religious affinities, and trying to uphold their official role as impartial guarantors of law, order, and justice. In this ambivalence, their pro-Arab biases had the upper hand and became inextricably tied up with their governmental role in the area. The result is that they penetrated and interfered on behalf of their allies at the levels of the family, the tribe and Arab-Dinka relations to promote hegemonic objectives of Arab dominance and domination over the Dinka. Nevertheless, they felt self-righteous about their governmental control and authority and claimed to be neutral third parties in the quest for conflict resolution.

The Arabs and the Dinka had interacted for centuries and had developed ways of coexisting in relative peace and of resolving their differences whenever they came into conflict. Left alone with the traditional balance of power or with a constructive third party mediation, as was the case under the British, they would most likely have endeavored to reconcile their differences and build on their conventional wisdom in preventing, managing, or resolving their conflicts. With the force of the government intervening in favor of one party, nearly always the Arabs since independence, the incentive for mutual coexistence in peace and harmony became eroded. The Arabs began to see advantage in adversity, since they often ended up on the winning side, and to make demands on the Dinka in areas of vital interest to them, such as access to land and water, which they would have had to request or negotiate deferentially in accordance with the established conventions of Dinka-Arab relations.

In this respect, the position of the provincial government was far more involved than that of the central government whose stakes were more remote. This accounts for the fact that the central government authorities were more able to see the justice of the Dinka cause against their neighboring Arab tribes than the provincial government and were prepared in principle to grant the area micro autonomy and a development program. On the other hand, when the vital concerns of the central government were threatened in any way, as was the case with the rising rebellion in the Ngok Dinka area that was fueling the resumption of hostilities in the South, the reaction of the central authorities became less impartial. And yet, even in that situation, they reflected the ambivalence of an interested party and an impartial government, which is why, despite the massive arrests and threat of trials for treason, they were still able to appreciate the point of view of the people of Abyei and their quest for justice and equality, as long as it was within the framework of the North and therefore did not unduly threaten the interests of the Arab tribes and the region of Kordofan.

In all of these cases, success or failure seems to depend on the degree to which there is an accepted framework of values and rules governing relations and established methods of resolving any conflicts that might arise. Within the family and the tribe this is clearly the case. In the relations between neighboring Arab and Dinka tribes, this is less the case, but conventional norms have evolved that have created a code of conduct which, left to themselves, they would be more inclined to observe. In the larger provincial and national contexts, however, the nation has not yet developed a consolidated framework for regulating relations among groups or for resolving conflicts in mutually accepted ways that are respected as legitimate, reliable, and sustainable. The fact that Sudan has been engulfed in a civil war since independence with only a pause resulting from the subsequently abrogated Addis Ababa Agreement underscores the fact that this lack of an agreed upon framework permeates all levels to the national context. It is further demonstrated by the fact that to this day, the Sudanese have not yet agreed on a permanent constitution. They have intermittently been governed by the transitional constitution bequeathed to them by the British, which has been abolished by military coups and restored, albeit with amendments, by democratic governments several times, and is now replaced by the current military regime with an Islamic agenda that has drawn the line even more sharply and made the prospects of national consensus, peace, and unity even more remote.

Negotiating Personal Relations Cross-Culturally

The interpersonal encounters abroad are less complicated than intergroup or interstate conflicts. But they particularly touch on the related issue of the degree to which the values involved in talking matters out are universal or culturally conditioned. What the episodes tell us seems to be that they are both. There are fundamental values which condition the pattern of behavior in each cultural context, but values may also have universal application and the potential of influencing behavior cross-culturally. It is anthropologically established that when people representing different cultures meet and interact, they are never the same as they were before the encounter. Quite the contrary, they influence one another in varying degrees, depending on a variety of factors. As the great American anthropologist and African specialist, Melville Herskovits (1962:6) put it, "Whenever peoples having different customs come together, they modify their ways by taking something from those with whom they newly meet. They may take over much or little, according to the nature or the intensity of the contact, or the degree to which the two cultures have elements in common, or differ in basic orientation. But they never take over or ignore all; some change is inevitable."

The challenge of moving in a cross-cultural international context is to balance delicately between knowing one's identity and potential contribution and one's ability to absorb and benefit from other cultures and situations. This was the essence of an article I wrote in 1963 (Deng 1965) in response to an invitation by the Oxford Institute on Race Relations for foreign students in Britain to write competitive essays on their experiences with racism in Britain. About one hundred students competed and the top ten were selected for publication in a book (Tajfel & Dawson 1965). I chose to write on the theme reflected in the title: "Racialism at the Meeting Point." My thesis was that racial consciousness, whether described as tribalism or racialism, was a universal phenomenon, which defined people's sense of identity in relation to others. I argued that in relative isolation, all peoples esteemed themselves as the ideal standard of God's idea of a human being in a cultural context. Others were of course human, but they all fell short of what, as defined by our own yardstick, was the ideal model. Although they deserved a degree of respect as fellow human beings, they did not merit the same worthiness that members of indigenous groups deserved.

Recent changes, I argued, had brought people who had been isolated in their mutual prejudices in contact with one another and the result was racialism at the meeting point. I particularly underscored the universality of racial consciousness and prejudice as features of identity, which all peoples shared in varying degrees. On the other hand, I distinguished between racial consciousness expressed in benign self-esteem and the racialism that entails active imposition of assumed superiority on others through domination, discrimination, and subjugation, the extreme example of which was the apartheid system of South Africa.

Essentially, my argument was that racialism was rooted in our ignorance of each other and the fear of the unknown. "As a result of our differences and mutual ignorance of each other, racialism occurs as a reaction at the meeting-point of races. The Dinka proverb says, 'In a strange home, the dogs bark'" (Deng 1965:99). I noted:

> Even when it is not a policy racialism is serious moral challenge – a problem which should no longer be treated as a series of isolated facts, but as a universal and deeply rooted vice of which we are all guilty, whoever and wherever we may be. Our moral weakness lies in our reluctance to judge ourselves by the same criteria by which we judge others. We all need to educate ourselves, to relax at the meeting-point and accept our differences as facts which are overwhelmed by the unifying factors of a common humanity. Let us then start by acknowledging ourselves as patients who all need treatment whether racialism is active or latent in us. Racial consciousness is the root of racialism, discrimination is only a shoot; destroy the roots and the shoots will wither away (Deng 1965:102).

The tool for doing that, I thought, was to expose ourselves to each other and to our mutual attitudes in order to realize that our prejudices were only human and mutual. If we recognized that others consider us as inferior as we deem them, then, perhaps, in that overestimation or underqualification, we might realize our common humanity with its ideals and shortcomings.

The policy implication of my thesis was that the sooner we meet, interact, and discover our mutual prejudices, the faster we will be able to realize our common ground of mutual prejudices and rise above them. How shocking and sobering it would be to discover that the people we look down upon as inferior do indeed have their own criteria of judgment that holds us inferior!? Humbly we may come to realize that while we still cherish our own identity and cultural values, we need to understand why others do not respect our self-evident virtues. In that understanding may lie a source of cross-cultural fertilization and enrichment.

Much of what has transpired since I wrote that essay does not particularly support my thesis. How can one explain the fact that the Serbs, Croats, and Muslims in the former Yugoslavia, who are, if anything, too historically familiar with one another, would be so violently and mercilessly torn apart by ethnic conflict? These are people who in most cases are indistinguishable racially and ethnically. Only their religions, revealed perhaps by their names, can distinguish them. A similar question can be posed with respect to ethnic conflicts in the countries of the former Soviet Union. And of course xenophobia has emerged as a pattern in Europe. Was I therefore totally wrong in my thesis of familiarity creating a bridging understanding among the races and cultures at the meeting point?

The answer I would venture to give is yes and no; yes in the sense that I had of course oversimplified the problem; no in the sense that the basic message of understanding one another even in a context of familiarity remains unheeded. Indeed, it may be that the closer the contact and familiarity, the more we clam up in self-defense, and the less we absorb in cross-cultural communication and understanding.[52] Proximity, therefore, becomes a paradoxical cause of mutual alienation, rather than a bridge in interracial and cross-cultural understanding.

What then is the answer beyond more of the same? Judging from my own experiences, the possible answer is to build on the dialectic premise that while we come from different, perhaps opposite quarters, compelling reasons of mutual interest in peace and security compel us to try to communicate, be keenly sensitive to the message we are communicating, recognize that this message is alien and therefore requires concentrated attention, and challenge ourselves to rethink our assumed positions toward one another. This is a tall order, which only a few may be able to undertake. But then only a few are prepared or able to undertake adventurous challenges outside the familiar framework. What is important is the realization that as human beings in an increasingly interactive world, we are all called upon in our varying contexts to face that challenge and to respond to it in individually incremental ways. The impact of what we do will of course be too small and subtle to gauge. But some influence over every individual interaction should be counted as a significant

---

52. This indeed seems to be the case in the relations between the Ngok Dinka and the Homr Arabs of southern Kordofan who combine a degree of cross-cultural fertilization and cooperation across the North-South borders with intense mutual prejudices and animosities.

accomplishment, even though the cumulative impact may not at all be visible.

The talking it out theme of my encounters abroad is built on the assumption that there is indeed a human dimension that transcends the barriers of race, culture, language, or national origin. That human dimension may need effort to uncover through interaction, communication, and mutual understanding.

I have no doubt in my own mind that the impact of my presence in the remote village of Zell-im-Wiesenthal in the Black Forest in Germany was phenomenal. Beyond my intrusiveness, the fact that I imposed on the school my presence and the values I represented challenged the entire system – the director, the teaching staff, the students, and the parents – beyond anything they had expected. What was even more gratifying was the dramatic shift in the conduct of the pupils. After I gave my lecture to the school, I was no longer frightfully strange; I was a friendly foreigner, a guest to be received hospitably, even by those with whom my only contact was the fact that their children had seen or heard me talk at the school.

While major international events are disproving my thesis on racialism at the meeting point in the bedrock of ethnic conflict and xenophobia, my own modest experiences gave me a glimpse of human potential to bridge formidable differences. How else can I explain the fact that after my talk at the school, children changed dramatically from running away in fear to eagerly holding my hands, accompanying me to my hotel, and prompting their parents to invite me to their homes? And how else can I explain the transformation of a four year old German girl who cried in fear when first confronted with me, but progressively changed to the point where she would call me her best friend?

Some of the intermediate stages with that child were quite humorous. Once persuaded by her parents to shake hands with me, she immediately looked at her hand, obviously afraid that the greeting might have left black stains. Then later, as we sat next to one another in a boat with our hands in the water, she noticed that the palms of my hands were lighter than the back. "The black color is washing off from your hands," she remarked. I later played a trick on her by rubbing my hands on her cheeks and then telling her that I had painted her face black. She rushed to the mirror to check and then returned and said smiling, "No, you did not." She then held my face in her hands and said, "Du bist mein bester Freund!" When I responded affirmatively, she remarked, "But you are no longer a child!" She now saw age rather than race as the possible barrier in our friendship.

There is no way of telling how much my discussion with the Italian-American in New Haven changed his world view; probably not much. But his attitude toward me seemed transformed from one of hatred and hostility to one of a relatively harmonious exchange of views. It is difficult to believe that in similar future situations that experience would not figure in his approach to people.

Race was not an overt factor in the behavior of the Woodstock "lawyer", although interacting with a racially mixed couple could have compounded his initially adverse reaction. But once that barrier was transcended by our subsequent interaction, cross-cultural perspective suddenly turned into an enriching potential. It is difficult to see how he too would be the same in his outlook, whether that outlook is based on race or merely on an adversarial predisposition toward people, whatever their racial or cultural identity. I would hope and think that he would have more faith in a cooperative interaction rather than assume that those situations are by definition adversarial and antagonistic.

More importantly, what these experiences show is that managing human relations, even in unfamiliar cross-cultural contexts, is not a task for the expert few, but a challenge for every individual. Since we must by the very nature of things interact with others, most of whom are strangers, we all have to find ways of doing so amicably and cooperatively in our mutual interest. While some will continue to be experts in the arts or skills of human relations, all of us have a stake in developing and applying our own ways of managing conflictual situations and reconciling our differences. To be aware of this need and the potentials involved for fostering a more peaceful and cooperative climate in human relations is both an empowerment and a source of security, if only because it makes us less helpless by assuming a degree of control over the dynamics of the situations in which we find ourselves. If individual efforts at fostering understanding and cooperation are multiplied by the countless numbers of people with whom we interact over the course of our lives, and conciliatory and cooperative attitudes generally have the effect of eliciting commensurate conciliation and cooperation, we can expect the cumulative impact to be considerable.

Negotiating Diplomatic Relations

The problems of bilateral and multilateral diplomacy are more formidable to analyze in this framework, but they represent a degree removed from the difficulties of intergroup conflicts within the national framework, accentuated by the foreign dimension. Even here, the challenge is how to recognize the added complication of state representation while still focusing some attention on the perspective of the individual in a dynamic cross-cultural situation.

In diplomacy, set policies of an impersonal nature aimed at serving the national interest tend to dominate. The collective psychology is geared toward winning the game of nations. Whereas in the family or in the more intimate circles, saving face is an honored expression of sensitivity to the position of the adversary, in interstate conflicts collective identities tend to be "dehumanized" and turned into impersonal abstractions. The aim tends to be to acquire the upper hand whether this is objectively the case or is a subjective, self-congratulatory perception, which often happens in post-negotiation appraisals of satisfactory outcomes, unless they are otherwise obvious failures, in which case the individuals involved are sacrificed and blamed as scapegoats.

The moral dilemma, functionally perceived as a dichotomy, is therefore one of being totally victorious against the enemy when a successful negotiation by definition implies a give and take. This is why after a negotiation with an adversary, there is either jubilation over total victory, or lamentation over defeat, for which blame must be placed on scapegoats. In the past, when the flow of information was rather limited to the immediate circle, such a self-indulging view of the outcome was benign. But now, with both sides having easy access to post-negotiation representation of the situation to internal audiences, such a partial interpretation of events and the results can become dangerously counterproductive.

If the parties thought about negotiations in cooperative human terms rather than with adversarial absolutism, their level of empathy about each other's situation would inevitably rise. It would then be a question of genuinely "talking it out", listening carefully, understanding the other point of view, and concluding with gestured or expressed responses to the effect that: "I see", "I understand", and "I would feel the same way". Such empathy would provide a common ground for bridging adversarial positions. This means that although the adversarial group psychology is absolutist and categorical, there is a potential for a bridging human factor. After all, groups are ultimately people, human beings, individuals. In that context, the shared elements of their common humanity are capable of bridging, bending, or even breaking the barriers between racial, ethnic, religious, or national groups.

The crucial question, then, becomes why it is that some people, indeed the majority, conform to the group orientation of absolutist right and wrong, while some individuals dare to see the barriers as "soft", transcendable, and even breakable to permit communication, understanding, and unity. This is where the functions of individuality and collectivity come into focus.

Being an individual means that even if people descend from the same family, there will be differences in their responses to similar situations. This applies to all levels. Bol and I, sons of one man, who were of almost the same age, went to the same schools, and lived together most of the time, still differed to a significant degree on issues relating to the family, the tribe, and the country. This could be the result of a wide variety of genetic factors, including our mothers' side of the family. It could also be the differences in the impact of the same environment in which we were raised and educated. After all, at Tonj Intermediate School, Bol had a dramatic experience in which I was relevant only as a mediator. We each went through experiences which could be formative at various stages of our growth, education, and occupation. To this day, I still find the story of my maternal grandfather's aspirations for me most proving, and to the extent that I have always been aware of his perspective, it could not have failed to influence my outlook.

These individualized, microcosmic instances can be collectivized to the tribal, national, and even global contexts, and yet the individual factor will come through in specific situations with consequences that can vary considerably from person to person and differentiate the individual from the group.

Let me now put this into the context of bilateral and multilateral diplomacy as reflected in the experiences included in this collection. Sudan's response to the Camp David Accords exemplified the diversity of the human factor, both individual and collective, in foreign policy decision making. The principles which governed both rejection and support represented contrasting perspectives of individuals and groups behind the values around which the domestic and foreign policies of the nation were shaped. To all the institutions that advocated rejection, Sudan, as an Arab country, had to follow the collective Arab stand. To me, representing the southern perspective, and President Nimeiri, who bridged the North and the South and in this case shared my view, the most important accomplishment of the Sudan for which it was internationally admired was the Addis Ababa Agreement. That agreement created a domestic framework of peace and national reconciliation which positively influenced our foreign policy and our bilateral and multilateral relations. For me, and in an acquiescing sense Nimeiri, support for the Camp David Accords was a logical extension of those domestic values and principles. In contrast to this perspective, northern Sudanese in general saw the Addis Ababa Agreement as a local arrangement for the South which had no significant bearing on national policy, and certainly not on foreign relations. Lack of an agreed upon sense of collective identity and a normative national framework was therefore a factor in the conflicting perspectives on the Camp David Accords.

In many ways, our efforts at moderating regional conflicts with respect to our bilateral relations with Ethiopia and Libya, the problem of Western Sahara, and the Tanzania-Uganda war reflected similar dynamics about the linkage between the domestic scene and the regional and international contexts as well as the role of the individual in the linkage.

For most Sudanese in the central power apparatus, the history of Ethiopian-Sudanese relations was one of adversity and Ethiopians could not be trusted as a matter of historical fact and cultural interpretation. That absolutism made whatever they promised or said questionable, if not absolutely dismissable. Whether the explanation lay in some inherent genetic differences or in environmental factors, such as the obstructive mountains or the expansive desert, as Nimeiri used to put it, the end result was virtually insurmountable prejudice. The categorical rights and wrongs reinforced the absolutist tone of the ultimatum I was supposed to present to the Ethiopian leadership. There could be no equivocation on the issue: Ethiopia was the culprit and innocent Sudanese the victims. That was the official version. The fact that to Ethiopia, Sudan provided sanctuary for its rebel movements and therefore might have a legitimate grievance against us did not figure in our apportioning blame.

My own perspective as an individual and a southern Sudanese was that there was a human dimension, which the official version missed or undervalued. Ethiopia was that neighbor which had helped us overcome a crisis of national unity that had afflicted our country with a seventeen-year civil war. They had been our peacemakers, cooperative neighbors, and friends in need and deed. We owed them a favor and I was in a public position to return that favor. Conveying the ultimatum in a mild language was only a small part of my sense of obligation and moderation.

That sense of moral obligation to Ethiopia was more revealed and pronounced in the negotiations before the OAU mediation committee. But the principles were the same: I had to represent my country to the best of my ability while also giving my Ethiopian adversaries their due as a proud nation and a friendly neighbor. Ethiopians who had participated in those negotiations would later characterize me as "a tough adversary". The Ethiopian chargé d'affaires in Khartoum, who had not even attended the discussions, told me face-to-face that I had given their delegation a very hard time. He even conspired behind my back with my international collaborators in the peace process to question my commitment to the South, thus undermining my credibility – a behavior which tempted me to believe the stereotyped views of my compatriots, northerners and southerners, about the Ethiopians. But I strove to see both him and me as individuals in a complex context of conflicting and contradictory perspectives.

I worked hard, whenever the occasion arose, to make Ethiopians understand and appreciate my standpoint and value judgment in our bilateral negotiations. Some assured me that they had always understood my position, others seemed surprised, and yet others remained oblique.

All said and done, while I was deeply conditioned by my appreciation for what Ethiopia had done to bring peace, justice, and reconciliation to our country, I was equally driven to promote the realization of the same ideals in their own national context with respect to Eritrea. This they apparently could not see or understand. As a result, an admiring and appreciative interlocutor, who wanted to apply the same ideals to a situation he thought comparable, was turned into an adversary. The conflict between the Ethiopian foreign minister and me in Freetown could not have been more adversarial, even though in later years he seemed to reveal more understanding of my perspective than he had felt or dared to show at the time.

All this goes to show that while the barriers between opposing groups stand taller than life, the human dimension remains an unbeatable challenge that will find subtle or crude ways of penetrating or transcending divisions. To be sure, this human dimension represents perhaps a small minority, but it is by no means negligible, for by its dissenting characteristics, it is capable of spotlighting a different point of view and setting an example that could potentially be pivotal in turning the tide.

The role played by the various personalities and representatives on the Western Saharan issue reflects similar dynamics between the set positions of states and the human challenge of bridging the differences which individuals tried to meet. Obviously, representatives of countries, and even of the Organization of African Unity, had their defined parameters within which they did their best to accomplish their set objectives. The collective and predetermined nature of these positions virtually divested them of the dynamics of the human factor involved. Certainly, neither of the parties, whether the Moroccans or Mauritanians, or their adversaries under the leadership of Algeria, could entertain human considerations above the instructions from their governments. But then, they could also not shed their fundamental human qualities that reigned underneath in defiance of any government policies or dictates.

King Hassan's expectations as revealed to Nimeiri represented the sterile, stereotypical perspective of international politics. So was the profile maintained by the representatives of Morocco and Mauritania right to the end of the deliberations. My own approach was to build on the human factor without any doubt or scrutiny. That factor meant that I had to cultivate and win those I thought were politically the most committed to the hard line in order to move them toward a middle ground. I could not afford to let either side know my objective or else my tactic or strategy would be exposed, discredited, and dismissed. At the same time, in order to be effective, the good intentions of the approach had to be recognized, accepted, and appreciated by all sides. This was in a sense a contradiction in basic terms. But the reconciling factor was trust in the personality and character of the individual involved. While the individual of course takes that for granted, those involved in the conflict, with their stereotypical positions, question it as a matter of principle. The crisis becomes almost zero-sum.

And yet, recognizing that there are indeed individual dynamics, which, given the opportunity and the correlative support, can challenge the stereotyped positions, these frozen representative positions can be thawed into a more fluid state that can redefine the issues and help the parties relocate themselves in a more creative search for a common ground. My close contact with the representatives of Algeria and Benin were no more than an effort to establish credibility with them to enable me to move them toward moderation. As I recalled, they turned out to be much more responsive to my bridging efforts than those I had assumed to be more moderate. On the other hand, while we did not succeed in finding that common ground, we certainly managed to defrost the positions and generate an optimistic perception of the situation in a manner that did not change the basic differences, but at least postponed the deadly collision and thereby allowed some time for thought and the on-going search for more workable solutions.

The bottom line, however, is that the OAU consideration of the case of Western Sahara is illustrative of a basic disagreement on the fundamental norms involved and there was nothing we could do to bridge that dichotomy. What we did on the case was an evasion tactic aimed at avoiding a divisive clash between the extreme positions represented by Algeria on the one hand and Morocco and Mauritania on the other hand. The differences focused on the issue of recognition for the Polisario. I thought that a genuine resolution of the conflict in an amicable way had to be more than just one of recognition. But looming large in my mind was the need to avoid anything that was sure to endanger the unity of the organization, not only because of my own personal values, but also as representative of a country that took pride in the principle of a negotiated settlement as evidenced by the Addis Ababa Agreement. Cecil Dennis of Liberia as president of the Council of Ministers supported my position but with his own genius for evasive tactics, facilitated by the developments in the political arena, in particular the Polisario's declaration of a government in exile. By upholding the principle of self-determination, the entitlement of the people of Western Sahara to that right, and declaring that they had indeed exercised that right, leaving the issue of recognition to each government as a sovereign right, he made both sides victorious. And so everyone applauded the outcome, not because they thought we had resolved the conflict, but rather because we had evaded an intractable crisis.

The conflict between Tanzania and Uganda underscored the hazards and potentials of the individual human factor in group dynamics. On the one hand, the lines were clearly drawn among several sets of conflicting partners: Idi Amin and Julius Nyerere (representing Uganda and Tanzania, respectively); those who condemned the initial invasion of Tanzania by Uganda, and thereby approved of Tanzania's overkill retaliation; and those who saw Tanzania's intervention and overthrow of Idi Amin as an unjustified and dangerous precedent. Nimeiri was caught in the web of these complex moral and legal standpoints. He obviously could not approve of Amin's aggressive initiative, even though secretly he seemed to resent what he saw as Nyerere's high podium as an intellectual and a veteran civilian statesman with some distaste for military dictators. By the same token he could not totally support Nyerere's onslaught of Amin, partly because of his instinctive biases, and partly because it set a dangerous precedent in favor of foreign, albeit regional, intervention.

In practical terms, Nimeiri's uncertainty made him wobble without a clear sense of direction. He particularly stumbled when he insinuated that the Tanzanian attitude toward Amin might be an anti-Islamic prejudice. Nyerere's articulate and didactic response threw Nimeiri even more off-balance. If confrontation between Nyerere and Nimeiri were seen in terms of a boxing game, there would be no exciting match as the victor far excelled the vanquished.

The duel was carried to the summit in Monrovia and there too, the alignment between the predominant African sentiment against Idi Amin and the Liberian press once more gave Nimeiri a deadly punch that threw him off the stage. Bruised and humiliated, he wanted to escape back home where he would have predictably created a self-serving atmosphere of rights and wrongs, dichotomizing between the virtuous and the villainous, translated into the national interests and the amalgam of foreign enemies, regional and international. From a proud chairman of the OAU, he would have emerged as a committed and dogmatic enemy of the organization.

In this high-stake game of nations, I emerged and dared to challenge what I saw as a dangerous escalation toward stereotyping. To do that, one had to build a human bridge across the dividing lines. Even that required finding human beings willing and capable to bridge. President Talbert of Liberia, being the host and a man inspired by both statesmanship and spiritual and religious idealism, was the first obvious choice. Despite his best intentions and moral drive, he failed dismally to move Nimeiri to change his mind from walking out of the summit.

A different kind of human being who did not plead humanity or idealism but invoked the imperatives of power politics, the Nigerian president, General Olusegun Obasanjo, succeeded by simply telling Nimeiri, "You cannot and dare not go!" When Nimeiri tried to plead practical considerations, arguing that he had already ordered the plane to fetch him and was expected to return by a certain time, General Obasanjo challenged him by asking whether there was a superior authority in the country to which he, the president, was responsible. The implication was not that the president should not be unaccountable, but that in such matters as his flight schedule, he could not be governed by the convenience of others. Nimeiri, overwhelmed by Obasanjo's assertiveness and challenged by his invocation of the rules of the power game, made the right decision to which he had been blinded by individualistic instincts, camouflaged as protection of national pride.

The thin line between that which is personal and that which is national was nearly exposed, but in the end was salvaged by ambiguity. The true salvation emerged the following day when Nimeiri participated with glowing colors in the summit as the proud outgoing chairman of the organization. The high moral ground he projected can only be appreciated in the light of a speculative perspective on what his dramatic withdrawal would have meant for the country and the organization.

Conclusion

As I noted at the outset, I have considered over the years documenting mediation or negotiation situations in which I have been involved, but have always hesitated, partly because I thought it would seem self-serving, and also because of time constraints. Now that circumstances have propelled me to present a selection of these experiences, I find their true value not in their autobiographical association, but in their generic potential for raising the level of consciousness about issues in human interaction and relations which most of us at best take for granted and do not give second thought.

Talking things out is clearly a conflict resolution phenomenon which is recognized by all peoples and cultures, but the degree to which it is practiced must vary with the cultural values and institutional practices of a given society or community. Among the Dinka, it is very pronounced, demanded, and expected. The mere fact of talking it out is considered a source of relief, and therefore is inherently remedial. But beyond that, the dialogue which talking it out implies, provides an opening that improves the prospects for conflict resolution.

The approach of reaching out to the adversary must not be viewed as glossing over issues or condoning wrongful behavior. Quite the contrary, the objective is to establish communication, enter into a dialogue, and hopefully correct the cause of conflict, wherever it may happen to be found after the investigation. This balance between opening up in a positive way and pointing out the wrongs involved was well illustrated by some of the examples which elders cited about Deng Majok's efforts in peacemaking. While we cooperated with the commanding officer at

Abyei, we also had moments of confrontation and tough talk. In virtually all my talking it out with people in Germany and the United States, the truth came out as I saw it. And that provided the basis for the constructive dialogue that ensued.

In intercommunal conflicts the fact that in the cases covered in this collection some agreement or understanding was reached (and I hasten to add that they were not selected for that reason, but merely as conflict and negotiation situations that stood out), is, I believe, a degree of success and a vindication that one must try where conflicts call for intervention. That most of them did not bring a lasting solution to the crisis is the result of structural flaws inherent in those situations and the lack of a reliable and sustainable framework of values and patterns of normative behavior. But that does not indicate a dead-end; the creation of a common ground requires a sustained effort and every case of a successful negotiation or a conflict resolution effort contributes toward that objective.

Since societies or communities have become nationally and even globally interactive and interdependent, it is no longer possible for the principles of conflict resolution that operate within a particular context to be effective in isolation. The potential for influence across the societal or communal boundaries has been immensely increased. Such influence could support or undermine the conflict resolution methods and outcomes of a particular context. What is achieved at one level becomes subject to scrutiny and possible counteraction at the next level up the ladder of national and international interaction and interdependence.

In this process, the ability of individuals to move across political, social, and cultural borders is particularly instrumental. The function of individuals in the process may take the form of an appeal to the higher level of authority, challenging the outcome of any measures taken at the lower level, or a counter-appeal aimed at reaffirming the same measures, or a more generic extension of the values and practices of a given culture into cross-cultural situations.

The role of the individual in transfusing talking it out as a method of conflict resolution is particularly challenging in interpersonal relations among people of very different cultural backgrounds. It is here that both the relativity and the universality of the concept become particularly significant. In some cases, perhaps the majority, the universal human factor allows for a narrowing of the cultural gap in applying the concept. But in some cases, hopefully the minority, the gap between those inclined to preserve their privacy in nursing internalized conflicts may be unbridgeable. Intergroup relations pose more complex sets of issues because of their collective orientation. In particular, interstate relations tend to be depersonalized and formalized in a manner that constrains individual initiatives. But even in intergroup and interstate conflicts there is an underlying human dynamic which offers the individual considerable potential in conflict resolution efforts.

Two major policy implications emerge from the interconnectedness and mutual influences across societies and levels. One may be to ensure the autonomy of each level and support its distinctive methods of negotiating or otherwise dealing with conflict. This would discourage individuals or groups from emotively resorting to outsiders, especially superior authorities, to intervene and undermine the internal processes of conflict management, which have been conducted in accordance with basic cultural norms and institutionalized practices of the community at that level. The opposite model would be to adopt a comprehensive approach to conflict management in accordance with basic principles of justice and human dignity, which are recognized as paramount and transcending any exclusive concepts.

The reality is of course more complex and varied than the dualistic model of autonomy and comprehensive global order suggests. Both models coexist in varying degrees. Within the national framework, a degree of autonomy exists in the family, the tribe, and the province, or the region. And yet, the authority of the central government penetrates through various levels into the family. And of course both the autonomy of the unit and the penetration of central authority are not wholesale but depend largely on the issues involved and the interests at stake. What is required and is indeed imperative is an eclectic arrangement whereby the legitimacy and the integrity of decisionmaking and conflict management methods within a given political, social, and cultural framework are recognized, supported, and sanctioned, while avenues for correction and pursuit of higher standards of equity and justice are opened.

The same principles apply with respect to the power of the central government. Under normal circumstances, the government as the responsible organ of the state, is expected to exercise independent authority over its citizens within the framework of national sovereignty and in accordance with its own cultures, laws, and code of conduct. To the extent that the cultural values and methods of conflict management in a given context and at any level of the national constitutive structure reinforce and strengthen the realization of the universal norms of justice and human dignity, the autonomous and inclusive models can be said to be complementary. But where they are in conflict, the universal norms, especially if formally adopted by the international community, must prevail.

This is the essence of the controversy between the relativists and the universalists in the debate on the applicability of international human rights standards cross-culturally. The argument of the relativists is in part motivated by a genuine concern about differences in cultures and values and their relevancy to the international protection of human rights. But to the extent that this argument is advanced by governments, which are the potential targets of human rights protection, the relativists use the argument to shelter them from international scrutiny. The genuinely cultural argument can be accepted only as a means of reinforcing and strengthening the application of the universal norms with sensitivity to a particular cultural context. The manipulative use of culture as a shield by violators of human rights cannot be accepted by the international community as valid. After all, no victims of human rights violations have ever been heard to claim that they are justifiably punished in accordance with the principles of their particular cultural or religious code.

The objective of this volume is, however, more modest than these global issues signify. The aim is to make available to the readers the experiences of one individual who carried with him his native values and cultures and applied them to human relations in cross-cultural situations, with varying degrees of success and failure. If these accounts challenge the reader to ask such questions as to whether the way I managed the situations reflected personal idiosyncrasies, culturally determined patterns, or universally valid human responses, or how they as individuals would have responded under similar situations, I would be satisfied that the exercise has been worthwhile. From these experiences, I hope that some conclusions can be drawn and lessons learned that might be useful in addressing the generic value of managing human relations, and therefore conflicts, through "talking it out".

Bibliography

Ahmed, Abdel Ghaffar M. & Sorbo, Gunnar M. 1989. *Management of the Crisis in the Sudan*, Proceedings of the Bergen Forum, 23-24 February, 1989. Bergen: Center for Development Studies.

Beshir, Mohamed Omer 1968. *The Southern Sudan: Background to Conflict*. London: C. Hurst & Co.

Brown, Radcliffe 1960. Introduction to the Analysis of Kinship System, in Bell, Norman W. & Vogel, Ezra F. (eds), *A Modern Introduction to the Family*. London: Routledge & Kegan Paul.

Burton, John W. 1980. Atuot Age Categories and Marriage, *Africa* 50 (2), 146-160.

Butt, Audrey 1952. *The Nilotes of the Anglo-Egyptian Sudan and Uganda*. London: International African Institute.

Buxton, Jean 1963. *Chiefs and Strangers: A Study of Political Assimilation among the Mandari*. Oxford: Clarendon Press.

Buxton, Jean 1973. *Religion and Healing in Mandari*. Oxford: Clarendon Press.

Carter Center 1992. Sudanese Conflict in Perspective: An Action Memorandum. The Carter Center Consultation of The International Negotiation Network Resolving Intra-National Conflicts: A Strengthened Role for Non-Governmental Actors, January 15-17, 1992. Atlanta, Georgia: The Carter Center.

Cole, David & Huntington, Richard 1985. African Rural Development: Some Lessons from Abyei. Unpublished manuscript. Cambridge,

Massachusetts: Harvard Institute for International Development, October, 1985.

Deng, Francis M. 1965. Racialism at the Meeting Point, in Tajfel & Dawson (eds) 1965, 87-102.

Deng, Francis Mading 1973. *The Dinka and Their Songs*. Oxford: Clarendon Press.

Deng, Francis Mading 1978. *Africans of Two Worlds: The Dinka in Afro-Arab Sudan*. Khartoum: Institute of Asian and African Studies, University of Khartoum.

Deng, Francis M. 1980. *Dinka Cosmology*. London: Ithaca Press.

Deng, Francis Mading 1982. *Recollections of Babo Nimir*. London: Ithaca Press.

Deng, Francis Mading 1986. *The Man Called Deng Majok: A Biography of Power, Polygyny and Change*. New Haven and London: Yale University Press.

Deng, Francis M. 1992. A Triple Approach to Peace in the Sudan, in Hunwick, John O. (ed), *Religion and National Integration in Africa: Islam, Christianity and Politics in the Sudan and Nigeria*. Evanston, Illinois: Northwestern University Press.

Deng, Francis M. 1993. Hidden Agendas in the Sudan, in Daly, M.W. & Sikainga, Ahmed Elawad (eds), *Civil War in the Sudan*. London: British Academic Press.

Deng, Francis Mading & Daly, W.M. 1990. *Bonds of Silk: The Human Factor in the British Administration of the Sudan*. East Lansing: Michigan State University Press.

Deng, Francis Mading & Gifford, Prosser 1987. *The Search for Peace and Unity in the Sudan*. Washington, D.C.: The Woodrow Wilson Press.

Deutsch, Morton 1991. Subjective Features of Conflict Resolution: Psychological, Social and Cultural Influences, in *New Directions in Conflict Theory*. London: Sage, in association with the International Social Science Council.

Evans-Pritchard, Edward E. 1940. The Nuer, in Evans-Pritchard, E.E. & Fortes, M. (eds), *African Political Systems*. Oxford: Clarendon Press.

Evans-Pritchard, Edward E. 1971. *Nuer Religion*. Oxford: Oxford University Press.

Faure, Guy Olivier & Rubin, Jeffrey (eds) 1993. *Culture and Negotiation*. Thousand Oaks, California: Sage Publications, Inc.

Henderson, Kenneth D.D. 1939. The Migration of the Missiria Tribes into Southwestern Kordofan. *Sudan Notes and Records* 22, No 1.

Henderson, Kenneth D.D. 1965. *Sudan Republic*. London: Ernest Benn Ltd.

Herskovits, Melville J. 1962. *The Human Factor in Changing Africa*. New York: A.A. Knopf.

Howell, Paul.P. 1951. Notes on the Ngork Dinka. *Sudan Notes and Records* 32, 239-293.

Howell, Paul P. 1954. *A Manual of Nuer Law*. Oxford: Clarendon Press.

Hutchinson, Sharon 1980. Relations between the Sexes Among the Nuer. *Africa*, 50 (4), 371-388.

Johnson, Douglas H. & Prunier, Gerard 1993. The Foundation and Expansion of the Sudan People's Liberation Army, in Daly, M. W. & Sikainger, Ahmad Alawad, *Civil War in The Sudan*. London: British Academic Press.

Khalid, Mansour 1985. *Nimeiri and the Revolution of Dis-May*. London: Kegan Paul International.

Khalid, Mansour 1989. *The Government They Deserve: The role of the elite in Sudan's Political Evolution*. Kegan Paul International.

Lienhardt, Godfrey 1958. Western Dinka, in Middleton, John & Tait, David (eds), *Tribes Without Rulers*. London: Routledge & Paul.

Lienhardt, Godfrey 1961. *Divinity and Experience: The religion of the Dinka*. Oxford: Clarendon Press.

Lienhardt, Godfrey 1963. Man in Society, in *The Listener*. London: B.B.C.

Malwal, Bona & Kok, Peter Nyot (eds) 1992. *Conflict in the Sudan*, Proceedings of the Adare Conference (September 1992).

Middleton, John & Tait, David 1959. *Tribes Without Rulers*. Oxford: Clarendon Press.

Niblock, Timothy 1987. *Class and Power in the Sudan: The dynamics of Sudanese politics, 1898-1985*. Albany: Albany State University of New York Press.

Saeed, Abdelbasit 1982. *The State and Socioeconomic Transformation: The Case of Social Conflict in Southwest Kordofan*. University of Connecticut. Ph.D. dissertation.

Seligman, Charles G. 1932. *The Pagan Tribes of the Nilotic Sudan*. London: G. Routledge & Sons, Ltd.

Tajfel, Henri & Dawson, John L. 1965. *Disappointed Guests*. London: Oxford University Press. An Institute of Race Relations publication.

Titherington, Major G.W. 1927. The Raik Dinka of Bahr el Ghazal Province. *Sudan Notes and Records* 10, 159-209.

Trimingham, John S. 1949a. *The Christian Approach to Islam in the Sudan*. London & New York: World Dominion Press.

Trimingham, John S. 1949b. *The Christian Church in Post-War Sudan*. London & New York: World Dominion Press.

United States Institute of Peace 1993. We Must End the War: A Soul-Searching Quest for Peace in the Sudan (United States Institute of Peace – House of Representatives Subcommittee on Africa symposium on Sudan, October 1993). Washington, D.C.: United States Institute of Peace.

Wai, Dunstan M. 1981. *The African-Arab Conflict in the Sudan*. New York and London: Africana Publishing Company.

Wolfers, Michael 1970. How Six Sudanese Died: A Family Massacre. London: *The Times*, October 19, 1970.

Zartman, I. William 1991. Conflict Resolution: Prevention, Management, and Resolution, in Deng, Francis M. & Zartman, I. William (eds), *Conflict Resolution in Africa*. Washington: Brookings Institution.

Zartman, I. William 1997. Governance as Conflict Management in West Africa in Zartman, William I. (ed), *Conflict Resolution in West Africa*. Washington: Brookings Institution.